DIVORCE WARS

Interventions with Families in Conflict

Elizabeth M. Ellis

Published by
American Psychological Association
750 First Street, NE
Washington, DC 20002

Copies may be ordered from
APA Order Department
P.O. Box 92984
Washington, DC 20090-2984

In the U.K., Europe, Africa, and the Middle East, copies may be ordered from
American Psychological Association
3 Henrietta Street
Covent Garden, London
WC2E 8LU England

Typeset in Goudy by EPS Group Inc., Easton, MD

Printer: Port City Press, Baltimore, MD
Cover Designer: Kathleen Simms Graphic Design, Washington, DC
Technical/Production Editor: Allison L. Risko

The opinions and statements published are the responsibility of the authors, and such opinions and statements do not necessarily represent the policies of the APA.

Library of Congress Cataloging-in-Publication Data
Ellis, Elizabeth M.
    Divorce wars : interventions with families in conflict / Elizabeth M. Ellis.—1st ed.
      p. ; cm.
    Includes bibliographical references and index.
    ISBN 1-55798-679-4 (alk. paper)
    1. Divorce therapy. 2. Divorce—Psychological aspects. 3. Children of divorced parents—Mental health. I. Title.

RC488.6.E45 2000
616.89'156—dc21

00-036205

British Library Cataloguing-in-Publication Data
A CIP record is available from the British Library.

Printed in the United States of America
First Edition

CONTENTS

ACKNOWLEDGMENTS

A literature review book such as this is a major undertaking for a clinician in private practice; at times, the task seemed impossible. I am indebted to the Emory University library system for allowing me to use the extensive collections of the graduate, health sciences, and law libraries free of charge. For those articles I could not obtain through Emory, I thank Dowman Wilson of the Atlanta Public Library for his diligent efforts in obtaining hard-to-find articles from other libraries in the region. Researching the literature has changed drastically since I was a graduate student. Internet resources such as *PubMed* and *PsycInfo* were useful in researching certain topics and providing me with abstracts.

Many experts in the field were considerably gracious in sending me copies of unpublished or hard-to-find articles. For that, I thank Dr. Janet Johnston of Menlo Park, California; Dr. Carla Garrity of Denver; Dr. Jeffrey Siegel of Dallas; Dr. Edward Hoppe of Beverly Hills, California; and Dr. Earl Schaefer of Chapel Hill, North Carolina. I also thank Dr. Ben Schutz of Silver Spring, Maryland, who gave me some good perspectives on the nature of this work.

This book was long in search of a publisher, and I thank my editors, Susan Reynolds and Ed Meidenbauer, of the American Psychological Association Books Department, who felt there was a market for this book and who guided me through the process of (re)writing and publishing my first professional textbook. I also appreciate members of the Forensic Interest Group of the Georgia Psychological Association who were willing to read and review chapters from the book: Dr. Bill Buchanan, Dr. Beth Moye, Dr. Ann McNeer, and Dr. David Proefrock. Atlanta attorneys Randy Kessler, Barbara Bishop, Bruce Steinfeld, Barbara Lassiter, Dianne Woods, and John Wilson III also provided helpful input. I also thank Emily McBurney, Barbara Rubin, and Judge Cynthia Wright of the Family Court

Division of the Fulton County Superior Court, and Anne Marie Timini and Susan Boyan of Cooperative Parenting for taking time out of their days to tell me about their programs.

Psychological research can be exciting and relevant to today's social issues. For that reason, we should give it away to the public and not keep it confined to academia. For giving me a love of research, I thank my professors at Emory University: Dr. Al Heilbrun, Dr. Dave Edwards, Dr. Marshall Duke, and Dr. Steve Nowicki.

Last, I thank my husband James and my children Andrew and Sarah, who put up with my late nights at the computer and Sunday afternoons at the library for several years. Their support has never wavered.

INTRODUCTION

For psychologists and other mental health professionals, testifying in court is one of those experiences that one either avoids, like trial by fire, or one thrives on. After many years of clinical practice, I found myself to be one of the latter. Much like the Tuesday afternoon case presentations we had in graduate school, one must face a critical audience and be prepared to articulate one's premises clearly and concisely, to justify one's conclusions with a mound of data, and to cite one's sources.

Forensic work requires an academic rigor that is not demanded by a general clinical practice. Over the years I have found myself doing literature reviews on special topics, preparing short summaries on these topics, or bringing to court textbooks with special selections flagged. Then a thought occurred to me: "Why not prepare a book that would be a literature review of the field on highly conflicted families of divorce?" Such a book could be a good single resource for the psychologist or guardian ad litem going into court. One could be prepared to answer questions such as "Are this child's symptoms congruent with parental alienation syndrome?" "What is the most likely explanation for why this child comes back from a visitation in a highly agitated state?" "What would be the best way for the parents to share custody of a 1-year-old? Why?" The field of child and family forensic psychology has matured over the past 20 years, I hope, from a field in which the expert is a clinician who espouses his or her personal opinions to a scientist–practitioner who can find some scientific basis for his or her argument. Clearly we are moving in this direction, and the courts will expect the expert to be just that.

Such a book would be helpful, too, to attorneys who cross-examine expert witnesses in this field. For that reason, I have made the writing style straightforward and accessible—posing questions of interest and answering them with brief summaries of relevant studies. The busy attorney can go to the sections in each chapter titled "What the Research Shows" to get a sense of whether the material in the chapter will be useful to his or her case. Clinicians—those psychologists and social workers and other family therapists who do not go to court but who conduct therapy with children enmeshed in the conflict, or with adults who are distraught, angry, and not always acting in the child's best interests—should find the book helpful, too. The chapters open with brief case studies and close with the outcome of the case. The case presentations are taken from my own work with families, although the names and other identifying information have been changed and, in some cases, two cases are merged. Each chapter concludes the review of research with a summary, followed by a section called "Guidelines for the Clinician."

In organizing this material, I sought to arrange the chapters roughly in the order in which the divorce process and its aftermath take place. It was necessary, however, to first do some review of the divorce literature in general. Chapter 1 reviews the history of divorce in the United States and, in doing so, explains why divorces have become so contentious. All the external factors that might have been considered in determining custody (such as gender) are now disallowed. Custodial decisions must be made on the basis of subtle, psychological, and unobservable factors. Our attitudes about the children of divorce have changed also. Whereas in the 1970s we believed as a nation that divorce was good for children, we now know otherwise. The results of several longitudinal studies show that the impact on children persists into adolescence, into young adulthood, and even into the marriages of the adult children of divorce. Some may say that a backlash has set in.

Chapter 2 attempts to put the results of these longitudinal studies into perspective. Smaller scale studies have examined the adjustment of children in highly conflicted intact marriages and found that it is not divorce per se that results in poor outcomes for children but the level of conflict in the home—before, during, and after the divorce—that is crucial. This finding establishes the importance of this book. One quarter of divorces end in high levels of conflict, and it is the group of children in those marriages who experience the most adjustment problems. Another body of studies is summarized that pinpoint why this is: The years of interparental conflict and subsequent second and third divorces deteriorate the child's relationship with both parents.

Chapters 3–8 follow roughly a chronological course. Chapter 3 explores the common avenues toward the failure and dissolution of marriages today. This provides a backdrop for those unresolved issues that become entrenched in postdivorce disputes. They reappear as part of children's psychopathology in Chapter 8 and parental psychopathology in Chapter 9.

Because mediation is still the best intervention for defusing hostilities in a pending divorce and avoiding litigation, this literature is reviewed in detail in Chapter 3. Information is provided not only for mental health practitioners who may mediate the child custody issues but also for attorneys who will want to know when mediation is most likely to succeed and when it is an exercise in futility.

Chapters 4 and 5 explore the ending of a marriage and the decisions that must be made. Chapter 4 begins with a review of trends in custodial arrangements since the divorce revolution and why mothers and fathers choose to pursue custody of the children. The review then moves into the various forms of child custody arrangements and their success rates. This material will be useful to the attorney who is consulting with a parent prior to litigating and will help the attorney with case strategy. The clinician–mediator–consultant will also find it useful in answering parents' questions about various forms of custody.

If the couple has not settled out of court and the issue of custody is litigated, the next phase of the process will be the custody evaluation. Chapter 5 opens with a historical review of the legal basis used by the courts to award custody. The chapter then reviews research on that small subportion of parents who litigate and their reasons for doing so. There follows an overview of the theoretical and scientific basis for the custody evaluation—the goals, rationale, elements, and use of psychological tests. The selection of tests covered in this section will be especially useful to the clinician, who will want to avoid using tests that have a shaky empirical basis, and to the attorney, who will be able to vigorously cross-examine the expert who uses shoddy tests. There follows a discussion of the criteria judges use to determine custody, so that mental health practitioners can understand where the two fields diverge. The chapter ends with a discussion of some principles for organizing the conclusions of the evaluation and a consideration of whether to testify to the "ultimate issue."

The custody evaluator or the expert in postdivorce disputes is often asked to propose a visitation plan. For this reason, Chapter 6 is next in the sequence. The bulk of the chapter reviews guidelines in the literature based primarily on age but also on how involved the two parents have been, how close they live to each other, and the child's temperament. There follows a discussion of the frequency of visitation conflicts and a summary of the controversial findings on whether children benefit from seeing their father when the visitations are hostile.

Chapters 7 and 8, which discuss child psychopathology, are next in the sequence, as they can be assumed to be the result of the failure of mediation, the custody recommendations, and the establishment of a good visitation plan to intervene in the children's lives effectively. Chapter 7 opens with a review of research on the reactions of children to parental fighting, especially at visitation exchanges. The chapter then reviews the large body of research by Janet Johnston and other researchers on the varying reactions of children to divorce conflict at different ages. These reactions are modified by the child's own internal resources, however, and the chapter closes with a review of the impact of the child's temperament, coping skills, and cognitive style on adjustment in high-conflict divorces.

A small number of children with postdivorce adjustment problems will go on to develop a more severe and entrenched reaction called *parental alienation syndrome* (PAS). Chapter 7 thus provides a natural lead-in to Chapter 8. Expert witnesses will want to review this chapter carefully as attorneys have become more savvy at cross-examining experts on the validity of this behavior pattern. First there is a discussion of how the term arose and some of the theoretical background and research that has been done to date. There follows a short summary on the disorder *folie à deux*, which is very similar in nature. These two sections are combined, along with further research studies, to construct a cohesive formulation of how this disorder (PAS) arises. The chapter closes with a review of interventions and treatments that have been proposed and their relative effectiveness. The proposed list of 12 characteristics of children with PAS, found in the "Suggested Guidelines" section, may be especially useful for evaluators and clinicians who are trying to determine whether a child's behavior fits this pattern.

Chapter 9 ties in naturally with Chapters 8 and 7 in that, in this chapter, we see the forms of parental psychopathology that are directly linked with child psychopathology. The chapter opens with a discussion of the observations of clinicians and researchers in the field about these parents: that they are individuals with personality disorders or subclinical levels of such. The origins of these disturbances are not clear; they may be due to losses in childhood or to characterological cognitive distortions. Research is reviewed that demonstrates that these parents are lacking in empathy and perspective-taking ability; that they engage in defensiveness and projection of blame; and that they have rigid thinking styles, interpersonal skills deficits, and are more self-oriented and less child-oriented. Two additional sections focus on the intensification of conflict that often arises with remarriage and the subgroup of highly disturbed parents who engage in child abductions.

Chapter 10 explores the complex area of accusations of sexual abuse that arise in custody and visitation conflicts. A large body of research has accumulated over the past 20 years on the sexual abuse of children, but I have made an effort to restrict the information to that which is needed by the clinician, especially one who is conducting an evaluation for the courts in a highly conflicted postdivorce case in which there are vague accusations of sexual abuse and little hard evidence. The material is organized around four areas in which the evaluator should gather information: the situation, the accuser, the accused, and the child. Information gathered on the child is organized under these headings: Physical Evidence, Mental State, Reports of Behavioral Symptoms, Behavioral Checklists, The Child's Verbal Account, Projective Tests and Drawings, and Consistency Among Sources of Data. Attorneys will find this outline useful in cross-examining witnesses for thoroughness and for challenging weak testimony for which there is no empirical basis.

Such a book would not be complete without a section on ethical problems and pitfalls, and those are the subjects of Chapter 11. Ethical issues can be dry when presented in the form of legalistic formulations of *dos* and *don'ts* but quite fascinating in the form of real cases. For that reason I have organized the material around several case scenarios, drawn from my own experience or that of colleagues, that illustrate some of the most common problems: going beyond the data to make conclusions unsupported by the data; failure to clarify confidentiality; failure to clarify what your objective is, as well as what you can and cannot say in court; failure to distinguish clinical from forensic roles; the dangers of doing average work; and the dangers of working with noncustodial parents and children.

I have not proposed specific treatments for families in postdivorce conflict in this book. These families are served, in large part, by standard forms of individual, family, and play therapy. In addition, support groups for children and parents going through divorce have been in existence now in churches, schools, and community centers for more than 20 years. Instead, I have offered personal commentary in most chapters in the form of guidelines for the clinician. Chapter 12 addresses the newer forms of intervention for the specialized population of highly conflicted families, programs that have come into being just in the past 8–10 years. It opens with a discussion of the backlash against divorce and the movement in churches toward keeping marriages together. I then review attempts to introduce new legislation aimed at divorce prevention. From there, the chapter covers changes in the court system itself once the parents file for divorce: specialized family courts, parent education programs, and mediation. Next it reviews new roles for mental health professionals in postdivorce resolution: court psychologist, special master, coparenting coordinator, and arbitrator. The chapter closes with a review of new treatment programs for children and a look toward the future.

If there is any doubt as to the urgency of finding effective therapy and counseling for conflicted families, consider this: Research shows that divorce doubles the risk of emotional and behavioral disorders in children. With the rate of divorce being what it is, the future emotional balance of a good portion of society depends on the kind of work reviewed in this book. I hope that the information and interventions I present here can be of service to other therapists, lawyers, and researchers who work with this ever-growing population of clients.

1

THE LEGACY OF DIVORCE IN THE POSTMODERN AGE

CASE STUDY

"It's Davis," the woman said on the telephone, "my 10-year-old son. He's been talking about wanting to die." Brooke went on to explain that she and her husband had separated 3 months previously. At first, Davis and his 7-year-old sister Beth Ann were shocked and angry. Then Davis became withdrawn. He would go off by himself more than usual and said that he only wanted to talk to God about his problems. He had lost interest in going places and no longer enjoyed riding his bike, playing computer games, or reading. He had been talking to his mother a little more lately but not to his father. Recently, he asked her if he could talk to somebody because he felt depressed and that his life was really bad.

I saw Brooke and her children together and asked Davis and Beth Ann to draw a picture of what the divorce felt like to them. Beth Ann drew a picture of a heart with two cracks running through it, dividing it into three sections, "Mom," "Davis," and "Beth Ann," accordingly, by size. Planted in the "Mom" section was an ax named "Dad."

Davis, a serious-looking, awkward preadolescent with thick glasses, asked me to help him draw a world map. I roughed out the continents for him, and he set to work with great intensity. He drew spiral shapes in all the oceans, indicating the formation of hurricanes. The spiral shape in the

Atlantic Ocean, he explained, was gaining in strength and was creating spin-off tornadoes on the Eastern seaboard. The spiral shape in the Pacific Ocean merged into a larger shape in red and a still larger spiral in purple that overshadowed the West coast. I asked him to draw where he would be in the picture. Without hesitating, he drew a red dot on Antarctica. "There," he said. "There in Antarctica. I'm a scientist. I live alone in a little hut, taking weather measurements."

Brooke explained in a later meeting that she and her husband Walker had always had a turbulent marriage. Both were subject to mood swings, and there was frequent fighting. There had been many threats and vicious things said between them, even some slapping and shoving. One time Walker had retreated to the closet with a gun to his head, threatening suicide. She knew the behavior was wrong but did not know how to stop it. She was not shocked when Walker left. He had done so before. She was unhappy, too, but she would have stayed in the marriage.

In a subsequent meeting, Davis again came in and, without speaking, sat down to work on his picture. He drew furiously, making lines running the length of North and South America, then throughout all the major continents. "These are earthquakes starting, fissures in the earth. They're occurring all over the earth." Then he made green dots around all the earthquake lines, then red xs over the green dots. "These are the earthquake sites. They're everywhere. The world is disintegrating." Davis went on to say that he felt his happiness was the family, and if the family is broken then his happiness is broken. "I will be sad for eternity," he said.

A month later, Brooke announced that the divorce was final. Walker was seeing the children erratically. He still did not have an address or telephone number, and his whereabouts were secret. She and Walker had argued about this when he came to get the children. Davis was very distracted in the office. His affect was flat. He announced, "The cracks are lessening, but the storms are widening. The end is coming. The end of life." He set to work drawing again. "Five asteroids the size of earth are coming into the sun. Boom! Everything is pitch black. The earth is smashed into bits. Antarctica is at first getting smaller and smaller due to global warming. Then it is broken off completely and goes flying through space."

What does the future hold for Davis and Beth Ann? Can we make reasoned predictions about how this divorce will affect children this age? Are their reactions typical? Are boys and girls affected by divorce in different ways? Will Brooke and Walker continue their conflict? If so, how will this affect their children?

THE BEGINNING OF THE DIVORCE REVOLUTION

To address these issues, we must go back to the beginning of the divorce revolution in the United States. In the late 1960s, American society began a great experiment with the structure and foundation of the family that has been unprecedented in modern times. In 1969 California passed the first "no-fault" divorce law, precipitating a surge in the divorce rate that moved eastward throughout the 1970s. Frank Furstenberg (1994) noted that the actual incidence of divorce had been steadily increasing up to that time since the mid-1800s. Studies show that the incidence of divorce after the Civil War, roughly 5%, had increased to an estimated 36% in 1964 (these are lifetime rates). Nevertheless, there was a sharp increase in the divorce rate from the mid-1960s to the late 1970s. Demographer Paul Glick (1979) noted that the proportion of children living with only one parent doubled between 1960 and 1978, from 9% to 18.6%. He predicted that the number would increase to 25% by 1990 at those rates. Although some of this increase was due to the rise in unmarried mothers raising their children alone, most of it was due to the increased divorce rate. Glick estimated that about 28% of all children younger than age 18 in 1976 had parents who would divorce during their childhood, as compared with 12.6% in 1960. He further predicted that this figure would increase to about 33% by 1990.

How do we account for this increase in the divorce rate? Furstenberg, of the University of Pennsylvania, and Andrew Cherlin, of Johns Hopkins University (1991), suggested that the roots of the divorce revolution can be found in what historian Lawrence Stone (1977) labeled *the rise of affective individualism* in early modern England. By this, Stone was referring to the greater valuing of emotional love in relationships and the pursuit of personal happiness. Americans have always prized personal fulfillment more highly than the bonds of kinship as compared with people in European societies. Family relationships in American society likewise focus more on emotional closeness and expressions of love than on the carrying out of sharply defined social roles.

The civil rights and women's movements further focused the nation on the principle that it was within the American birthright to pursue individual interests so as to maximize our potential as persons. The *human potential movement*, as it came to be called, was held to be as much in keeping with the American spirit as life, liberty, and the pursuit of happiness. With this newfound campaign to develop one's potential to the fullest came a succession of new ideas: that pregnant teenagers should be allowed to bear their children without shame and to keep and raise them, that mothers should be allowed to work if they so chose, and that people who have been chronically unhappy in a marriage should be allowed to end the marriage and pursue their happiness without the social stigma that had been previously attached to divorce.

Before 1969, in all 50 states one could be granted a divorce only if he or she could establish that one party was at fault through one of the following: adultery, desertion, physical or mental abuse, drunkenness or drug addiction, imprisonment, or insanity (see Furstenberg & Cherlin, 1991, for a good summary). Before this time, it was common for a man to allow one of these shameful labels to be applied to him in order to obtain the legal grounds for a divorce, even if it may not have been true. Once divorced, a wife was referred to as "a divorcee," and children were said to be "from broken homes." Of course, husbands tried to make new lives and live down their reputations as adulterers, deserters, wife beaters, and so on. Such falseness and shame did not fit into the new society of tolerance.

These changes in divorce laws reflected many changes already going on in U.S. society. Families had become smaller, with only one, two, or three children. Americans had moved off the farms and into the cities. Americans were much more affluent than our ancestors and had more education and leisure time. People were more educated and more informed about the world. Television had broadened our knowledge about segments of society whose lives differed from ours.

HISTORY OF DIVORCE AND PARENTHOOD IN THE UNITED STATES

In the late 1800s, the United States was an agricultural society. Men married to have someone to bear their children, and women married to be economically supported during their childbearing years. Children, many of them, were born to run the family farm and to inherit the land. Boys were often sent away as apprentices or to work on farms or in factories. Girls were sent away to work as household help at the home of a relative. Fathers died in wars, mothers died in childbirth, and the extended family had a great part in raising children. Family relationships were not the intense emotional bonds that exist in families today (Furstenberg & Cherlin, 1991; Stone, 1977).

The families of the late 20th century are smaller, more stable, and more intimate. Parents have children to feel fulfilled, to give love to them, and to devote a newfound affluence and leisure time to them. The vast majority of children now live past infancy, and parents become deeply attached to them. If the purpose of having children has changed, the purpose of marriage has changed as well. Americans now view marriage as based on mutual love, companionship, and compatibility. We marry to find happiness, to fulfill ourselves. If we are not happy and not fulfilled, then what is the point of staying married?

With the passage of no-fault divorce laws in nearly every state, married couples can now divorce without the rancorous, stigmatizing, and even false accusations of the past. Mutual unhappiness, written into law as "irreconcilable differences" or statements that "the marriage is irretrievably broken," now provides a way out for thousands of unhappy couples.

Changes in social attitudes are a circular process. As no-fault laws permitted more divorces, the increasing frequency of divorce made it more acceptable. The growing acceptability of divorce eased the way out for still greater numbers of couples.

With this increased tolerance, the old language of divorce has been replaced by the new language of acceptance. A "divorced woman" now conjures up images of strength and independence. Children are not from "broken homes" but have "binuclear homes." Single fathers are considered virtuous and self-sacrificing. We seldom hear the terms "adulterer" or "deserter." The new language now stigmatizes those whose behavior is unacceptable after the divorce, for example, "deadbeat dads" and "absent fathers."

As Americans embarked on this experiment of no-fault divorce, few people anticipated what was down the road. At first, the process was straightforward: Parents separated as amicably as possible, the mother took custody of the children, and the father gave generous financial support and consented to playing a secondary role in the children's lives.

Even in the early 1970s, however, further changes were taking place in U.S. society. Women were working in larger numbers—some because it was more acceptable, some because of economics. In the workplace, women were demanding equality. Equality before the law and the easing of sex role stereotypes for women were buzzwords in the 1970s. Furstenberg (1994) suggested that the erosion of gender roles has played a large part in the increasing divorce rate. The increasing focus in society on emotional and personal fulfillment in marriage has occurred concurrently with the opening of opportunities for women to support themselves economically in the workplace. Thus, while marriage has become increasingly disappointing for women, the prospect of raising a child or children alone has become a more viable alternative.

Sex role stereotypes have been easing for men as well. In the 1970s, men were allowed in the delivery room and invited to care for infants. Many men began to participate in the physical care of young children and found that they liked it. Men discovered that the mutual love and sharing of fatherhood was satisfying and began to see it as part of their basic right to fulfill their potential as persons. Dual-career couples became increasingly egalitarian, with more men than in the 1960s acquiring the domestic skills of running a household. Thus, men came to view divorce as more palatable as they were no longer so reliant on the domestic services of wives. Even being the primary custodial parent of the children became increasingly acceptable and doable, thus making the option of divorce more attractive for men as well.

By the mid-1970s, the first judicial opinions began to be handed down in regard to gender equity—that is, the regarding of mothers and fathers as equal before the law in their petition for custody of their children following a divorce (Derdeyn, 1976). A 1974 Illinois opinion stated "Equality of the sexes has entered this field. The fact that a mother is fit is only one facet of the situation, and standing by itself, it does not authorize a denial of custody to the father." (Marcus v. Marcus, 1974)

By the mid-1980s, gender equity laws had been passed in most states (Wyer, Gaylord, & Grove, 1987). Again, Americans had embarked on a bold new experiment with the family, with unforseeable consequences. A wave of litigation that began in the mid-1980s still has not begun to abate. Now that fathers are able to assert in court their rights to custody of their children, with some confidence that they will not be rejected outright because of their gender, approximately 15%–25% of couples divorcing with children now engage in bitter emotional disputes over who will obtain the right to raise the children and to make the most important decisions about their well-being (Maccoby & Mnookin, 1992). More than one third of these divorced parents are going back to court years after the divorce to reconsider the custody issues—many of them fathers seeking to reverse custody, to share custody, to alter the decision-making arrangements, or to alter the visitation plan (Foster & Freed, 1973; Scott & Emery, 1987). Father support groups have sprung up around the country to provide information, education, legal advice and referrals, and validation for men who want an enhanced role in their children's lives.

Fathers' Right to Custody

Although we Americans think of ourselves as progressive in terms of honoring fathers' rights to be parents, few people realize how the views of mothers' and fathers' rights and responsibilities have changed over the centuries (see Derdeyn, 1976; Warshak, 1992). Most American and English jurisprudence traces its origins to Roman law. In Rome, the father had absolute control over the family, including the children, and they were regarded as the property of the father. The father had the right to sell his children and, under some conditions, even to kill them.

This acceptance of absolute paternal supremacy continued through the Middle Ages. Children were valued as economic assets to the family in much the same way as were servants. Children provided free labor to the family and were put to work by age 7. Because the father was obligated to support the children financially, he was seen as having the right to their labor and their economic value.

It was not until the 16th and 17th centuries that children began to be seen as people who deserved love and affection and some measure of protection. The English courts began to adopt the position that the government had a vested interest in seeing to it that children were protected from harm if the parents failed to do so. Fathers began to be seen as having the obligation to provide education and training as well as some level of appropriate care and concern.

However, as long as mothers were completely dependent on husbands economically and had few to no legal rights, custody was still automatically awarded to fathers through the 19th century. Children were still valued through the 1800s as a financial asset and as laborers to whose services the father had the rights.

In 1817, the case of poet Percy Bysshe Shelley shocked Great Britain because he was one of the first fathers to lose custody of his children. Viewed as a radical in his day, the court cited his "vicious and immoral" atheistic beliefs as just cause for awarding custody to the children's mother.

Few of us appreciate the different society that existed 100 years ago with regard to parents' roles. In 1857 a New York judge found that, although a husband was abusive to his wife, this did not justify a divorce, and added

> The only difficulty, if any, in the present case, in regard to the right of the father to retain the child, arises from the child being of tender age, and deriving its sustenance, in part, from the breasts of the mother. But, upon the evidence, I think these circumstances form no obstacle to the father's rights. (People v. Humphries, 1857)

The rights of fathers to custody of their children were unquestioned throughout the 1800s. Women had few to no rights before the law, and children's rights were nonexistent. An 1881 Arkansas opinion held that

> It is one of the cardinal principles of nature and of law that, as against strangers, the father, however poor and humble, if able to support the child in his own life style, and of good moral character, cannot, without the most shocking injustice, be deprived of the privilege by anyone whatever, however brilliant the advantage he may offer. It is not enough to consider the interests of the child alone. (Verser v. Ford, 1881)

Mothers' Right to Custody

By the 1900s an entirely new conception of childhood had evolved in American society. As the country became industrialized, fathers left the home to go into the cities to work. Mothers stayed in the home. Their roles diverged so sharply as to be mutually exclusive. Whereas childhood used to be seen as a limited time in which the child was nursed, weaned, toilet trained, and sent to work, childhood in the 20th century came to be seen as a special time of innocence and freedom; of vulnerability and protection; and of playing, exploring, and learning. Children's toys were first mass marketed around this time, as were children's furniture, children's clothing, even children's literature.

"Childhood" as we know it today had arrived. Child labor laws were enacted to banish children from the mills and factories, and educational laws were passed to keep them in the classroom. Now that childhood had been "invented"—and extended from birth to age 16—a specialized role had to be developed for the nurturance, protection, education, training, and guiding of children for those years, and that was motherhood (Ellis, 1995).

The idea of motherhood, as it was developed in the early 20th century, was elevated to a level comparable to sainthood (see Kagan, 1984, for an overview). Mothers were viewed as selfless, tender hearted, honest, gentle, devoted, protective, sympathetic, religious, and so on. One writer went to sentimental extremes in this 1938 opinion:

> There is but a twilight zone between a mother's love and the atmosphere of heaven, and all things being equal, no child should be deprived of that maternal influence unless it be shown there are special or extraordinary reasons for so doing. (Tuter v. Tuter, 1938)

Although Americans are somewhat embarrassed by sentimental soliloquies on the virtues of motherhood today, we were not in the 1920s. A 1921 legal opinion reads,

> For a boy of such tender years nothing can be an adequate substitute for mother love—for that constant ministration required during the period of nurture that only a mother can give because in her alone is duty swallowed up in desire: in her alone is service expressed in terms of love. She alone has the patience and sympathy required to mold and soothe the infant mind in its adjustment to its environment. The difference between fatherhood and motherhood in this respect is fundamental. (Jenkins v. Jenkins, 1921)

In the legal opinions that were handed down in the late 1800s and early 1900s, the term *tender years* was used often. This term referred to the period of a child's intense vulnerability and dependence on the mother, specifically thought to be from birth to about age 7 or 8. The courts took the position that society had a compelling interest in seeing to it that children were well cared for during this time. Because mothers were seen as the parent who was specialized in addressing the needs of children of tender years, this legal position became synonymous with the preference for mother custody (Derdeyn, 1976; Warshak, 1992; Wyer et al., 1987).

Two legal opinions of this era, *Chapsky v. Wood* in 1881 and *Finlay v. Finlay* in 1925, laid the groundwork for the concept of "the best interests of the child." In these opinions, the court took the position that the state should look out for the children's best interests rather than assume that fathers ought to be granted custody automatically. Although in some ways these were radical opinions at the time, they also became synonymous with mother custody. Because mothers were considered uniquely qualified to care for children, the best interests of the child was automatically assumed to be the placement of him or her with the mother.

A third development in the early 20th century was the ordering of fathers to pay child support to mothers who were awarded custody of children. Before this time, if in rare cases mothers were awarded custody, no child support was to have been paid by fathers. It was held that if fathers lost the custody of a child, and thus the economic asset value of the child, then they certainly would not be expected to pay for the economic maintenance of the child. This began to change in the 1920s (Derdeyn, 1976, cites two key cases: *Waller v. Waller*, 1926, and *Ross v. Richardson*, 1928).

A fourth development has been changing attitudes around the issue of parental fault and subsequent custody. It has long been the trend that the parent who was clearly at fault in the divorce—through abuse, alcoholism, insanity, adultery, or desertion—had no right to ask the court for custody of children. Because men typically voluntarily assumed the fault for the divorce, this principle further buttressed the supremacy of mother custody. In the rare case in which the mother committed adultery or deserted the family, she relinquished any reasonable right to custody of her children. Derdeyn (1976) noted that the importance of "parental culpability" has diminished in importance as a guide to determining custody. Similarly, Wyer et al. (1987) noted that the trend has been toward separating proof of unfitness in a custody proceeding from proof of misconduct in a divorce action.

With these several elements in place—the supremacy of motherhood, the tender-years presumption, the best-interests-of-the-child concept, the awarding of child support, and the linking of custody with lack of fault in the marriage—mothers were awarded custody of children almost unchallenged for 70–80 years—from about 1910 to the 1980s.

CURRENT VIEW OF DIVORCE IN THE UNITED STATES

With the bold social experiments of the 1970s and 1980s, much of the previous thinking is gone. Lyrical sentiments about the virtues of motherhood are considered sexist. If Americans are lyrical now at all, it is about the gender-blind term *parenthood*. The tender-years presumption is gone. No studies have shown that mothers are capable of caring for children due solely to their being born female. Many fathers are entirely capable of and competent at caring for children of tender years.

Child support is not automatically given now from father to mother. A mother may be ordered to pay child support to the father if she has a good income and the father is the custodial parent. The parents may share custody and, in some cases, no child support payments may be made, although the details of expense sharing must be worked out.

Being at fault for the failure of the marriage is now considered a separate issue from the right to have custody of the children. This is a concept that most parents, aching from rejection and bitterness, find baffling. A parent who was clearly in the wrong and may have committed a moral offense now has a right to ask the court for custody and, in many cases, will be granted custody if he or she can make a case that he or she is a good parent.

Modern jurisprudence in family law is dominated by the concept of "the best interests of the child," but this idea has been separated from the assumption that mother custody is automatically the best situation. The best interests of the child may now be to reside with the father, or perhaps the grandparents, the stepparent, or even none of the above.

In less than 20 years, the dissolution of marriage and the shifting roles of parents toward their children has altered the character of the family court from a situation where rulings are handed down unchallenged to one where virtually anything can happen. While promoting the greatest level of freedom for parents to pursue what they feel is right for themselves and for their children, we have unleashed a torrent of anger, bitterness, and repeated litigation never before seen in U.S. courts.

In my own practice, I have seen cases that illustrate this deep sense of betrayal. In one instance, a mother had an affair during the marriage and even had the man move in with her while the husband was away on business trips; she also took the children with her to motels to buy drugs. Yet the mother retained custody of the children because she had been the primary caretaker of the children and because the father traveled in his work. The father in this scenario was bitter beyond words and considered not keeping up child support payments, having lost his wife, children, and home through no fault of his own. Another mother divorced her husband because he was a poor provider, yet lost custody to him because, even during periods when he was not working, he provided the majority of the children's day to day care. She was shocked and embittered and felt punished for having been the family breadwinner. One father had an affair with a woman while his wife was pregnant, showing no interest in the birth of the child. Yet he demanded and was accorded regular overnight visitations with the infant while she was still being breastfed. In two Chicago cases, a judge ordered children to see their father on their regular visitations or face a jail sentence. The judge then placed one 8-year-old on house arrest and shackled the 12-year-old and ordered her jailed for 36 hours ("Send them to jail," 1996). Mothers as well as fathers are kidnapping their children and going to jail or into hiding with the children to prevent contact with the other parent (see chapter 9).

IMPACT OF DIVORCE ON CHILDREN

What has been the resulting impact on children of this social experiment? In the late 1960s and early 1970s, Americans optimistically assumed that what was good for Mom and Dad was good for the children. If the parents were free to pursue their happiness, unconstrained by a loveless marriage, then surely the children would benefit from the new level of parental personal fulfillment. If the marriage were dissolved because of long-standing conflict, then surely the children would benefit from ending the years of conflict.

Large-scale studies on children of divorce began almost when the divorce rate began rising. The California Children of Divorce Study began in 1971 under the direction of psychologists Judith Wallerstein and Joan Kelly. These authors published their results at the 5-year follow-up mark (Wallerstein & Kelly, 1980b), and Wallerstein took over the study and published the results at the 10- (Wallerstein, 1985; Wallerstein & Blakeslee, 1989; Wallerstein & Corbin, 1989) and 15-year follow-ups (Wallerstein, 1991). These researchers took an impressionistic approach— interviewing only the children of divorce and their parents, not children in intact families as a comparison group, and they did not measure the children's problems with precise, quantifiable scales. However, their biographical sketches of the children of divorce are compelling.

They reported that the 131 largely White, middle-class children from well-educated families were profoundly sad and troubled by their parents' divorce for many years. At 5 years postdivorce, moderate to severe depression was reported in over one third of the sample. How the child had fared depended overall on how well the newly reconstituted divorced family had managed to find stability and happiness. Boys, overall, were doing more poorly than girls, with more problems with poor school performance, poor peer relationships, and angry acting-out at home with family members. The girls who had not yet reached adolescence seemed to be doing well.

At 10 years postdivorce, the children who were very young at the time of the divorce were doing reasonably well in school and had adjusted to the divorce. A significant number were still sad about the divorce, and over half wished to see their parents together again. Those who were now teenagers continued to express sadness about the divorce, resentment toward their parents, and a feeling of having missed out on something important by not having grown up in an intact family. Most of the group felt deprived or needy. They felt that their lives had been more difficult and less pleasurable than the lives of their peers who grew up in intact families.

The children's relationships with their fathers declined substantially over the years, and at the 10-year mark only a fraction of the children had strong, positive, enriched relationships with their fathers. Wallerstein and Blakeslee (1989) observed that how well the children were doing seemed to be a reflection of how strong their relationship was with their mother at that point.

During this same time, psychologist Mavis Hetherington and her colleagues at the University of Virginia began a study of children of divorce that started in 1982 and continued through 1988, 6 years after the divorce (Hetherington, 1989; Hetherington, Cox, & Cox, 1985; Hetherington, Stanley-Hagan, & Anderson, 1989). This group studied both children of divorce and children in intact families. The 144 families that began the study were White, middle class, and well educated. The child followed in each family was 4 years old at the time of the legal divorce, which was typically 1 or 2 years after the separation. At the 6-year follow-up, the groups were more complex, as many of the intact families had divorced and many of the divorced mothers had remarried.

In this more rigorous study, the researchers found that shortly after the divorce, mothers were irritable and tired, and the quality of parenting, in terms of time and attentiveness, substantially declined. "It is not uncommon for custodial mothers to become self-involved, erratic, uncommunicative, non-supportive, and inconsistently punitive in dealing with their children" (Hetherington, Stanley-Hagan, & Anderson, 1989, p. 308). (There were no custodial fathers at the time who could be similarly observed.) There was disarray in the household, routines were disrupted, and discipline was erratic and inconsistent.

Given what was happening at home, it was no surprise that in the first few years following divorce the children showed more antisocial, impulsive acting-out behavioral problems and more aggression and noncompliance, both at home and at school. This was particularly the case for boys. Boys in mother-headed households were less self-controlled and less able to delay immediate gratification. They were more rebellious against adult authority figures than were the boys in intact homes. Divorced mothers and their sons were particularly at risk for chronic conflict in which the boy was refusing to comply with directions, and the mother was becoming increasingly threatening, hostile, and verbally abusive.

This phenomenon of boys' increased aggression and acting-out has been noted by numerous researchers who have examined the long-term effects of divorce. Many have speculated that these children have much to be angry about. First, the children often feel abandoned or rejected by the parent who leaves—in most cases, the father. They may also feel angry at the parent (usually the mother) who asked that parent to leave. Some children are angry at both parents because they could not resolve their differences and stay together and then chose to pursue their own personal agendas and move on to new interests in life. Many of these children come to view their parents as motivated by self-interest and caring little for the children's needs.

For most children, the involvement of the parent who left (again, usually the father) may continue for approximately a year or two, then usually drops off sharply. Furstenberg and his colleagues studied several thousand children of divorce in the National Survey of Children (Allison & Furstenberg, 1989; Furstenberg & Cherlin, 1991; Furstenberg, Peterson, Nord, & Zill, 1983) and found that 35% of the children had had no contact with their fathers over the past 5 years. Another 16% had not seen their fathers during the previous year. Only one third of the group had an ongoing relationship with their fathers in which they saw them at least once a month.

Children of divorce who do see their fathers often have to contend with canceled and shortened visitations, missed birthdays, absences from school events, and the inclusion of the father's girlfriend and her children during the visitations. By 10 years postdivorce, two thirds of the children in the National Survey of Children had not seen their fathers in over a year. Children living with their fathers reported more ongoing contact with their noncustodial mothers. Seventy percent had seen their mothers at least monthly or more often, and only 7% of the mothers had dropped out of their lives altogether.

Mothers also move on with their lives, and the children must contend with mothers being away from home more as they return to work. When mothers are home, they are likely to be emotionally absent because they are doing double duty as provider and homemaker. Soon mothers are dating and developing a social life. Many children feel increasingly unimportant in their parents' lives as these shifts occur (see Wallerstein & Kelly, 1980b, for a review of case material).

One must add to this scenario the often continued hostility between the parents. One parent may describe the other in derogatory terms, perhaps as justification for the divorce. The child is increasingly conflicted by this as he or she struggles to form a new and positive bond with both parents. Furthermore, the child feels maligned, too, as they see themselves as an extension of both parents.

Effects on Boys

Neil Kalter (1987) and Richard Warshak (1992) have both proposed that boys are "developmentally vulnerable" to the lack of a father in the home because of divorce. As a boy moves into late elementary school age, approximately 7–12 years, he naturally wants to push away from his mother and identify more with males. At this time of "male bonding" boys refuse affection from their mothers and express an aversion to girls. Interest in Boy Scouts, athletic activities, and other traditionally male activities is at an all-time high. Developmentally, boys feel a new sense of power and aggressiveness at this age, and it has traditionally been fathers who provide them with a role model for handling aggression in a socially acceptable manner and an effective presence in the home toward curbing the boys' aggression without demeaning them.

When fathers are absent or are maligned, both of these influences are gone. Boys resist the mother's discipline, yet there is no male presence to effectively contain their acting-out behavior. Neither is there a role model of how to be a man who is assertive and effective who yet maintains self-control. Boys in these situations often look to their peer group for models and identify with older and more aggressively defiant boys.

Mothers may try valiantly to be that controlling presence and role model, yet boys may view giving in to their discipline as signifying that they are weak and unmanly. Thus, mothers with boys this age often feel particularly frustrated, tired, ineffective, and angry. Hetherington (1989) described the relationship between single mothers and their sons as evolving into a coercive cycle: As the boy continues to act out and defy her authority, she in turn becomes more hostile and critical toward her son and more withholding of affection. Hetherington found that when mothers did not remarry, boys continued to have more problems with aggressive, acting-out behavior problems even 6 years after the divorce (Hetherington, 1989; Hetherington, Cox, & Cox, 1985).

Many studies show that approximately 80% of fathers remarry and 75% of mothers remarry, and the majority of those marriages occur 2–3 years after the divorce. Thus, most children of divorce are eventually living with stepparents. Hetherington and her associates (Hetherington, Cox, & Cox, 1985; Hetherington & Parke, 1979) found that in the remarried families strong shifts occurred. Boys seemed to have settled down with a stepfather in the home, and there was a sharp decline in behavior problems, compared with boys in homes where the mother did not remarry. In fact, rates of problems in boys who had stepfathers did not differ from those of boys in intact families. Hetherington et al. theorized that boys yearn for a male figure in the home and for the most part form a good attachment to a stepfather. Somehow their aggression is curbed when there is a male presence in the home, even when he is not the disciplinarian, as is the case for most stepfathers (Hetherington, 1989; Hetherington, Cox, & Cox, 1985).

Keep in mind that the boys in Hetherington's study (Hetherington, Cox, & Cox, 1985) were only 10 years old at the time of the follow-up. Neil Kalter, a researcher at the University of Michigan, found in his study of 387 children that boys younger than age 12 from divorced homes were more angry and aggressive toward others and had poor school performance (Kalter, 1977). This pattern of problems decreased when the mother remarried and a stepfather was in the home. However, Kalter found that these problems reasserted themselves in adolescence. These boys, in spite of having stepfathers, had higher rates of aggression toward parents, delinquent behavior, drug use, and conflict with the law than did boys from intact homes. Kalter concluded that the presence of a stepfather in the home was advantageous to boys in middle childhood but did not provide a lasting resolution to the problem of the lack of a father.

It seems that in experimenting with the American family we have not brought about much happiness for boys. Instead we have gathered some new insights about male development. About half of the fathers in these families do not stay involved with their sons after divorce, and these boys are deeply angry and often out of control.

Effects on Girls

These researchers also found higher rates of problems with dependency, anxiety, and depression and more difficulties in social relationships among the children of divorce. These rates were somewhat higher for girls than boys, although in general girls were described by their mothers as less of a problem. Girls' levels of anger, noncompliance, and demandingness were generally lower and usually dropped off considerably by 2 years after the divorce. All three major studies cited above found that in cases where the mother did not remarry, girls had no more behavior problems than the girls in intact families (Allison & Furstenberg, 1989; Hetherington, 1989; Kalter, 1977). In fact, many of these girls reported becoming closer to their mothers during the years after the divorce, confiding in each other and spending long hours together engaged in traditionally female activities (Kalter, 1984).

Hetherington found a "sleeper" effect for these girls, however, when they reached adolescence. Hetherington was most likely not surprised by this observation, as she had observed similar findings in earlier research done on girls who had lost a father through divorce, as compared with girls who had lost a father through death (Hetherington & Deur, 1971). Daughters of widows were found to be anxious, exceptionally shy, and uncomfortable around males. When observed in activities at a recreational center, the girls avoided the activities that males led or participated in and gravitated toward all-female groups. In contrast, girls from divorced homes sought attention from males the most, were very forward with them, touched them, sat close to them, and acted in sexually provocative ways (Hetherington, 1972, 1973; Hetherington & Deur, 1971).

Kalter (1977) found similar results among a group of adolescent girls whose parents had divorced when they were young. These girls were more likely to engage in aggressive behavior toward adults, precocious sexual activity, substance abuse, and running away. They also had more behavior problems at school. In a second study (Kalter, Riemer, Brickman, & Chen, 1985), Kalter and his colleagues found that adolescent girls from divorced homes were more likely to engage in delinquent activities such as using marijuana and other illicit drugs, skipping school, and committing larceny.

As in Hetherington's study (Hetherington, 1972; Hetherington & Parke, 1979), this was particularly true if the girls' parents had divorced in early childhood, before the girls began elementary school.

Both Hetherington (1989) and Kalter (1987) theorized that in father-absent homes girls develop intense, enmeshed relationships with their mothers. This may not present problems in childhood, but it does make for difficulties when it is time for the girl to separate from her mother and form relationships with males. Because of their overly close relationship, girls must separate from mothers in these homes through angry conflict and rejection. They want to form a close tie with a father but often cannot do so. Not only may girls not see their father because he is far away and a marginal player in their lives, but also girls from divorced homes often harbor more negative feelings toward their fathers than do girls from intact homes. These girls may have angry feelings toward the father about his absence and lack of involvement.

Unlike girls from widowed homes, whose mothers idealized their lost husbands and who received emotional support throughout the community, these girls mothers' often expressed negative attitudes toward men and marriage. They had often felt alone and unsupported by family and friends. They were more unhappy with themselves and with their lives in general. These girls more often viewed their fathers and all males as less competent than women, and they had lower expectations for happiness for themselves.

Hetherington and Kalter theorized that fathers must be important to girls' development in terms of offering them opportunities to interact positively and nonsexually with males and to be reinforcers of the girls' growing female identity. Without this, these girls seem to bring into dating relationships a hunger for male approval, coupled with a basic insecurity and lack of trust in a boy's interest in them. They appear to hold a basic belief that males may not be capable of a sustained and committed, nonsexual interest in and acceptance of them. Having grown up with a perception that their mother was rejected by their father, they seem to expect this same rejection by males in their own relationships.

Hetherington, Cox, and Cox (1989) found that when mothers remarried, the effect on these girls appeared to be the reverse of that for the boys. These girls deeply resented the stepfather, and much higher rates of conflict were reported between mother and daughter. The girls often viewed the stepfather as an intruder, someone who could take away their closeness and position of importance with the mother. These daughters were found to be more sulky around, resistant to, ignoring of, and critical toward stepfathers than were boys. Conflict was particularly high in terms of the daughters' refusal to accept discipline from stepfathers, their acting-out behavior with boys, and their continued conflict with mothers.

In fact, among adolescent girls with stepparents, Kalter (1977) found that 35% had problems with being aggressive (hostile and argumentative) with their stepparents, 41% had problems with drug use, and 47% had acted out sexually. The corresponding figures for girls in intact homes were 4%, 7%, and 11%, respectively.

Hetherington (1989) observed that even after several years of positive effort on the part of stepfathers, these girls, as a group, still rejected them. She suggested that these girls have difficulty forming close relationships with stepfathers because of the fear in both of them of the development of a sexual interest between them.

The Search for Gender Differences

All the above-mentioned researchers have concluded that, when evaluating the results of divorce on broad groups of children, one must be careful to consider the age of the child, whether the child is male or female, and whether the mother remarried or remained single.

The studies cited above are a small but representative sample of the extensive research that has examined the adjustment of children of divorce. A large number of these studies explored the question of sex differences. Are boys more affected by divorce than girls? The answer, as one might expect from the studies above, is "it depends." Martha Zaslow (1988, 1989), with the National Academy of Sciences in Washington, DC, examined this question in exhaustive reviews. She found that studies that do not take into account the child's age at the time of the divorce, the type of symptoms measured, and the parent's marital status subsequent to the divorce generally do not find any sex differences. However, the more carefully done studies with large samples and that do take these variables into account find consistent differences.

Zaslow determined that virtually all the studies that found that boys fare more poorly than girls examined boys who were seen for the first few years after the divorce, when their mothers were single and had not remarried. Boys growing up in single-mother homes were consistently more at risk for behavior problems than girls.

Zaslow also found that the types of symptoms measured also produced different results. It is widely known among clinicians that boys tend to respond to stress with more *externalizing* symptoms (acting-out, disruptive, aggressive behavior) and that girls tend to respond with more *internalizing* behaviors (anxiety, sadness, withdrawal, worrying). When the custodial parent remains unmarried, the studies are consistent in indicating that boys show more externalizing problems than girls in the preteen years. The results on internalizing behaviors are not as clear, with both boys and girls having higher than normal levels of internalizing problems.

Effects on Children in Remarried Families

What do we know about the effects of remarriage? Many parents divorce and remarry with the simplistic expectation that the new parent will simply replace the old one, sort of like trading in a "lemon" for a new model car, but this is not the case. Children develop intense bonds with the parent who raised them, even if he or she was a failure as a wife or husband. Younger children may bond to a new stepparent, but older children are likely to show strong resistance, as well as resentment, toward stepsiblings.

Zill, Morrison, and Coiro (1991) examined the effects of remarriage on children and concluded that although children benefited from the financial advantages of remarriage, the data failed to show a beneficial effect for children in terms of their achievement or behavior. They stated that "there is no clear evidence that remarriage has a protective or ameliorative effect against the negative consequences of family discord or disruption" (p. 99). There was some support in the data for remarriage having a positive effect on the children if it occurred when they were very young and if it was stable. Remarriages in the teen years were more problematic.

Zaslow (1988, 1989) examined a large number of studies that took the custodial parent's remarriage status into account and found that there was an interaction with the child's gender. In a series of major studies, girls (who typically were in their teens when mother remarried) adjusted more poorly than did boys to the mother's remarriage. Girls reacted with elevations of internalizing symptoms such as depression and withdrawal as well as acting-out and disruptive behaviors.

The one consistent finding, Kalter (1977) reported, across all age groups and gender groups, whether the children were in single-parent homes or remarried homes, was that these children were angrier and more aggressive toward their parents. Like other researchers, Kalter found that the children of divorce had poorer relationships with their parents than the children from intact homes. It is this strong bond with parents that seems to act as a buffer, protecting children from the strong (and sometimes negative) influence of the peer group in adolescence.

Effects on Young Adults

How do these children of divorce fare as young adults? Many of these researchers have followed children into young adulthood and college life to review the long-term effects of divorce. Wallerstein found her group to be rather troubled, drifting, and underachieving (Wallerstein, 1985; Wallerstein & Blakeslee, 1989; Wallerstein & Corbin, 1989). She found that young men endorsed the ideas of love and marriage but were afraid to make commitments themselves for fear of repeating their own parents' mistakes. Some avoided dating altogether. Although the boys were no longer a behavior problem, many were underachieving as young men. Although they expressed a desire to fall in love, they had deep reservations about making commitments out of a fear of failure at marriage.

As a group, these young men had failed to match the socioeconomic aspirations of their parents. Half of these 19- to 29-year-old men were still in school full-time. Many had dropped out of high school and college, although they came from upper-middle-class families, who traditionally support higher education for their children. Of those who were out of school, one third were unemployed, and most of the remainder had drifted from one low-wage job to another.

Wallerstein and Corbin (1989) were able to locate 64 of the original 68 girls who had been young at the time of the divorce and were now in their teens and 20s, 10 years later. They found that the younger the girls were at the time of the divorce, the better they seemed to be doing. Three quarters of the girls who were now ages 11–15 were seen as "doing well" in that they had good grades in school, had good relationships with peers and adults, and were viewed as emotionally responsible and flexible. However, only 40% of the girls who were now ages 16–18 were seen as doing well, and 25% were doing poorly. Even more striking was that only 27% of the older adolescents—ages 19–23—were doing well, and 60% were doing poorly.

The girls' postdivorce relationships continued to be better with mothers than with fathers, and a good relationship with mothers often predicted good outcomes for these girls 10 years later. A good mother–child relationship was defined as one that included mutual affection, firm but flexible limits, emotional support, and clear parent–child boundaries. Whereas 80% of the girls had a good relationship with their mothers after the separation, this figure had dropped a bit, to 67%, 10 years later. One third of the mother–daughter relationships faltered primarily because of a decline in the mother's emotional well-being or the daughter's substance abuse or promiscuity.

The girls from divorced families had weaker relationships with their fathers, and poor relationships were associated with poorer adjustment at the 10-year mark. Whereas 50% of the girls had a good relationship with their fathers at the time of the marital breakup, only 18% did 10 years later. Girls who were the most likely to sustain a good relationship with their fathers were those who were the youngest at the time of the divorce (Wallerstein & Corbin, 1989).

At the 10-year mark, Wallerstein (1991; Wallerstein & Blakeslee, 1989) also found that many of the young women who had done well when they were younger experienced a sleeper effect as they moved into late adolescence. They were more likely to have impulsive, promiscuous sexual relationships. One third of the group became pregnant outside of marriage.

Wallerstein (1985) found the young women in her study to be caught up in a lifestyle of drifting from one man to another, unable to find a fulfilling relationship. They expressed an intense wish to be loved and cared for by a man yet were unable to find such a relationship. Wallerstein and Blakeslee (1989) wrote:

> The sleeper effect is particularly dangerous because it occurs at the crucial time when many young women make decisions that have long-term implications for their lives. Entering young adulthood, they are faced with issues of commitment, love, and sex in an adult context—and they are aware that the game is serious. (p. 61)

As young adults, at the 15-year mark, these women often were embarked on multiple relationships and impulsive marriages that ended in early divorce. Wallerstein (1985) reported that many of these young women had deep fears of abandonment, betrayal, and not being loved by a man. Two thirds reported a fear of betrayal by their partner, and some were preoccupied with this fear. As one woman said, "How can you expect commitment when anyone can change his mind at any time? Divorce destroyed my fantasy of love and life" (p. 552).

Hetherington and Parke (1979) found this same phenomenon. The young women from divorced homes in their sample were more likely to have married at an early age, to have been pregnant at the time they married, and to have chosen less adequate husbands than the women from widowed and intact homes. Kalter et al. (1985) studied a group of young women from divorced homes who had gone on to college and were doing well academically. Even though these women were succeeding at life (more so than their peers who had dropped out of high school or gotten pregnant outside of marriage), they had more negative views of men and of women than did their peers from intact homes. They viewed men as more unfeeling and less strong. They viewed women as less sensitive and less mature. They were significantly less hopeful about their future and were less certain of having an enduring marriage.

In a more recent study, Rosemary Dunlop and Ailsa Burns (1995) of Macquarie University in Australia challenged the sleeper effect. These researchers had already gathered a large amount of data on the lives of adolescents in earlier studies and then re-examined the data to gain information about adolescents whose parents had divorced when the children were between ages 13 and 16 and compared outcome data on those adolescents 10 years later with data from a matched sample of adolescents whose parents had not divorced. There were no reported differences in the groups by virtue of their parents' divorce status. However, both groups of young women reported higher rates of anxiety and depression than both groups of men. Dunlop and Burns noted that the children in the Hetherington and Wallerstein studies had experienced their parents' divorce at an earlier age.

Thus, the sleeper effect, if it does exist, may be characteristic of American samples and may be lessened if divorce occurs later in the child's life.

Wallerstein's work has been criticized for methodological flaws and for her overdramatization of the dire effects of divorce on children. Seeking to improve on her work with a larger sample and much stricter statistical sampling and precise measurements, Nicholas Zill and his associates at Child Trends in Washington, DC, completed a longitudinal study of the 240 children whom they followed in the National Survey of Children (Zill, Morrison, & Coiro, 1993). One group of the children had experienced their parents' divorce at the age of 5 or younger. The second group did so between ages 6 and 16. All were interviewed years later, at ages 12–16 for the first group and 18–22 for the second group.

Overall, Zill et al. (1993) concluded that the children had fared badly, that Wallerstein was not so far off the mark. In most categories of problems, the children of divorce had rates of occurrence that were roughly twice that of the children in intact families. Table 1.1 is a condensed version of Table 2 from Zill et al. (1993).

The results in Table 1.1 were obtained while controlling for race, social class, and parents' education. Not all comparisons were significant. For example, there were no strong differences in the two groups of young adults in rates of completing high school or delinquency. Zill et al. (1993) made the cogent point that the doubling of a hazard, in epidemiological terms, is a significant risk factor: "The increase in risk that dietary cholesterol poses for cardiovascular disease, for example, is far less than double, yet millions of Americans have altered their diets because of the perceived hazard" (p. 101).

Effects on Adult Children

What have we learned about the adult children of divorce, now 30 years into the experiment? An early study (Kulka & Weingarten, 1979) tracked the children of divorce 20 years later by analyzing the results of national cross-sectional surveys conducted in 1957 and 1976. Data collected by the Survey Research Center of the University of Michigan from nearly 5,000 adults were analyzed. Although the differences were small, the researchers found that the adult children of divorce were less likely to report being very happy than the adults from intact families and were more likely to report psychological problems and to have sought psychiatric treatment. More striking was the finding that the adult children of divorce reported lower levels of marital happiness and a higher divorce rate. For men and women who grew up in intact homes in the 1940s, 1950s, and 1960s, the divorce rate was about 2%. Yet men and women who grew up in divorced homes had adult divorce rates of 38% and 34%,

TABLE 1.1
(Adjusted) Proportion of Children Exhibiting Problems in Young Adulthood (Age 18–22 Years) by Developmental Area and Parental Divorce Status

Developmental area	% Parents divorced	% Intact family
Poor relationship with father	65	29
Poor relationship with mother	30	16
High Behavior Problem score	19	8
Received psychological help	41	22
Dropped out of high school	27	13

Note. From "Long-Term Effects of Parental Divorce on Parent–Child Relationships, Adjustment, and Achievement in Young Adulthood" by N. Zill, D. Morrison, and M. Coiro, 1993, *Journal of Family Psychology, 7*, p. 91. Copyright 1993 by the American Psychological Association. Adapted by permission.

respectively. This finding led to the term *intergenerational transmission of divorce*.

Following up on this dramatic finding, Norval Glenn and others at the University of Texas at Austin conducted a series of later studies on the adult children of divorce (N. Glenn & Kramer, 1985, 1987; N. Glenn & Shelton, 1983). These sociologists investigated the results of face-to-face interviews conducted with more than 1,500 people each year from 1973 to 1985. Along several dimensions of emotional well-being, such as happiness, health, and satisfaction with their lives, the adult children of divorce consistently scored lower than adults who had been raised with both parents (N. Glenn & Kramer, 1985). Again, the most striking finding was that these adults, as a group, were more likely to divorce than adults who grew up in intact homes or homes in which a parent had died (N. Glenn & Shelton, 1983). The percentage of adults who grew up in intact homes and went on to divorce in adulthood was 21.6% for men and 22.6% for women. The comparable divorce rates for those who grew up in single-parent homes because of divorce were 27.3% for men and 34.4% for women. The divorce rate for adult children who grew up with one parent and a stepparent was 31.5% for men and 38.9% for women. These figures were thus 50%–70% higher than those for adults from intact families.

N. Glenn and Kramer (1987) speculated on the finding that adult children of divorce are more prone to divorce when they reach adulthood. Although the differences are somewhat small, they are consistent from one study to another. Glenn and Kramer considered the possibility that this occurs because the children of divorce marry at younger ages, and it has been known for a long time that those who marry at a younger age divorce at higher rates. Glenn and Kramer also considered the possibility that educational opportunities are lessened for children of divorce and that lower levels of education correlate with higher rates of divorce. They found that the proportion of the indirect "parental divorce effect" that could be attributed to early marriage or years of school completed was small.

For many children, the home situation in families of divorce is more likely to be unhappy and thus brings about the expectation in these young people that marriage will provide an escape. N. Glenn and Kramer (1987) considered the reports of Wallerstein and Kelly (1980b) that adolescents in divorced homes are more "emotionally needy" and that this neediness impels them toward early establishment of close, heterosexual relationships. Wallerstein (1985) found that these young adults often insisted that they would never marry because they did not believe in the permanence or security of marriage.

Yet N. Glenn and Kramer (1987) found that adult children of divorce married at the same high rates as those from intact or widowed homes; what they did not seem to have was a commitment to marriage. Glenn and Kramer concluded that, as a group, these young adults often threw themselves into marriage, hoping for the best yet expecting the worst. It seemed that they often felt a need to minimize their expected failure by holding back their full commitment to the marriage.

As did the researchers who studied adolescents and young adults, N. Glenn and Kramer (1987) also found a greater negative effect for women than for men. (Again, only White Americans were studied, as Glenn and Kramer determined that the life course of Black Americans around marriage and divorce is much different.) These women were 59% more likely to divorce than were their counterparts from intact homes; the men were 32% more likely to divorce than were men from intact homes. Glenn and Kramer suggested that because it is women who have greater adjustments to make to marriage, the success of a marriage depends more on the commitment of the woman to make it work. Adult women of divorce, it seems, come into marriage more cynical, more distrustful, and more prone to find the disappointment that they are expecting. Glenn and Kramer suggested that mothers who are divorced are, as a group, more unhappy than fathers and that mothers may socialize their daughters to be distrustful of the benefits that marriage may hold for women.

Paul Amato (1996) of the University of Nebraska has continued to conduct research on the intergenerational transmission of divorce in an effort to find the link between childhood divorce status and adult divorce rates. Using telephone interviews with more than 2,033 married people in the United States, Amato looked at variables such as educational achievement, age at marriage, attitudes toward marriage, and interpersonal behavior problems as moderating variables. It is interesting that Amato picked 10 behaviors on the basis of clinical hunches (as opposed to an established set of indicators of interpersonal functioning): gets angry easily, has feelings that are easily hurt, is jealous, is domineering, is critical, will not talk to the other, has had a sexual relationship with someone else, has irritating habits, is not at home enough, and spends money foolishly. He reasoned that growing up in a home marked by disturbed marital and parent–child relationships might cause children to develop personal traits such as emotional insecurity and a lack of trust in others—traits that could increase the likelihood of a divorce.

Amato (1996) found that, as in previous studies, a marriage in which one of the partners had come from a divorced family was more likely to end in divorce than when both partners had grown up in intact families. However, when both partners had grown up in divorced homes, the risk for divorce was triple the rate of that for couples from intact families. When both members of the couple had come from divorced homes, they were also more likely to have had less education, to have lived together before marriage, and to have married at a young age. Finally, when both husband and wife had come from divorced homes, the rates of behavioral problems in the marriage were much higher.

The fascinating aspect of this study is that Amato (1996) determined the causative factor among all these variables to be the high rate of behavioral problems. He concluded that what seems to be transmitted from one generation of divorce to another is a disturbed pattern of interpersonal behavior such as problems with anger, jealousy, hurt feelings, infidelity, and so on. Each problem behavior appears to have an additive effect of increasing the risk of divorce in marriages of short duration. Amato concluded that this finding explains why the children of divorced parents have an increased risk of divorce in the second and third marriages as well as the first marriage. The risk is due to fundamental deficits in their capacity for interpersonal relationships. Amato's finding also explains why the risk of divorce is greatly increased when both members of the couple come from divorced backgrounds: Neither of the spouses has good interpersonal skills in intimate relationships. Finally, Amato concluded that his finding dovetails with the findings of other studies that have concluded that children whose parents divorced when they were very young appear to have more negative sequelae than those whose parents divorced when they were in their teens. These children have had even less time to learn how to function in close, interpersonal relationships.

These findings have been corroborated in large part by a recent study by Hetherington and her colleagues, Margaret Bridges and Glendessa Insabella (1998). Comparing adult children of divorce and remarriage with adult children of intact marriages, Hetherington et al. also found what seems to be the transmission of maladaptive behaviors—escalating, mutual, negative exchanges, or a pattern of chronic, unresolved conflict. During these exchanges, couples displayed denial, belligerence, criticism, contempt, and poor problem-solving skills.

Overall Effects

What the social scientists have concluded, now that America is 30 years into the divorce revolution, is that the national experiment with divorce has been a failure for the children. We can now say, with some degree of reliability, that Beth Ann, whom we met in the opening paragraphs of this chapter, is likely to show few problems now but will have a difficult adolescence. She is at risk for having fears of being abandoned and betrayed by the men in her life. She may accept a stepfather at age 7, but she is likely to reject a stepfather if her mother remarries in Beth Ann's adolescence. As a young woman, Beth Ann will approach marriage with feelings of insecurity and expectations of disappointment.

Davis is likely to continue to feel angry at his father and abandoned by him. He may have increasing conflicts with his mother as he moves into adolescence. He may do well if his mother remarries and if he accepts a stepfather's authority. Both Beth Ann and Davis's own marriages may be more prone to chronic conflict over feelings of insecurity. They both will be at greater risk for divorce, especially if they marry someone from a divorced family.

In the early 1970s, the general rule about divorce, at least for mental health professionals, was that it was better to divorce than to subject children to the tension of a chronically unhappy marriage. In the late 1990s most professionals would have to admit that divorce is a transition that benefits the adults involved but not usually the children. Children benefit from the security of an intact home and both a male and a female parent, and they are not generally better-off after divorce unless one of the parents was chronically abusive, had a severe mental illness, or was addicted to alcohol or drugs. Yet how much do parents actually benefit from divorce? Wallerstein and Blakeslee (1989) found in their California survey that only 10% of the divorced parents could state that both they and their former spouses were better off after the divorce.

Divorce has come to be viewed as a transition in children's lives—a period of stress and instability that requires the child to use coping mechanisms and to make lifestyle adjustments in order to reorganize his or her relationships with significant adults and reassess his or her trust in others. Furstenberg and Cherlin (1991) found that, by 1983, 41% of children were having to cope with the stress of growing up without both parents in the home by age 15, and up to 50% were having to do this by age 18. More troubling was that 26% of the children had to contend with two or more transitions—the loss of one parent through divorce, being the product of an out-of-wedlock pregnancy, the custodial parent's remarriage, and so on. One in 10 children had to cope with three or more transitions—the loss of a parent, a parent's remarriage, loss of the stepparent through a subsequent divorce, and so on. At the time of the study, the figures for children undergoing two, three, and four major life transitions were steadily rising. Furstenberg and Cherlin estimated that for children born in the 1990s, the number of children living for a time in a single-parent household could reach 60%, if the divorce rate remains high and the incidence of having children outside of marriage continues to increase in frequency. As demographers, they noted that if the number and range of casual unions become more frequent, then calculating marital stability will be become less meaningful, as a majority of "marriages" will be nonevents.

The figures for African American families are even less optimistic. Furstenberg (1994) noted that as far back as the 1800s, African Americans married earlier, had a higher incidence of premarital childbearing, and had less stable marriages, though scholars disagree as to whether this pattern was a holdover from kinship patterns in Africa, arose out of slavery, or began after Emancipation. Only about 75% of African Americans do marry, as opposed to 90% of White Americans. Of those who do, African Americans have a substantially higher rate of divorce—48% after 10 years of marriage, as opposed to 28% for White Americans. Although most White Americans remarry, the majority of African Americans do not. Among African American families, the proportion of children who grow up with both birth parents is less than 1 in 5. Furstenberg estimated that it may be as low as 1 in 10.

Are children today better off than the children of earlier generations? Furstenberg and Cherlin (1991) reviewed several demographic studies and determined that, of those children born around the turn of the century, about 25% lost a parent through death by the age of 15. This high death rate, coupled with a low divorce rate, meant that about one third of these children grew up in a single-parent home at some point.

However, by the 1950s only about 5% of children lost a parent through death. Only 11% went through a parent's divorce, and as few as 6% were born to unmarried mothers. If we add these together, about 22% of children experienced a single-parent home.

By the 1980s the percentage of children born out of wedlock rose to 24%. When this figure is added to the divorce rate, the figure for children born between 1970 and 1984 rises to 44% living in single-parent homes. For children born in the 1990s the estimates are as high as 60%. Furstenberg and Cherlin (1991) concluded that "whereas children may be no worse off today than a century ago, very possibly they are worse off than they were thirty or forty years ago" (p. 8).

WHAT THE RESEARCH SHOWS

Demographers indicate that although the rate of divorce had been increasing since the Civil War, it took a dramatic jump upward in the

1970s with the passage of no-fault divorce laws and the entry of women into the workforce. With the overvaluation of motherhood and the tender-years doctrine, custody was traditionally awarded to mothers from the late 1800s until the late 1970s. Since then, gender preference has been replaced with the "best-interests-of-the-child" standard. With gender and marital misconduct no longer grounds for custody, the awarding of custody has become less predictable and more rancorous.

Large-scale studies of the effects of divorce on children are largely in agreement in indicating that boys are at greatest risk, especially for disruptive behavior in single-mother households. Many boys show improved adjustment, however, when the mother remarries. Girls show far fewer adjustment problems, especially in mother-custody homes, but do not adjust well to the mother's remarriage. They appear to show delayed effects of the divorce in adolescence, with more acting-out and antisocial behavior. The most consistent outcome across age and gender groups was that the children of divorce are angrier and have a poorer bond with both their parents. Divorce appears to double the rates of a wide variety of adjustment problems in children.

Large-scale studies that followed the children of divorce into young adulthood found that they have lower educational and occupational attainment than their parents. They rate themselves as more unhappy and as having more problems in life than their counterparts from intact families. The most striking finding has been that these children have far greater rates of divorce in their own marriages, leading researchers to hypothesize about the intergenerational transmission of divorce.

GUIDELINES FOR THE CLINICIAN

This overview of divorce is provided for the clinician who may be asked questions by a client with children who is considering divorce. If a client is primarily interested in what is in the children's best interests, he or she should pause and think carefully about this decision. So often parents have presented children to me following a difficult divorce and have asked me to provide some short-term counseling "so that the divorce won't affect her (or him) in a negative way." Such a statement is naive at best and does not appreciate the overwhelming changes the children will experience for years to come. Furstenberg and Cherlin (1991) explained that the divorce is not simply one simple event but a transitional event. It initiates a series of multiple changes in roles and family structure that occur throughout the child's development into adulthood. Some of the transitions may be easy and beneficial, but an equal number may be stressful. For many children the divorce is the first in a series of ongoing losses.

The studies described here are broad in scope and by their nature report on group, not individual, differences. Clinicians know through their own experience that many children of divorce do well. If a client is firm in his or her decision to divorce or is already divorced, you may want to inform him or her about which factors predict good adjustment and which predict bad outcomes for children. A theme that will come up in study after study is that of conflict between the parents and its role in children's adjustment to divorce.

CASE STUDY UPDATE

Davis was evaluated by a child psychiatrist and prescribed antidepressant medication, although he showed little benefit. A visitation schedule was established when Walker finally leased an apartment. However, the children often spent their weekends at his new girlfriend's home, with much dissatisfaction. Brooke and Walker continued to have hostile interchanges when Walker arrived at the house—over his girlfriend, over financial problems, and with regard to Davis's growing refusal to see him.

Six months into treatment, Walker discontinued all contact with the children with no explanation. Davis accepted his father's silence at first with relief, then with anger: "He's not a father to me any more. He's a stranger to me." His moods became darker and more brooding. He became briefly paranoid, stating, "People are against me," and took a knife to school one day. However, this passed. Davis spent the summer with his mother and sister at his grandparents' home in North Carolina.

One year into treatment, Davis had not seen his father for 6 months. Although he voiced hatred of his father and said he wished he were dead, Davis was making a good adjustment to school and good grades. His affect was animated, and he enjoyed his hobbies again—bike riding, playing Nintendo, and following weather reports. His mother had met someone new, who owned a farm in North Carolina, and the children were expressing eagerness for her to remarry and move.

2

IMPACT OF PARENTAL CONFLICT ON CHILDREN'S ADJUSTMENT FOLLOWING DIVORCE

CASE STUDY

Sixteen-year-old Mark took a long drag on his cigarette and threw it to the pavement, where he ground it out with his shoe as if in defiance. He stared straight ahead, with his arms folded. "I'm not going in," he said. "I'm not going into your office. You and my mom are just trying to use me against my dad. I want to live with him, and I don't care if she gets custody; I'm not living with her. I'll run away."

Mark's mother Janice had brought him to my office for their third visit. He had announced at the first two visits that he did not want to be there but that he had come out of respect for her. This time he got into the car but refused to come up to my office. Instead, he stood in the corridor below, smoking. Janice had requested counseling for her and Mark but also wanted an opinion as to whether it was in her son's best interest to be in her custody. Janice's attorney also called me before their first appointment to let me know that Janice had filed a petition to reverse custody and that Mark's parents would be in court some time in the next few months.

Janice explained to me that she and her ex-husband Brad had argued over custody and child support for the 6 years since their divorce and that they had been to court many times. For a while, she had custody of Mark and his two older sisters, both of whom were defiant and skipped school. She sent one girl, then the other, to live with Brad, and one by one they dropped out of high school. One had a baby out of wedlock. The other married but was divorced with two small children. Janice remarried. Then Brad took her back to court and won custody of Mark.

Initially, Janice paid child support to Brad. Then, when she became disabled, she stopped the payments. Brad took her to court for back child support, requesting that she forgo part of her disability check. He also alleged that her disability was fraudulent.

In the meantime, Brad married a woman who was mentally unstable. Both Brad and his new wife worked a night shift, necessitating that Mark be alone and unsupervised for blocks of time at night. Janice would sometimes call the house at 11:00 at night to find that there was no one home. One night Mark got into a fight with an older boy who hit him over the head with a bottle and gave him a mild concussion. Mark's grades began to go down in ninth grade, and she saw all the elements gathering for another school failure.

"I made a mistake in letting the older two go live with their father," Janice said, her eyes filling with tears. "I didn't try hard enough to keep them in school. Now it's too late. I want Mark to know that I'm not going to give up on him without a fight. I'm not working. I've got the time to get him to school every morning and follow up with his homework every afternoon."

But for Mark it was too late. His relationship with his mother had deteriorated over the years. He blamed her for letting his sisters get pregnant and for letting them skip school. He did not trust Janice's motives. He had heard a great deal of anger from his dad about how Janice had been unfaithful in the marriage, how she was to blame for the divorce, and how she had falsified her disability. Janice had pointed out to Mark in frustration that when his sisters had dropped out of school and became pregnant they were living with their dad, but Mark refused to hear it. He was squarely aligned with his father.

"That's where I've lived for the last four years. That's where my home is. That's where my friends are, where my school is. I don't care if I'm alone at night. I can take care of myself. My father respects me as a man. He lets me do what I want to do."

Mark's face hardened into a glare as he stood in the corridor refusing to go upstairs, yet not retreating to the car. I asked him, "More than anything—never mind what your mother wants, what your father wants —what do you want right now? What can I do to help you?" Mark's voice softened as he said, "I just want the fighting to stop. I don't want to go back to court. It seems like all my life they've been fighting. That's all I've ever known. Fighting over my sisters, fighting over me, fighting over custody, fighting over child support. I'll do anything to stop the fighting and keep this thing out of court."

From there, I began a new approach to postdivorce conflict counseling: "shuttle diplomacy." I took Mark's requests upstairs to Janice, then back downstairs to Mark, and upstairs to Janice again, until we had hammered out an agreement with which both could live. Mark agreed to joint physical custody, alternating periods of 2 weeks in each home, with his mother having the final say with regard to educational and medical decisions. Janice agreed to drop her petition for a change of custody and to move into a home in Mark's school district. Brad would have to drop his petition for back child support as well. Neither parent would litigate any further.

Unfortunately, Mark's case illustrates what often happens as a consequence of divorce. Although most studies suggest that as many as 90% of divorces involving children are settled through negotiations (Mnookin & Kornhauser, 1979), many go back to court later to solve a custody or visitation dispute. Pearson and Thoennes (1982) found that 20% of their sample who were not offered mediation relitigated within 1 year of the divorce. Foster and Freed (1973–1974) found that one third of divorcing parents eventually relitigated custody and visitation issues. Many, such as Mark's parents, relitigate for 4, 6, or even 10 years. What do psychologists and sociologists know about these children?

As we saw in chapter 1, many large-scale studies, particularly those that followed children for years after divorce, have found that children of divorce do more poorly as a group than children from intact families. These results are consistent from one study to the next and are generally accepted as part of the knowledge base about the effects of divorce on children.

However, we also have learned that the degree of differences in adjustment between children of divorce and children of intact families is not that large. In other words, when all children of intact families and all children of divorce are compared on a number of measures, children of divorce come out as doing more poorly, but not by much.

Moreover, these studies report only on group differences. There are large individual differences in how the children of divorce are doing, with some doing rather well and some doing very poorly. Likewise, there are broad differences among the children of intact families, with many doing very well and some doing very poorly. In this chapter I take a closer look at the effects of divorce on children to better determine what accounts for these differences. Is it the absence of a parent? The reduced financial circumstances? The conflict the children experience? Several studies are reviewed that separate the effects of family conflict from divorce status. Finally, a body of research is summarized that explains how parental conflict has a corrosive effect on the parent–child relationship and children's emotional well-being, often exerting its effect long before the divorce occurs.

GROUP DIFFERENCES BETWEEN CHILDREN FROM INTACT AND DIVORCED HOMES

What theories account for the broad group differences between the children of divorce and the children in intact families? Can these theories help determine which children will do well and which will not?

Paul Amato and Bruce Keith (1991), sociologists at the University of Nebraska and West Virginia University, respectively, surveyed more than 90 studies conducted on children of divorce over a 20-year period. Amato and Keith surmised three theories about why the children of divorce fare more poorly: parental absence, economic hardship, and family conflict.

Parental Absence

The parental-absence perspective starts from the assumption that the family is the foundation for nurturing, teaching, and guiding children. Naturally, two parents should have more to offer than just one parent. One would hope that a father and a mother have two different sets of skills and perspectives. If this is true, then children who have lost a parent through death should fare no better than the children of divorce. Also, children whose parents remarry should have consistently better adjustment, as they now have two parents in the home. Last, children who see their noncustodial parent often should do much better overall than those who do not.

Amato and Keith (1991) found that although children who lose a parent through death do more poorly on many measures of adjustment than children in intact families, they function much better overall than the children of divorce. As shown in chapter 1, children in stepfamilies do not necessarily fare better than those in single-parent families. Generally, young boys fare better, and girls fare worse.

Children who see their noncustodial parent often have always been assumed to fare better, yet the studies do not bear this out. Many studies have found no differences in children's adjustment regardless of whether they saw their (primarily) father often. Some studies found that the children were doing better, but just as many found that they were actually doing worse the more often they saw their out-of-the-home parent. (This issue is reviewed in more depth in chapter 6.)

What we can conclude about parental absence is that it matters but that conflict also plays a major role. Children who survive a parental death may have much to cope with, but re-experiencing ongoing conflict is not a problem. Many studies indicate that children who have frequent visitations with a noncustodial parent in a harmonious atmosphere benefit enormously. But when the child must "cross the firing line" to get to the out-of-home parent, the child's adjustment goes down as the frequency of visits goes up.

Economic Hardship

Many studies have found that, following divorce, women's standard of living does down, whereas men's usually goes up. Keep in mind that 90% of children reside primarily with their mothers following divorce. Many studies on the children of divorce have found that children, as a group, are more economically disadvantaged following divorce than when they lived in an intact family. Also, children who are economically disadvantaged have poorer adjustment following divorce than children who are financially well off. However, in many studies in which children of divorced families were matched in income level with children of intact families, the children of divorce still scored higher on measures of poor adjustment and behavior problems.

If economic hardship were the biggest factor affecting children of divorce, these children would all fare better when the mother remarries and thus brings a second income to the family. This is not necessarily the case. It would make sense, too, that children of divorce would all have better adjustment if they lived with their fathers, who typically make much more money than mothers. The studies in this area generally indicate that boys do better staying with their fathers than with their mothers but that girls fare worse in father-custody homes than in mother-custody homes. (More will be said about this in chapter 4.) Therefore, there is valid but modest support for the economic-hardship factor.

Economic hardship may affect children following divorce and may lower their quality of life; however, it is likely to be an additive factor. This was seen in a study by Daniel Shaw and Robert Emery (1987) of the University of Virginia. Children's functioning at the time of their parents' separation was best predicted by parental discord, followed by mother's level of depression, and then by family income.

Family Conflict

Divorce has negative effects on children primarily through exposing them to conflict before, during, and after the divorce. If this is true, then it should be the conflict between parents per se that is detrimental to children and not necessarily whether the children live in an intact family or a divorced home. Also, children whose parents have low conflict following divorce should have fewer adjustment problems than children whose parents have high levels of conflict.

These results are, in fact, exactly what Amato and Keith (1991) found in their survey of more than 14 research studies to date. When intact families are categorized as "high conflict" versus "low conflict," the children in the high-conflict families have been shown to have significantly more behavior problems, more anxiety and depression, and lower self-esteem than children in low-conflict families. In fact, they show significantly more problems than groups of children from divorced homes that are low in conflict.

FAMILY CONFLICT AND DIVORCE STATUS

Although studies that compare family conflict and divorce status are not widely known, they are not new to psychiatric research circles. British psychiatrist Michael Rutter conducted a well-known series of studies in the late 1960s—now known as the "Isle of Wight" studies—on children who were separated from their parents. An island is an ideal place for studying child development because it is a stable society, and researchers can easily obtain needed information from the courts and schools and track the children over a period of years (see Rutter, 1971, 1987; Rutter, Tizard, Yule, Graham, & Whitmore, 1976).

Seeking to determine if short-term and long-term separations from mothers and fathers were as harmful as prevailing attitudes held them to be, Rutter (1971) found that short separations of a few weeks or months, when a parent was ill or away, had no effect on long-term adjustment in children. Long-term separations, when a parent was out of the home on a permanent basis, did appear to result in higher rates of antisocial (law-breaking) behavior—but only if the parent was out of the home because of a marital separation or divorce and not because of a death. In fact, parental conflict was a strong factor in predicting problems of acting out and unruliness, even when the home was intact. Rutter found the rate of antisocial behavior in boys to be 0% in homes where the parents' marriage was rated as "good," 22% when the marriage was "fair," and 39% when the marriage was "very poor." When boys were separated from both parents and the home had been characterized by a very poor marriage, nearly 70% of the boys engaged in antisocial behavior.

As Rutter searched his data for answers to such questions as "What kind of conflict?" and "How much conflict, and for how long a period of time?" he found straightforward answers. Although active quarrelling predicted poor outcomes in children, active fighting between parents combined with a lack of warmth toward each other and a lack of concern for family members tripled the rate of juvenile delinquency in these children. When children experienced parental discord followed by a divorce and then a second very poor remarriage characterized by more conflict, the rates of psychiatric disorder and delinquency were double those of children who experienced only one home marked by chronic conflict.

What happened when the conflict stopped? Rutter (1971) found no children who were separated from a parent through divorce who went on to live in happy, harmonious homes. Those who lived in family situations that were rated as fair, however, had half the delinquency rates as those who lived in poor home environments. Rutter concluded that children were at greater risk for antisocial behavior if they lived in quarrelsome homes with both parents than if they lived in happy and intact homes. He did not have enough of the latter type of participant to measure this directly, but he cited an early study by William McCord and Joan McCord (1959). These researchers, pioneers in the field of juvenile delinquency, found that children from harmonious but "broken" homes had lower rates of juvenile delinquency than children from homes marked by high levels of conflict and neglect in which the parents remained married. Incidentally, Rutter noted that all of these effects held only for boys and not for girls.

Nicholas Long of the University of Arkansas Medical School, along with coauthors Elisa Slater, Rex Forehand, and Robert Fauber (1988), sought to follow up on this type of finding by comparing three groups of adolescents: teens from intact families, teens from divorced homes whose parents had stopped fighting, and teens from divorced homes in which the conflict continued. He found what we might expect: that the first two groups were doing about equally well. The third group, however, had more difficulty with poor grades, anxiety and withdrawal, and acting out. Long et al. reasoned that these adolescents may have been affected by growing up in a more tense environment and by feelings of neglect due to less supervision and less help with homework.

These findings seem to contradict chapter 1, in which we were awash in data about the deleterious effects of divorce on children. As research studies on the effects of divorce on children have become more refined in the past 15 years, we are realizing that the divorce itself is but one part of a troubled life pattern for these children. The major stressor on children of divorce appears to be that they grow up in families marked by chronic conflict, which escalates to the rupture of their parents' marriage, followed by continued conflict after the divorce. Many children experience a second or even third home that is marked by high levels of tension again, unresolved problems with stepparents and stepsiblings, deep resentments, and a lack of warmth.

Kathleen Camara and Gary Resnick of Tufts University (1988, 1989) conducted extensive interviews with children and parents in mother-custody homes, father-custody homes, and two-parent households. They also explored how the parents resolved conflict, categorizing the resolution styles as verbal attack, avoidance, compromise and negotiation, and physical anger. Their results indicated that family type was not a good indicator of children's adjustment; rather, the best indicators were the parents' conflict resolution styles combined with the child's gender. When a parent (especially the father) used a verbal attack when faced with conflict, the children were more likely to be aggressive, to have trouble cooperating with other children, to have lower self-esteem, and to have more behavior problems (especially the boys). Mothers who used compromise and negotiation were more likely to have children with high self-esteem, regardless of whether they were divorced or married. The overall amount of conflict did not predict how the children were doing; the way in which conflict was expressed was the important factor.

Marsha Kline, a researcher at Yale University, with coauthors Janet Johnston and Jeanne Tschann (1991), re-examined much of the data from Wallerstein and Kelly's (1980b) study and found that families that had higher levels of conflict before the divorce tended to have higher levels after the divorce as well. The children who were most at risk for poor outcomes in these hostile environments were those who were younger, male, an only child or one of two children, and more often exposed to the conflict.

EFFECTS OF INTERPARENTAL CONFLICT ON CHILDREN'S
POSTDIVORCE ADJUSTMENT

What exactly is it about parental conflict that accounts for emotional and behavioral problems in children? Most divorcing parents make clear to their children that they are not angry at the children and that they are rejecting not the children but the other parent. Kline et al. (1991) found that mothers who were involved in higher levels of conflict in the marriage were less warm and more rejecting toward their young children. They were also less happy themselves and often had poor control over their emotions. In addition, they had lower expectations for their children's self-control. Overall, these mothers had poorer relationships with their children than mothers in low-conflict marriages.

Christy Buchanan, with Eleanor Maccoby and Sanford Dornbusch (1991) of Stanford University, explored this subject further with adolescents. Buchanan et al. determined the degree to which adolescents were "caught up" in their parents' conflict by asking them these questions: "How often do you feel caught in your parents' conflict?" "How often does your mother (father) ask you to carry messages?" "Does your mother ask questions you wish she didn't ask?" "Does your father ask questions you wish he didn't ask?" "How often do you hesitate to talk about your mother in front of your father (and vice versa)?" Buchanan et al. found that the more "caught" the adolescents were, the more likely they were to say that they did not feel close to either parent. Also, they were more likely to be depressed and anxious and to engage in reckless, law-breaking behavior.

A researcher at the University of Virginia, Robert Emery (1982), who is widely known for his studies on the effects of parental conflict on children, summarized the research to that date on the effects of interparental conflict on the children of divorce. His main findings on American children are similar to those from the children on the Isle of Wight:

- Parental discord is associated with behavior problems in children of intact families as well as families of divorce.
- Behavior problems are more strongly associated with coming from a divorced home than with experiencing the death of a parent.
- Children from intact but high-conflict homes have more behavior problems than children from divorced but conflict-free homes.
- Children from divorced parents who continue to experience conflict are worse off than those who do not.
- Open conflict is worse on children than emotional distance or apathy.
- The parents' own emotional problems tend to interact with the level of conflict to be especially destructive to children's emotional and behavioral adjustment.
- Parental conflict is more predictably associated with problems of undercontrol (i.e., acting out, running away, argumentativeness, defiance, using drugs, dropping out of school) than overcontrol (i.e., anxiety, worry, withdrawal, depression) in children.
- Boys in conflict-ridden homes have more behavior problems than do girls, but this may be due to the fact that boys tend to respond to stress with problems of undercontrol, whereas girls respond more with symptoms of overcontrol.
- The child's relationship with his or her mother is perhaps the strongest predictor of how well he or she will function under the chronic stress of a conflicted home.
- The child's relationship with his or her father is not a strong predictor of how he or she will do under conditions of conflict; rather, the amount of conflict between the parents seems to shape whether the child has a good or poor relationship with the father.
- Divorced parents tend to be poorer parents in that they make fewer demands on their children to act maturely and independently, they are less affectionate with them, they communicate with them more poorly, and they are more inconsistent in their discipline.

- There is some evidence that poor parenting style is evident years before the divorce.
- Boys tend to have poorer relationships with mothers in homes marked by conflict than do girls, most likely because of boys' acting-out behavior.
- A good relationship with one parent may mitigate the effects of the divorce and the chronic conflict on the child, but it must be a very good relationship and most likely must be with the mother.

IMPORTANCE OF THE PARENT–CHILD RELATIONSHIP DURING AND AFTER THE DIVORCE

The last conclusion above is intriguing and comes up in nearly every study of the effects of chronic parental conflict on children. Almost every parent going through a divorce resolves to work toward a good relationship with his or her child, no matter what hard feelings may remain toward the ex-spouse, yet it is this crucial factor that often plays a large part in how children adjust to the divorce. Jeanne Tschann of the Center for the Family in Transition in Corte Madera, California, and coauthors Janet Johnston, Marsha Kline, and Judith Wallerstein (1989) studied 80 middle- and upper-middle-class divorcing families with several predictions as to how children's adjustment would be affected by six factors: demographic variables, temperament, marital conflict, postseparation parental conflict, amount of time with the visiting parent, and parent–child relationships. Tschann et al. found that the strongest correlation overall was between marital conflict before the separation and postseparation parental conflict, as might be expected. High levels of conflict before the divorce predicted high levels of continued conflict after the divorce. They found significant correlations between both of these types of conflict and the children's emotional adjustment; however, the correlations between "warm relationship with mother" and "children's emotional adjustment" were twice as high. In other words, although postseparation parental conflict predicted to some degree how children would respond to the divorce, it was mediated by how it affected the parent–child (particularly the mother–child) relationship. Relationships between "warm relationship with father" and "children's emotional adjustment" were significant but much lower. Being female and having an easy temperament predicted good emotional adjustment to a slight degree. In predicting which children were likely to have behavioral problems after the separation, marital conflict and postseparation parental conflict were again significant factors. Warm relationships with both the mother and father predicted better outcomes, but to a lesser degree here than when predicting emotional adjustment.

As part of a series of studies on adolescents' response to divorce, Amanda McCombs and Rex Forehand (1989) of the University of Georgia followed the progress of a group of 71 adolescents whose parents had recently divorced. Using grade-point average as a measure of good adjustment, McCombs and Forehand found that the mothers of the students with good grades had higher education levels, which might be expected, but they were also less depressed and had less conflict with the adolescents' fathers. The adolescents who had the best grades reported the least conflict with their mothers. McCombs and Forehand found that the best predictors of students' academic performance following divorce were the reported levels of conflict to which the adolescent was exposed. In a follow-up study, Amanda Thomas and Forehand (1993) found significant correlations between divorced fathers' reports of good relationships with their teenage children and teachers' low ratings of anxiety and withdrawal. A poor relationship with the father after the divorce predicted teacher ratings of conduct problems in the classroom.

Robert Hess of Stanford University and Kathleen Camara of Tufts University (1979) conducted an intriguing study in which they compared children in intact and divorced homes categorized as high or low in "parental harmony." They found what might be expected—that the degree of parental harmony was a better predictor of how the children were doing than whether the children's parents were married or divorced. The most aggressive children were those with low parental harmony, a poor mother–child relationship, and a poor father–child relationship.

However, when Hess and Camara (1979) compared the effects of parental conflict against the strength of the parent–child relationship, they found that the quality of the parent–child relationship was an even stronger predictor of how happy the children were than was the amount of parental conflict. Some of the children had good relationships with both parents in spite of much conflict between the parents. As a group, the children of divorce and the children of intact marriages did best when they had good relationships with both parents, worse when they had a good relationship with just one parent, and far worse when they did not have a good relationship with either parent.

DETERIORATION OF PARENT–CHILD BONDS DURING DIVORCE

Although it may be heartening to know that a good relationship with one's child may ease the effects of the divorce as well as the effects of the ongoing conflict, the reality is that many parent–child relationships deteriorate under these conditions. Recall the National Survey of Children study cited in chapter 1 (Furstenberg & Cherlin, 1991; Furstenberg et al.,

1983) in which several thousand children were interviewed. In Wave 1 of the study, the researchers compiled information as to how often children saw their parents following a divorce. In Wave 2, James Peterson and Nicholas Zill (1986) of Child Trends compiled information as to how often these children described having a positive relationship with their parents. Altogether, 49% of the children (from both intact and divorced homes) reported a good relationship with both parents—19% with the mother only, 12% with the father only, and 20% with neither parent.

When broken down by family type and amount of disruption and conflict, however, the numbers are very different. Table 2.1 contains the numbers for intact families, categorized by level of conflict. The figures give a stark realism to what happens between parents and children who are caught up in chronic conflict. Children living in conditions of chronic parental conflict enjoyed good relationships with both parents at a level that was one third of that seen in the homes of children whose parents had low conflict. Likewise, the percentage of children who were alienated from both parents, and thus at risk for psychiatric and behavioral problems, made up 28% of the sample.

Next, Peterson and Zill (1986) compiled figures on the children of divorce, categorized by type of living arrangement (see Table 2.2). The figures are lower still than those for intact families. Most dramatic are the figures for children living with mothers who have divorced a second time: In these cases, less than 1 child in 10 reported having good relationships with both parents. Forty-six percent of this group is seriously at risk for emotional problems, acting-out behavior, and poor academic performance.

EFFECTS OF EXPOSURE TO CHRONIC PARENTAL CONFLICT

To fully understand how the parent–child relationship often deteriorates following divorce, we must look at the process of chronic conflict in the family and its psychological impact on children and parents. A body

TABLE 2.1
Children's Relationship With Parents, by Degree of Conflict

Degree of conflict	% Children having positive relationship with			
	Both parents	Mother only	Father only	Neither
Low	62	13	12	13
Moderate	51	14	12	23
High and persistent	20	29	14	28
All families	55	15	12	18

Note: From "Marital Disruption, Parent–Child Relationships, and Behavior Problems in Children" by J. Peterson and N. Zill, 1986, Journal of Marriage and the Family, 48, p. 295. Copyrighted 1986 by the National Council on Family Relations, 3989 Central Ave. NE, Suite 550, Minneapolis, MN 55421. Reprinted by permission.

TABLE 2.2
Children's Relationship With Parents, by Children's
Living Arrangements

Child's living arrangement	% Children having positive relationship with			
	Both	Mother only	Father only	Neither
Living with mother[a]	25	35	11	29
Mother separated or divorced	26	32	12	30
Mother remarried	32	39	9	20
Mother redivorced	8	36	10	46
Living with father[a]	36	22	33	9

Note: From "Marital Disruption, Parent–Child Relationships, and Behavior Problems in Children"
by J. Peterson and N. Zill, 1986, Journal of Marriage and the Family, 48, p. 295. Copyrighted 1986
by the National Council on Family Relations, 3989 Central Ave. NE, Suite 550, Minneapolis, MN
55421. Reprinted by permission.
[a]Full-time.

of research has now established the negative effects of marital conflict in intact families on the behavior and adjustment of toddlers (Jouriles, Pfiffner, & O'Leary, 1988), school-aged children (Shaw & Emery, 1987), and young adolescents (Long, Forehand, Fauber, & Brody, 1987). What is the specific connection between chronic marital conflict and poor adjustment in children?

Insecurity and Agitation

Patrick Davies and E. Mark Cummings (1994) of West Virginia University theorized that children who grow up in harmonious homes derive a strong sense of security from the confidence that their parents' marriage will endure. They grow up to believe that their parents will be there when they need them and that their parents will not be constantly preoccupied or overly stressed. When they see their parents having small arguments, they are not threatened or frightened. They expect that ordinary family feuds will be resolved.

Chronic conflict, on the other hand, causes chronic distress and agitation in children as well as a loss of emotional control. Some parents might think that children who witness chronic parental conflict will "get used to it." However, the opposite seems to be true. Children become sensitized over time and begin to perceive even small arguments as danger signs of major blowups that might be about to happen, so that over time their emotional reactions get more tense with each argument. Children often try to intervene in the conflict, only to end up feeling useless and inadequate. They feel more out of control and sense that their home and family life are more unpredictable. In a home marked by conflict and unpredictability, children form insecure attachments to their parents. They do not have a deep and abiding trust in their caretakers.

Shame and Guilt

The content of parental conflict appears to matter to children in that conflicts over child-rearing or the child's own misbehavior elicit in children the greatest amount of shame, responsibility, self-blame, and fear of being drawn into the conflict. These children, whose own out-of-control behavior may have contributed to the parental conflict, react with more acting out, which contributes to more parental conflict, more guilt and shame, and so on.

John Grych and Frank Fincham (1993) of the University of Illinois demonstrated that the content of parental fighting matters to children. They studied children in middle-class, two-parent families and found that when children were exposed to marital conflict that was not about them, they had higher levels of anger, sadness, and worry. However, when the conflict was about them, they experienced more self-blame, felt more shame, and had more fears of being drawn into the conflict. Grych and Fincham suggested that fighting over a child has direct effects on his or her self-evaluation.

Helplessness

Davies and Cummings (1994) suggested that when conflict is unresolved, children experience much more distress than when it is resolved. Thus, it is not just the conflict that is stressful for children but also the meaning of the conflict. Unresolved conflict means to the child that such conflict is going to happen repeatedly and that there will be no end to it. The conflict seems to be inevitable, and the children, even their parents, are helpless to stop it.

Fear of Abuse

Physical violence between the parents is the most severe form of conflict to which children are exposed. Davies and Cummings (1994), in their review of 12 studies on this subject, found that among the various forms of conflict, physical aggression between parents was associated with the most behavioral and adjustment problems. Severe emotional problems are four times more common in children of battered women than in children raised in nonviolent homes. Fear of seeing one's parent hurt or injured stirs up the most distress and agitation. It also causes the child to fear that he or she will be abused as well. In fact, in homes where parents abuse each other, children are more likely to be abused.

Less Parental Involvement

Davies and Cummings (1994) found in their review that in 13 of 13 studies, parental conflict (whether in married or divorced families) was associated with parental rejection, hostility, and unresponsiveness toward the children. Parents who are caught up in high levels of conflict simply have less to give to children in that they are more preoccupied, more impatient, more stressed, more agitated, and more discouraged. They, too, feel hopeless and inadequate. It seems likely that they become more sensitized over time to stresses of all kinds, including the children's own misbehavior.

Davies and Cummings found that, in general, children who grow up with marital conflict tend to grow up with poor attachments to both parents. These parents also tend to be poorer parents in terms of lax discipline and less consistency, much as Robert Emery (1982) found. Instead of focusing on children's schoolwork and friends, parents focus more on with whom the child is allied and how to win over the child as an ally. Instead of being listened to, these children tend to be relied on as confidantes. Acting out and slipping grades tend to be ignored as the parent mobilizes all of his or her energy for the struggle to cope with the spouse or ex-spouse.

Rejection

Daniel Shaw of the University of Pittsburgh, along with authors Robert Emery and Michele Tuer (1993), addressed the question, "What is the association between predivorce parenting practices and a young adult's adjustment, and how is it affected by the parents' divorce?" Shaw et al. re-examined archival data from the New York Longitudinal Study conducted by A. Thomas, Chess, and Birch (1968; Thomas & Chess, 1977) and found that boys from families who went on to divorce did have poorer life outcomes in adolescence and adulthood. As one would expect, these families also had higher levels of marital conflict. What was intriguing was that parents who would go on to divorce behaved differently toward their sons when the boys were as young as age 3. They were less concerned about their sons and more rejecting toward them.

Robert Fauber of Temple University, with coauthors Rex Forehand, Amanda Thomas, and Michelle Wierson (1990) of the University of Georgia, as part of a series of studies on the influence of divorce on adolescents, developed a statistical model to answer the following questions: (a) Is it the exposure to parents' conflict itself, or the reduced adequacy of parenting, that has a negative impact on adolescents just following a divorce? (b) If it is the lowered level of parental functioning that is the problem, what, specifically, is going on? Is it that the parents are lax in their control of the children? Is it that they are using shame and guilt to discipline them? Or is it the degree of rejection the adolescent experiences, the lack of acceptance and closeness? Fauber et al.'s results supported the hypothesis that it was low quality of parenting per se, more than the level of conflict, that predicted both internalizing and externalizing problems in the adolescents from divorced homes. Furthermore, the degree of rejection the adolescents felt, far more than any other parenting factor, accounted for their high scores on emotional and behavioral problem inventories.

These findings were echoed by John Fantuzzo, a researcher at the University of Pennsylvania, and his associates (Fantuzzo et al., 1991) at California State University. Fantuzzo et al. studied a group of 107 preschool children who were living in a home that was not violent, living in a home marked by verbal abuse, living in a home where there was physical violence, or living with their mothers in a shelter for battered women. The shelter group, which presumably had been exposed to the most violence at home, displayed much higher levels of internalizing behavior problems and much lower levels of social competence than the other three groups. Beyond that, however, these children gave self-reports of much lower levels of maternal acceptance. These ratings were obtained when the children responded to 24 pictures of a more competent or more accepted child versus a less competent or less accepted child and were asked "Which one is like you?" Like the adolescents described above, these children, who had been exposed to high levels of conflict, also had high levels of emotional problems, but the key that linked the two was the sense these children had of being unloved and rejected.

Janet Johnston (1992, cited in Johnston, 1994a) reported on the adjustment of 75 children (ages 3–12) whose families were referred by a court because of chronic conflict between the parents. The findings strongly and consistently demonstrated that physical aggression in the family was associated with emotional and behavioral problems in the children. They also revealed diminished parenting, in that these parents were found to be less warm, less affectionate, and more threatening with their children.

EFFECTS OF PARENTAL CONFLICT BEFORE DIVORCE

An intriguing finding of many studies is that boys with difficult, hard-to-manage temperaments or personalities seem to be most at risk for poor outcomes when growing up in families marked by conflict, followed by divorce, followed by more conflict. Over the past 10 years, a number of researchers have conducted studies in which information was gathered about these boys before the divorce—in some cases, as much as 11 years before the divorce. For example, Jeanne Block, Jack Block, and Per Gjerde (1986) of the University of California, Berkeley, found that 3-year-old boys from families who were more likely to divorce when the boys were 13 or 14 were already identified as more moody, difficult, stubborn, and restless. They were more disorderly, more inconsiderate of other children, more impulsive, and more likely to try to take advantage of other children.

Similarly, Andrew Cherlin of Johns Hopkins University and other researchers in the United States and England (Cherlin et al., 1991) were able not only to study boys after the divorce, when they were ages 11 and 16, but also to obtain information on the boys 4–5 years earlier, when they were ages 7 and 11. They found that the boys who had more behavior problems following the divorce (as rated by both parents and teachers) and lower reading and math grades were the same boys who had more behavior problems and poorer school performance several years before the divorce.

These studies point to the need to identify the children who are most at risk for problems stemming from parental conflict and divorce—for example, boys who, at preschool ages, are already aggressive and difficult to manage. However, they also raise the question of how much the child's behavior may contribute to the marital conflict.

Ernest Jouriles of the University of Houston and others (Jouriles, Murphy, Farris, Smith, Richters, Waters, 1991) raised this question in a study of 3- to 6-year-old boys. They found that the degree to which parents disagreed about child-rearing was strongly associated with behavior problems in these young boys—even more so than the degree of general conflict between the parents. They suggested that boys with difficult temperaments seem to cause more parental conflicts over how to discipline the child. As the level of conflict escalates, the child's behavior tends to worsen, perhaps because the parents are inconsistent in their handling of the child. Although we cannot determine just how much one causes the other, these studies do point to the need for parents and family therapists to be particularly aware of these high-risk children: boys who are characterized, as early as preschool age, by disruptive, out-of-control behavior in a family that is marked by conflict and appears headed for divorce.

EFFECTS OF PARENTAL PRE- AND POSTDIVORCE CONFLICT ON ADOLESCENTS AND YOUNG ADULTS

In chapter 1, I reviewed a number of studies that indicated that experiencing the divorce of one's parents as a child has broad group effects on those children as young adults. Do the separate effects of parental conflict on children persist into adulthood? Paul Amato, along with Laura Loomis and Alan Booth (1995), followed up a large group of children in 1992 whose parents had been interviewed in 1980, before divorce occurred. The average age of the sample was 23, and they had experienced their parents' divorce between ages 9 and the early 20s. Amato et al. explored the young adults' feelings of emotional stress, their happiness in intimate relationships, and their perceived closeness with family and friends. They found more negative outcomes for individuals from high-conflict families who did not divorce, as compared with those from high-conflict families who did divorce.

It is interesting that Amato et al. (1995) also found high ratings of emotional problems in adulthood for individuals from families with low conflict who did go on to divorce. They cited a paradigm by Wheaton (1990), who suggested that life transitions were perceived as not upsetting, and even as beneficial, when they are preceded by acute stress. Yet when there is low stress—such as in a family where the children are not aware of any intense conflict—transitions out of these roles are painful, because they are associated with the loss of a quality of life that was gratifying. Joan Kelly (1998), reviewing this intriguing finding, suggested that when parental conflict is low, adolescents neither have reason to anticipate divorce nor see any benefits to themselves coming from their parents' divorce. These adolescents may enjoy positive, supportive parent–child bonds and may come to view the divorce only in terms of loss—of time and attention from their parents and a reduced standard of living.

In a follow-up to Amato et al.'s (1995) study, Amato and Alan Booth, of Pennsylvania State University, retrospectively examined the quality in 1980 of the parent–child relationship of those families who went on to divorce by 1992 (Amato & Booth, 1996). They found that low ratings of marital happiness, along with reports of problems in parents' relationships with their children, were present 8–12 years before the divorce. These parents were more likely to report that they felt their children gave them a lot of problems, that they did not like the way their spouse handled the children, and that one of them had been abusive to the children. Furthermore, the study found that having a poor marriage with high levels of conflict 8–10 years before divorce was associated with parent–child relationships that were less close and less affectionate after the divorce and that further deteriorated during early adulthood.

WHAT THE RESEARCH SHOWS

We now know that there is a broad range of outcomes for the children of divorce. Some do quite well, some do poorly, and a small proportion do very poorly. Researchers in the field of divorce have stopped conceptualizing divorce as a *cause* of adjustment problems in children but rather as a *process*. By this we mean that divorce often occurs in the context of many factors that are co-occurring both before and after the divorce.

In this chapter we have seen why divorce has a stronger impact than the death of a parent on children's adjustment. It is not the absence of a parent or a reduced quality of life that affects children the most, but it is the level of conflict associated with divorce that is key, both before and after the divorce. "Good" divorces, in which parents fight very little or which bring the marital fighting to an end, have much less impact on children than do "bad" divorces. A good relationship with both parents acts as a buffer against the losses of divorce. Chronic parental conflict corrodes the parent–child bond over time and more so with each subsequent divorce. Children caught up in this cycle of chronic conflict experience chronic distress and agitation, feelings of insecurity and helplessness, fears for their own safety, a lack of parental involvement, and an overwhelming sense of rejection. Children with difficult temperaments respond to chronic conflict even more negatively than do other children and can be identified in distressed families long before the divorce occurs.

GUIDELINES FOR THE CLINICIAN

Clinicians are often asked by parents whether it is better for them to stay together for the sake of their children or to end an unhappy marriage for the benefit of all. More often, parents ask clinicians how they can go about the divorce process in a way that will minimize negative outcomes for their children. The clinician may want to explore with the parent a series of questions regarding the five major factors that we have come to believe determine the outcome of divorce for children.

The first and most obvious question is "To what degree are the children experiencing active, open quarrelling; chronic disagreements; verbal abuse; and even physical confrontations in the home right now?" A corollary to this is "Will the divorce bring an end to this conflict?" If the parent can determine that the divorce will bring an end to open, rancorous conflict, then clearly the children will be relieved and will benefit greatly. However, the parent who seeks a divorce and custody of children after a long and conflicted marriage must realize that the conflict may not end. It may only narrow and become focused on issues surrounding the children. For these children, there may be no relief; in fact, the conflict may intensify.

Some marriages that end in divorce are not characterized by open conflict. Instead, there may be a lack of warmth and common interests between the parents, and this degree of emotional distance may be very painful to them. However, these problems may go relatively unnoticed by the children and are clearly not as meaningful to the children as open conflict, unless the lack of warmth extends to them as well. When, finally, one party sues the other for divorce with little warning, the resulting bitterness on the part of the spouse who is left, as well as the children, results in conflict that was not experienced before. These children will fare poorly as well.

The second most important factor is the parent's relationship with the children. An important question to ask the parent who is anticipating divorce is "Will you be able to maintain a good relationship with your children in the emotional wreckage of a hostile divorce?" A parent must consider his or her own absence from the children, his or her own emotional distress and preoccupation, and the emotional distress and preoccupation of the other parent. Will he or she be able to nurture as well as discipline children—wear both hats, so to speak—as a single parent? Even when the children may be angry, disruptive, and bitter? Parents must ask themselves whether they can maintain a positive parent–child bond in the face of bitterness toward them by the other parent, and sometimes the children as well, and the children's loss of respect for them as their faults are laid bare by angry and blaming attacks. Many parents are able to be better parents when they can function as a single parent in a home that is no longer marked by conflict. In these cases, the children will experience an improved relationship with one or both parents.

A third factor is the emotional stability of the primary caretaker for the children after the divorce. One must ask "Will the custodial parent for the children be able to cope with enormous stress with patience, emotional control, and a positive outlook?" If this parent, before the divorce, was chronically unhappy, impatient and explosive, inconsistent in his or her approach with the children, drank alcohol excessively, and had a negative outlook toward life, then this person is likely to be more so under stress. If the children are to live with this person, then odds are they will not fare well. If, on the other hand, this emotional instability in one partner led to the divorce, and the children will reside with the healthier partner, then life may begin to improve as the children can begin to live with more security, consistency, and predictability.

A fourth factor is economic hardship. Although this is not a psychological factor per se, it is one with emotional consequences. A decline in standard of living for children results in more stress, more resentment toward the parent who initiated the divorce, and a poorer quality of relationship with the parent who is constantly preoccupied with money worries. Economic hardship also results in more battles over child support, triggering more hostility, more litigation, and withholding of visitations in retaliation for economic suffering.

The last factor to consider is the number of disruptions the children will experience. This factor has not been directly studied by researchers because disruptions are hard to specify and quantify. Indirectly, the studies of Rutter in England and Peterson and Zill in the United States found that children who experienced a second divorce did more poorly than those who experienced only one.

However, disruption for the children of divorce means much more than simply a parent's second divorce. By "disruptions" I mean moves—from a home to an apartment, across town, to another school district, to another state—as well as changes of caretakers—to grandmother's home temporarily, then to Mom's, then to Mom and Dad's together while they try to reconcile, then to Mom's again, then to Dad and his girlfriend's for a few months. Disruptions also include having to adjust to new people—Mom's boyfriend, Dad's girlfriend, Dad's girlfriend's son, Mom and her new husband's baby, and so on—as well as ongoing stressors—Mom's new husband's drinking problem, not getting along with a very strict stepmom, Mom taking Dad back to court over child support. Disruptions can even mean more losses—Dad moving away to a distant part of the country, Mom getting divorced again, Mom working two jobs and being gone all the time, Brother leaving home and moving in with Dad several states away. From these lists it is obvious that the disruptions and stresses children of divorce experience are numerous. Although children in intact families experience stresses, transitions, and losses as well, the numbers are smaller. It is rare for two parents to divorce amicably, live within a mile or two of each other, never move, never remarry, and so on.

Again, the divorce is not a precipitating event in itself; it is not a cause but a process—a series of dominos cascading in several directions. Each of these events requires the child to put emotional energy into coping with life—energy that ordinarily would be put into the business of growing up.

Last, I conclude with Table 2.3, which lists the worst-case scenarios and the best possible outcome scenarios of divorce, what epidemiologists call "the pluses and the minuses." Parents should consider both in their divorce decisions.

TABLE 2.3
Children of Divorce: Best and Worst Outcomes

Best possible outcome	Worst-case scenario
Conflict may be ongoing, but children are shielded from it	Conflict is open and acrimonious
There is no violence	Children are witness to violence
Children are not verbally or physically abused	Children are verbally or physically abused
Conflict is short lived	Conflict goes on for years
Conflict is not about the children	Conflict is about the children
Children are not involved in the conflict	Children are drawn into the conflict
Conflict is often resolved	Conflict is never resolved

Table continues

TABLE 2.3   (*Continued*)

Best possible outcome	Worst-case scenario
This is a large family	There are only 1 or 2 children in the family
Child is a girl or a boy with an easy temperament	Child is a boy with a difficult temperament
Divorce is wanted by both parties	One party does not want the divorce and is bitter
Parents settle custody out of court	Parents fight bitterly over custody
Conflict does not continue	Conflict, litigation continue after the divorce
Child does not have behavior problems	Child, especially a boy, acts out and becomes disruptive
Custodial parent remains patient, calmly in control, and consistent	Custodial parent engages in angry, coercive battles with child; parent is angry, rejecting, preoccupied
Child continues to feel a strong, close bond with the custodial parent	Child perceives a deterioration in relationship with custodial parent; feels distant, rejected
Noncustodial parent continues regular visitation	Noncustodial parent visits irregularly, infrequently, or not at all
Visitations take place smoothly	There is much conflict, tension surrounding the visitation
Custodial parent has few money worries	Custodial parent experiences continued economic hardship
Custodial parent is content with the divorce and how his or her life is going	Custodial parent is depressed, discouraged, and unhappy about his or her prospects for the future
Child's relationship with both parents remains good	Child's relationship with both parents is poor
Parents remain in same school district	Child experiences multiple moves and changes of homes, schools, friends, etc.
Child remains mostly with one parent, with no more than one transfer to the other home	Child moves back and forth between parental homes because of disruptive behavior or family instability
Mother (of daughter) does not remarry	Mother (of daughter) remarries
Mother (of son) remarries	Mother (of son) does not remarry
Parents' new marriages are stable and harmonious	Parents' new marriages are marked by conflict
Parents do not divorce again	Child experiences a second divorce, third divorce, etc.

CASE STUDY UPDATE

It would be encouraging to report that Janice and Brad's agreement was adopted and that Mark was doing well, but this was not the case. Brad refused to agree to the terms, and he and Janice went to court. As of this writing, the case is still in litigation. Mark is continuing to have excessive absences from school and to fail to turn in work. He continues to drift back and forth between his two homes as he feels the need.

3

THE ROAD TO DIVORCE

CASE STUDY

Scott and Laura were ordered by the court to have an evaluation to determine who would have primary custody of their two young daughters Nicole and Jeanette. The couple had married in 1977, had two children, Tim and Denise, then divorced in 1984. They remarried in 1985, had the two younger girls, and separated again in 1995.

By the time Scott and Laura came for the evaluation, their family was well known to the local courts. The marriage had been stormy from the beginning. Scott, a police officer, had always been somewhat moody and distant and was prone to blowups when he felt threatened. Laura, who had devoted herself to being a full-time mother, had always been highly emotional, needy, and demanding of Scott. The neighbors had heard the angry exchanges over the years—some from the kitchen window, some out in the street—and all were interviewed as part of the evaluation.

Laura saw Scott as self-centered, uninvolved as a parent, and too harsh with discipline. Scott saw Laura as manipulative, constantly critical of him, too lax with the children, and mentally unstable. When Laura was angry at Scott, she would pursue him doggedly with verbal attacks and accusations. He would avoid her as long as he could, then finally blow up. Scott denied that he was abusive to Laura, but the children told stories of him saying abusive things to her and pinning her against the wall.

Tim, the older son, allied himself with Scott. He would soon graduate and did not want to get involved in the conflict. The older daughter Denise was solidly allied with Laura. Nicole and Jeanette had become afraid of Scott and would cling to Laura during the parents' arguments. The event that triggered the final separation was one where Scott observed Laura talking with a man and then grabbed her, with a loud argument ensuing. Laura insisted that he physically abused her, filed a family violence petition, and had the papers served to him at the police station.

When they separated, Scott moved out, and Laura stayed with the children in the house. However, the visitations did not take place peacefully. Scott reported that Laura had called the police on him four times (Laura said it was two times) for coming early to pick up the children.

By the time the family came for the evaluation, the temporary hearing had been held, and Nicole and Jeanette had been placed with Scott. Denise stayed with them in Scott's home to "protect" them from his angry blowups and harsh punishments. Ordinarily, Laura would have received temporary custody, but her contempt for Scott was her undoing. She had talked to all the neighbors about how awful Scott was until she had few supporters. She had fired her attorney when he refused to carry out her unreasonable requests for sole custody, high child support and alimony payments, and more than half the couple's assets. To add to this, she had become embroiled in an angry dispute with the judge, who took offense and reasoned that in her contempt for her husband she would block visitations and alienate the children from their father.

By the time of the evaluation, Laura was grief stricken at the loss of her children and at being forced from her home. However, all of her energies fueled her antipathy toward her husband. She had further confrontations with Scott over visitations and had called the police to the home yet again to arrest him. She had fired another attorney. Most questions to her were answered with a laundry list of Scott's deficiencies as a husband and father.

What had happened to Scott and Laura in their 18-year history together? Could all of this have been avoided? Could they have resolved the custody dispute out of court?

In chapter 1, I discussed how the effects of divorce are not the same for all children and that they do not begin only at the time of the divorce. Longitudinal studies indicate that high-conflict families are embroiled in unresolvable disagreements, often for years, before the final break. Some experts feel they can predict which couples will be divorced and which will have lasting marriages.

In this chapter, I examine the interpersonal patterns and personality traits that are highly associated with divorce. Understanding these behaviors will give clinicians a sense of why negotiations break down in divorcing families before and at the time of the divorce and later as couples enter into visitation disputes, custody battles, and endless relitigation. Women are typically more unhappy than men with marriage and are usually the ones to initiate divorce. In this chapter, I look at some of the reasons for this trend. Last, I survey the rise of mediation and review whether it has fulfilled its promise to end the "divorce wars."

INTERPERSONAL PATTERNS THAT LEAD TO DIVORCE

John Gottman (1994), a researcher at the University of Washington in Seattle, has studied more than 200 couples in his laboratory for the past 20 years, from those who are newly wed to those who have been married for a long time. Each couple was videotaped having a conversation in which they attempted to solve a problem while hooked to machines that monitored their physical reactions. After the session, each person watched the videotape separately while explaining their private thoughts and feelings during the heated moments of the encounter. Then the videotape was subjected to hours of microanalysis of voice patterns, facial expressions, and even changes in heart rate. Gottman's team followed up with the couples years later to determine which ones had divorced. On the basis of these results, the members of Gottman's research team claimed that they could predict divorce correctly 94% of the time.

Gottman found that conflict, surprisingly, was not the problem. Conflict in a marriage is like the weather—it is an inevitable feature of the environment. Whether the couple resolves conflict, however, can make all the difference in the world. As a marital therapist, I can attest that virtually all couples who present themselves for counseling state that they have "communication" problems. What they mean by this is that they have areas of chronic conflict that have been impervious to resolution.

Conflict Resolution Patterns

Gottman (1994) identified three patterns of conflict resolution. The *validating* couple speak openly and comfortably, compromise often, and calmly work out their differences. The *volatile* couple vent anger intensely and engage in passionate disputes. The *conflict-avoiding* couple is one in which both individuals are low keyed and reticent; they find conflict unsettling, and they "agree to disagree."

Gottman found that although the volatile couples and the conflict-avoiding couples had their difficulties, many had stable and satisfying marriages. When the volatile couples were not fighting, they laughed more and were more affectionate than the other couples. They expressed more negative and more positive emotions.

Likewise, many of the conflict-avoiding couples were doing well. They seemed to value peace and harmony over openness and honesty. They silently agreed to overlook their differences and respect the other's position. They valued separateness and autonomy and led calm, pleasant lives.

The key, Gottman found, was that in the marriages that lasted, the positive interactions between the spouses occurred five times more often than the negative interactions. This was true regardless of the type of marriage. When the negative interactions began to consistently outnumber the positive interactions, the marriage seemed doomed.

"The Four Horsemen of the Apocalypse"

Gottman (1994) also profiled the downward spiral of marriages that fail. He identified "the Four Horsemen of the Apocalypse"—the four elements of marriages headed toward divorce: criticism, defensiveness, contempt, and withdrawal. Not surprisingly, they tend to follow a certain order and are interrelated.

The first horseman is *criticism*. Although couples may complain about what is not right about their lives or each other, criticism involves an unrestrained attack on the worthiness of the other person. It is broad and deep and implies that the other person is inferior. An example is "You're always doing that. You only think about yourself and no one else." Gottman (1994) found that women are more likely to complain about and criticize their spouse. Men are much more likely to be emotionally flooded by criticism than women—to experience a rise in heart rate, an outpouring of adrenaline, and a feeling of being out of control. Gottman concluded that this physiological reaction made men more likely to withdraw from conflict.

When complaining about a problem does not yield results, it often moves into frequent criticism. When criticism does not yield results, *contempt* is used. "Contempt is a very corrosive thing in a marriage," Gottman said to reporter John Stossel in an ABC news program (Baylor, 1993). "It ought really to be banned and outlawed in marriages." To show contempt toward one's partner, one is intentionally trying to insult or degrade him or her. Contempt is derision in any form—a rolling of the eyes, name calling, a disgusted sigh, insults, hostile humor, mockery, and so on. Gottman (1994) found that when women get completely swamped with emotion, they are more likely to start "kitchen-sinking"—bringing up all sorts of past and present complaints, even unrelated ones, and mixing them with sarcasm and derision. This often overloads the man, causing further withdrawal.

What is toxic about contempt, Gottman (1994) found, is that the person who is showing contempt is also brooding over negative thoughts about the other person, for example, that he or she is stupid, disgusting, incompetent, foolish, and so on. All positive qualities or memories are forgotten. This internal one-sided conversation takes its toll: If a husband shows contempt toward his wife often, Gottman found, she will be more prone to a range of health problems such as colds, flus, bladder and yeast infections, and gastrointestinal symptoms. When a wife's face shows disgust four or more times within a 15-minute encounter, it is a silent signal that the couple will be divorced within 4 years.

The third horseman, *defensiveness*, is the inability to listen sensitively to a complaint or a criticism. It is the refusal to take responsibility for a mistake, a failing, a lapse in judgment. It is the putting of blame back on the one who first raised the problem. Defensive partners engage in denying responsibility ("It wasn't my fault"), making far-fetched excuses, cross-complaining ("Well, you do it, too"), "yes, but-ting," and whining ("Why are you always picking on me?"). Defensiveness is particularly corrosive because it shuts down any hope on the other person's part that an issue that is raised might get settled. It provokes the other person toward contempt and, finally, withdrawal.

The fourth horseman Gottman (1994) identified is *withdrawal*, or stonewalling. Stonewalling happens when a partner's response to conflict is stony silence, changing the subject, refusing to talk, or leaving the situation. Most stonewallers, about 85%, are men; and this type of response is extremely physically upsetting to women. Like defensiveness, it is a response that causes the other person to give up all hope of resolving conflict. Withdrawal and stonewalling send a powerful message—a combination of superiority, distance, and even hatred.

Personality Traits

As a marital therapist, I would add that some additional danger signs that may be related to the above problems: rigidity, a lack of empathic ability, unrealistic expectations, and a lack of problem-resolution skills. These are problem areas for people in many walks of life, but especially in a marriage, and they come under the heading of what Daniel Goleman (1995) called *emotional intelligence*. The ability to be flexible and adaptable when solving a problem, to empathize with another person's point of view, to scale back one's wants to a reasonable level, and to be able to generate alternative solutions to problems in order to work toward a common goal are survival skills in everyday living. People who are lacking in these skills have repeated failures in social interactions with others. These people are likely to go on to postdivorce conflict as well.

Rigid personalities approach marriage like they approach life in general—with fixed ideas about what is the right way and what is the wrong way. They tend to take control and push through their own agenda. They also tend to take a strong stand on sex role stereotypes, that is, "this is what a woman does, this is what a man does not do." Such rigid roles also predict marital failure, according to Neil Jacobsen and Andrew Christensen (1996), also at the University of Washington. When times change—a baby arrives, he loses his job, she wants to make more of the decisions, they get older—rigid personalities are not able to make shifts in the marriage. They are likely to insist on maintaining the status quo.

It is not surprising that rigid people are often seen as lacking empathy; rigidity and lack of empathy are related problems. People who are lacking in empathic skills have an inability to put themselves in another person's place and compare that person's experience with one that they have had, and so they are unable to feel a commonality with others. People who are married to unempathetic people feel frozen out, not understood, or not listened to. Unempathetic people tend to alienate not only spouses but also children, in-laws and relatives, and even friends and acquaintances.

Rigid and unempathetic partners tend to be, but certainly are not always, men. Women, on the other hand, often come into a marriage with strongly felt needs for comfort, protection, support, and reassurance that cannot be met by their partner. Their expectations are so high that they are often disappointed. When a marriage is in trouble, and one partner is saying "You don't meet my needs," it is nearly always the wife who is reporting this.

Jacobsen and Christensen (1996) found that couples who benefited from marital therapy and went on to experience satisfying marriages had worked toward acceptance of the other to a very great degree. This was a powerful conclusion for Jacobsen, who early in his research on marital therapy focused on how couples could change each other's behavior. Over the course of 20 years of research, he had to conclude that he was headed in the wrong direction. Satisfied couples learned to overlook shortcomings, minimize their partner's limitations, focus more on the partner's positive qualities, and even turn a "negative" into a "positive" by taking a different perspective on it. Chronically unhappy partners, who are mostly but not exclusively women, appear to be rigid individuals in the sense that they are unable to find creative and workable solutions to their disappointments with their partner.

Last, many partners who are headed for divorce lack problem-resolution skills. It is a simple observation from my 20 years of practice that couples headed for divorce rarely get to the point of asking "Now, what do we do about this problem?" They do not brainstorm, put ideas on the table, focus on what they do agree on, offer compromises, or formulate simple goals. They do not make a commitment for change, negotiate a contract with each other, or agree on a deadline.

Volatile couples, especially, ventilate their feelings in a virtual blood-letting of emotion, as if in doing so the initial disagreement would be solved. They finally stop, feeling broken and wounded. Conflict-avoiding couples may be coaxed out of their shells to open up a bit, but they quickly retreat before getting to an agreement. Most couples agree that these tactics do not pay off, but they are unable to stop using them.

Inner Scripts

Gottman (1994) discovered in his research that couples who are headed for marital breakdown develop inner scripts in which they make statements to themselves that consolidate their position and vilify their partner. He referred to these as *distress-maintaining scenarios.* (Couples with good marriages engage in *self-soothing scenarios* in which they make excuses for their partner's bad behavior, rationalize it, or attribute it to some short-lived, isolated incident.) These scripts fall into two categories: scripts of the innocent victim and scripts of righteous indignation. For example, the wife may engage in an internal script in which she is the victim of a cold, heartless, unsupportive husband who cares only about making money. The husband may engage in a script in which he is indignant over his wife's failure to keep the house in order, maintain her attractive appearance, and be an interesting and lively companion.

The cycles of contempt and withdrawal continue until both feel the situation is hopeless. They both begin to live parallel lives. As they do so, they consolidate their negative views of each other and begin to turn to others outside the marriage to validate their point of view. Each is at risk for extramarital involvement with others. Outside relationships are not marred by chronic conflict, they do not stir up anxiety, and they are not mired in feelings of hopelessness.

The last step in the process, Gottman (1994) found, is that each partner begins to revise history. "Nothing foretells a marriage's future as accurately as how a couple retells the past," he wrote (p. 127). Gottman found that couples headed for divorce looked back on the beginning of their relationship in distinct ways: They viewed the decision to marry as an impulsive one, made under pressure; they could not recall positive feelings about each other; they felt the decision to marry was one sided. They reviewed early slights and disappointments as harbingers of bad times to come. It was as if they were revising the story of the marriage so that it was congruent with their internal scripts.

GENDER DIFFERENCES THAT LEAD TO DIVORCE

Sociologists Linda Thompson and Alexis Walker (1989) conducted a review of many studies that focused on the different ways that men and women experience marriage and marital conflict. They found that women were, on the whole, more expressive, communicated more clearly, and were better at understanding their partners than were men. Thus, most men have an advantage over women when in conflict with their partners. Women tend to be more sensitive to what is going on in the marriage, to monitor it closely, and to bring up and confront problems. Men tend to bring up problems only when things are clearly going poorly. In fact, ignoring problems tended to benefit husbands but contributed to poor physical health in women.

Thompson and Walker (1989) demonstrated that women often use more emotional appeals than men when approaching conflict. They reasoned that women do so because of their subordinate position in most marriages. Like other groups who lack power, women must use moral persuasion, manipulation, emotional appeals, coercion, begging, and indirect methods to get what they want. Men, on the other hand, by virtue of their dominant position in marriage, are more likely to remain calm and reasonable and to be problem focused. They are more able to be chivalrous and conciliatory. They interrupt their partner more successfully, use more bullying tactics, and assert their dominance more successfully.

Conflict Resolution

Thompson and Walker (1989) found that when conflict is resolved, it is most often the women who are submissive and willing to compromise. Men tend to see their own personality traits as permanent, thus giving themselves credit for their positive qualities. However, this stance also enables them to see their shortcomings as "just the way I am" and therefore not subject to change. On the other hand, men tend to see their wives' personality traits as malleable, thus giving women little credit for their positive qualities and enabling them to see their wives' shortcomings as something that the wives should change about themselves.

Marital Satisfaction

In marriages that eventually end in divorce, women generally know the marriage is headed for disaster long before men do. Therefore, it should come as no surprise that women initiate the majority of divorces. Wallerstein and Kelly (1980b), in their early study of divorcing families in California, found that women initiated three fourths of the divorces, and nearly half of their husbands opposed the divorce. Paradoxically, they found that many of these women bitterly opposed the divorce, although they felt pressured to be the one to file. Amy Koel and her colleagues with the Middlesex Divorce Research Group in Cambridge, Massachusetts (Koel, Clark, Phear, & Hauser, 1988), followed 700 divorcing couples and found that women initiated divorces at a rate of 3 to 1 over that of men. Frank Furstenberg and Andrew Cherlin (1991) found that 80% of the marriages in their study ended unilaterally, usually at the wife's initiation. They, too, suggested that often the husband provoked the wife into filing so that he would not be responsible for ending the marriage.

Julie Fulton (1979) also found this pattern in her study of 278 divorcing families in Minnesota. Like Thompson and Walker (1989), she found that when men and women are interviewed about what happened in the marriage that led to divorce, one gets a "his" viewpoint and a "hers" viewpoint, which may be distinctly different. Most of the men in Fulton's sample viewed themselves as average to above average as a husband and felt that their contribution to the marriage was about equal to that of their wives. The women, however, described themselves as the partner making the most effort in the marriage. They were far more negative about their ex-husbands than the men were of their ex-wives. When asked how many years of the marriage were happy ones for them, only 6% of the wives said they were happy most of the time, whereas 19% of the husbands said they were happy most of the time.

Parenting Roles

Different viewpoints also emerged in regard to parenting roles. When Fulton (1979) asked divorced parents who was responsible for eight areas of parental responsibility in their former marriages, the wives were far more likely to say that they did each task alone or with very little help from their husbands. The husbands, however, rated themselves as having been much more involved. They saw themselves as the one who had most often disciplined the child and felt they had equal participation in social activities, homework, and religious training. Although they saw their ex-wives as having done the lion's share of the other roles—diapering, making doctor visits, keeping bedtime routines, shopping—they saw themselves as helping out a great deal. Wives, on the other hand, saw their ex-husbands as helping out very little, and when the men did discipline the children, the women disapproved of how they handled it.

Although these different viewpoints emerge in many studies, the research indicates that mothers are the more accurate raters of who did what in the marriage. Michael Lamb, a national expert on the role of the father in the American family, and his colleagues at the University of Arizona (Lamb, Pleck, Charnov, & Levine, 1987) summarized a large body of research on mothers' and fathers' roles in the family and found that fathers, on average, are available to their children for about half as much time as mothers. Mothers spend about three times as much time in face-to-face interaction with the children as do fathers.

Lamb et al. (1987) concluded, however, that spending time with one's children is not the same as being responsible for them. In one study, the average father was solely responsible for the children for 1 hour a week, compared with 40 hours for the average mother. Furthermore, 60% of the fathers of preschool-age children had never taken sole responsibility for them. Only 20% had done so on a regular basis.

Lamb et al. (1987) reviewed a study by Grace Baruch and Rosalind Barnett (1983) of Wellesley College in which 160 fathers were asked for which of 11 household and child care tasks they were responsible. Seventy percent of the fathers reported that they were responsible for none of them. Twenty-two percent said they were responsible for 1 of the tasks, and only 7% said they were responsible for 2 or 3 tasks.

Lamb et al. (1987) designated as the *responsible parent* the one for whom the buck stopped (i.e., who stayed home with the children when they were sick) and who was the arranger, coordinator, and decision maker. They determined that mothers outweighed fathers 9 to 1 in time spent as the responsible parent.

Even more dramatic is the difference in which parent is designated to stay home with a sick child. Lamb et al. (1987) cited a study by Quinn and Staines (1979), the Quality of Employment Survey, in which two-wage-earning families were asked who usually stayed home with a sick child. The mother was the designated parent 80% of the time, the father 15% of the time. Only 5% of the parents said "it depends."

PREDIVORCE PARENT–CHILD RELATIONSHIPS

By the time a marriage ends, all goodwill is lost between the couple, and there is little to rehabilitate. According to published studies, parent–child relationships have begun to suffer as well. Recall from chapter 2 that parents who are locked in conflict and going through a divorce make fewer maturity demands on their children. They communicate with them less well, express less affection, and are less consistent and more lax in terms of discipline. They are less likely to reason with the children and are more likely to issue commands to their children and to give them less attention. One study (Peterson & Zill, 1986) found that only 20% of the children in intact families in which there had been chronic conflict had positive relationships with both parents.

Psychologist Jack Block and his colleagues at the University of California (1988) conducted a unique study in which 110 families were followed for 10 years to try to determine which would go on to divorce and what the parent–child relationships were like long before the divorce. Mothers in families who went on to divorce described their husbands in largely negative terms, as distant and unaffectionate, not helpful, critical, and stubborn. These mothers reported more conflict with their sons, were strict and tense with their sons, and wished their husbands were more interested in their sons.

The fathers' ratings did not differ greatly, in that they described themselves as having more anger toward their sons, as being less involved in disciplining their sons, and as more forgetful of their promises toward their sons. The mothers who went on to divorce were a more unhappy group overall than the ones who stayed married, in that they rated themselves as more likely to get upset easily, to not be calm and relaxed, to be more vulnerable and less assertive, and to have lower self-esteem.

PREDIVORCE NEGOTIATIONS

Once a couple decides to divorce, and as it becomes clear that they will have conflicts over custody of the children, many assume that they will take their battle to the courtroom. However, in most states, at present the couple will be mandated by the courts to undergo mediation first in an attempt to settle their dispute out of court. California, in 1981, was the first state to enact a statute ordering that all families litigating over custody and visitation first enter into mediation before going to court. Donald Saposnek (1998), director of Family Mediation Services in Santa Cruz, California, reported that 39 states now have provisions such that a judge can order parents into mediation as soon as the court is made aware that they are in dispute over custody. However, much mediation is still sought voluntarily before going to court hearings or may be recommended by the parents' private attorneys before going to court. Much can be gained through mediation if it is successful. The adversarial process of a custody dispute in which children are at stake is extremely stressful; few other legal confrontations involve such emotional intensity. Also, they are time consuming and costly to the taxpayer. Jessica Pearson and Nancy Thoennes (1982), psychologists and mediators in Denver, Colorado, reported that the average "bench time," or courtroom time, for contested custody cases is between 4 and 10 hours per case. Pearson and Thoennes (1984) also cited waiting periods of up to 1 or 2 years because of a backlog of cases in some districts.

An Overview of Mediation

The goals of mediation, according to Robert Emery and Melissa Wyer (1987), are the "four Cs": to reduce *conflict*, to increase *cooperation*, to give people more *control* over the important decisions affecting their lives, and to reduce public *costs*. Although mediation is similar to family counseling, it is different in many ways. It is short term, lasting from 1 to 4 or 5 sessions, and is specifically goal oriented. Unlike in the adversarial process of a custody dispute, the mediator is acting as an advocate for both parties and for the children indirectly. Mediation, ideally, is not a win–lose situation but a win–win scenario—one in which both sides potentially can maximize their positions. The agreement that is entered into is completely voluntary. If the couple cannot reach an agreement, then mediation has failed, but unlike a judge, the mediator has no authority to force the two into a final agreement. Finally, mediation is like psychotherapy in that the information revealed is confidential. The mediator cannot be called into court to testify, although on occasion judges have overruled on this matter.

Elizabeth Koopman and Joan Hunt (1988) of the Institute for Child Study in College Park, Maryland, view mediation as an approach that comes out of the field of negotiation, a prime example of which is the book *Getting to Yes* by Roger Fisher and William Uhry (1981). Mediators start from the position of identifying what is similar about the two parents' positions—that both are good parents, that they want what is best for the children, that they want to be meaningfully involved in the children's lives, and so on. Mediators encourage parents to focus on issues rather than on personal positions (e.g., not "What is your position with regard to . . ." but "What are the pros and cons of this option . . . ?"). They then attempt to separate the person from the problem by a careful choice of vocabulary (e.g., not "Dad failed to keep the agreement" but "This part of the agreement did not work out"). They also try to get parents to back off from fixed demands ("I want the children all but four nights per month") to more general positions ("I want a meaningful involvement in school activities and Boy Scouts"). From there mediators work toward brainstorming alternatives, even unusual or outlandish ones, to attempt to get the parties to loosen their positions and think more flexibly. They push for the participants to come up with alternatives that maximize gain for both parties. They further build in an outline for objectively evaluating the effectiveness of a specific plan. They anticipate problems as well as developmental changes as the children get older and plan for those as well. Last, they work with the participants to finalize the details so that there is no need for confusion or debate at a later point.

Saposnek (1998) viewed the mediation process as one in which couples are at an impasse over custody and visitation because they have strong needs and goals they feel compelled to meet. These may include the need to reunite, to disengage, for power or retaliation, or to control financial aspects of the divorce that are tied to custody. He also reviewed the need to save face, to survive the loss of contact with the children emotionally, and to appease a new spouse. Saposnek likened the role of the mediator to that of one who practices the martial art of aikido. The goal of aikido is to neutralize and redirect the aggression of the attacker so that no one is harmed. The core principle is "turn when pushed and enter when pulled" (Saposnek, 1998, p. 64). Couples in custody mediation are known to be highly emotional, unpredictable, and intensely hostile. Saposnek detailed how the mediator must neutralize hostile attacks through a range of clever maneuvers such as deflecting, putting the individual in a double bind (i.e., giving the person only two choices, both of which work to the mediator's advantage), offbeat behaviors, and changing the subject.

Acceptance by Parents

Will parents accept mediation? Pearson and Thoennes (1984) found that 44% of those who were offered free mediation by the courts rejected it. They found this fact to be common, citing data from the Brooklyn Dispute Resolution Center, at which 32% of referred parents failed to appear and another 12% refused mediation altogether. Pearson and Thoennes also reviewed data from Neighborhood Justice Centers, which report dropout rates as high as 60%.

Pearson, Thoennes, along with attorney Lois Vanderkooi (1982) conducted a study of parents in their local Denver population who were offered free mediation but nevertheless rejected it. They found that the largest group of women who rejected mediation did so because they mistrusted or feared their spouse or ex-spouse or wanted to avoid him. Men who rejected mediation tended to be in semiskilled occupations and to have partial custody of their children. As a group they seemed to feel that they would fare better in court than in mediation. The majority of the couples who rejected mediation reported that they had little to no communication and had avoided each other for a long time. Also, they tended to be more embittered by the separation and more ambivalent about ending the relationship. Couples who readily accepted mediation and used it tended to be better educated and to have higher incomes. They had more experience with psychotherapy and with talking out their problems. As a group, they had accepted the divorce in large part and moved on to develop new lives. They tended to want joint legal custody and shared parenting.

Robert Emery and Melissa Wyer (1987) found that men favored mediation more than did women. They assigned 20 couples to mediation and 20 couples to litigation. Interviewing them afterward, they found that the men were more likely to receive joint custody when they mediated and to feel that concern was shown for them and that their rights were protected. Women who mediated were more likely to feel that they won less and lost more than the women who went to court. Re-examining the data carefully, Emery (1988) concluded that mothers were about equally satisfied with mediation and litigation, but fathers who litigated formed an outlying group of individuals who were particularly unhappy with their experience. Despite the advent of legislation in which judges are directed to be blind as to the gender of a parent, fathers felt that judges still tended to favor mothers in custody decisions.

Success Rates

Is mediation successful? This question has a three-pronged answer. First, there is the issue of whether parents who mediate feel positive about the process. Pearson and Thoennes (1982, 1984) reported that, of parents who successfully reached an agreement, 70% of their sample were "highly satisfied" with mediation and 93% would mediate again in the future. Ninety-two percent would recommend mediation to someone they knew. Of those who did not reach an agreement, only 22% were happy with mediation, although, oddly, 81% would recommend mediation to a friend, and 64% said they would try mediation again in the future.

Other mediators have reported similar praise for mediation. Donald Saposnek, Joanna Hamburg, Claire Delano, and Hila Michaelson (1984) conducted a study of approval ratings given by 148 parents seen by the Family Mediation Service center of Santa Cruz, California. These parents rated their own personal experience with mediation as a 6.0 out of 10 points or higher. Sixty percent were generally pleased with mediation, and 33% were generally unhappy with it. However, when asked to rate the effectiveness of mediation in general, they gave an average score of 8.2 out of 10. Charlene Depner of Stanford University, along with co-authors Cannata and Simon (1992), reporting on parents who mediated successfully as well as those who did not, reported that 90% rated mediation "a good way to develop a parenting plan" (p. 199).

Second, there is the question of what percentage of parents who mediate make a final out-of-court agreement. Attorney Elizabeth Scott and psychologist Robert Emery (1987) reviewed several studies as to how many parents actually resolve their dispute through mediation. One Los Angeles study of court-ordered mediation found a success rate of 55%. A Connecticut study of 3,272 cases of voluntary mediation found a success rate of 64%. In Emery and Wyer's (1987) study, 75% of the couples who mediated reached an out-of-court settlement. This resulted in a considerable cost savings in court time compared with the control group, in which only 25% of parents settled out of court. Saposnek et al. (1984) reported a success rate of 75% among their court-mandated group who underwent mediation. Still another 15% reconciled their marriage or went on to settlement on their own.

Pearson and Thoennes (1982, 1984) found that of the parents who voluntarily accepted mediation, 50% reported successfully reaching an agreement out of court. Of those who did not, 65% of the failed group settled on a parenting agreement before going to court. Thus, a total of 80% of those who mediated were successful in keeping their dispute out of court.

The success of mediation can be measured in still a third way. Pearson and Thoennes (1982) found that at 6 weeks after the settlement, three times as many people who went through mediation reported that "things had gotten much better" as those who had gone through litigation. They also reported lower rates of adverse actions, as seen in Table 3.1.

Relitigation Rates

Even more important to consider is whether parents return to court to litigate after the initial agreement is made, thus incurring more court time, court costs, and attorneys' fees. Pearson and Thoennes (1982) found that among the families who mediated successfully, none initiated court actions to modify custody or visitation in the 6–12 months following the decree. On the other hand, among parents who failed to reach an agreement through mediation, 14% went on to initiate more litigation. Among the control group who were never offered mediation, 20% had filed court motions. When asked if they expected to go back to court regarding their agreement in the future, only 22% of the successfully mediated group reported they planned to do so, whereas 77% of the control group planned to do so.

Scott and Emery (1987) cited several other smaller studies in which the return rate to court was from one-sixth to one-third the rate of parents who went on to litigate over custody and visitation. Emery and Wyer (1987) found that 8 members of their mediation group of 20 parents (mostly those who had failed to reach an agreement) and 7 members of the litigation group of 20 parents returned to court in the 6 months following the reaching of a settlement. However, the litigation group as a whole had more overall contacts with the court and more problems with unpaid child support. Three families in the litigation group went to court repeatedly.

TABLE 3.1
The Denver Custody Mediation Project Results

Action	% Group who mediated successfully	% Group who litigated
Temporary restraining order or contempt citation in effect	15	35
Parents who reported "serious problems" with the agreement	13	40
Parents who reported the spouse is in compliance with agreement	66	34

Note. From "The Benefits Outweigh the Costs" by J. Pearson and N. Thoennes, 1982, *The Family Advocate, 4*, p. 26. Copyright 1982 by the American Bar Association. Reprinted by permission.

Children's Adjustment

Mediation clearly has not solved the growing national problem of couples locked in court battles over children. Carol Bruch (1992), professor of law at the University of California, Davis, penned a controversial piece on the limitations of mediation that received several rejoinders from experts in the field. Citing an unpublished study by Pearson, Thoennes, and Hodges (1984), Bruch noted that children's adjustment did not differ as to whether they were in the successfully mediated group or the litigation group. Neither were there any long-term differences between the two groups with regard to compliance with the agreement, spousal cooperation, and relitigation. Thoennes and Pearson (1992), in their response to Bruch, agreed that "we find that mediation does not guarantee greater divorce adjustment on the part of children, nor does mediation eliminate later problems with visitation and ensure parental cooperation" (p. 142). Robert Emery (1988), in his study of mediating and litigating couples in Virginia, found no differences in self-reported levels of conflict over coparenting, levels of depression, or acceptance of the end of the marriage. He concluded that early proponents of mediation were quick to hail it as the solution to divorce conflict and that "it would seem that some of the most optimistic claims about mediation need to be tempered" (p. 54).

In the first effort at examining the longitudinal effects of mediation, Peter Dillon and Robert Emery (1996) of the University of Virginia recontacted their sample 9 years after the custody dispute was settled. Twenty-five parents were referred to mediation and accepted it, whereas 28 parents were assigned to litigation and accepted it. (Dillon and Emery did not state what the nonaccepting families elected to do.) They relied on parents' reports for their results, finding that parents in the mediation group reported greater contact between the noncustodial parent and child, more involvement on the part of the noncustodial parent, and better communication between the two parents. There were no differences in relitigation rates, and there were no differences between the two groups as to the mothers' report of children's behavior problems. Although Dillon and Emery described these groups as randomly assigned, each group had voluntarily accepted the method in which to settle their dispute. Thus, presettlement differences cannot be ruled out. In fact, Dillon and Emery noted that the mediation group was much more likely to be employed, work at white-collar jobs, and have a higher family income than the litigating group. Such a group may comprise parents who are healthier individuals, with less hostility at the time of the divorce. Nevertheless, the fact that there were any differences 9 years later is rather remarkable.

Overall Effectiveness

Joan Kelly (1996) surveyed the existing research on the effectiveness of mediation and concluded that, although mediation cannot cure all problems of postdivorce conflict, it has been moderately successful. The following is a summary of her findings:

- Mediation is considerably less expensive and takes less time than litigation.
- Parents are more likely to comply with mediated agreements than those reached in court.
- Relitigation rates are lower among groups who mediate versus those who litigate.
- Parents who mediate are considerably more satisfied with their experience than are those who litigate.
- Parents who mediate appear to report less conflict during the separation, at the time of the divorce, and at 1 year postdivorce. Long-range reports of conflict do not consistently show less conflict with divorce mediation.
- Child psychological adjustment may not be affected by mediation versus litigation.
- Parent psychological adjustment may not be affected by mediation versus litigation.
- Mediation may be appropriate for cases in which domestic violence has been brief, was initiated by the wife, or did not occur before the separation.
- Mediation may not be effective with parents who are severely disturbed or have serious character disorders.

Kelly's (1996) review may be more supportive of mediation than those of other reviewers, reflecting her position as Executive Director of the Northern California Mediation Center and as past president of the Academy of Family Mediators. She suggested that the next wave of research focus on the specific process of variables of mediation—that is, which strategies or techniques and which mediator behaviors are most effective in bringing about good results.

Saposnek (1998), in the most recent review of the research, and reflecting his own lengthy experience as a mediator, agreed with Kelly (1996) that mediation has been modestly successful. He, too, cited greater client satisfaction, significant cost savings, better compliance with orders, and modestly lower rates of relitigation. However, he also concluded that mediation does not seem to have any lasting effect on children's adjustment or on parents' anger toward each other and their ability to solve disputes informally. He concluded that "The ability of mediation to increase ongoing cooperation between the parents has not consistently been found in the research" (p. 15). He pointed out that families at an impasse over custody issues often have histories of being in conflict for many years and have behavioral patterns that may not be amenable to treatment. It would be highly unlikely that any form of brief mediation could be successful in bringing about permanent changes in such behaviors.

Type of Couple

Should we conclude that mediation is for everyone? Not necessarily, says Atlanta attorney Deborah Lubin (1995). The success of mediation depends greatly on the motivation level of parents to work out their differences. For those who are not motivated to be cooperative, mediation may simply be one more step that is required along the way to court, which adds more time, frustration, and costs to an already stressful process. Pearson and Thoennes (1982) found in fact that, whereas parents who successfully mediated proceeded fastest through the court process, at an average length of 8.2 months, those who failed to mediate successfully took the longest—14.2 months. Those who went straight into litigation were the middle group, at 10.8 months. The breakdown by legal fees was similar, with the successful mediation group paying less than those who had failed to mediate successfully and went on to litigate as well.

Lubin (1995) pointed out that whereas court-mandated mediation is likely to be brief and less costly, it also tends to be less successful. Mediation that is pursued privately is likely to be done by a professional with more training who charges higher fees and to extend over many more sessions. In such a case, where an attorney reviews the final agreement and may even sit in on the individual sessions, the cost savings for the client overall may be nil.

In a recent study, Catherine Lee of the University of Waterloo, Ontario, and others (Lee, Beauregard, & Hunsley, 1998) surveyed 161 Canadian attorneys as to their opinions about mediation. The participants strongly agreed that parents needed to maintain their own attorney throughout the process, that mediation was preferable to litigation, and that parents should be screened for domestic violence before mediation. They only mildly agreed that mediation enhanced family relationships, increased parental compliance, or strengthened shared parenting. They were neutral as to the advisability of mandatory mediation and agreed that custody evaluations should not be mandatory.

Mediation may be contraindicated for many couples. Most attorneys suggest that cases in which there is a great discrepancy in bargaining power are not suitable for mediation. Parents who may be at a disadvantage would include those who have been battered or who may have been passive or submissive in the marriage as well as those who are at a financial disadvantage. Carol Bruch (1992), a professor of law at the University of California, Davis, reviewed numerous studies and concluded that even a skilled mediator cannot undo the sharp divisions of power and influence that exist between some couples. Subtleties such as the way men tend to monopolize the speaking time and interrupt women frequently give them an advantage in mediation that may not even be noticed by the mediator.

Neither is mediation appropriate for cases in which there are allegations of child abuse or neglect; substance abuse; mental instability; or violent, antisocial behavior. Those cases are best left to the courts to order outside evaluations by expert witnesses.

In a later article, Bruch (1993) went on to delineate still other scenarios in which mediation may not be the best alternative. For example, mediators tend as a group to push for joint custody and for compromise. A parent who has a good chance of getting sole custody in court and who may not need to compromise might fare better in court. Mediators are not investigators and may not have all the facts. Here one may be wise to engage an investigator, have a home study done, or pursue a custody evaluation in order that all the factors may be known to the court. Also, Bruch advised against mediation if one's client is in the dark about financial matters, is shy or unassertive, is feeling guilty about leaving, or finds talking to the recently estranged spouse simply too painful. Last, she pointed out the merit of traditional dispute resolution for some populations. Parents who have been betrayed or abused and those dealing with child abductors, for example, may benefit from the "clarity, moral force, or symbolic dignity" of a judge's verdict handed down in a courtroom (p. 105).

In the future, the courts may wish to consider screening candidates for mediation to make the best use of the court's time. The court may want to send on to mediation cases in which (a) the partners are not too hostile, (b) they can communicate reasonably well, (c) they are both resigned to the divorce, (d) they are fairly close in agreeing on such issues as joint custody, and (e) domestic violence has been nonexistent or brief.

The courts may want to send on to litigation cases in which (a) the couples are deeply hostile and embittered, (b) their requests for custody are sharply divided, (c) the seriousness of allegations that have been made necessitate that outside evaluations be done, and (d) there has been a long history in which the wife has been battered.

WHAT THE RESEARCH SHOWS

In this chapter, I have examined how and why marriages so often end in divorce. Longitudinal research studies have found common pathways to divorce. Chronic, unresolved conflict, according to Gottman (1994), leads to cycles of contempt, criticism, defensiveness, and withdrawal. During this process, couples construct increasingly negative inner scripts about each other and have increasingly higher rates of negative interactions. These patterns are important in understanding the entrenched patterns of unresolved conflict seen in some parents long after the divorce. Similarly, personality traits associated with divorce, such as rigidity, a lack of empathy, unrealistic expectations, and poor problem-solving skills, are reviewed again in chapter 9, which covers the psychopathology of adults in chronic postdivorce conflict.

Women in American culture at this point in time are far more likely than men to be dissatisfied with marriage and to initiate divorce. Studies indicate that women are likely to feel that they bear an unfair burden with regard to responsibility for the children, to feel disappointed in their partners, and to feel that their partner will not communicate with them in resolving conflict and that he is unlikely to change.

Mediation has grown both in acceptance and prevalence as a means of negotiation before divorce. Studies indicate that although mediation is often preferred by parents and can result in workable out-of-court settlements at a cost-savings to the parents and to the court, it has not been a solution to parental conflict. Long-range studies indicate that relitigation rates are about the same between parents who mediate and those who litigate, and children's emotional adjustment does not appear to be affected by mediation. Couples with severe conflict and emotional disturbance cannot mediate effectively, and those who have been violent are inappropriate candidates for mediation.

GUIDELINES FOR THE CLINICIAN

Many clinicians understand how the crisis of an impending divorce, along with fears of losing one's children, bring out latent forms of character disorders in normally stable individuals. The issue was reinforced to me several years ago while testifying about a mother's irrational and violent behavior when she learned that her husband was having an affair. The judge asked me to specify whether such behavior had occurred in this woman's past. I replied "no," and the judge sighed as if to dismiss the woman's erratic behavior altogether. I learned from that interchange to always ask myself "Did this behavior ever occur before the separation?" If not, it is probably uncharacteristic of this individual and unlikely to occur in the future, except under extremely stressful circumstances.

The clinician who is treating an individual who is in this most irrational and fragile mental state should anticipate some common patterns and provide a stable ego to lend to the divorcing parent-in-crisis. One pattern is the paranoid individual who has become convinced that the other parent is somehow abusing the children. This parent—usually, but not always, the mother—has a history of feeling dependent, trapped, and defenseless in the marriage. She has thought of "escape" but cannot conceive of a way to take charge of leaving because of her emotional and financial dependency. Noticing some unusual behaviors or signs of stress in her child, she considers the possibility that the child is being abused by her partner. On the other hand, she may feel threatened or coerced into staying in the marriage and arrives at the conclusion that she herself is being mentally abused. Some individuals may then leave the home abruptly and go into hiding.

Abuse allegations bring an individual into contact with many public and private agencies—shelters for battered women, social services agencies, private foundations for abused children, the mental health community, and the courts. As such, allegations are easy to make, the accuser is likely to receive much concern and sympathy, and many agencies readily offer housing and counseling. Soon a protective community forms around the parent making the allegations and this protection enables her to feel strengthened and empowered.

If the allegations are false, however, the accuser is in a dangerous position. Not only do the offers of help stop abruptly, but also these same individuals who made the offers may be called on to testify against the parent in court. It may even be their testimony that causes the accusing parent to lose custody of the children and be allowed only brief, supervised contact with them. This parent may be portrayed in court as mentally unstable, at risk for kidnapping the children, and determined to alienate the children from the other parent.

For this reason, clinicians should proceed carefully with allegations of abuse. The advocate for this type of patient should help determine if there is a realistic basis for the accusation, as well as be sympathetic and compassionate. As an advocate, the clinician should also prepare this individual for possible negative consequences of making allegations that are later ruled unfounded. This individual has a narrow focus and is not able to evaluate their actions from a different point of view. The clinician must enlarge this focus and help the patient view the situation from the perspective of the courts, the social services agencies, the children, and the other parent.

A second type of distraught parent whom the clinician may see in crisis is one who has learned of an affair and is thus hurt and explosive. He or she may order the adulterous parent out of the home and bar the children from seeing him or her. He or she may have been audiotaping the other parent's telephone calls, following his or her car, stalking him or her, or having him or her monitored and videotaped by a private investigator. This parent may have threatened the offender in front of the children or verbally denigrated him or her to the children. Physical altercations may occur also.

The clinician working with such parents must help them enlarge their perspective as well and anticipate possible negative consequences of their actions. Such individuals may feel so righteous in their indignation that they feel that any retaliation is justified. However, the courts may see the situation otherwise. The courts may see this parent's actions as a willful disregard for the children's feelings in the matter and view him or her as a high risk for interfering with visitation with the other parent. Such individuals' arrogance and sense of entitlement often alienate the judge and elicit a rebuke from the bench.

Last, the clinician may encounter some parents who present as extremely defeated and demoralized once they have been served with divorce papers. Although these individuals may have been highly involved, even the primary parents, they may be extremely accommodating to the other parent—allowing him or her to have sole custody and move the children out of state, for example—in order to placate the other parent and possibly avert a divorce. These individuals feel so diminished by the failure of the marriage that they are unable to sort out what is in the best interests of the children.

The clinician working with this type of parent must lend ego strength and bring in other supports. Referral to a good attorney is a beginning toward helping these parents secure their legal rights and not make unwise decisions or sign papers prematurely. Enlisting the aid of relatives is sometimes necessary to provide a safety net around such parents to encourage and support them.

Most individuals look to escape the marriage as a way out of the isolation, loneliness, and despair that they feel. Many parents simply move out, then meet with an attorney and draw up a petition for custody of their children. If a parent is planning to seek custody, however, he or she should stay in the home for several reasons. The clinician working with this parent should understand some of the legal ramifications of such a move.

Most parents attend a temporary hearing once they file for divorce, at which time issues of financial maintenance and visitation are established. If a parent has left the home and has begun a visitation relationship with the children, they may continue this pattern for 6 months or as long as 2 years, until the divorce is final. Most judges dislike to make changes in a visitation arrangement that seems to have been working adequately, as the disruption would be difficult for the children. A parent who leaves the home at the time of the temporary hearing is not likely to get final custody of the children.

This is especially true for fathers. Eleanor Maccoby and Robert Mnookin (1992), in their study of more than 1,000 divorcing families in California, compared residence of children at time of separation with residence at the time of the divorce in cases in which mothers and fathers were in conflict about custody issues. Of those children who were living with the mother at the time of the separation, about 70% went on to stay with her (about half of the rest went into joint-custody arrangements). Of those children who were living with the father at the time of the separation, only about 30% remained primarily with father at the time of the divorce (about 50% went on to joint-custody arrangements).

Second, the parent who remains in the home provides stability and continuity for the children. He or she may be a good parent, perhaps the primary parent to the children. Staying in the home establishes to the children and the courts that this parent has an interest in the children. It may also offer him or her time to establish himself or herself as the primary parent if the other parent has moved out.

Many clinicians are drawn into the coalition of supporters during an intensely conflicted divorce. However, a competent clinician does well to serve in a more neutral and impartial capacity—as an advocate for the children and one who can provide clear boundaries for the parents. The clinician can help the client sort out whether his or her pursuit of custody of the children is being done out of fear and revenge or whether it is a real desire to raise the children. The most genuine reason to seek custody is because this person has been the responsible parent and the executive manager for the children and thus has a strong and healthy bond with them. The clinician may want to review with the parent the difference between "helping" with the children and assuming primary responsibility. Studies show that though fathers help with the physical care of the children, even to the extent of doing 50% of the tasks when both parents work, it is typically the mother who makes the executive decisions about the children, schedules appointments, and is the repository of information about them. The clinician should ask clients "Who selected the caregiver?" "Who attends the school conferences?" "Who knows where to find the children's immunization records?" "Who can name their children's friends and their friends' parents?" "Who maintains the children's scrapbooks?"

The clinician must also help clients separate personal needs and troubles from their obligations as parents to work in the best interests of their children. This point comes up repeatedly in postdivorce litigation. Many cases that return to family court do so out of vendettas, bitterness, and wounded egos. Judges, caseworkers, guardians, attorneys, mediators, and evaluators sift through the myriad accusations and allegations, looking for the parent who can delineate and maintain this clear boundary. As the clinician, you may have to redirect your client to this issue often. The weeks and months just before and just after the separation are intensely emotional times, and this boundary can be blurred.

Janet Johnston and Vivienne Roseby (1997) made the sanguine observation that distressed parents, particularly at the time of an abrupt and particularly humiliating separation, often rewrite history in the sense that they revise their previous account of the marriage and their perception of their spouses, reconstructing a much more negative and malicious scenario. The passionate romance or the deep companionship is revised into a plot to manipulate the aggrieved spouse. The "soul mate" is transformed into a "con artist."

Recall that John Gottman (1994) made this same observation about couples headed toward divorce—that they begin to alter their cognitive perception of the marital relationship as they begin to make preparations to leave the marriage in order to validate their position, reduce dissonance, and justify their actions. Clinicians who are able to intervene at this vulnerable point in the marital breakdown have an important role to play in halting this process. A skilled clinician will help the client tolerate dissonance and ambivalence, reviewing what is both good and bad about the spouse, reminiscing about the happy times in the beginning of the marriage, and grieving the loss of the many positive aspects of the marriage and of the intact family unit.

CASE STUDY UPDATE

Laura was difficult to interview. She answered each question with a long account of her contempt for Scott and all she felt she had suffered in the marriage because of his actions. In spite of this, I recommended that the younger children be placed with her, as she had been the primary parent and the children had a much stronger bond with her. The examiner cautioned the court that Laura was a risk for blocking visitations and that the court should administer strong sanctions if she did so.

However, the judge saw otherwise at the hearing to determine custody of the two younger children. It seems that he, too, saw Laura's never-ending contempt for Scott as an impediment to the two parents' being able to develop a working relationship around the children. He awarded primary custody of the children to Scott, even though Scott's unusual shifts as a police officer meant that they were largely being raised by their aunt, who had come to live with Scott.

Six months after the hearing, Laura appeared at the evaluator's office. She was hoping to file an appeal. She could not bear to be apart from the girls, who missed her terribly, were doing badly in school, and were often fussy and irritable with Scott. However, Laura had fired yet another attorney. She still could not answer questions without going into long, detailed asides about her contempt for her ex-husband.

Twelve months after the hearing, Laura and Scott were still not finally divorced but were having a hearing to determine the financial settlements. Laura was still distraught over her loss of the children and hoped that somehow she could raise the issue again with still a third judge at this last hearing. In the lobby of the courthouse Laura greeted the evaluator who was to testify yet again. And as she had done continuously in the past, Laura began to go into her long litany of contempt for Scott.

Two and a half years after the initial separation, Laura was still petitioning the court for custody of her children and was still intensely hostile toward Scott. As of this writing, and after several more court actions, Laura was awarded custody of her two daughters, 4 years after the initial separation. She related that she and Scott were still intensely hostile toward each other, although she stated that she "still loved him."

4

DIVIDING THE CHILDREN

CASE STUDY

Terry and Bill were unusual for a couple going through a custody dispute—they were not hostile toward each other. The two parents were profoundly sad about their failure to make a sustaining family unit. Terry, age 34, was a dental hygienist, and Bill, age 38, worked as a senior systems analyst with a large company. They had one child, Bill Jr., age 5.

Bill knew that Terry had a drinking problem when he met her. In the early days of their courtship, she had been in recovery but had begun drinking again around the time that they married. They were living in a small town in the Midwest, and Terry had no friends there. They both attributed Terry's drinking problem to her loneliness and isolation. There was also a time during the courtship when Terry moved to Florida for 6 months to see if a relationship with an old boyfriend might work out. Bill was relieved when Terry returned and decided to make a commitment to him. Bill was a shy and passive individual. He did not feel that he could be demanding with Terry and could only wait for her to decide to settle down with him.

Terry openly admitted that she drank through the first 3 months of pregnancy but insisted that she stopped at that point out of fear that she was going to harm the baby. When Bill Jr. was born everything seemed fine. Terry went back to work when he was 8 months old and left him with the family caregiver down the street. In the course of taking care of Bill Jr., the caregiver noticed that the child was developmentally delayed. A full evaluation yielded the diagnosis of fetal alcohol syndrome.

When Bill Jr. was age 2½, Terry lost her job and began drinking again. After 4 months of binge drinking, she left suddenly. Bill located her through her parents in Florida and found that she was having an affair with a man there. He drove to Florida to get her and had her hospitalized in a drug and alcohol rehabilitation program. She felt much improved but began drinking again 6 months later and went back into the hospital.

Finally, Terry filed for divorce. Bill was ready to forgive her and to try again, to wait for her "to come to her senses." Terry said that the marriage had always been lifeless, that she had never been happy. Bill married her in order to "fix her," and she had hoped that he would, but it did not work. She found him to be uncommunicative, lacking in passion. He never even got angry at her.

Terry was asking for sole custody of Bill Jr. She had been in Alcoholics Anonymous (AA) for 1 year at the time of the evaluation, and she felt that she had recovered. She felt that she was the more nurturing parent and had a stronger bond with her son. She alleged that Bill was depressed and that he blew up occasionally at minor inconveniences. Bill was asking for sole custody, as he was the more stable parent who had more consistently cared for his son. He had spent more time with him overall than had his mother. Also, he did not want Terry to take Bill Jr. with her to nightly AA meetings.

Interviews with caregivers and neighbors revealed that Bill appeared to be a quiet man who had become more withdrawn since Terry had resumed drinking but that he was always warm and friendly in one-on-one situations. They had observed Bill playing in the yard with Bill Jr. much more than they had Terry.

When Bill Jr. was observed with both parents, he appeared to relate warmly to both of them, and they were both patient and nurturing with him. Projective tests with the child revealed a stronger attachment to his father than to his mother.

I noted that although both parents were now stable and providing good care for Bill Jr., it was Bill who was more likely to provide a stable home in the future. Terry had not yet been put to the test of facing a life crisis to determine if she could get through it sober. I also noted that in abandoning Bill Jr. for several months, Terry had demonstrated a weak bond with him. She was currently attending AA meetings every night but was staying late afterward to socialize with members and also had begun to date someone. I felt that Terry's energies were more focused on finding a love interest and controlling her drinking than on parenting her son.

Are Terry and Bill suitable for joint custody? For joint legal custody, or for joint physical custody? Is Bill a suitable candidate for primary custody of his son? Is there any basis for suggesting that Bill Jr. might do better with Bill than with Terry because he is a boy?

These are the kinds of complex questions that arise when couples litigate over the issue of dividing the children. Unlike the financial issues, which can largely be resolved by state laws that provide formulas for calculating child support, division of property, and even alimony, the issue of dividing children must be sorted out case by case.

In this chapter, I first examine the trends in custodial arrangements, which have moved away from exclusively mother custody to a range of new patterns, such as father custody, split custody, and joint physical custody.

The courts and families themselves have experimented with different forms of the division of children's time in an attempt to find the arrangement that works best for the child and the parents. This chapter looks at some of the controversial literature that suggests that boys may fare better in father custody. Also, split custody—the dividing of the children, one (or more) to each parent—is not often chosen by the courts but at times is opted for with some benefits. Joint physical custody, at first hailed as the solution to interparental conflict, is examined to see if it has lived up to its promise.

HISTORICAL TRENDS IN DIVIDING THE CHILDREN

When the divorce revolution began in the late 1960s, the method of dividing the children was relatively simple: to allot each parent time with the child in a similar manner in which the children had lived in the intact home. All fathers worked and saw their children mostly on the weekends. Nearly all mothers stayed in the home and functioned as primary parents throughout the week. Thus, mothers were granted custody, and fathers were granted weekend time. So that mothers were allowed some weekend time, the children alternated weekends between the mother and father.

By the mid-1970s many experts in the field had concluded that this arrangement had many major flaws. Family therapists were encountering children, especially boys, who felt abandoned by their fathers. A large proportion of fathers had been relegated to such a minimal part of their children's lives that they drifted away, both in terms of their time with the children and their financial support of the family. Fathers who kept up visitations on alternate weekends found their role and importance to the children drastically altered. No longer were they the head of the household, the breadwinner, the disciplinarian. Setting aside weekends for fun and play time, they had become "Disneyland dads." Their primary function was reduced to that of providing child support, and many objected to having become "just a check" to their children.

Fathers also found that their access to information about their children was sharply curtailed. When the mother had sole custody, the father did not have to be notified about the children's illnesses. He could be barred from speaking to the pediatrician. He did not have to be notified about important school events or the child's grades in school. He could be blocked from speaking to the teacher or picking up the child from school. When the mother had sole custody, the father had no say in how the child was to be raised, educated, disciplined, or provided with religious training.

Faced with an avalanche of sad children and angry fathers who had begun to form support groups, the courts began to pass laws allowing divorcing parents to have *joint custody*. As late as the mid-1970s, only one state, North Carolina, recognized joint custody. However, by 1981, according to law professors Doris Freed and Henry Foster (1981), writing for the Family Law Section of the American Bar Association, 11 states had passed laws permitting courts to provide for joint custody of children. By the late 1980s, Doris Freed and Thomas Walker (1988) found that 35 states had by then enacted laws recognizing joint custody. In doing so, the courts began to differentiate more succinctly between *joint legal custody* and *joint physical custody*. Nearly all 50 states now recognize that it is desirable, even preferable, for parents to share legal custody of the children—that is, for both parents to be actively involved in the decision making about the child's well-being and for both to have access to important information about the child.

Eleanor Maccoby and Robert Mnookin (1992) of Stanford University provided figures for one area—Santa Clara County, California—as an example of the shift toward joint legal custody. In the 1979 divorce decrees in that county, only 25% of the judgments awarded some form of joint custody. By 1981, the figure had risen to 37%. Between 1985 and 1989, however, 79% of the decrees involved joint legal custody of the children. About 20% of Maccoby and Mnookin's sample were awarded joint legal and joint physical custody. These figures for northern California are much higher than in other parts of the country. As a comparison, Amy Koel and associates (Koel, Clarke, Phear, & Hauser, 1988), with the Middlesex Divorce Research Group in Massachusetts, reported an increase in joint legal custody awards in that state from 15.9% in 1978 to 45% in 1985. During that same time span, awards of joint physical custody increased from only 2% to 4.5%.

In a side note, Maccoby and Mnookin (1992) noted that the presence of attorneys had a significant effect on the outcome of sole or joint custody. When both parents had legal representation, the parents received joint legal custody 92% of the time. When only one parent had an attorney, the percentage fell to 77%. On the other hand, only 50% of the families with no attorney present in the courtroom received joint legal custody. (This may be an artifact of income. Higher income fathers are more likely to hire an attorney and to request an attorney.) In fact, when no lawyer was present, when the mother requested sole custody, and when the father did not object, the judge awarded joint legal custody only 11% of the time.

WHAT DO PARENTS WANT, AND WHAT DO THEY GET?

What do parents want when dividing the children? Most parents want joint legal custody, and that is in fact what they usually get. Maccoby and Mnookin (1992) reported that 60% of the mothers and 75% of the fathers wanted joint legal custody. Overall, 79% of their sample obtained joint legal custody.

The difference between what mothers and fathers want and what they get with regard to physical custody, is, however, striking. Maccoby and Mnookin (1992) reported that 82% of the mothers in their California study wanted sole physical custody—that is, for the mother's home to be the primary residence. Only 15% said that they wanted joint physical custody —the nearly equal splitting of the children's time between two fully established residences—and only 2% requested that father have primary physical custody. Maccoby and Mnookin (1992) examined the divorce decrees for the hundreds of California families in their sample and found that the mother in fact received primary physical custody about 67% of the time, the father received sole physical custody about 9% of the time, and the parents had joint physical custody about 20% of the time (4% were in "other" arrangements). Even so, these figures are somewhat deceiving. When those children who were legally decreed to split their time equally between homes were followed to see where they actually lived, only 45% were actually abiding by the pattern agreed to in the divorce decree. Fully 38% were living primarily with their mothers. In other words, joint physical custody often means mother custody.

When fathers were interviewed as to their wishes, their responses were about equally divided among mother custody, joint custody, and father custody with regard to the child's living arrangements. Given the broad differences in these numbers, one might expect that a large number of divorces would result in contested custody battles over physical custody. However, only about 25 of the couples in Maccoby and Mnookin's (1992) sample were in dispute as to custody. The reason seemed to be that of those fathers who said that they wanted joint physical custody, only 40% requested it in their petition for divorce. Another 43% made no request at all. Of those fathers who said that they wanted sole physical custody, fewer than 38% actually asked for it in their petition and 30% made no request at all.

Why do the fathers not pursue what they want more aggressively? Some experts suggest that fathers may not feel as intensely about having custody of the children as do mothers. Certainly many who would like custody do not have work schedules that would fit around the children's needs. They may be living in an apartment located out of the children's school district and thus not be able to provide transportation to and from school. They may not feel as sure of their parenting capabilities as are mothers. The majority, however, may be dissuaded from seeking custody because of the perceived bias of the courts toward mother custody. Although fathers enjoy a more equal footing with mothers in court battles than they did in the past, the numbers still indicate that mothers have an edge over fathers in winning contested custody.

Why do the vast majority of mothers seek sole physical custody? Is it to retain control over the children? The Maccoby and Mnookin (1992) study, which started out studying more than 1,000 divorcing families, found that mothers asserted their desire for custody largely on the premise that they had been the primary parent responsible for the children, regardless of whether they worked, and they wished to continue in that role. The majority of mothers, even working mothers, have formed their lives around the children's needs. Mothers take lower paying jobs to work daytime hours and to work close to their homes. Studies show that fathers typically have not done so, and the changes that fathers would have to make to facilitate the transition to father custody would be much greater.

Two thirds of the mothers in Maccoby and Mnookin's (1992) study had concerns about whether the father could be an adequate caretaker of the children. This is not surprising in that the mother was the one to initiate the divorce in two thirds of the cases. No doubt many of the women had found the father lacking as a provider, spouse, or parent. The mothers asking for custody had been far more involved with the children than the father had and tended to be more hostile toward the father.

Fathers' reasons for seeking custody are more complex. First, there are economic factors. Several studies show that fathers who ask for joint legal and physical custody, or even sole custody, tend to be more educated and have higher incomes. They tend to be in professional occupations or own businesses, such that they have more control and flexibility over their schedules. They are in a better position also to hire attorneys, to pay for high-quality child care, and to buy a larger home for the children than are lower income fathers.

Fathers who seek sole physical custody tend to have more forceful personalities and are accustomed to asserting their power over others. They are unlike many of the fathers who may have wished to ask for custody but were reluctant to go against the mother's wishes. They are more likely to have shared parenting with the mother in the past and to be fully committed to the principle of coparenting.

Another subgroup of fathers who seek sole physical custody are those who have had a history of being more involved with the children than most fathers. Likewise, the mothers in these families tend to be less involved. Many of these same families are those in which the father has deep reservations about the mother's ability to care for the children adequately, both financially and emotionally. In many cases the mother has gone through a period of emotional instability, impulsive decisions, or neglect of the children.

Still other fathers were likely to assert custody out of anger toward the mother. These were cases in which the mother wanted out of the marriage and the father did not, and the mother was perceived to be at fault for ending the marriage. Although most divorces are legally "no fault," in reality many parents do seem to ascribe blame. Maccoby and Mnookin (1992) found that when mothers were perceived to be to blame for the divorce, fathers were more likely to seek and to obtain sole physical custody. Robert Felner of the University of Illinois, along with his associates Terre, Farber, Primavera, and Bishop (1985), found that a substantial percentage of attorneys (but not judges) believed that fathers sought custody out of revenge or to obtain leverage in negotiations over financial settlements.

James Turner (1984) of the Wright Institute in Berkeley, California, interviewed 26 fathers who had won custody of their children. He found one group who did so at the time of the divorce. As a group, these fathers had been involved in their wives' pregnancies and the births of their children, had bonded with their children through infant care, and had had an active and close relationship with their children. The fathers felt that the separation and divorce were a devastating loss and had attempted to reconcile with their ex-wives. They were not likely to be hostile, but rather to have amicable relationships with their ex-wives.

A second group identified by Turner (1984) waited 2 years after the divorce to seek custody. These fathers had not wanted a child initially, had not been involved in physical care of the children as infants, and were not in a close father–child relationship during the marriage. These men had been unhappy in the marriage from the start and were relieved to be out of it. After the divorce, the coparenting relationship had been hostile and bitter. The fathers in this group pursued visitation out of anger at the mothers for restricting their visitation or out of concern that the mothers were poor parents. These concerns focused around issues of the children's poor hygiene, poor diet, living in an unsafe environment, lack of structure, lack of discipline, and being left alone too long.

When the divorce revolution began, mothers received both legal and physical custody in about 90% of the cases, and fathers did so about 10% of the time. Much has been written about single-parent mothers, and the studies that have tracked the effects of divorce on children are largely studies of children in single-mother homes (although most go on to live in remarried homes). It is well known, for example, that the standard of living for mothers drops substantially after a divorce, that mothers are overburdened with having to carry out multiple roles, and that fathers' involvement and financial support fade away in time in large numbers of cases.

FATHER CUSTODY

What is known about father-custody families? The small numbers of fathers who sought and were awarded custody in the 1970s and 1980s were regarded as curiosities by the media and researchers alike. Society held its breath, wondering if fathers could in fact take over basic household chores and the parenting of young children. Fathers did, in fact, take over these tasks, albeit with some start-up difficulties. What we have also learned is that single-father homes, as a rule, are very different environments from single-mother homes. A big factor is the proportion of single-mother homes headed by young women who dropped out of high school with unplanned teenage pregnancies. These women are extremely disadvantaged both economically and emotionally and also are subject to the stresses of poverty, isolation, hopelessness, and lack of support from family and community.

Even when this group is removed from consideration and only divorced single mothers are compared with divorced single fathers, we still find that single fathers are more educated, have substantially higher incomes, and can provide a better home in a better neighborhood. For example, researchers Reuben Schnayer and Robert Orr (1988–1989) of Windsor, Ontario, studied a sample of 42 parents in which single fathers earned twice the income that single mothers did. Ann-Marie Ambert (1982) of York University in Toronto, Ontario, could not find any low-income single fathers with custody of their children. The seven custodial fathers that she did find were a banker, a financier, a commercial artist, a skilled worker, and three other professionals. With the exception of one father who was a millionaire, the yearly income of the group averaged $50,000 in 1982, the year in which the study was conducted.

These researchers saw not only large financial discrepancies between the two groups, but also subtle differences. The fathers benefited from more visitation by the noncustodial parent than did the mothers with custody. They also were invited out socially more often and were offered more help by people in the community. The fathers were frequently "set up" with dates and were more likely to have a companion living with them than did the mothers, and their girlfriends helped with child care, whereas mothers' boyfriends did not.

Schnayer and Orr (1988–1989) found that children in mother-custody homes tended to be more successful academically, whereas children in father-custody homes tended to have more behavior problems. All in all, they found that how the children were doing was more related to family income than to the type of custody arrangement.

Ambert (1982) found that her sample of children in father-custody homes had fewer behavior problems than those in mother-custody homes by a great margin. When she compared children in father-custody homes with children in mother-custody homes that were more upper middle class (although the mother's income was still only $33,000 on average), the differences narrowed considerably. Even so, the mother's income was only two thirds that of the father's, and the mother was not benefiting from the subtle social advantages of father custody that were mentioned earlier.

Richard Warshak, a professor at the University of Texas Southwestern Medical Center in Dallas, Texas, reviewed nine studies and concluded that father-custody children do not appear any more or any less well adjusted overall than mother-custody children (Warshak, 1992, see chapters 6 and 7)—that is, until the gender of the child is examined. Warshak did his doctoral dissertation under the supervision of Richard Santrock, a researcher known for his work on father-absent boys. The two were aware of the common behavioral problems of mother-custody boys and were interested in determining if boys from divorced homes had fewer behavior problems when they were being raised by fathers. In a well-planned study (Santrock & Warshak, 1979), they compared the social development of children, both boys and girls ages 6–11, from father-custody, mother-custody, and intact families. Their most intriguing finding was that children living with the opposite-sex parent were more poorly adjusted than children living with the same-sex parent. Boys living with fathers were rated as more mature, sociable, cooperative, and independent. They were less anxious and less demanding and had higher self-esteem. Santrock and Warshak found them to be more satisfied with their living arrangements. Girls living with mothers received similar ratings. In contrast, boys in mother-custody homes and girls in father-custody homes were seen as less mature and more demanding.

In a later study, Warshak and Santrock (1983) used pictures and a storytelling technique to determine children's preferences with regard to custody. They found that all of the father-custody boys wanted to live with their fathers. Likewise, all the mother-custody girls wanted to live with their mothers. Of children who lived with the opposite-sex parent, over half expressed an indirect wish to live with the same-sex parent.

Warshak's original research (Santock & Warshak, 1979) vaulted him into the glare of the news media because he seemed to offer some hard evidence as to how to divide the children, boys especially. Fathers and attorneys quickly sought him out as an expert to testify that fathers ought to be the custodial parents of their sons. Some have critiqued Warshak's work on the basis that his father-custody families were far more affluent and stable than his mother-custody families. Warshak said in his original article (Santock & Warshak, 1979) only that his families were "matched as to socioeconomic status" (p. 116).

What is even more intriguing about Warshak's findings is that they have been supported by similar findings by different researchers in other parts of the United States. Recall researchers James Peterson and Nicholas Zill (1986) from Child Trends in Washington, DC, who studied the effects of divorce, as well as subsequent divorces, on children. An unexpected finding was that the negative effects of divorce were lessened if the child lived with the same-sex parent. When boys lived with their fathers, they were a little less depressed and withdrawn than boys from intact families, whereas girls living with their fathers were an unhappy group.

Several years later, Kathleen Camara and Gary Resnick (1988) of Tufts University in Massachusetts conducted a similar study of the effects of divorce and conflict on children. They also compared children from three family types: intact homes, mother-custody homes, and father-custody homes. Although Camara and Resnick were not looking specifically for a gender difference, that is what they found. Mother-custody boys and father-custody girls were the most aggressive of all the groups of children and had the most behavior problems and the lowest levels of self-esteem. Mother-custody girls appeared to be doing about as well as girls from intact homes, whereas father-custody boys were actually doing a little better than boys from intact homes on many measures.

Viewed together, these studies make a persuasive argument for placement of a child with the same-sex parent in a custody dispute, provided the home is a suitable one and the child is at least equally attached to that parent as to the other. The observation that boys have fewer behavior problems when living in the custody of the father is one that dovetails with earlier findings about the high incidence of behavior problems of boys in mother-custody homes, which were reviewed in chapter 1. It also meshes with the observation that families themselves tend to shift boys to the father's custody as they enter preadolescence. As stated earlier, boys developmentally push away from maternal authority at this age but are more likely to inhibit their aggression when confronted with male authority. Maccoby, Depner, and Mnookin (1988) of Stanford University tracked the living arrangements of 1,884 children and found that the trend toward living with the same-sex parent was typical of children of all ages. However, it was strongest for boys older than age 11. From about ages 10 to 13, the number of boys living with fathers increased from about 12% to 25%. During this same period, the percentage of girls living with their fathers decreased from roughly 14% to about 8%.

A note of caution should be sounded here. Douglas Downey and Brian Powell (1993) challenged these conclusions about the advantages of same-sex custody. They pointed out that the sample sizes in the three studies cited above were small. The total number of children in father-custody homes in all three studies numbered only 60. Downey and Powell focused on data obtained from the National Education Longitudinal Study of 1988 collected by the National Center for Education Statistics. They culled data from the sample profiles of 3,483 children living with mothers only and 409 children living with fathers only. They examined 35 different outcomes by gender and found no differences between children in same-sex parental homes and children raised with the opposite-sex parent. In attempting to explain this discrepancy, Downey and Powell noted that the three studies described earlier examined elementary-school-age youngsters, whereas Downey and Powell's study examined only eighth graders ages 13–14. They questioned whether the same-sex parent effect holds only for younger children and diminishes with age.

SPLIT CUSTODY

On the basis of the research findings presented above, it seems that it might make sense to split the children in some cases, for example, having sons live with fathers and daughters live with their mothers. This is called *split custody*. Although it seems to make sense on the surface, in actuality it is rarely the court's decision to split children, and little is known about whether it is good for the children. Geoffrey Greif (1990), a professor of social work at the University of Maryland at Baltimore, wrote that split custody "is an unstudied phenomenon" (p. 15). The 1987 report by the U.S. Census did not even count split custody when counting homes with various custodial arrangements. Greif reviewed 75 consecutive divorce decrees granted in Baltimore County in a 3-month period in which at least two children were involved and found only three cases of split custody.

Maccoby and Mnookin's (1992) study of 783 divorcing families in California found that less than 1% of mothers requested split custody at the time of the divorce, along with less than 2% of the fathers. Even in California, which usually leads the nation in trends toward new and different family arrangements, less than 4% of the divorce decrees resulted in split custody.

Virginia Simons and others (Simons, Grossman, & Weiner, 1990) at St. Luke's Medical Center in Chicago reviewed the results of their study of 22 divorcing families who were seen for evaluations and recommendations to the court. They recommended split custody in only 2 cases, considering the choice "extreme" and to be made only when it was clearly the best solution for all involved. They based this recommendation on factors such as the siblings providing little or no support for each other and the siblings having strong alliances with the respective parents.

Why is split custody so rarely awarded by the courts? This may be due to the influence of the social work field on the juvenile court system.

The prevailing model in foster care and adoption work is that children should never be split up following the loss of the parents or removal from the parental home. This model came into fashion in the 1950s and 1960s, when caseworkers realized that children who were raised in different homes without any contact with each other suffered a double trauma: first the loss of their parents and then the loss of their siblings. Children do form strong emotional bonds with each other, and "having each other" was thought to offset some of the traumatic loss of their parents.

However, is a divorce the same sort of trauma? Children who are in split custody are not removed from their parents permanently. At worst, they still live with one parent most of the time and continue to see the other parent occasionally. In many cases, they continue to see both parents on a regular basis. Some children in split custody see each other every weekend—spending two weekends a month with the father and two weekends a month with the mother. So in reality they do not undergo a traumatic loss of parents or siblings.

Greif (1990) observed in his research that although the courts rarely award split custody at the time of the divorce, the arrangement occurs on its own over time following the divorce as the parents and children together move toward split custody. He interviewed families with father custody and split custody to determine why this is the case. The most common reason that the families moved toward split custody is that one or more children chose to live with the other parent. One typical scenario is the boy who becomes too difficult for the mother to handle, needs a male role model, and is sent to live with his father. Another common scenario is one in which the children may be living with the father, he remarries, and his daughter does not get along with the new stepmother and opts to move into the mother's home. The few children who chose split custody from the outset seemed to have formed strong coalitions with one parent at the time of the divorce.

Barry Bricklin (1995, see pp. 236–239), a psychologist in private practice in Pennsylvania and the developer of many tests now used in custody evaluations, reviewed the existing literature and concluded that he could find no research on whether split custody was a good or bad idea. Barbara Hauser (1985) cited an unpublished paper by Beck, Clark, Whitney, and Hauser (1985) of the Middlesex Probate Court Family Service Center in Cambridge, Massachusetts, that examined split custody. Although the number of split-custody cases was small—6 out of 35—they received significantly lower ratings for family outcome and child adjustment.

Bricklin polled the readers of his *Custody Newsletter* as a means of sampling opinions from other clinicians in the field. The responses he received generally indicated that many clinicians feel that split custody is appropriate under certain circumstances. One example is when the match-up between parent and child is such that one parent and child are an exceptionally good match in terms of personality and interests and so are the other parent and other child. Many of his readers referred to the child's age as an important variable. Younger children may need and derive more of a sense of security from being together. Adolescents may not have the same need to be together and may even be happier to be away from each other. Age may be important, also, in that younger children may need to be with the parent who has more time available for them, whereas older children do not. A third factor comes down to logistics: If there are several children, money is tight, and space is at a premium, the children may do better to be split between two parents so that each can have a private room, more financial resources, and a less exhausted parent. The last factor mentioned was one of safety: One child may be at risk of being abused sexually or physically by an older sibling. Transferring that child to the other parent may be best for everyone in the family. Until more research is done, clinicians will have to review recommendations for split custody on a case-by-case basis.

JOINT CUSTODY

The 1980s heralded a large shift from mother custody to joint legal custody as well as the beginning of experimentation with joint physical custody. What have we learned so far about the pros and cons of joint legal and physical custody? In the initial phases of this trend, many groups were quick to hail this experiment as the best solution for dividing the children. Judges were enthusiastic about joint custody because it provided a standard against which to apply cases—a standard that was obviously fair to all. The courts hoped to see a decrease in petitions for unpaid child support once fathers had more access to their children and more involvement in making day-to-day decisions. Fathers' rights groups hailed the trend as a way to open the door to fathers to be whole parents, involved and meaningful in their children's lives. Even many women's groups saw this as a positive development as it offered more relief to single mothers from the overwhelming physical and emotional responsibilities of sole parenting.

Advocates for children largely saw positive gains coming from the opportunity for children to have two fully involved parents in their lives who participated in decision making and whom they saw often. Some saw boys as standing to benefit particularly from having more frequent access to their fathers. No longer would fathers simply drop out of children's lives after the first couple of years, as they had in the past, when they were relegated to the position of children's "playmates."

There were, however, naysayers from the outset. What would be the effect on the children, they wondered, of frequently shifting back and forth between two separate-but-equal homes? Nothing had been tried like this in American history. Children had always had a primary home plus secondary residences for brief periods of time with relatives, for example, the grandmother at Christmastime or the aunt and uncle in the summer. The concept of a binuclear home was new. Do children need a primary home base to feel a sense of stability and security? No one knew the answer.

How would the parents coordinate these frequent transitions, and how would they split decision making? In most homes, the mother is the executive manager of the children's lives, and the father follows her lead. Sharing decision making equally in an intact home requires a great deal of flexibility and goodwill on each parent's part—even when they are married to each other. How, then, could divorced parents, who may be hostile to each other, accomplish this with equal finesse? Would a parent's ability to make swift, executive decisions be sabotaged by the parent who is quick to feel slighted? Would there be more conflict? Would the children be caught up in this conflict?

Also, what would be the effect on the parents? If the mother and father are seeing each other and talking to each other several times a week, will they be able to effectively end their relationship—and all of the painful emotions that went with the divorce? Will they be more likely to have feelings of ambivalence about each other? Will seeing each other often stir up all of the old feelings? Will the children engage in fantasies of their parents getting back together if they see them fighting and making up frequently?

At the outset of the experiment with joint physical and legal custody, few people anticipated these outcomes: that fathers would propose giving mothers much less child support if they had the children half the time and thus mothers' financial status would drop even lower. Some women received so little support under joint custody that they were forced to give up the children altogether to the father. In some cases, joint physical custody has exposed women to their abusive ex-husbands much more often and put them in positions of having to negotiate decision making with them, which exposed them to further abuse.

The earlier studies on joint custody, usually taken to mean joint physical custody, were marked by strong bias, both on the part of the researcher and the type of parents studied. For example, the earliest study, conducted by Alice Abarbanel (1979), a psychologist in Berkeley, California, studied only six children in four families. She observed that two of the children accepted their life situation and that two were quite distressed (and the other two were not mentioned). Yet she concluded that joint custody was a resounding success. In this and in other studies to follow, the parents were a well-educated, more affluent sample who had both decided that they wanted joint custody and were highly motivated to make it work. As stated before, the father is more likely to have the economic assets and the flexible schedule to make it work. The mother, too, is likely to have a career and be more invested in matters outside the home. She does not have as strong of a need to be the executive manager of the children's lives. They tend to have usually one child, at most two. When there are a large number of children, the mother is more likely to be a stay-at-home mom and to push for sole custody.

Are fathers more involved now? Has joint custody stemmed the tide of deadbeat dads and absentee fathers? Pearson and Thoennes (1990) reanalyzed data from four projects in Denver and Northern California that they had collected from 1979 through 1985. Examining data from more than 1,700 parents, the largest and most varied sample at that time, they concluded that under joint-custody arrangements fathers were indeed more accessible to children and continued to be accessible for a longer period of time. Their time with the children increased from 20% of the child's time to 28% with joint legal custody and usually increased to about 40% with joint residential custody. Thus most children still maintained a primary residence—in which they lived about 60% of the time—and a secondary residence.

The mothers in this sample reported that canceled, sporadic, or missed visitations were a problem only about 25% of the time, a figure that is about half that reported by sole-custody mothers. The parents in the joint-custody group were less likely to move away, thus providing further stability for the children. Also, the incidence of petitions for back child support were substantially less. All in all, the goal of greater and more equal involvement seemed to be obtainable with joint custody.

The parents in the joint-custody group even seemed to have better opinions of each others' parenting capacity as well. Whereas 50% of the sole-custody mothers reported that their children had a good relationship with their father, 90% of the joint-residential-custody mothers cited this as a positive outcome. Similarly, whereas only 30% of the sole-custody mothers reported being "very" or "somewhat" satisfied with how the father was doing as a parent, 65% of the joint-residential-custody mothers were pleased with how the father was doing.

So far, mothers as a group would seem to be pleased with joint legal and physical custody. Indeed, these mothers were not reporting the feelings of being overwhelmed, as were sole-custody mothers. Whereas 40% of sole-custody mothers often reported being overwhelmed, only 13% of the joint-custody mothers did (25%–30% of fathers with custody reported being overwhelmed).

However, the joint-custody mothers seemed to still be taking on much of the executive manager functions with the children. Where parents had joint legal custody, the primary residential parent (usually the mother) reported feeling responsible for getting tasks done for the children in 75%–85% of the cases, depending on the task. In joint-residential-custody families, only about half the mothers reported that the responsibility for the children was shared equally. Staying home with the children when they were sick was the last pillar to fall to equality. Fewer than 35% of the parents having fully joint custody reported that they shared this job equally. (Only 10% of parents in other custody arrangements shared this job equally.)

Barbara Rothberg (1983) of Lutheran Community Services in Brooklyn, New York, found parents to be equally favorable to joint custody. Her sample comprised 30 parents and 25 children who were drawn from the enrollment of a private school in New York City. All of the children spent at least 3 days of the week with the parent who was not the primary-residential parent. Sixty-seven percent of the sample had good feelings about joint custody, 13% had negative feelings, and 20% had ambivalent feelings. Eighty percent of the sample said that they would recommend joint physical custody to others, although it depended on the couple. The biggest benefits that they cited were the children having a "real father" and the mothers having more free time. The biggest drawbacks that they listed were difficulties with transitions, coordinating the specific logistics of frequent pick-ups and drop-offs, and the stress on the children of having to adjust to two different environments. Dealing with the ex-spouse was also high on the list of drawbacks, followed by the financial strain of having to maintain two full households and both parents having to remain living in the same neighborhood.

Like the California sample, the New York parents also agreed that the mother was still in large part the executive manager of the children, even when the parents' time was almost evenly split. Over a third of the group felt that the mother had the primary responsibility when it came to caring for sick children, buying the children's clothes, and going to school to meet with teachers.

Does the enthusiasm of parents for joint custody mean that, as was hoped, the court dockets have been cleared of family disputes over child-related issues? Not necessarily. Deborah Luepnitz (1986) of the Philadelphia Child Guidance Clinic looked at a small sample of parents with various custodial arrangements and found that although half of the sole-custody parents had returned to court to fight about money, none of the joint-custody parents had done so. Also, the joint-custody parents reported less conflict.

Frederic Ilfield and Holly Ilfield of the University of California at Davis School of Medicine and attorney John Alexander of the Superior Court of Los Angeles County (1982) examined 414 consecutive custody cases in Los Angeles in the early 1980s to determine which parents had returned to court more often. They found that whereas 32% of the sole-custody families had returned to court, only 16% of the joint-custody families had done so. Even when the judge had awarded joint custody against the wishes of one parent, only about one third had returned to court.

Catherine Albiston of the Stanford Child Custody Center, along with Maccoby and Mnookin (1990), asked the question "Does joint legal custody matter?" Albiston et al. re-examined Luepnitz's (1986) and Ilfield et al.'s (1982) data and noted that the joint-legal-custody families actually had less time to litigate—a factor that may have explained their favorable results. In fact, Phear, Beck, Hauser, Clark, and Whitney (1983) found different results. These researchers, using a different sampling method and following a different population, found that parents with joint custody relitigated at rates higher (20%) than those with sole custody (12%).

Albiston et al. (1990) examined the data from the Stanford Child Custody Study, a set of interviews with 1,145 northern California families who had gone to court seeking a divorce and to resolve custody issues between 1984 and 1985. They asked the question whether in fact conflict was actually lessened in joint-legal-custody families. They divided their sample into three groups, which they labeled *cooperative* (high cooperative communication and low conflict), *conflicted* (high conflict and low cooperative communication), and *disengaged* (low conflict but also low cooperative communication). The results were clear: There were no differences in levels of cooperation or conflict when the groups were divided by type of custody arrangement (see Table 4.1).

The three groups were amazingly unalike. One would expect that the joint-legal-custody families would at least be less likely to be disengaged, but this was not true. In reviewing myriad factors, Albiston et al. (1990) concluded that the best predictor of conflict at 18 months after the divorce was not custody type but the level of conflict between the parents at 6 months postdivorce. The best predictor of conflict $3^1/_2$ years postdivorce was the level of conflict at 18 months postdivorce. In other words, parents who were prone to high levels of conflict at the time of divorce tended to be the same ones entrenched in conflict years later, regardless of custody arrangements.

Koel et al. (1988) found few differences among their sample of 700 families. About 19% of mother-custody families relitigated, but so did 17%

TABLE 4.1
Percentage of Families With Coparenting Patterns in Each
Residential Group

	Children's residence		
Coparenting style	With mother	With both	With father
Cooperative	24	33	20
Conflicted	36	31	33
Disengaged	29	23	37

Note. Adapted from "Coparenting in the Second Year of Divorce" by E. Maccoby, C. Depner, & R. Mnookin, 1990, *Journal of Marriage and the Family,* Copyrighted 1990 by the National Council on Family Relations, 3989 Central Avenue NE, Suite 550, Minneapolis, MN 55421. Reprinted by permission.

of the joint-custody families. Only 5.3% of the father-custody families had come back to court. Pearson and Thoennes (1990), the custody mediators and researchers in Denver, found few differences in their large sample of families in mediation. Visitation conflicts occurred in about 30% of all the various custody arrangements. Although sole-custody mothers complained about missed or canceled visitations, 38% of the mothers with joint physical custody complained that the father had the children too much of the time. Furthermore, the joint-custody families were much more likely to return to alter the visitation arrangements. Fully 29% of the joint-legal-custody and joint-residential-custody families returned to court with petitions to modify custody. (The figures were even higher for families in which the father had the most control. Thirty-three percent of the joint-legal/paternal-physical-custody families and 39% of the sole-paternal-custody families went back to court with requests for modifications.)

In summary, it seems that although the financial disputes in joint-custody families are substantially diminished, such families still return to court in high numbers—with conflicts over requests for more time or less time with the child, petitions to move out of state, requests to modify custody altogether, complaints about what goes on in the other parent's home, and so on. Some of the relitigation rates are determined by economic and social factors. Fathers who seek joint legal custody, joint physical custody, or both tend to be more educated, more affluent, and have access to legal representation. They are more likely to demand that their parental rights be acknowledged from the outset and to continue to do so when they feel that they have not been given an adequate voice in decisions made about their children.

DO CHILDREN IN JOINT CUSTODY FARE BETTER THAN THOSE IN SOLE CUSTODY?

How are the children doing? From the early large-scale studies described in chapter 1, which reported negative effects of father absence, it was assumed that the children would benefit by having a more involved father in their lives. But here again the answer is not necessarily.

Susan Steinman (1981) of the Jewish Family and Children's Services in San Francisco conducted perhaps the first study to follow the children of the experiment with binuclear living. The 32 children that she studied were not caught up in the loyalty conflicts that children in sole-custody arrangements often are, but she did find them to be overly sensitized to loyalty issues. That is, they scrupulously maintained a position of neutrality and fairness toward each parent, being careful not to express a want or complaint that might slight one parent. She found 25% of the children to be experiencing confusion and anxiety about their schedules and switching houses. She found that the confusion about where they were to be and when left them frustrated, anxious, and unhappy with themselves. The most stressed groups seemed to be the 4- and 5-year-old girls and the 7- to 9-year-old boys. Although some had mastered the demands of the situation, clearly a significant portion of the children had not, and their stress about the complex living arrangements appeared to add to their already sad and "burdened" feelings about the divorce.

Several more recent studies have compared the adjustment of children in different custody arrangements. Luepnitz (1986) studied 91 children in Philadelphia who came from mother-custody, father-custody, or joint-custody homes. These families were "normal" samples, recruited through newspaper ads and word-of-mouth. The researchers measured the children's self-esteem, psychosomatic problems (aches and pains caused by mental distress), and behavior problems. Leupnitz found that adjustment was not related to custody type, but it was related to level of conflict between the parents. When their parents remained locked in conflict, children did poorly on all three measures regardless of custody type. This is not surprising in view of the wealth of findings (reviewed in chapter 2) that reveal that the level of conflict between parents predicts children's adjustment regardless of whether parents are married.

Kline, Tschann, Johnston, and Wallerstein (1989) investigated the effect of custodial arrangement on 93 children ages 3–14. At the outset of the study, 65 children were in mother's physical custody, 23 were in joint physical custody, and 5 were in father's physical custody. At the 2-year follow up, 58 were in mother-physical-custody and 35 were in joint-physical-custody. These families, too, were a normative sample, recruited through letters sent to couples in the San Francisco Bay area who had filed for divorce. These researchers found that, in general, boys did more poorly than did girls, children ages 6–11 did more poorly than did children who were older or younger, and children who were only children did more poorly than did children from larger families. Second, mothers' emotional states, such as depression and anxiety, and the level of conflict between parents also were predictive of children's adjustment. The children in joint physical custody were functioning neither better nor worse than were children living in other arrangements.

Pearson and Thoennes (1990) re-examined their data on more than 150 families whom they followed for 15 months after divorce mediation. They found that children in all custody types scored about the same on measures of depression, aggression, delinquency, social withdrawal, and physical complaints. When they statistically analyzed their data, they found that children were functioning better in families in which parents were cooperative, had no history of violence, and were not having financial problems. They also found an association between better adjustment and more frequent visitation with both parents, fewer changes in the child's life, and less conflict between the parents. But again, children in joint custody were doing neither better nor worse overall than those in sole-custody arrangements.

Janet Johnston (1995) reviewed a total of 14 studies on this topic. She concluded that there were "few, if any" significant differences in the adjustment of children by virtue of the type of custodial arrangement in which they lived. In her commentary she noted that children had a tendency to self-select into the type of custodial arrangement that they wanted over a period of time, with about one third of the children changing homes over a 2- to 4-year period. Children in joint residential arrangements tended to drift back into the primary care of their mothers. (The tendency for boys to drift into father custody in preadolescence has already been noted.) Children with behavior problems tend to be deposited into the custody of their fathers in adolescence. This may make father-custody samples appear to be more maladjusted, although this was mostly true for adolescent girls in father-custody homes.

Should we presume that joint legal and physical custody should be the standard for all divorcing families? Most experts in the field would answer that "it depends." First, there are the obvious cases to rule out—ones in which the father has been abusive and the mother is afraid to encounter him. For these families, it may be best for the mother to have sole custody to retain control of decision making and not have to encounter the father as often.

The verdict is out still on couples in which one parent wants sole custody, the other wants joint custody, and the judge awards joint custody. Are these arrangements likely to fail when one parent is coerced into an arrangement that he or she did not want? This is hard to answer because nearly all the studies on joint-custody families are biased in several ways: the majority of families with joint custody (both legal and physical) chose this form of custody enthusiastically, both parents believed fully in co-parenting, both were committed to the children, and both tended to be well educated and to have high incomes. It is not known how well joint custody would work for other samples.

Couples who are extremely hostile toward each other may not be suited for joint legal and physical custody. Studies show that these couples are entrenched in hostility years before the divorce and continue to be immersed in conflict for years afterward. Joint custody, although it may inject a dose of fairness into the situation, does not seem to reduce the conflict. The focus of the conflict simply changes to the myriad decisions that have to be negotiated to make joint custody work effectively. As discussed in chapter 3, out-of-court mediation has been tried as a solution to reduce conflict, and it has failed with these couples. So has joint custody.

Recall Susan Steinman of the Jewish Family and Children's Services of San Francisco. She and her colleagues (Steinman, Zemmelman, &

Knoblauch, 1985) conducted a 3-year study of 51 joint-custody families, looking at which families were successful and which were not. The "successful" group included families who were pleased with joint custody, had maintained it for 3 years, and had not returned to court. The "failed" group began with a joint-custody arrangement that subsequently broke down, the mediation had failed, and they were back in court litigating over custody. Steinman et al. found that parents in the successful group responded to the divorce with mild depression and feelings of guilt about the breakup. Not only was the intensity of their anger low, but also they actively suppressed their anger toward the former spouse rather than act it out. These parents were characterized by a high level of trust in themselves and high levels of self-esteem. They had good control of their emotions and were able to moderate their aggression and control their temper. They were able to work cooperatively, to be rational, and to problem solve. They also expressed an aversion to going to court and used every means possible to settle their disputes without attorneys.

The failed group, in contrast, responded to the marital breakup with intense feelings of anger, unassuaged by guilt or sadness. They blamed the ex-spouse for the divorce, for their own personal problems, and for the children's behavior problems. Many of the parents in this group had a low sense of self-worth, and the anger and blame at the ex-spouse seemed to serve to protect themselves from depression and humiliation. Last, they were rigid in general and in their view of the divorce.

Steinman et al. (1985) concluded that several personal traits are necessary in parents for joint custody to work. Among them are an appreciation of the bond between the child and the other parent; an objectivity with regard to the child; an ability to empathize with the point of view of the child and the other parent; an ability to view the ex-spouse as a co-parent and not as a mate; and generally high self-esteem, flexibility, and openness to help.

WHAT THE RESEARCH SHOWS

When the divorce revolution began in the United States, custody was automatically awarded to the child's mother, unless she was an unfit parent. Fathers' rights groups, feeling marginalized, soon brought changes in the law, moving custody away from gender preference and toward more flexible, adaptable arrangements. In 30 years, joint legal custody has become the standard arrangement, although mothers still bear the larger burden of primary residence and responsibility for the children's care. Fathers have shown that they can be adequate primary caregivers, and a series of studies indicates that they may be the preferred caregiver for boys. Likewise, mothers may be the preferred caregiver for girls. Split custody, although not often pursued, may be a good option for families in which children have been neglected, may feel jealous or resentful of each other, or present a danger to each other.

Joint physical custody, hailed as the solution to interparental conflict, has been largely a disappointment. Parents in this arrangement relitigate as often as when one parent has primary custody of the children. Children do not fare better in joint physical custody, and many fare worse when they are exposed to frequent, ongoing conflict at times of transition. Joint physical custody appears to be most successful when both parents want it and when both show high levels of emotional adjustment and low levels of anger, blame, and distress.

GUIDELINES FOR THE CLINICIAN

Clinicians who are asked by the courts to determine whether joint legal and physical custody is the best arrangement for a particular family should first consider whether the parents are described in the paragraphs above. Couples in whose marriages abuse or violence has occurred are not good candidates. Couples in which one person wants joint custody and one is firmly against it are probably not good candidates; neither are couples whose contempt and resentment toward each other run deep. Many parents in custody disputes are controlling and obsessive individuals who will insist that the other parent comply with their wishes about minute aspects of the children's care. In these cases, the clinicians and the courts are in a quandary. Such individuals do not adapt to joint legal custody easily—yet if one parent is given primary custody, the nonfavored parent is likely to feel so personally offended and disenfranchised that he or she will launch a new round of litigation. The ideal couple for joint custody is one in which each parent has forgiven the other for their failings and moved on with their lives with some degree of contentment. Although such couples no longer desire the other as a partner, for them the ending of the marriage has not been traumatic or humiliating, and each respects the other as a parent. If this describes the parents being evaluated, the clinician should keep in mind that both parents will need to communicate with each other often, be flexible in rearranging schedules at the last minute, and be willing to compromise endlessly.

Next, if the couple seems suitable for joint custody, both parents will need to consider certain demographic and logistical factors. The parents must live in the same approximate area and be able to afford two adequate homes. Both must be committed to remaining near each other for a long time. Both must have careers that allow for the flexibility to take time off from work for school functions and the care of sick children. Neither parent must travel extensively in his or her work.

Next, the needs of the children must be factored in. Generally, joint custody is not recommended for very young children. However, it can be gradually phased in, and children in the age range of 8–12 years tolerate it best. Children ages 13 and older will want to make their own choices as to custody and visitation (see chapter 6 for a fuller discussion of these issues).

Studies show that joint legal custody is typically no different from sole custody in how decision making is handled. This is because most divorce agreements specify that in the event of an impasse between the parents, the parent who has primary physical custody of the children (usually the mother) will have the final say. This amounts to de facto sole custody, and the secondary-residence parent is in fact only a token coparent in this form of dispute resolution.

Some families with joint legal custody attempt to circumvent this problem by opting for a demarcated form of joint custody—that is, they lay out the various areas of parental control and determine who will have the final say in each area. For example, one parent may have the controlling vote as to which school the child attends, whereas the other parent may have the controlling vote as to the child's after-school enrichment activities. One parent may have the authority to select the pediatrician and health plan in which the child will be enrolled, and the other parent may have the vote on whether and with whom to seek counseling for the child. Religious upbringing is another area that could be demarcated, as well as the form of child care that is provided. Although each parent may feel more empowered by this arrangement, each will still have to make decisions with the other parent in mind. For these plans to work, the arrangements will have to be geographically accessible to the other parent and fit in with the other parent's schedule.

Although split custody is rarely awarded by the courts, it may present some distinct advantages and should not be ruled out. Boys, especially, may benefit from living with fathers, particularly from the age of 11 on. Adolescents in general may tolerate split custody better than younger children. Many families, over the course of time, move through a series of custodial arrangements with the developing needs of the children, often gravitating toward split custody on their own. I have worked with many families in which the children live with the mother when they are young, then move to the father's home one by one as they reach adolescence, completing high school in the father's home. They express the desire to "get to know" the father before they are grown up and it is "too late."

Whereas many families adopt this plan in a de facto way through a series of crises in early adolescence during which the child is sent away from the mother's home, some families anticipate this problem and plan for an orderly move to the father's home as a kind of "rite of passage," eliminating the turmoil of family crises. Parents who prefer not to litigate may consult with a mental health professional every few years to evaluate the children's changing needs and to get an opinion on what custody arrangement would best suit their needs at that time. The clinician may want to recommend this option to the court and the respective attorneys. In fact, many custody evaluators now routinely recommend that the parents consult with a psychologist or psychiatrist who is knowledgeable in child development every 2–3 years to re-evaluate the custody plan.

CASE STUDY UPDATE

I recommended that Terry and Bill have joint legal custody of Bill Jr., as they both seemed suitable candidates. I also recommended that Bill Jr. live primarily with his father and have regular visitations with his mother. In particular, I recommended that Bill Jr. spend 1 day each weekend with Terry and 1 overnight stay during the week with her on a night when she did not attend an AA meeting. Bill and Terry were quiet and tearful at the feedback session and took the recommendations somberly. After consulting with their attorneys, they decided to accept the recommendations and settle out of court. Terry stated that she agreed with my opinion that Bill Jr. belonged with his father. Bill had more stamina for family life than she did, and she, too, felt that she was searching for something that she could not find. In some ways, she said, she had pursued custody because she felt she ought to as Bill Jr.'s mother, although she had her own doubts about whether she was suited for the job.

5

RATIONALE AND GOALS OF THE CUSTODY EVALUATION

CASE STUDY

By the time Ted and Jennifer began their custody evaluation, each had accrued an arsenal of witnesses and documents to be used in their campaign. Ted submitted to me, as the examiner, 23 documents and no fewer than 37 affidavits from friends and neighbors testifying as to his outstanding qualities as a father. Jennifer submitted 4 documents and 27 personal affidavits on her behalf. In the 2 months that it took to complete the evaluation, I spent $6\frac{1}{2}$ hours interviewing Ted and 5 hours interviewing Jennifer. I also spent a total of 4 hours with 5-year-old Tyler, the subject of their battle. One hour was spent with Jennifer's teenage sons from a previous marriage, and I also interviewed eight other people: Jennifer's first husband, one caseworker, three neighbors, one minister, one counseling psychologist, and a marital therapist. Ted insisted that I interview still more people on his list, but I refused out of fairness to Jennifer.

In the months leading up to the evaluation, there had been numerous petitions and three court rulings. Jennifer had kidnapped Tyler and hidden him for 4 weeks. When Ted regained access to his son, Tyler had dark circles under his eyes and muttered bizarre statements such as "You're a son of a bitch. I want to kill you. Mama has a stun gun. She will spray gas on you." Ted had been following Jennifer in his van and videotaping her through a darkened window. Both had compiled lengthy diaries detailing the breakdown of the marriage, which they submitted to me. How had they come to this point?

Only 6 years previous to that time the couple had met and become enthralled with each other immediately. They married after a 6-week courtship. Both had felt that the other was the "answer to their prayers." Ted had gone on disability because of a work-related injury and had obtained a sizable settlement. Jennifer saw in him someone who would be devoted to her, take care of her financially, and be a father to her children. Ted, who had been out of work and lonely and was in his 40s and childless, saw an opportunity to gain a ready-made family. Each was thrilled when 1 month into the new marriage Jennifer became pregnant with Tyler.

Over the years, however, the settlement money ran out, and Ted did not seek employment. He said that his disability discouraged anyone from wanting to hire him as an accountant. He became depressed and sat on the front steps many evenings drinking beer. He and Jennifer argued over Tyler. Jennifer insisted on keeping Tyler in their bed; Ted wanted Tyler in his own bed. They argued over Jennifer's teenage sons, who were rude and disrespectful. Ted tried to discipline them, but Jennifer would rush to their rescue. They argued over money, now that Jennifer had become the sole breadwinner in the family. They went through a series of attempts at marriage counseling, with no success.

The description of Ted that I gave in my report was that he is "a very obsessive and meticulous individual who has made the campaign for custody of his son a full-time job." Ted was, in fact, difficult to interview because he continually digressed into long-winded and detailed stories that had little direct bearing on the questions at hand. Nevertheless, he also applied this same degree of obsessiveness to his care of Tyler. I summarized Ted's assertion that he is the better parent (obtained from the interviews with Ted and others, observations, affidavits, and documents) with the following outline (shortened here from the original):

1. Ted insists that he is the better parent in that he is less likely than is Jennifer to alienate Tyler from his other parent. Jennifer has attempted to alienate Tyler from Ted by (a) kidnapping him for 4 weeks, (b) saying abusive things about Ted to Tyler, (c) using her other children to ally with her against Ted, (d) blocking his telephone calls to Tyler, (e) changing her work schedule to break up his visitation time with Tyler, (f) alienating Tyler from the neighbors who have supported Ted, (g) blocking Ted's efforts to seek speech therapy for Tyler, (h) encouraging Tyler not to play with toys given to him by Ted, and (i) leaving Tyler with babysitters rather than let

Ted care for him. I also listed seven points under which Ted alleged that Jennifer had alienated her two older sons from their father in a similar manner.

2. Ted alleges that Jennifer has poor boundaries with the children. Specifically, (a) she allows Tyler to watch R-rated movies, (b) she sleeps with Tyler every night, (c) she has allowed Tyler to touch her breasts, (d) she has discussed her legal proceedings with Tyler, and (e) she allows the older boys to make adult decisions in the household.

3. Last, Ted alleges that Jennifer is a lax and neglectful parent. His assertions here were summarized under 11 points in which Jennifer is said to be neglectful of Tyler's hygiene, does not get him to bed on time, lets him eat milkshakes for dinner, does not discipline him, sees no need for speech therapy, lets him be supervised by teenagers, and has no control over her teenage boys.

When Jennifer was interviewed, she was very hostile and defensive. She did not see why she needed to "be on trial." Ted did not and would not work and was a poor provider and a poor role model. He had abused alcohol on a regular basis. He could not get along with her children because he was ridiculously rigid and strict, almost abusive, when it came to his expectations for children. She saw him as depressed and paranoid and in need of psychiatric help. Tyler needed to stay with her and her children in her home, where he had always lived and where he "belonged."

What is to be done when mediation fails and the mother and father cannot agree on how to divide the child? How should the courts intervene? This is a weighty matter—deciding the future of a child's life—and one that judges do not take lightly. In the past, as was stated in chapter 1, judges simply awarded the children to the mother, especially if the child was of tender years—under the age of 7 or 8. Mothers were considered so specialized for the job that a mother had to be proven to be unfit in order for the father to be considered for custody of his children. As the tender-years doctrine was challenged, new guidelines had to be developed to provide standards for the court—standards that could be reasonably free of bias. Because these standards have incorporated many psychological factors that are not readily observable, a new industry was born—that of the psychological expert in family and child forensic cases. In the 1970s, and even into the 1980s, these experts rendered opinions to the court that were largely informal and based on "clinical experience." However, the development of increasingly greater standards in the field has forced evaluators in this field to rise to the level of other forensic evaluators—a level that demands scientific expertise, verifiable conclusions, and a familiarity with family law and the court system.

In this chapter I begin by briefly reviewing the development of legal standards for recommending custody. Then I review what is known about that 5%–10% of families who litigate over custody and why they do so. From there I review the American Psychological Association's (1994) *Guidelines for Child Custody Evaluations in Divorce Proceedings* and the essential components of a thorough evaluation. The use of psychological tests in custody evaluations is somewhat controversial, and several tests will be reviewed in detail. Given that custody evaluators are being held to a more rigorous, scientific standard, the evaluator is cautioned to use tests judiciously and carefully. After conducting numerous interviews and collecting a large array of data, the evaluator must sort through and prioritize this information to come up with recommendations. In this chapter I not only review the research on guidelines used by other mental health professionals, but also compare them with guidelines actually used by judges. Finally, I will propose several sets of guidelines as well as provide a discussion of whether it is ethical to make an actual recommendation for custody.

The Guidelines for the Clinician section at the end of this chapter is divided into two parts. Clinicians may first want to review information on the impact of the evaluation on the family and the guidelines for helping the client weigh the costs and benefits of undergoing the evaluation. Then a number of pointers are offered to improve the quality of one's evaluation.

DEVELOPMENT OF GUIDELINES FOR RECOMMENDING CHILD CUSTODY

The Uniform Marriage and Divorce Act, which was written in 1970 and finally passed by the American Bar Association in 1973, proposed that gender no longer be the criterion for obtaining custody of young children. It introduced the concept of "the best interests of the child" as the standard by which to make decisions regarding child custody. Section 402 set forth five factors to be considered as contributing to the best interests of the child:

1. the wishes of the parents
2. the wishes of the child
3. the interaction and interrelationship of the child with his parent or parents, his siblings, and any other person
4. the child's adjustment to his home, school, and community
5. the mental and physical health of all individuals involved.

It also proposed that the behavior of the parent, no matter how morally objectionable, should not be considered when making custody decisions, unless it directly affects the child.

In the early 1970s a handful of states passed statutes outlining criteria for custody decisions. The most detailed was the Michigan statute adopted in 1972, which recommends that the best interests of the child should be determined by the sum total of the following factors:

1. the love, affection, and other emotional ties existing between the parents and the child
2. the capacity and disposition of the parties involved to give the child love, affection, and guidance and continuation of the education and raising of the child in his or her religion or creed, if any
3. the capacity and disposition of the parties involved to provide the child with food, clothing, medical care, and other material needs
4. the length of time that the child has lived in a stable, satisfactory environment, and the desirability of maintaining continuity
5. the permanence as a family unit of the existing or proposed custodial home or homes
6. the moral fitness of the parties involved
7. the mental and physical health of the parties involved
8. the home, school, and community record of the child
9. the reasonable preference of the child, if the court deems the child to be of sufficient age to express a preference
10. any other factor considered by the court to be relevant to a particular child custody dispute (Foster & Freed, 1973–1974).

Law professors Doris Freed and Henry Foster (1981) determined that by the 1980s the tender-years doctrine had lost ground and been rejected in 37 states. The laws favoring mothers remained on the books but could be subordinated to the best interests of the child in 8 states. Two states still had laws stating that the mother was to be preferred in the event that both parents were equally fit to care for the children. Foster and Freed also found that by that time, about 25 states had adopted guidelines for custody decisions.

Updating their review of child custody law in the late 1980s, Doris Freed and T. B. Walker (1988) found that 31 states had statutory guidelines delineating the basis on which custody decisions should be made. These standards were largely taken from the Uniform Dissolution of Marriage Act. Most were similar to the Michigan statute outlined above. However, one additional factor had been added:

11. The willingness and ability of each of the parents to facilitate and encourage a close and continuing parent–child relationship between the child and the other parent.

Law professors Linda Elrod and Robert Spector (1996) updated the changes in family law in their more recent review. At this writing, 38 states now have statutory guidelines by which the courts can award custody to litigating family members. A total of 41 states now have laws on the books recognizing joint custody, and 44 states can by law consider the children's wishes when making custody dispositions.

Along with the passage of these statutes, many laws have been adopted in various states that have struck down the use of criteria such as the parent's income, sexual orientation, and religious faith or lack of church involvement. Even the parent's race in the case of a mixed-race marriage or relationship is not to be considered a criterion for custody; neither is the presence of a health problem or physical disability. In addition, the parent's having committed adultery may be proof of misconduct in a divorce action, but it is no longer used as proof of unfitness when making custody decisions.

With the passage of all of these state laws between 1970 and 1996, the effect has been to eliminate from consideration nearly all criteria that are easy to determine—gender, religion, sexual orientation, wealth, race, disability, and past history—and to base custody decisions instead on subtle, psychological factors. Thus, by the early 1980s mental health professionals were being called on by the courts to serve as information gatherers and behavioral scientists when sorting these subtle issues. A new subspecialty for psychologists and psychiatrists has evolved around rendering custody evaluations, making parental fitness evaluations, offering opinions to the court as to visitation arrangements, and even offering opinions as to when a parent is abusive or neglectful or should have his or her parental rights terminated. Some mental health professionals have moved even further into quasi-legal areas such as divorce mediation and arbitration of visitation disputes.

WHO SETTLES AND WHO GOES TO COURT?

What portion of divorcing families with children go to court to resolve the division of the children? Are these the most hostile, embittered families? What are the factors that predispose some families to settle peacefully and some to go to war, despite the financial and personal costs to themselves and, possibly, their children? Law professors Robert Mnookin and Lewis Kornhauser (1979) estimated that only a small percentage of divorces, "probably less than ten percent" (p. 951) involved disputes that were contested through the courts. Rohman, Sales, and Lou (1987) reviewed several studies and concluded that the vast majority of cases—83%–90%—settle out of court and that only a fraction go into litigation.

Maccoby and Mnookin's (1992) study of 1,100 divorcing San Francisco families is the only study that carefully tracked the disposition of custody disputes through the court system. They found that 50.4% of the families settled out of court and that custody was uncontested in these cases. These families reported low levels of conflict, and most had agreed from the start that the mother would have primary physical custody.

Another 29.3% of these divorcing families contested the custody issues but finally settled out of court with the help of negotiations through attorneys. Although they appeared to have low levels of conflict because they did not actually appear before a judge to settle a custody dispute, this was deceptive in that many had filed petitions for child support or had filed restraining orders. Twenty percent of these families reported high levels of conflict between the parents.

Another 11.1% went into mediation and did settle their dispute with the help of the mediator. Although these families did not have to go into a courtroom to resolve custody issues either, they were reporting much conflict. Twenty-one percent of this group reported moderately high levels of conflict, and 29% reported severe conflict. Thus, 50% of this group reported high levels of conflict, even though they eventually settled.

In California, where Maccoby and Mnookin's (1992) study was conducted, cases not settled by mediation go into mandatory custody evaluations. Approximately 10% of the entire sample did so, although not all these disputes were decided by judges. Some families—5.2% of the total—settled out of court after the evaluation was conducted. Most likely, the evaluator presented the recommendations to the parents, who felt it best to avoid a court battle by abiding by those recommendations. This was a conflicted group, with the majority reporting moderate to severe levels of conflict.

The last 3.7% of the sample did go to trial. Of these, 2.2% of the total settled during the course of the trial—literally in the waiting area of the courthouse. Of these families, 95% reported moderate to severe levels of conflict.

The last 1.5% of the sample completed a custody trial, and the final adjudication regarding custody was made by the judge. Of this group, 86% reported moderate to severe levels of conflict.

Maccoby and Mnookin (1992), surveying the large amount of data that they had collected, determined overall levels of conflict for their sample. They found that although half of the families resolved amicably the issue of how to divide the children, 24% had mild levels of conflict, 10% had moderate levels of conflict, and 15% had intense or severe conflict. Thus, they concluded that about 25% of their sample could be described as involved in entrenched legal battles over the children.

Who are the individuals who make up this 25%? Maccoby and Mnookin (1992) assumed that it would be the most affluent parents who, after all, could afford the attorneys, mediators, and custody evaluators.

However, they were wrong. Parents' race, age, education, and income were not good predictors of who made up this subsample. They did find that mothers who did not work outside the home were more represented in this sample, and they theorized that these mothers may have had a larger investment in being the primary parent and had the most to lose in a custody battle.

Maccoby and Mnookin (1992) also found that the age of the child was a relevant factor. The high-conflict families were much more likely to be fighting over custody of a child younger than age 3 and much less likely to be attempting to get custody of a child older than age 11. It may be that parents feel a strong protective bond toward a child who is very young. They may also have a concern that if they do not have primary custody of a young child, they will never establish a strong bond with that child. Older children, on the other hand, have already established, one would assume, strong bonds with both parents. These children are able to look out for themselves or at least speak up for themselves in the event of mistreatment. They are also able to express a preference for custody, which in some states is binding.

Psychologist Ellen Dixon (1991) is a custody evaluator in Springfield, Virginia, and coauthor of the book *Solomon's Sword*. She described the subset of families that she sees for custody evaluations as upper-middle-class families who are hostile and who are poor interpersonal problem solvers. She noted that they are usually litigating over only one or two children and that the children are typically quite young. She commented that families with three children or more feel such a strain that parents do not litigate over custody of them.

I agree with Dixon's claim that families seen for custody evaluations are nearly always litigating over one or two young children. Older children, ages 12 and up, usually make strong alliances with one parent and are outspoken in stating their preference. It would be difficult, or even impossible in some cases, to oppose a 12- or 14-year-old child's adamant choice of residence. However, these families, as Maccoby and Mnookin (1992) found, are not necessarily wealthy. I practice in a suburb that borders a rural area. Even relatively poor families have presented for custody evaluations. Some cashed in retirement plans, many were financed by gifts or loans from their parents, and some were given money from their church. Maccoby and Mnookin reported that their high-conflict families spent, on average, 13% of their combined incomes on legal fees, with one family spending $81,000. I have heard quotes of $25,000–$50,000 spent on court battles. Researcher Janet Johnston (1994b) with the Center for the Family Transition in California, reported the case of a man who spent $125,000 on his custody battle, which he took to the U.S. Supreme Court.

What are the reasons parents give for litigating over custody? The answer to this question usually must be answered by the father because in the vast majority of cases, the mother requests primary physical custody and the father relents. When a battle over custody does ensue, it is usually one that is initiated by the father and is dependent on his motivations. Maccoby and Mnookin (1992) found from their interviews of families in California that the most common reason given for the father's motivation was the concern over the child's well-being in the mother's household. These concerns commonly focused around the perceived lack of the mother's capacity to discipline the children, lack of financial means to provide an adequate home for them, or objections to the mother's male companions. The second most common reason was hostility toward the mother. Most commonly, the hostility arose around the mother's rejection of the father in requesting the divorce or arose out of the mother's infidelity. A third factor was the father's perception of his involvement with the children as having been much more extensive than the mother felt it was. These fathers saw themselves as having been full partners in parenting and facing a greatly diminished role in the children's lives. I would add that a fourth motivating factor is the father's concern that the mother will block his access to the child by canceling visitations, withholding important information about the child, and even moving away. These fathers view the mothers as extremely hostile toward them and determined to alienate the children from them.

OVERVIEW OF THE CUSTODY EVALUATION

"Warring" parties who come to mental health professionals for evaluation have expectations and agendas that are unique and unsettling. Each contestant is, by that time, highly emotionally and financially invested in his or her own position and in winning. They see the issues in black and white, good and bad. They have lost all perspective—all capacity to see the situation from the other person's point of view. They see their position, and only their position, in crystal-clear terms and expect the evaluator to do the same. The evaluator, on the other hand, is cautioned to be neutral and objective and to not be sympathetic and understanding—as he or she would as a treating therapist—because this would send the message that he or she is allying with a particular parent. The evaluator's role is to serve as an extension of the courts and an advocate for the child—a behavioral scientist who gathers and analyzes evidence.

In an ideal situation, the two parties and their attorneys negotiate among a list of names of professionals to agree on one person or team to conduct the evaluation. The name is then entered into a court order, and the order is signed by a judge. Typically, the order stipulates that the expert has access to any and all information or persons necessary to conduct the evaluation. It may also stipulate who will pay for the evaluation, the date by which it is to be completed, that a written report will be filed, and to whom it will be submitted. The court order compels all parties to participate and to do so cooperatively.

This ideal is reached, however, in probably fewer than half of the cases. William Keilin and Larry Bloom (1986) of Colorado State University surveyed 190 custody evaluators to better understand their work. They found that although 90% of these professionals preferred to be appointed by the court or retained by both parents and their attorneys, this was achieved only 49% of the time. The other half of the time they were retained by only one parent and attorney. Marc Ackerman of the Wisconsin School of Professional Psychology, along with Melissa Ackerman (1997), repeated Keilin and Bloom's study and found that 100% of the evaluators preferred to be retained by both parents or by the court.

When there is no written and signed court order and the evaluation is voluntary, the parties are free to drop out of the evaluation at any time, which often happens. In some cases, one party does not have the financial means to complete the evaluation and declines to participate or stops keeping appointments before the evaluation is finalized. When only one party is available to be evaluated along with the children, the evaluator can make no recommendations to the court as to custody. This point is still unclear to many attorneys and parents. The 1994 APA *Guidelines for Child Custody Evaluations in Divorce Proceedings* bars psychologists from making any statements about custody when one of the parties has not been available to be interviewed or to be observed with the children. A limited evaluation can be done in which the expert comments only on the available parent's relative strengths and weaknesses, which is referred to as a *parental fitness evaluation*.

In still other cases, there is no order specifying the date by which the evaluation is to be completed, and one party delays the completion of the evaluation as long as possible or does not make the final monetary payment. If that parent has temporary physical custody of the children, he or she may be hoping that by doing this, the judge, when the case is finally heard, will simply leave well enough alone and order that the children remain in the home where they have been since the separation.

Evaluators who have an "ideal" case must conduct an evaluation around three central issues: (a) the needs of the child, (b) the abilities and capacities of the parents, and (c) the best fit between the two (APA, 1994). Many parents are surprised at both the length and cost of such evaluations. Believing as they do in the absolute simplicity and clarity of their position, many assume that a 1- or 2-hour interview in which they state the issues will be sufficient. However, the evaluator, knowing that there are always two sides to the issue, is aware that the parents are often the least objective informants. Others must be interviewed to corroborate each parent's and the children's story. Most evaluations involving two children and two parents can take 20 hours or more for the evaluation and report write-up. The respondents in Keilin and Bloom's (1986) sample, who were surveyed 10 years ago, reported a mean of 18.8 hours per evaluation. Ackerman and Ackerman (1996) reported an average of 29.7 hours (including report write-up and testimony), with an average total cost of $3,668.50.

The fact that the parents are often the least objective informants must be underscored. Parents distort their view of themselves as parents, seeing their good qualities only and viewing their partners or former partners in terms of their deficits. Parents also distort their impressions of their children. Peter Ash and Melvin Guyer (1991) demonstrated this empirically in a novel study of families referred to a forensic clinic in a child psychiatry program. They demonstrated that parents who had physical custody of a child reported fewer behavioral problems in the child who was the subject of litigation, whereas the noncustodial parent emphasized the child's symptoms. They had hypothesized that the custodial parent would minimize symptoms because it supported his or her need to retain custody, whereas the noncustodial parent needed to denigrate the quality of the existing custodial arrangement in order to support his or her need for a change of custody. These data go against most clinicians' findings in treatment that children exhibit more acting out in the custodial home than in the noncustodial home. In contrast, parents did not differ in ratings of children's behavioral symptoms in cases of visitation disputes in which distortion of the children's problems gave the parent no legal advantages.

Although there is no standard as to exactly what must occur in a custody evaluation, the 1994 APA guidelines emphasize that information must be collected from multiple sources and through multiple means in order to obtain the most thorough overview of the issues. Typically, multiple sources include the parents individually, the children individually, the children together, the children interacting separately with the mother and with the father, the father's new wife or live-in companion, the mother's new husband or live-in companion, and the caregivers for the young children. Ancillary people may include pediatricians, teachers, grandparents, other relatives, and neighbors. *Multiple means* refers to the way in which information is obtained, which may include interviews, observations in the office, questionnaires, standardized psychological tests, the evaluations of other professionals, depositions and legal documents, and home visits in some cases. The evaluations of other professionals may include a home study done by a social worker, a drug and alcohol screen done by laboratory personnel, an academic evaluation done by a school psychologist, an examination for physical or sexual abuse done by a physician, a summary of treatment done by another mental health professional, results of a polygraph, a police report, and even a discharge summary from a psychiatric hospital. The evaluator may want to read depositions inasmuch as the deposition, by its very nature, is adversarial. The parent being deposed is forced to give information about himself or herself under questioning by the opposing attorney that he or she might ordinarily not be inclined to reveal.

There are many textbooks available for professionals to use in conducting these evaluations. The mental health professional may want to consult those by Richard Gardner (1982, 1989); Dianne Skafte (1985); Benjamin Schutz, Ellen Dixon, Joanne Lindenberger, and Neil Ruther (1989); Barry Bricklin (1995); and Marc Ackerman (1995). All are good resources, although the last two books reflect more well-developed guidelines than do the earlier books. William Hodges's 1991 textbook *Interventions for Children of Divorce* provides a thorough overview and synthesis of the nuts and bolts of a custody evaluation for the professional while drawing many techniques from the authors mentioned above.

What are evaluators looking for? When evaluating the parent's capacities as a parent, the evaluator is first gathering information about the parent's life stability and whether he or she has been able to persist in the pursuit of long-range goals. Sources of information include whether the parent has completed his or her educational goals; how many jobs he or she has held and how long he or she was employed in each one; residential stability; military service record; and how many times the parent has been married and how long those marriages lasted. Emotional stability is important also, and questions are asked about the parent's physical health, psychiatric treatment, alcohol and drug abuse, and arrests for law-breaking behavior. The evaluator also gathers information about the parent's past history as a parent, both with children from previous marriages and the child or children at issue. The evaluator should gather evidence of the parent's capacity for perspective taking: to see his or her own part in the downfall of the marriage, to see strengths and assets in the other parent, to understand what the other parent has to offer the child and why contact with that parent is important, and to view his or her own weaknesses and mistakes as a parent. Many evaluators conduct a lengthy and detailed history of the parent's involvement with the child and explore his or her knowledge of intimate details of the child's life; inquire as to the kind of home the parent intends to provide, or is providing, for the child; and determine the parent's future plans. Many evaluators conduct a thorough assessment of the parent's knowledge and skills about parenting situations.

USE OF PSYCHOLOGICAL TESTS IN CUSTODY EVALUATIONS

Evaluators most often administer psychological tests in their work. For example, Keilin and Bloom (1986) found that, among custody evaluators, 71% administered the Minnesota Multiphasic Personality Inventory-2 (MMPI-2), 41% used the Rorschach inkblots, 38% used the Thematic Apperception Test, and 29% used the Wechsler Adult Intelligence Scale with parents. The tests most frequently used with children were intelligence tests (45%), the Children's Apperception Test (39%), the Rorschach inkblots (29%), and various projective drawing tests such as the draw-a-person test and the house-tree-person test (33%).

This factor notwithstanding, the use of psychological tests in custody evaluations is regarded with skepticism by many experts in the field. Melton, Petrila, Poythress, and Slobogin (1997) stated that such tests are only indirectly linked to issues such as parenting capacity and the parent–child relationship. They recommended that standardized tests play only a limited role in custody evaluations. Weithorn and Grisso (1987) opposed the use of projective tests, finding that they "have not been shown to have the requisite psychometric properties to render them reliable or valid for predicting custodial functioning" (p. 165). Brodzinsky (1993), while acknowledging that selective tests can be useful to answer specific questions, concluded that "psychologists routinely misuse test data in this type of forensic case" (pp. 213–214).

These caveats aside, these same experts have suggested limited and careful use of tests, with the caution that the evaluator should always stay within the data. For example, unless allegations have been made that the parent is mentally disabled, administering an intelligence test to the parent would not be appropriate, because intelligence has no direct bearing on parenting capacity. Most evaluators will administer a test such as the MMPI–2 to assess overall truthfulness, significant mental illness, or the presence of a group of personality traits that are highly maladaptive. For example, a parent who tests with high L and K scores on the MMPI–2 tends to see himself or herself only in the most virtuous light and is hostile and blaming toward the other parent. Likewise, a parent with a high Pd score, indicating a severely reckless and thrill-seeking personality, is often impulsive in decision making and is a high risk for pursuing gratification of his or her own needs at the expense of the children (see chapter 9, this volume, on parental psychopathology for more information on MMPI–2 profiles of parents in custody litigation).

The difficulty with the use of such tests is that they were not designed to measure parental capacity. The 1994 APA *Guidelines for Child Custody Evaluations in Divorce Proceedings* suggest that factors measured by such tests be directly related to parenting capacity. Schutz et al. (1989) reviewed many tests and concluded, "We found no tests that directly measure the domain of functional parent abilities" (p. 69). Grisso (1986) evaluated 10 current parenting measures in use at that time and concluded that none fully addressed the issues of matching parental capacities to children's needs. None had been validated in such a way that high scores translated into predictions of current parenting behavior or the success of one's parenting in the future.

To address this need, several evaluators have developed some of their own tests over the past 10 years and have begun to market them commercially to custody evaluators.

Ackerman–Schoenderf Scales

One such test is the Ackerman–Schoenderf Scales for Parent Evaluation of Custody (ASPECT; Ackerman, 1995). This measure, which is not actually a scale, is a compilation of information derived from a battery of tests administered to the parent. Although this effort is a good start, reviewers such as Gary Melton (1995) and Joyce Arditti (1995), writing for the *Twelfth Mental Measurements Yearbook*, concluded that the scale is poorly conceptualized and lacks validity. In other words, scores on these tests have not been shown to correlate with parental behaviors or the outcomes of custodial arrangements. Melton concluded that "clinicians who use the ASPECT are not likely to improve the quality and ethical propriety of their work. Instead, the ASPECT incorporates and exacerbates most of the problems that have attracted commentators' criticism" (p. 22). Michaela Heinze and Thomas Grisso (1996) reviewed the ASPECT and concluded that normative and validity data were inadequate: "At present . . . it is unknown whether ASPECT scores are related to the quality of parenting" (p. 297).

Bricklin Scales

Barry Bricklin (1995) developed several scales that purportedly measure parenting abilities; they include the Parent Awareness Skills Survey (PASS) and the Parent Perception of Child Profile (PPCP). Lisa Bischoff (1995) noted that the PASS has no norms and no reliability data and that no attempt has been made to validate it. In other words, high scores on the PASS have not been demonstrated to carry over into good parenting at home. Similarly, Robert Hiltonsmith (1995) and May Lou Kelley (1995) noted that the PPCP manual has little to no information about norms, reliability, or validity. They concluded that it cannot be considered a psychometric instrument.

Parent–Child Relationship Inventory

One scale that has some validity is the Parent–Child Relationship Inventory (PCRI; Gerard, 1994). This 78-item scale was designed to assess parents' attitudes toward parenting and their children. The items are grouped into seven content scales—Parental Support, Satisfaction With Parenting, Involvement, Communication, Limit Setting, Autonomy, and Role Orientation—plus a Social Desirability scale. Validation studies indicated that high scores were associated with parents' use of good discipline practices; low scores were typical of parents referred for court-ordered mediation and those at risk for child abuse. Heinze and Grisso (1996) reviewed the PCRI and concluded that it had good reliability, that the scores were stable over time, and that several studies pointed to good validity. One good feature is the Social Desirability scale. Roger Boothroyd (1998) considered the PCRI "a sound measure." Gregory Marchant and Sharon Paulsen (1998) concluded that the PCRI is "well conceived and well developed, and fills a much needed role in both research and clinical assessment" (p. 721).

Parenting Stress Index

Another well-validated scale is the Parenting Stress Index (PSI; Abidin, 1990). The purpose of this test is to identify the presence of stressful factors within the child, stress within the parent's life, and the resulting interaction or relationship between the two. Although the PSI was not developed for the purpose of child custody evaluations, it does closely match some of the goals outlined by the 1994 APA guidelines. The Child domain consists of temperament variables such as adaptability, demandingness, mood, and distractibility/hyperactivity, as well as how acceptable and gratifying the child is to the parent. The Parent domain consists of at-risk factors such as depression, sense of competence, level of attachment to the child, spousal support, parental health, level of role restriction, and social isolation.

Heinze and Grisso (1996) gave the PSI high marks for reliability and validity. The scale does appear to predict which parents feel highly stressed by a particular child. The Defensive Responding scale identifies parents who are attempting to create a favorable impression. One of the drawbacks of the scale is that mothers and fathers tend to score differently on the PSI; thus their scores cannot be directly compared. Julie Allison (1998) concluded that the scale has strong validity. Nearly every one of the items are directly related to at least one research study on parental stress or dysfunction.

Informal Measures of Parental Attachment in Young Children

When meeting with the children, the evaluator has a number of issues to explore. With younger children, the most immediate question is, "To whom is the child most strongly attached?" Usually, but not always, the answer is the primary caretaker. Children as young as 3½ years can be assessed with informal methods. Some may involve completing a series of stick figure drawings in which the child places himself or herself in relation to each parent and other family members. Others may involve having the child act out everyday family situations with dolls and a dollhouse and noting how the child places each parent in various roles. Some evaluators have the child act out scenarios with a toy telephone. Evaluators are looking not only for which parent is preferred but also for information as to the quality of the attachment. Is the child overly dependent on the parent? Is the child intimidated or afraid of the parent? Does the child view the parent as a source of security and comfort?

Perception of Relationships Test

Bricklin (1995) developed the Perception of Relationships Test (PORT) as a measure of parental attachment, and it too is commercially available. However, reviewers of this test (Carlson, 1995; Conger, 1995) have noted that it has no psychometric properties. The test was developed on the basis of Bricklin's psychodynamic assumptions and has not been validated. Heinze and Grisso (1996) agreed with the reviewers, noting that "the test user has no meaningful basis for interpreting the scores, or for meeting scientific and legal standards for expert opinions based on the test" (p. 300).

Informal Measures of Parental Attachment in Older Children

Children from ages 7 to 13 years can be directly interviewed about their perceptions of each parent. These children can even answer direct questions as to what each parent's home is like, what each parent's liked and disliked traits are, and what each parent has to offer the child. They can give adequate information as to the parent's personal habits, such as whether the parent drinks excessively, works long hours, is prone to angry outbursts, leaves them unattended, and so on. (In addition, when seen with younger children, an older sibling can explain what the younger child is having trouble articulating or can corroborate a younger child's allegations.)

Bricklin Perceptual Scales

The Bricklin Perceptual Scales (BPS; Bricklin, 1995) assess older children's loyalties; the child rates each parent on his or her competence at a large number of parenting behaviors and social skills by punching a card with a stylus. Marcia Shaffer (1992) questioned the assumption that children who stick a stylus into a long black line have unconsciously chosen a parental preference. Rosa Hagin (1992) noted that the sample sizes used to develop the BPS were small and that the descriptive statistics are "missing." Heinze and Grisso (1996) likewise found the BPS completely unacceptable as a psychometric measure. High and low scores can be categorized as accurate or completely distorted, as the evaluator chooses. There is no reliability, because a child's perceptions are thought to change from moment to moment and from day to day.

Children's Reports of Parental Behavior

Brodzinsky (1993) suggested that evaluators use an old, little-known parent-rating scale, the Children's Reports of Parental Behavior (CRPB; Schaefer, 1965), which has been validated. This rather lengthy (260-item) scale assesses parenting attitudes on 18 scales, which have been found in study after study to cluster statistically around three main themes. Schluderman and Schluderman (1970) and Teleki, Powell, and Dodder (1982) shortened the scale to 108 items; Margolies and Weintraub (1977) shortened it further to 56 items measuring six dimensions of parenting. Schaefer demonstrated that children's scores on the CRPB differentiated the ratings of children from normal families from those of delinquent boys. Grisso (1986) reviewed the CRPB's internal consistency favorably but noted that children's ratings of their parents' behavior did not correlate highly with the parents' ratings of their own behavior. Nevertheless, the scale has applicability to questions that are relevant to the court in child custody evaluations. It may offer a standardized, well-validated indication of the child's perception of each parent's level of such positive factors as warmth, acceptance of autonomy, limit setting, and positive involvement, as well as such negative factors as rejection, hostile control, intrusiveness, and inconsistent discipline.

Test Difficulties

In his thorough analysis, Grisso (1986) pointed out the difficulties with all of these aforementioned tests. Conceptually, all are flawed in that they measure parenting attitudes in particular, on the basis of the assumption that parents who endorse good attitudes make good parents. It is simply not known that this is true. Almost no studies have clearly demonstrated that parents who endorse certain attitudes on a test actually engage in those behaviors in the home. Second, by concentrating on parenting attitudes evaluators omit the measurement of functional parenting abilities. We do not know, for example, which parent has the best handle on the child's nutritional needs or which parent is better at helping the child with homework. Third, which type of parenting skill is needed depends on the particular child (and there may be several in the family) and the child's age. No test can assess whether what a child needs today is what he or she will need 6 years from now. Finally, a test has yet to be developed that addresses the goals of the custody evaluation as set out by the APA—to address the best fit between the child's needs and the parent's abilities. The ideal test would somehow measure each child's particular needs, then assess the parental qualities that would be instrumental in meeting those needs, so that the final score would indicate good congruence or a lack of congruence. Such a test at present eludes us.

EVALUATING THE CHILD

Many parents assume the evaluator will simply ask the child with which parent he or she would like to live. What could be simpler? Yet much controversy surrounds this issue. First, most children are not assumed to be capable of making reasonable and informed decisions until they are about age 14. By 1991, nine states had age-based guidelines, and the typical range given by these statutes was from 12 to 14 years. Most psychologists agree with these guidelines because, developmentally, the 14-year-old mind is capable of solving higher level problems than is the younger mind. The adolescent is capable of objectivity, of stepping back from his parents and seeing them as people. Adolescents are also more able to weigh future consequences of day-to-day events. For example, they can see that the parent who makes them study is more likely to facilitate their getting into college. They can deal with hypothetical questions such as "What if?" Cognitively, they are more able to see a situation in shades of gray and to see it from another person's point of view.

Ellen Garrison (1991) of the University of Illinois conducted an interesting study in which she compared the ability of children from ages 9 to 18 to make reasonable and informed decisions about parental custody. She drew up two written scenarios involving parents locked in a custody dispute and asked 144 children, ages 9 to 14, to answer questions as to which custodial arrangement they would prefer and their reasons for this preference. She did the same with a small group of 18-year-olds. Raters read the children's answers and divided them into seven categories. Last, a group of 44 Illinois domestic-relations judges rated the children's answers for reasonableness. What Garrison found was rather surprising: The 14-year-olds were rated as high as the 18-year-olds in the reasonableness of their decisions, which confirms predictions based on cognitive developmental theory. However, the scores of the 9- to 13-year-old children were not far below those of the 14-year-old children, and on some measures they were as good.

Of equal interest was the way in which the reasons given changed with increasing age. The younger children tended to give reasons that focused on the closeness of the parent–child relationship, the time and attention available for the child, being able to stay in the same place, and a desire to maximize time with both parents. The 12-year-old children focused more on the parent's financial situation. The 14-year-old children, with their greater objectivity, were more likely to cite the parent's stability and commitment and the nature of the relationship between the parents.

Given Garrison's (1991) findings, we can assume that many children from ages 9 to 13 are capable of making reasonably informed choices as to custodial arrangements. One can determine how informed their choice is by asking them to give the basis for their reasoning and assessing the maturity level of their answers. In many states 14-year-olds can make decisions that are binding, given that they seem reasonably mature and that the homes are adequate.

But should children be asked to state a preference? Most evaluators think not for children who are younger than ages 12–14. For these children, although they may have a preference and although their preference may even be reasonable, they might make the false assumption that the ultimate decision about custody will be based solely on their statement. This is simply too great a perceived responsibility for a young child. Young children are highly dependent on both parents and do not wish to make any statements that might separate them from a parent or provoke a parent's anger. The school-age child, from ages 9 to 12 years, may be engaged in a strong alliance with one parent, and being asked to state a preference may foster an even stronger alliance. Some judges do interview children *in camera*, or in the judge's chambers, which is entirely at their discretion. Law professor Cathy Jones (1984) provided a good overview of when these interviews are appropriate and how they can be done sensitively.

Beyond the issues of attachment and the quality of the bond with each parent, the evaluator is also assessing other issues with the child, such as his or her particular needs. It is well understood among parents that some children need more of certain kinds of parenting skills than do other children. For example, the unusually active and rambunctious youngster will need a parent who can be firm and consistent and yet who can be so with love and acceptance.

The child who may have a disability, such as a speech defect or a learning difficulty, benefits most from a parent who is gentle and patient. A child who is exceptionally anxious and shy is not well served by a parent who is also phobic and uses avoidance to cope with stresses; he or she needs a parent who will give him or her a gentle push into new and anxiety-producing situations. Similarly, a child who has a prodigious musical talent is best cared for by a parent who appreciates the child's talent and has the time and energy to give to music lessons, endless practice sessions, and concerts.

EVALUATING THE PARENTS

Evaluators must also assess parents' strengths and weaknesses as parents and determine how skilled they are as parents. Some evaluators may have the parent describe his or her own parents and explain how they were or were not role models for parenting. Others may have the parent complete a structured questionnaire that has been developed for measuring skills or parenting style. Still others may offer the parent a series of hypothetical parenting situations and ask how he or she would handle that situation. Some may simply ask the parent to talk about the child and their day-to-day interactions in great detail.

DEFINING A "GOOD PARENT"

Parents may ask, "How can the evaluator determine what is a good parent? Isn't that a very subjective question?" The answer to the last question is, "No, not really." Fifty years ago there might not have been clear measures of what a good parent is, but decades of research have clarified these issues. Child development researchers began to study this area as early as the 1940s by examining children who were juvenile delinquents and following up with interviews and observations of their families and home environments. Many studies have also examined the parenting skills and traits of parents with severe alcoholism or who are abusive. These parents have a number of traits that show up in study after study: They are unpredictable and have impulsive personalities, and their home life is chaotic and disorganized. The home atmosphere is tense, with frequent hostile outbursts. There is an increased level of violence between parents and between parent and child. There is a higher incidence of neglect, a lack of nurturing, and little attention to the child's friends and activities. These parents are highly inconsistent with discipline, sometimes ignoring misbehavior and other times responding with excessive punishment. The parents are often irresponsible and fail to act in the child's best interests. They seem chronically unable to make the sacrifices necessary to meet the child's needs when they conflict with the parent's needs.

Child psychologists have studied what kinds of parenting work well by again starting with the children. One good way to select children who are succeeding at life is by going into a classroom and asking the children to write down the names of the people whom they most admire—those who are the leaders and the ones with whom they would most like to be friends. Teachers are then asked to list the names of the children whom the teachers most enjoy teaching, the ones who appear to be well liked and to be looked up to by their peers. Then these children are evaluated to see what traits they have in common and what it is about their families that contributes to these traits.

What researchers have consistently found is that most of these families can be described as those with an *authoritative* parenting style, a term coined by researcher Diana Baumrind (1971) to describe families who, among other things, provide clear and consistent limits while promoting independence and individuality and allowing children leeway to make choices for themselves. Neither overly strict nor overly permissive, these parents are known for being consistent in their rules and discipline.

Dixon (1991) surveyed the available research in this area and found that authoritative families also have a strong, positive emotional attachment to their children and are able to communicate this to them. The parents convey closeness and warmth, and the children know that they are loved. These parents also have a large fund of knowledge about their children—their interests, activities, and likes and dislikes. They have a good sense of what is typical and appropriate for a child of a given age and gear their expectations accordingly. These parents are sensitive and responsive to any of their children's special needs. The parents have an ability to communicate openly and respectfully with their children and are capable of showing understanding of and empathy with them. They demonstrate a willingness to be flexible and adaptable in responding to their children's demands; they are able to bend when it seems appropriate. They are able to make shifts when the situation calls for it, to adapt to their children's needs in different situations and at different ages.

These parents are also characterized by their capacity to establish healthy boundaries. They can see children accurately as individuals in their own right and with their own thoughts and opinions. They can see their children's needs as being separate from their own needs, and they can place their children's needs first. They encourage their children to separate from them appropriately and to be more independent. They are able to encourage their children's relationship with the other parent, because it is a good thing for their children. Last, they are able to provide a protective buffer between their children and the stresses of the world outside of the home.

Finally, good parents are role models of successful living in the world. They are self-confident and self-assured. They have good social skills and relate well to others. They like who they are and what they do, and they have an overall positive outlook on life.

ORGANIZING AND PRIORITIZING DATA

When the above information has been gathered, evaluators have the task of determining whether sole or joint custody would be the best arrangement and how the child's time should best be allocated between the two homes. By now the reader has a better sense of how much information is gathered and of the complexities of this recommendation. Most evaluators, either formally or informally, sort through 5–10 important factors, looking to see the relative number of pluses and minuses in the "father" and in the "mother" column, as well as the relative importance of each factor.

Rankings of Factors by Mental Health Professionals

Keilin and Bloom (1986) found that their sample of custody evaluators gave the most weight to these factors, in the following order, when comparing one parent with the other for sole custody: (a) the wishes of the child, if age 15 or older; (b) the parent's attempts to alienate the child from the other parent; (c) the parent with whom the child has the closer emotional bond; (d) the parent who seems more psychologically stable; (e) the parent who has the better parenting skills; (f) the parent who is more likely to allow the child access to the other parent; and (g) the parent who had primary care-taking responsibility prior to the divorce. All statutory guidelines aside, the evaluators in Keilin and Bloom's sample also gave a ranking of ninth place to whether the parent was engaged in a homosexual relationship. They gave little weight to the gender of the parent and child (19th place), whether the parent was cohabiting with another adult (17th place), and the age of the parent (21st place).

When Ackerman and Ackerman (1997) repeated Keilin and Bloom's (1986) study, they found that, among their sample of custody evaluators, that some of the rankings had changed. They gave the greatest weight to whether the parent was an active alcoholic—a new item that had been added. Items ranked 2nd through 5th most important were essentially the same. This group ranked whether the parent had been cooperative with previous court orders as the 6th most important factor and whether the parent was threatening to move to another state as the 7th most important variable. Whether the parent was gay was ranked 32nd in importance out of 40 variables.

Other psychologists have cited the importance of establishing who has been the primary caretaker if the child is very young, on the basis of the premise that one must assume that the child has the closer bond with the primary caregiver. Many evaluators also consider the parent's time and availability to be a parent. Naturally, a parent who works long hours, works weekends, and travels, no matter how good a parent he or she may be, will have less to give a child than will a parent who has limited work hours or who is self-employed and has control over her or his schedule. Also, most evaluators take into consideration the quality of the home and how suitable it is for raising children; the surrounding neighborhood; and the child's proximity to school, church, friends, grandparents, and other relatives while living in that particular home.

Rankings of Factors by Judges

Although mental health professionals make recommendations to the court in custody cases, judges have the authority to rule. Judges may view custody situations with a different set of standards than those used by mental health professionals. In an early study, Carol Lowery (1981) of the University of Kentucky surveyed 80 judges and commissioners as to their ranking of 20 factors. Six parental factors accounted for half the variance in the sample: (a) sense of responsibility toward the child, (b) mental stability, (c) ability to provide access to schools, (d) ability to provide continuing involvement in the community, (e) moral character, and (f) financial sufficiency. They gave the least weight to keeping a child with a parent of the same sex.

Researchers Felner et al. (1985) surveyed 74 attorneys and 43 judges to determine the guidelines that they used in weighing each parent's merits in custody battles. Legal professionals gave the greatest value to the emotional stability of the parent and his or her ability to care for the child, followed by time availability, the stability of living arrangements, child care arrangements, and financial resources. Many still favored mothers as a rule. One half felt that the child's wishes were important, and one third gave importance to the child's gender.

This last factor is interesting in view of the observation that many mental health evaluators do not give weight to the gender of the child. Yet, as discussed in chapters 1 and 4, there is a growing body of research that indicates that, all other things being equal, boys do better with fathers and girls do better with mothers. It is interesting that Felner et al. found that these judges gave little weight to the recommendations of the mental health expert who conducted the custody evaluation.

Erik Sorensen and Jacquelin Goldman (1989) of the University of Florida questioned 96 family law judges about the factors that they used in making custody decisions and asked them to rank those factors in order of importance. These judges ranked highest in importance items that centered around family unity—providing access for the child to his or her relatives and keeping siblings together. These judges also gave strong weight to the parent's lack of a history of substance abuse and the wishes of the child older than 12. In contrast to the judges in Felner et al.'s study, these judges gave the least weight, out of 20 factors to consider, to placing the child with the parent of the same gender. When asked if they favored mothers in general over fathers, 40% said that they did. Sorensen and Goldman (1990) and Sorensen et al. (1997) concluded that although judges' criteria are becoming more specific and do not differ to a great degree from the variables held as important by mental health professionals, judges still have wide latitude in making custodial decisions, and the relative weights given to different factors vary greatly from one judge to another.

Last, Reidy, Silver, and Carlson (1989) conducted a survey of 156 judges in the superior courts of California, asking them to rank the importance of various types of information when making their decisions. The judges considered the wishes of adolescents age 15 or older as most important, followed by the custody investigation report done by the probation department (the recommendations of the guardian would be equivalent in other states) and the testimony of the parents. These judges rated the report of the court-appointed psychologist as 4th; when the psychologist was retained by only one of the parties, the report was ranked 7th out of 11 factors.

The judges were then asked to rank 24 variables in order of importance in reaching their decision. These were the same variables used in Keilin and Bloom's (1986) study. Reidy et al. (1989) posted the rankings next to the rankings of mental health professionals obtained by Keilin and Bloom. It is encouraging to note that the same 7 variables appeared at the top of both lists, indicating congruence between the viewpoints of mental health professionals and judges. However, custody evaluators should be aware of the differences. There were wide discrepancies between the valuations of the expressed wishes of 5-year-old and 10-year-old children, with mental health professionals giving much more weight to them. If one parent were living alone and the other cohabiting, a quarter of the judges would award custody to the parent living alone. If one parent were married and the other parent were living alone, half would award custody to the married parent. If one parent had moved away and the other parent remained in the home, half the judges would award custody to the parent who remained in the home. Last is the issue of homosexuality. Although mental health professionals ranked it 32nd in order of importance, the judges would tend to rule otherwise: 71% of California judges said that if one parent were gay, they would award custody to the other parent.

GUIDELINES FOR RECOMMENDING A PARENT FOR PRIMARY CUSTODY

In summary, many writers in this field have proposed factors that the evaluator should use in considering which parent can provide the better home for the children in a divorce. Because a greater number of divorcing parents now have joint legal custody, and each parent is more likely to pursue a meaningful relationship than may have been true in the past, most evaluators do not focus on which home should be the single residence for the children but rather on which home is best suited to be the primary residence. A good evaluator's report will include a section outlining the factors that he or she felt were the most important to consider. For example, the American Academy of Child and Adolescent Psychiatry (1997) recommended that the evaluator gather information in 16 areas and suggested that 7 factors should be considered when making the final recommendations:

1. continuity and stability of living arrangement
2. child's preference

3. child's attachment to each parent
4. each parent's sensitivity to and respect for the child
5. parent and child gender
6. each parent's physical and mental health
7. parental conflict.

Recently, a group of Canadian psychologists—Barbara Jameson, Marion Ehrenberg, and Michael Hunter (1977), of the University of Victoria, British Columbia, conducted a study in which they attempted to develop an assessment model or framework that would organize many individual criteria for custody into an outline for evaluators. Through statistical analysis of responses from 88 custody evaluators, 60 items clustered into three major assessment areas that mirror the 1994 APA *Guidelines for Child Custody Evaluations in Divorce Proceedings*: I—Relational, II—Needs of the Child, and III—Abilities of the Parents. The Relational area includes four subareas: (a) the level of conflict and cooperation between the parents, (b) the history of shared parenting, (c) the quality of relationship between the parent and child, and (d) the parent's commitment to the child. The Needs of the Child area includes the child's basic needs and his or her views and preferences. The Abilities of the Parents area incorporates three subareas: (a) parental stability, (b) relevant parental history, and (c) parenting skills. Although it is not the final word in systematizing a recommendation for custody, the Victoria model is a beginning in standardization.

I recommend the following outline of considerations:

1. Which parent is more likely to permit the nonresidential parent free and easy access to the child and to foster a healthy relationship between the child and the nonresidential parent?
2. Which parent has better parenting skills? These include having good communication skills, being good at setting limits, being consistent with discipline, being able to express warmth and affection, having an appreciation for the child's age and gearing expectations accordingly, fostering independence, and giving praise where appropriate.
3. Which parent is least likely to be abusive, neglectful, or unstable, on the basis of a past history of psychiatric problems, alcohol or drug use, abusiveness or neglect with this child or other children, or a pattern of choosing partners with such a history?
4. Who has done the work of primary caretaker and knows best the child's needs, aversions, and likes and dislikes? The primary caretaker also knows best the child's medical history, teachers' names and reputations, friends' names, secret fears, favorite toy, favorite method of getting to sleep, and other idiosyncratic information that is important to the child.

5. To whom is the child more attached (if the child is age 11 or younger)? Who does the child prefer (if the child is age 12 or older and mature)?
6. Who has the most time and energy available to give to the child? Which parent travels, works at night, is on call for emergencies at work, or has a physical limitation that impairs his or her daily activities?
7. Which parent has the healthier relationship with the child? In this relationship the parent is not enmeshed and not disengaged, sets appropriate boundaries, separates the child's needs from his or her own personal needs, and carefully weighs the impact of his or her decisions on the child before acting.
8. Which parent can provide a better quality of life for the child in terms of siblings, stepparents, grandparents, home and neighborhood, schools, church ties, and so on?
9. Does the child have special needs? For example, does the child need medical treatment, psychological treatment, a great deal of structure and firm limits, a lot of one-on-one attention? Does the child have an intellectual gift or a learning disability? Which parent can better address these needs?
10. Which parent is a better fit on the basis of a number of factors? What is the child's temperament and personality? Is he or she outgoing and boisterous, reserved and bookish, very physical and athletic? Which parent is a better fit temperamentally? Which parent is a better fit in terms of mutual interests? Which parent is a better fit purely on the basis of gender?

Whatever the criteria used by the evaluator, the burden is on that individual to specify how each parent fares along each guideline and to what degree one parent is more favorable than the other on that standard. The evaluator must also give evidence for why he or she has made each of the conclusions, based on the rule of multiple sources and multiple means. A good evaluation is at least quasi-scientific and keeps personal bias to a minimum by demanding that several lines of evidence be given to back up each conclusion. Usually the preponderance of the evidence will lean toward one parent. When it does not but appears to be evenly divided, the evaluator can state only that both parents appear to be equally good (or bad) custodians for the children.

TESTIFYING AS TO THE "ULTIMATE ISSUE"

In concluding their report, should evaluators recommend a specific parent for primary custody? Although this question may seem obvious on the surface, the answer is rather complex.

Keep in mind that the final decision as to who gets custody of the children and under what conditions is a social, moral, and legal one that is made by the courts. The awarding of custody is considered an "ultimate legal issue," much like determining whether a defendant in a criminal case is sane or insane. The judge or jury is the "trier of fact" about ultimate legal issues. Therefore, many attorneys and judges see it as presumptuous for a mental health professional to tell the courts how to make a legal decision. This is viewed as an intrusion into the domain of the courts.

Many psychologists agree with this position. John Monahan (1980) of the University of Virginia Law School, writing for the APA, said, "Since it is not within the professional competence of psychologists to offer conclusions on matters of law, psychologists should resist pressure to offer such conclusions" (p. 9). Weithorn and Grisso (1987) argued that evaluators, although they may be experts in custody matters before the courts and may have relevant and important information to offer, should stick to the facts and draw no ultimate recommendation. The evaluator might, for example, present each parent's strengths and weaknesses on the 10 factors listed above. The evaluator might make observations about the effects of one parent's behavior on the children and make predictions about future consequences of that behavior. The evaluator might draw from the published research literature to present information on a particular issue, such as the advisability of joint physical custody for infants or the relative merits of mother–son versus father–son custody. Psychologist Theodore Blau (1997), nationally known as a forensic expert, emphasized that the evaluator should never, under any circumstance, conclude with a specific recommendation as to custody, because that is the court's prerogative.

Many other professionals, however—more typically, psychiatrists— take the position that the mental health professional is in a better position to determine the relative merits of one family structure versus another than are the courts. Psychiatrists Robert Solow and Paul Adams (1977) suggested that the evaluator "freely take sides and feel strongly about his partisan opinion" in custody matters. They asserted that the psychiatrist is far better able to make custody decisions than the judge and so should take over this role. In Solow and Adams's model, the two parents enter into a custody evaluation agreement in which the psychiatrist's opinion is binding and supplants that of the judge. The early guidelines drafted by the American Psychiatric Association (1981) for child psychiatrists in child custody evaluations specify that the evaluator make a specific recommendation and suggest that the inability to come to a conclusion is due to a lack of comprehensiveness on the part of the evaluator. Psychiatrist Richard Gardner (1989), perhaps the most well-known and prolific writer in this field, strongly advocates that evaluators make custody decisions for the court: "the impartial evaluator must commit himself (or herself) to providing an opinion . . . Not to do so is an abrogation of the evaluator's responsibility"

(p. 333). He makes this strong case on the basis of the premise that clear-cut cases are easy for the courts to decide. It is the difficult and complex cases, when both parents are equally qualified (or unqualified) for custody, for which impartial experts are called in to offer assistance to the court. The expert who simply compiles the merits of each parent offers nothing of use to the court.

Weithorn and Grisso (1987) pointed out that many attorneys and judges, far from objecting to such a recommendation, actually ask for an impartial expert and put pressure on the evaluator to offer one. Attorneys are interested in such a recommendation if it strengthens their client's position. Judges may ask for a specific recommendation as to custody, as it clarifies and summarizes the evaluator's findings. It also enables the judge to put part of the responsibility for his or her decision on the evaluator's report, minimizing the hostility of the parent who was not favored for custody and further validating the judge's opinion. I, myself, have even been ordered by the judge to provide a visitation plan for a disputing couple—a clear abrogation of the judge's responsibility in the case. In summary, whether the evaluator makes a specific recommendation of one parent or the other may depend on the evaluator's background, the complexities of the case, and the judge's interests in the matter.

WHAT THE RESEARCH SHOWS

The trend away from favoring mothers for custody began with the ABA's Uniform Marriage and Divorce Act, written in 1970. These standards for awarding custody became the model that was adopted, with modifications and additions, by nearly all states by the mid-1990s. These changes in the law not only made custody uncertain in many families, they also spawned a new industry—that of the child and family court expert. Families that do go into full custody evaluations are the most contentious 5%–10% of all divorcing families. They are typically middle- to upper-middle-class families battling over one or at most two small children. Litigation is largely triggered by the father's concern over the mother's care of the children, the father's hostility toward the mother, or the father's feelings of being excluded from the children's lives.

The ideal scenario for a custody evaluation is one in which all parties agree to participate (and by court order), but this is attained only about half of the time. Evaluations can be lengthy and will necessarily involve many interviews with the parties, psychological testing, interviews with collateral witnesses, review of documents, and compilation of this information into a well-organized report. Interview material provided by parents is notoriously biased and should be validated with interviews with children and collateral contacts. Studies show that interview material from children age 14 is quite sound in most cases and from children ages 9 to 13 is reasonably sound.

Misuse of psychological tests in these cases is common, and the reader is cautioned. Many tests developed for use in these evaluations have been reviewed. Those that meet an adequate standard of validity are the PCRI, the PSI, and the CRPB.

The evaluator should look for a good fit between the child's needs and the parent's skills and situation. The good parent is authoritative with regard to discipline, conveys warmth and positive regard, knows the child well and is responsive to the child, communicates well, and is flexible and adaptable. The good parent provides healthy boundaries, provides a role model of successful living, and encourages a healthy relationship with the other parent.

Evaluators can organize their data in many ways. Mental health professionals and judges agree for the most part on the importance of most factors. However, evaluators tend to give more weight to psychological factors and relationships, whereas judges tend to be more conservative, giving more weight to family ties and roots in the community and viewing alternative lifestyles more negatively. Although it is permissible for experts to give opinions on "ultimate issues" in civil cases (as opposed to criminal cases), many forensic psychologists suggest that the expert not do so. In these matters the expert may be best advised to organize the report so as to lead the reader to obvious and clear conclusions without actually making them. Another option is to ask the judge if he or she would like the evaluator to make a specific recommendation.

GUIDELINES FOR THE CLINICIAN

Custody litigation and evaluation are costly and time consuming. Both also are very stressful in that parents' personality traits, moral character and past decisions, behavior, and life experiences are subject to intense scrutiny by dispassionate strangers. The parent–child bond is often more intense than any other relationship into which human beings enter. For that reason, attorneys assert that custody cases entail more stress, tension, and highly charged emotion than do murder trials. "When you come into a family court, you can lose your money, your family, your property, and your freedom to see your children when you want to," said Judge Merrill Hartman of the 192nd Judicial District of Dallas, Texas, in *USA Today* (cited in Cordes, 1993, p. 13). In addition to the threat of tremendous losses that occur in divorce and custody cases, people who once loved each other are now faced with a partner who is engaged in lies and slander, revenge and counterattack. In fact, divorce wars and custody disputes are said to have as much potential for courtroom violence as do criminal trials.

A 1993 episode of the ABC news magazine *20/20*, "Deadly Decisions," reported that in 16 months' time 12 people had been wounded and 6 killed in courtroom shootings involving family disputes.

Impact of the Evaluation Process on the Family

Parents who are considering a custody dispute may ask the clinician "Won't it hurt the children to go through a court battle?" The answer is a surprising one. Psychologists Richard Wolman and Keith Taylor (1991) of Harvard Medical School tracked the children of both contested and uncontested divorces, first at the time of the initial separation (or custody battle) and then 18 months later. Their results were unexpected: The children caught up in the custody battles felt more stressed and anxious at the time of the separation; however, after the divorce was over, the children of the custody battles felt more in control of their lives, less anxious, and less angry than did the children in the uncontested group. The children in the uncontested divorces were more likely to feel rejected and lonely and to see their families as less warm and less close emotionally. It seems that these children derived some measure of self-esteem in being "prizes" over which the parents fought. Wolman and Taylor reasoned that these children may have felt more in control because they were kept informed of so many details and future plans, their opinions were sought, and they had an opportunity to share their thoughts and feelings with interested adults.

Although surprising, these results support the findings of an earlier study conducted by Julie Fulton (1979) of the University of Minnesota Law School. She found that among her sample of 278 families, 17% reported that their divorces were contested and that their children were aware of the battle. However, only 1 parent in 5 felt that the custody battle had affected their relationship with their children in a negative way. Most said the legal warfare over the children had no effect on them or may have even made their relationship closer. Peter Ash and Melvin Guyer (1986) conducted follow-up interviews with 100 families whom they had seen 4 years earlier in the context of a custody battle or an uncontested divorce. After inquiring as to how the children were adjusting, they concluded that there were no differences between the two groups. The quality of the children's current relationship with the parents appeared to be the major determining factor in their adjustment.

Recently, attorneys were asked their opinions of child custody assessments and the impact that they felt such assessments had on the family. Catherine Lee, with coauthors Beauregard and Hunsley (1998) of the University of Ottawa, Ontario, analyzed survey results from 161 Canadian family lawyers. As a group, the lawyers agreed that assessment was preferable to litigation and that litigation should be pursued only after mediation has failed. However, they were uniformly negative as to the advantages of this phase of negotiations. They did not feel that the custody assessments had beneficial effects on the parties in terms of improved compliance with the divorce settlement, improved family relations, or an improved ability to parent cooperatively. These attorneys also agreed that assessment should not be mandatory.

Helping Clients Decide Whether to Undergo a Custody Evaluation

Clinicians are often faced with parents who ask if it is wise to pursue a custody battle. Clinicians will want to examine with a parent his or her reasons for doing so. The following are good reasons:

1. The parent has been the primary caretaker for the children, and having primary custody would provide continuity and stability for them.
2. The parent has not been the primary caretaker, but the children are older, and circumstances have changed. The parent is able to work less and devote more time to the children. The other parent's life circumstances have changed as well —for example, he or she has remarried, is moving away, has started a business, or has returned to college and he or she is now less able to devote time and attention to the children.
3. The parent genuinely feels that he or she can provide a better home and environment for the children. He or she lives in a better neighborhood with a good local school. The parent's current spouse or own parents can provide child care for the children when the parent is away. The children are better able to attend church, music lessons, after-school activities, and so on.
4. The parent is genuinely concerned about the children's well-being in the custody of the other parent. The other parent is emotionally unstable, has a drinking problem, is moody and unpredictable, or invites undesirable people into his or her home. The element of risk or danger in the other parent's home is real.
5. The parent is genuinely concerned that the other parent will alienate the children from him or her or block his or her visitations, or these actions have already taken place. The threat did not occur only once during a heated argument but has been part of a pattern for some time.

The following are not good reasons:

1. The parent feels that he or she has been terribly hurt in the marriage because the partner has been consistently uninter-

ested in the marriage or has been unfaithful. Losing the children would be the final humiliation. Getting the children would punish the other parent and be a vindication.

2. The parent has done the majority of child care for years and feels that he or she has "earned" the children, that the children "belong" to him or her. He or she feels that the other parent has no right to the children.

3. The parent feels that the costs of child support are too high. The parent feels that he or she would be better off financially to keep the children and receive child support from the other parent.

4. The parent wants to move on to other goals in life—such as getting more education or pursuing a career—but he or she feels that it would be embarrassing to allow the other parent to have primary custody without putting up a good fight. People would wonder what kind of parent he or she is if he or she were to seem too disinterested in having custody.

5. The parent considers himself or herself to be an exceptionally moral person. The other parent is involved in dating relationships or is seeing someone seriously, and the parent is considering pursuing custody on the basis of the premise that the children are being exposed to "sexual promiscuity" or immoral behavior. However, the children appear to be doing well in the other parent's home, and others are suggesting that the parent is acting out of jealousy.

6. The parent is very dependent on an adolescent son or daughter who is expressing a wish to live with the other parent to see what it would be like. That child has become like a best friend and confidante to the parent, who would be overwhelmingly lonely without him or her. The parent opposes the change in custody on the basis of "Why not leave well enough alone? Everything is fine the way it is."

7. The parent shows signs of paranoia and has developed irrational beliefs about the other parent. The parent has become preoccupied with looking for clues that the children may be in some danger when with their other parent, even though family, friends, and mental health professionals assure them that their fears are groundless.

Parents who have clear, good reasons for seeking custody and who do not fit any of the seven unacceptable scenarios mentioned above should be prepared for the hidden costs of custody litigation. Clinicians should discuss that parents may feel publicly humiliated by the information that is brought into the courtroom and is used against them; this may fuel the anger between parents and make future negotiations around child care arrangements impossible. The children may become caught in the struggle and feel forced to take sides. Children who ally with one parent may resent the other parent for taking that parent to court. The legal costs may consume savings that otherwise would have provided for the children. In addition, parents who lose their battle may feel angry, mistreated by the justice system, and financially depleted.

On the other hand, parents who may have a good chance at custody but are too despondent to assert their interests present with a different set of issues. Clinicians can help such parents consider the hidden costs of not pursuing custody. First, the parent's greatest fears may be realized—that the children will be poorly taken care of or that the other parent will live with someone unsuitable, and he or she will be powerless to do anything about it until there is some dramatic evidence of physical abuse, neglect, or maltreatment. The children may feel abandoned by the parent and may wonder why he or she did not care enough to fight for them. The parent may have to return to court to get custody reversed, involving extensive additional court costs and attorneys' fees and necessitating more disruptions for the children. Also, the judge may question the sincerity of the parent's motivation, because he or she never raised any objections or voiced any concerns at the time of the divorce. The parent's attorney should mention that it is much harder to get custody reversed than to obtain it at the time of the divorce.

Finally, parents who pursue the evaluation and litigation must be prepared for the likely possibility that the courtroom experience will be a disappointment. Many parents view the procedure as their opportunity to have their day in court—to tell their whole painful story, to read from their lengthy diary, to play their audiotaped telephone conversations, to call all of their witnesses, and to be ultimately vindicated. However, the harried judge with an overloaded schedule may wish to settle the case as quickly as possible with a minimum of testimony by the parents and their allies and experts. The matter may even be settled in the judge's chambers with no witnesses called at all.

Parents should be prepared for the possibility that they might lose. If this occurs, clinicians can help a parent to be heartened that he or she put forth the best effort on behalf of the children. If nothing else, the parent has begun to establish a track record with the court, which will stand him or her in good stead if he or she returns to court to try to reverse custody. This effort may also put the winning parent on notice that he or she could lose custody if he or she does less than a stellar job at parenting. If, as feared, the children become alienated from the parent, he or she can document that his or her love and concern for the children have existed from the outset of the divorce by virtue of the great personal sacrifices made in the failed custody. This is discussed in more detail in chapter 8.

TIPS FOR A HIGH-QUALITY REPORT

As stated before, there are many detailed texts available for custody evaluators that outline specific techniques, tests, and questionnaires that many in the field use. The following is a list of hints for doing a top-notch evaluation regardless of technique used:

- Note the docket number on the report. This number helps the court match the report with the other legal filings in the case.
- List all of the participants and their ages, the dates seen, and the amount of time spent with each. Similarly, list the collateral contacts interviewed, the dates seen, and the length of the interview. List the documents read, along with author and date, in chronological order. Document telephone conversations with each parent. Attention to detail in these matters informs the court and the attorneys that the report is highly organized and meticulous. A report that is less than thorough calls into question the validity of the findings. To keep track of all of this information, keep a diary of everything done in the case.
- Begin the report with a section on how the evaluation originated. What were the circumstances that led up to it? Who ordered it, and why? Inquire about these events, and summarize them, how they may affect the current mental state and behavior of the parties being evaluated, and how they have a direct bearing on the referral questions.
- Outline the major issues addressed in the report so that they can be easily reviewed. These may be put in the form of questions (e.g., "Is Ms. Smith's use of alcohol such that it impairs her performance as a parent?" or "Did Mr. Smith have a pattern of emotional abuse of the children?"). This section also can be organized in the form of each parent's basis for why he or she should have custody (e.g., "Ms. Jones asserts she should have custody on the basis that she has been the primary parent and has been successfully rehabilitated from alcohol for 6 months" or "Mr. Jones asserts he should have custody of the children as he has been the primary caretaker of the children, while Ms. Jones, who is a corporate executive, travels frequently and is rarely home"). Another way to organize the central issues is in the form of the allegations that have been made (e.g., "Ms. Brown alleges that Mr. Green has never had a meaningful role in the children's lives and is interested in custody only to punish her" or "Mr. Green al-

leges that Ms. Brown is mentally unstable, having been in continuous psychotherapy for the past 3 years and being dependent on medication").

- Interview multiple individuals to verify and cross-validate every important piece of information relevant to the central issues or allegations of the case (e.g., If Mr. Black asserts that Ms. White is always screaming at the children, ask the neighbors what they have seen and heard. If Ms. Adams asserts that Mr. Adams drinks too much, ask the housekeeper whether she has collected empty beer bottles when emptying the trash. Interview Mr. Adams's supervisor about whether he has smelled alcohol on Mr. Adams's breath or about Mr. Adams's work habits).

- De-emphasize test scores. Although some psychologists favor the administration of tests and analysis of responses (Ackerman, 1995; Blau, 1997), the fact is that the tests are not that reliable. The majority of tests that are well validated and standardized have no direct bearing on parenting issues. The newer tests that have been developed to measure parenting skills or parent–child attachment, for example, have not yet been rigorously validated. Use only those tests that are relevant to the central issues, and use them only to check clinical opinions and observations. Describe the results in a tentative fashion, with many qualifiers, including apologies for their limitations. If the weight of the tests points to a strong conclusion, cross-validate with data from several other sources.

- Stay away from jargon (e.g., it is better to say, "The child described an instance in which she was left alone with the father on a visitation and saw him drink until he passed out. She described being alone in the house and said, 'I was frightened. I couldn't wake him up. I called 911'" than to say "The elevated score on the MacAndrews scale suggests that Mr. Thomas may have proclivities toward being an addictive personality").

- In the conclusion, outline the responses to the main questions in the introduction. If everything in the body of the report has been directed toward those questions and cross-validated thoroughly, the conclusions should be obvious. To avoid making a recommendation as to custody, draw up lists in a clear and concise way so that the judge will be left to come to the same conclusion as to custody as would a mental health professional (e.g., "List A: Mr. Smith's assets and liabilities as a parent"; "List B: Ms. Smith's assets and liabilities as a parent" or refer to a list of 10 factors to consider for the custodial parent and explain how Mr. Smith is the stronger parent on a certain number of factors, whereas Ms. Smith is the stronger parent on the remaining factors).

CASE STUDY

In my 23-page report to the court, I recommended, in my evaluation, that Ted have primary custody of Tyler. My findings are summarized with a 10-point outline:

1. Ted would be the parent more likely to allow his son access to the other parent. Although Ted had once driven around town with Tyler contemplating to kidnap him, Jennifer had followed through with this plan. She had also done the same with her older sons when she had divorced from her first husband.

2. Ted seemed to have the better parenting skills. Tyler was observed in the office to be very hyperactive and oppositional with both parents. The social worker also observed this on two visits to the parents' homes. Ted was able to control Tyler with firm limit setting and by shifting him to a new activity, even physically restraining him at one point. Jennifer, however, had no control over him. Several times in the office, Tyler hit Jennifer in the face and called her names. She responded by smiling and talking sweetly to him.

3. Psychological testing and interviews with Ted and Jennifer and the people who knew them did not reveal any serious psychological disturbance on the part of either parent. Also, the reports of neighbors and previous therapists, as well as drug screens, did not reveal Ted to be an alcoholic.

4. By Ted's report and those of the neighbors, Ted had been the primary caretaker of Tyler. Ted's unemployment enabled him to stay home with Tyler full-time for the first 3 years of his son's life. (This fact, although it clearly rankled Jennifer, often works in favor of mothers who stay home full-time with small children.)

5. Psychological testing with Tyler revealed that he was more strongly bonded to Ted. This was consistent throughout measures involving picture drawing, storytelling, and dollhouse play.

6. Ted had more time to give to Tyler; he was working only part-time, getting by on work from his father's accounting firm. Jennifer, however, worked full-time and cared for two other children.

7. Ted clearly had the healthier relationship with Tyler. Jennifer behaved in a seductive fashion with Tyler, slept with him, and used baby talk with him. The caseworker also observed these actions in the home. The caseworker, too, was alarmed when he discovered that Tyler had no bedroom of his own in his mother's home but slept with her in her room.

8. Both parents could provide an adequate home for Tyler. In addition, in Jennifer's home he would have access to older brothers. However, the caseworker noted that Ted's home was set up for raising a small boy. Tyler had his own room, a playroom with an electric train, educational tapes and videos, and an area set aside for schoolwork. Also, Ted was taking Tyler to speech therapy and to a divorce recovery group at his church, as well as to Sunday services. Thus, Tyler had a wider network of friends and supportive adults in his father's home.

9. Tyler was felt to have special needs. The examiner expressed concern about his hyperactive and oppositional behavior, his feelings of loss and abandonment, and his unintelligible speech. Ted was concerned also and was addressing these issues, whereas Jennifer dismissed them as inconsequential.

10. Ted would be a better fit with Tyler in a number of ways. Tyler seemed gifted at mechanical things, and the two were electric train enthusiasts. Also, the evaluator saw difficulty ahead for Tyler in developing a male identity in Jennifer's enmeshed relationship with him, her poor discipline of him, and her attempts to alienate him from his father.

The custody hearing lasted for 3 days. The judge concurred with my evaluation and awarded primary residential custody of Tyler to Ted. Jennifer was outraged and threatened retribution. Yet Tyler did well. Over the following year, Ted continued to take Tyler to speech therapy and divorce counseling and had him evaluated for attention deficit hyperactivity disorder (ADHD) and placed on medication. By the second year, Tyler's speech and behavior were much improved at school. Ted kept Tyler involved with educational activities, train shows, and visits to see his own family.

At the same time, the hostilities between Ted and Jennifer did not lessen. Jennifer continued to have Tyler sleep with her during his visitations, was lax about his meals and bedtimes, and refused to participate in Tyler's ADHD treatment or give him his medication. Ted renewed his campaign through the courts (fueled by family money) to reduce or restrict Jennifer's visitations with Tyler.

6

WORKING OUT A VISITATION PLAN AND RESOLVING PROBLEMS

CASE STUDY

"These are my children," Monica, age 30, blurted through tears explaining what had happened. "I had never been apart from them since they were born." Hudson was 4 years and Rebecca was 2 months old when their father Dan, age 36, came to get them for their first overnight visitation. Dan had announced that he wanted a divorce when Monica was 8 months pregnant with Rebecca and had moved out when the baby was 7 weeks old. Monica was stunned; she had thought that Dan had been content in the marriage, although she noticed that he had been rather quiet for a few months and not excited about having Rebecca.

For moral support, Monica had asked her mother and sister to be with her when Dan came to get the children. Dan, on seeing the three women huddled together and crying, immediately tensed and braced for a confrontation. Hudson took one look at the standoff and began to cry and cling to his mother. Dan grabbed Hudson's arm and said tersely, "Come on Hudson, let's go." Monica's mother pulled Hudson back. Soon the three adults were fighting over Hudson as he wailed "Mama!" Monica's sister headed for the telephone and called the police.

When the dust cleared the next day, the lawyers were busy filing motions back and forth. Dan asserted that Monica had her family there to intimidate him from exercising his legal rights to visitations with the children. Monica alleged that Dan had hurt her and cursed and threatened her. They both agreed to have psychological evaluations done to validate their claims.

Dan insisted that he should have sole custody of the children or at least joint custody with liberal visitation, stating that Monica was overly protective and possessive. He felt that she had pushed him aside to develop in the children a strong dependency on her, just as Monica was overly dependent on her mother and sister. He stated in his petition that Monica was mentally unstable and prone to unpredictable rages. He scoffed at her attorney's request for 5 years of alimony. Monica felt entitled to stay at home with the children until they began school. "She just doesn't want to work. Get real. This is the 90's. Mothers work. Monica is codependent, narcissistic, and manipulative."

Monica was deeply bitter about the divorce. She strongly suspected that Dan had begun seeing another woman during her second pregnancy and that he had had another affair in the past as well. She saw Dan as totally self-centered, not wanting to be burdened with the demands of a family. She insisted that he had never been involved in Hudson's life to any extent. He worked 80 hours per week in his career as vice president of a computer software company and played golf on the weekends. She felt that he was using the custody issue as leverage to bargain with her on alimony and child support. She further did not want Dan to have the children any more than a few hours once a week. Hudson was uneasy about the visitations, and she was adamant that the child not go overnight to Dan's house until Hudson communicated to her that he was ready. Sending Rebecca for visitation was out of the question. Dan had no experience in caring for her since she was born, and she feared for Rebecca's safety if Dan were to keep her overnight. Monica wanted full control of the children's lives, as she had always had.

My evaluation had to address three questions: Was Monica mentally unstable and therefore unable to make rational decisions about the children's well-being? Was the current visitation schedule, established at the temporary hearing, appropriate for the children? Was Dan capable of caring for the children alone, and were they safe with him?

It is easy to see from the above scenario that Dan is not serious about wanting sole custody of the children—after all, he often works 80 hours per week and enjoys golf on the weekends. Yet his assertion that Monica may be overly dependent on the children and that he may become a marginal figure in their lives may have some merit. Their roles in the family have already become so polarized—he, the breadwinner, and she, the parent and homemaker—that he will have a hard time establishing a strong relationship with the children. If, then, the issue is more one of what sort of visitation plan is suitable, the court is faced with these questions: What sort of visitation plan is appropriate for a 4-year-old child or for a 2-month-old infant? Should the children always accompany each other? If both go together to Dan's home, for example, do they follow a plan suitable for a 4-year-old or one suitable for a 2-month-old? Should the judge award the standard visitation—alternate weekends and one evening per week, regardless of the child's age, the child's familiarity with the noncustodial parent, the number of children, or the child's personality and temperament? What if the angry standoffs at the time of visitation continue? How will that affect the children? If they continue, should Dan's visitations be shortened or decreased? Is that fair to Dan? If the visits are hostile, should they be lengthened but decreased in frequency? Can the children tolerate longer-than-usual visitations? Are the children better off seeing Dan often, even if the visits are hostile, or is it better to diminish their contact with Dan until Monica and the children can better tolerate the visitations?

In this chapter I review the challenge of assisting parents and the courts with guidelines for a visitation schedule. The major criterion currently used is a developmental model, based on the child's age. However, other factors are usually considered as well: the child's familiarity with the parent, the level of conflict involved, and the child's temperament. Visitations by noncustodial fathers are often blocked, and visitation rates typically drop off during the aftermath of divorce. I review some of the reasons for the decrease and explore the controversial research findings on whether children benefit from increased contact with noncustodial fathers.

DEVELOPING GUIDELINES FOR A VISITATION PLAN

In chapter 5, I discussed how custody disputes primarily focus on young children, not on older children, and usually on only one or two children. Therefore, the courts are often faced with the questions raised above, and the parents' respective attorneys call on their experts in child development to address these issues.

These experts must contend with the fact that, as of this writing, there are no scientific studies on the subject of which visitation patterns work best for children of different ages. It would be unethical to conduct a study in which, for example, 100 divorcing families who have 2-year-old children are divided into two groups. One group has two brief visitations of 4 hours during the week and one long visitation of 24 hours. The other group spends alternating weeks with each parent. Then the children are evaluated to determine which are faring well and which are doing poorly. Similarly, it would be interesting but unethical to separate a parent from the child in the first 2 years of the child's life, then reintroduce that parent (as is happening naturally in some cases in which a biological father challenges the rights of adoptive parents to parent a child) and determine which visitation pattern is best for the child.

Because mental health professionals cannot conduct experimental studies on children to determine how visitation patterns affect them now, we also cannot answer questions about how these arrangements might affect them as adolescents or young adults. In other words, we cannot predict long-range consequences.

Thus, the experts in the field are left to make educated guesses on the basis of what is known about how children grow and develop in most families. Experts also have to make guesses about long-range consequences of different living arrangements on the basis of the longitudinal studies that do exist. For the most part, clinicians in practice also draw on their store of knowledge about the patients that they have seen in the past and on general guidelines adopted by experts in their field.

For child mental health experts, the way in which guidelines are developed for a visitation follows a stepwise process (see Figure 6.1). First, one must determine if the parents have joint or sole legal custody. The parent who has sole legal custody will also have primary physical custody of the children. Therefore, the noncustodial parent will have a visitation arrangement in which he or she is with the child less than 40% of the time. If this is the case, the next question to ask is whether the noncustodial parent is emotionally stable and not a danger to the child. If it can be established that the noncustodial parent presents a risk of harm to the child, the expert must recommend to the court some restrictions on that parent's time with the child. Typically, these restrictions involve (a) limiting the visitation to a brief period of time, (b) requiring the visitation to be supervised by an outside person, (c) requiring the parent to undergo some sort of treatment or to maintain sobriety, or (d) requiring that a family therapist gradually introduce the parent and child to each other and oversee the process of visitation. Ultimately, the court will decide the appropriate restrictions.

If, as in most cases, the noncustodial parent is emotionally stable and not dangerous, then the next issue to determine is whether the parent lives near the child and whether the parent has had an active role in the child's life in the past so that the child is familiar and comfortable with him or her. In most cases the visitation plan is developed at the time of the divorce when the noncustodial parent is familiar to the child and lives within a few miles of the primary custodial parent. In such cases the mental health expert can follow developmental guidelines based on the child's age.

If, however, the parent has been absent from the child's life for an extended period of time, that parent will need to be introduced to the child gradually. This may even have to be done in the presence of someone who is familiar to the child or be overseen by a child psychotherapist.

If the parent moves such a distance away that visits will be infrequent,

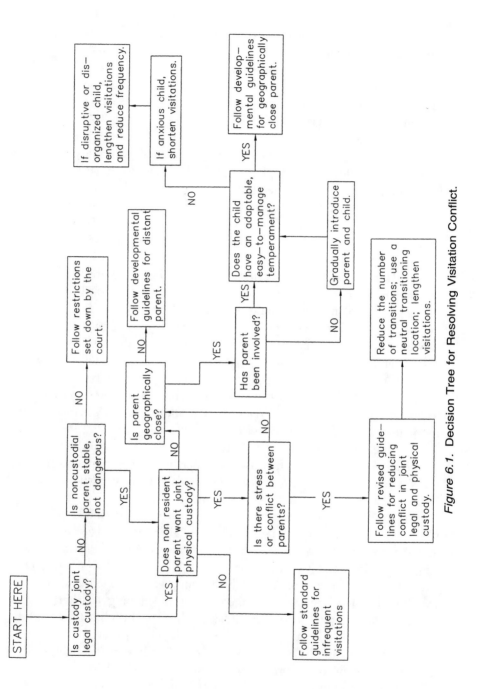

Figure 6.1. Decision Tree for Resolving Visitation Conflict.

that parent may request unusually long visitations to "make up" for his or her absence in the child's life. It is common for a parent who lives several states away to request to have his or her 2- or 3-year-old child for the entire summer. Such visitations may be inappropriate for very young children. The expert may require that the noncustodial parent fly to the city of the child's primary residence several times a year to have frequent, short visitations, returning the child to the custodial parent each night. Likewise, the custodial parent may be required to fly to the noncustodial parent's city and allow brief visitations, with the child returning to the custodial parent each night.

Parents who have joint legal custody have shared decision-making privileges regarding the child, but they may or may not have shared physical custody. If one parent clearly has a secondary role in the child's life, his or her visitation may range from 10% to 30% of the child's time, with relatively infrequent visits. In these cases, many experts still recommend visitations that are geared to the child's developmental level, although it is common for many judges to award "standard" visitations—alternating weekends, for example—regardless of the child's age or the expert's recommendations.

The most common scenario in which experts are asked to give opinions is that in which both parents have agreed to joint physical custody. However, it may also be the case that one parent wanted joint physical custody and one did not, but the court awarded joint physical custody over the objections of the one parent. If joint physical custody has been agreed to or determined by the court, it is assumed that both parents are mentally stable and do not present a danger to the children. It is also assumed that the parents live geographically close to each other.

In these cases, it is important to determine if there is a moderate to severe level of conflict. If there is, the expert will propose a plan in which transitions are minimized and are conducted by neutral parties at neutral locations. More will be said about this later.

If conflict is mild or minimal, the expert will recommend a residential plan that considers the child's age, the child's temperament or personality, and the presence of older siblings. By *temperament* psychologists are referring to personality traits with which the child is born, the enduring characteristics that are present in the child from a very early age and continue into adulthood, relatively unchanged. When developing a visitation plan, the important variables to consider are whether the child is easygoing, flexible, and self-reliant. Such children tolerate separations well, make transitions easily, and can keep up with their physical belongings. They may enjoy having two homes, develop attachments to both families, and adjust remarkably well.

Other children have difficult, or "fussy," temperaments. They are more vulnerable to life changes and stress in general—a factor that puts them at a higher risk for psychological problems. Researchers such as Mavis Hetherington (1989; Hetherington, Stanley-Hagan, & Anderson, 1989) and Michael Rutter (1971, 1987) have suggested that these children have greater adjustment problems following divorce. Children with difficult temperaments have more behavior problems before, during, and after each transition. They become agitated and act out when under stress, and they are prone to having long readjustment periods following each transition. For rigid or disruptive children, transitions may have to be less frequent and longer in duration (this issue will be explored further in chapter 7).

Some children become unusually anxious when separated from the primary parent for any length of time. Anxious children may need visitations that are shorter but more frequent to desensitize them to separations. They may also benefit from increased telephone contact with the parent who is not present. Some young children enjoy taking photographs and keepsakes of the absent parent with them.

Still others, particularly children with attention deficit hyperactivity disorder, have such organizational problems that they are continually confused and disoriented by frequent transitions, seldom knowing where they are in space and time, and lose track of belongings along the way. These children need maximum consistency between the homes. Easily disorganized children may also need less frequent and longer visitations.

If, as in most cases, the parents have joint legal and physical custody, there is a minimum of conflict, they live close to each other, and the child has an easy temperament, then psychologists can look to general developmental guidelines when making recommendations to the court as to visitation arrangements. The following are general guidelines, arranged by age group.

Category 1: Birth to Age 6 Months

Because scientific studies have not examined the effects of separating infants from their primary custodians for any period of time, for such young children to reside with the secondary parent, child custody experts are left to explore the research on the impact on children of being in day care for the closest approximation to sharing custody. In the middle of this century, it was taken as a truth that only one attachment was formed in infancy—the mother–child bond. It was taken that separations from the mother, or having care provided by other caregivers, was highly detrimental to young children. However, with the influx of women into the job market in the 1970s and 1980s, a large body of research has been conducted on the effects of paid group care on young children—research that has largely discredited this myth (see Mussen, Conger, Kagan, & Huston, 1984, and Galinsky & David, 1988, for reviews). It was feared that the presence of multiple caregivers would disrupt the mother–child bond and render children anxious and insecurely attached, perhaps even impairing their ability to trust others and to develop a moral conscience.

What has been learned is startling in some ways, yet obvious in hindsight. It is now known that infants form multiple attachments to caregivers. The attachments are not formed only with the mother but also with anyone who feeds the child; provides soothing touch and physical care; provides opportunities for learning and stimulation; and interacts with the child through playing games, rocking, smiling, and verbalizing. This person is often the mother but may also be the father, sisters and brothers, aunts and uncles, grandparents, and paid caregivers. This is the model for child rearing in all developing countries, as it was in the United States when the country was not yet industrialized. In these societies children are born into large, extended families in which many family members, mostly young girls, childless aunts, and grandmothers, all share in the child care responsibilities.

What appears to be important to the infant is that the caregivers are the same from one day to the next, that they actively engage the infant, and that routines are regular and predictable. Ideally, in paid day care arrangements, there should be no more than three infants per caregiver. Harvard child psychologist Jerome Kagan, along with coauthors Richard Kearsley and Philip Zelazo (1978), compared two groups of infants—one group was raised at home, and the other spent their first year in full-time day care—and found that they showed similar growth in language, perceptual skills, and quality of attachment to the mother. "If these conditions are met, children raised in day-care centers and those brought up entirely at home seem to be equally mature, socially competent, and attached to their mothers" (p. 91).

In the 1980s, three studies (Bargelow, Vaughn, & Molitor, 1987; Schwartz, 1983; Vaughn, Gove, & Egelund, 1980) found that a small but statistically significant number of children who were in nonmaternal care more than 20 hours a week had insecure attachments to their mothers. Vaughn et al.'s (1980) study found that infants from low-income, high-risk homes who attended day care in their first year were insecurely attached to their mothers. However, the findings were held to be nonrepresentative of more normal samples, because these children came from highly stressed homes. Schwartz (1983) evaluated children from middle-class homes and found similar results. Bargelow et al. (1987) corrected for bias even further by studying infants from middle-class homes whose mothers went to work before they were 8 months old and who were cared for in their homes by a nonfamily paid caregiver. Of those infants whose mothers worked (all were firstborns), 31.5% were rated as insecurely attached or avoidant with their mothers after a separation, and 54% were securely attached. Of those with at-home mother care, the comparable percentages were 9% and 71%, respectively. These studies made news headlines as they tapped into parents' worst fears about the negative effects of day care.

Alison Clarke-Stewart (1988) reviewed 16 studies on this issue and concluded that 38% of children who spent their first year of life in full-time day care were insecurely attached. The comparable figure for children who remained at home their first year with a full-time mother was 28%. Although the difference was statistically significant, it may not be very meaningful. Ellen Galinsky and Judy David (1988) pointed out that children who were enrolled in day care may have come from families that had other stressors impinging on them as well—divorce; parental conflict; economic problems forcing the mother to work; and an unstable life that resulted in frequent moves, job changes, and changes in day care arrangements. Also, it is still not known fully what the implications are for children who are insecurely attached to their mothers at age 12 months. Vaughn, Deane, and Waters (1985) noted, in a follow-up study of their earlier sample, that being securely or insecurely attached at age 1 year was not predictive of later social and emotional competence in the children whose mothers worked, even though it was predictive in the sample of children whose mothers stayed at home. Apparently, the children of working mothers develop these competencies through some other route.

From this research on child care in infancy, experts now believe that infants can adapt to having two homes and separations from the mother, if the number of caregivers is kept small overall, if the noncustodial parent has frequent and regular contact with the infant, and if routines are stable and predictable and roughly the same from one home to another. Overnight visits for infants are not recommended because they would disrupt the maintenance of regular routines around eating, sleeping, and bathing (Ackerman, 1995; Bray, 1991; Garrity & Baris, 1994; Hodges, 1991; Skafte, 1985). The ideal living arrangement for an infant of divorced parents is one in which the number of caregivers is kept low, such as no more than three persons. This can occur when the primary-residence parent remains at home full-time or when child care is provided by a nanny or a grandparent who comes to the home. The next-best option is one in which the child adjusts to three caregivers and three homes. For example, both parents work, and the child is dropped off at the grandparent's home or a family child-care home for the day. For many parents, these arrangements are not an option, and the only choice is group care. It simply is not known what the possible effects will be on a given child of experiencing three living environments and up to five or more caregivers. Some parents cannot agree on a day care center and enroll the child in different programs when they have possession of the child. Thus, some children may be shuttled among four environments and perhaps eight or more caregivers. In situations such as this, the mental health expert must be able to articulate for the court the point that every child presumably has some limit as to how many transitions, caregivers, and environments to which he or she can adapt. Such arrangements may suit the parents' needs but are likely to be confusing at best and probably stressful to a young child.

If the child must be in day care, the best arrangement is one in which the staff-to-child ratio is low—no more than three or four infants per caregiver—there is little turnover in staff, and the caregivers have training in early childhood development. If these arrangements can be made, the secondary-residence parent should have the infant for several hours at least every 2–3 days (Bray, 1991; Garrity & Baris, 1994; Hodges, 1991; Skafte, 1985; Teyber, 1992). Such contact with the secondary-residence parent would allow the infant to become familiar with that parent over time without providing any major disruptions in daily routines. The important variables are that (a) the routine is kept smooth and consistent, and (b) the infant is able to become familiar with the sight, sound, smell, and feel of the parent.

If the secondary-residence parent cannot make such arrangements, it is common for him or her to request to keep the child for the weekend. This is not recommended. It would be preferable to allow brief visitations each day of each weekend.

Unfortunately, this ideal is often not attainable. After a divorce, many custodial parents move several times. Drops in family income may necessitate long work hours and placement of the infant in the least expensive day care environment in which several staff care for too many children, and turnover is high. Often, the secondary-residence parent, who is typically the father, may have infrequent visitations with the child because of his discomfort with feeding, bathing, and diapering.

Again, there are no published studies on the long-range outcomes of these situations. However, day care research has suggested that infants in poor-quality day care are anxious, irritable, and insecurely attached to their custodial parents (Mussen et al., 1984). Therefore, one can only guess that infants who have long visitations with the secondary parent or irregular visitations will be predisposed to insecure, anxious attachments as well. James Bray (1991) of the Baylor University College of Medicine went so far as to suggest that infants who experience disruptions in attachment to a primary parent figure during the first year of life are likely to have later psychological problems. However, there is only indirect support for this assumption in the research literature.

Category 2: Age 6 to 18 Months

By 6 months of age most infants know and respond to many caregivers in their environment if they have interacted with them on a frequent and regular basis. Infants at this stage are developing a sense of security and predictability in their world and feelings of trust in their caretakers. They differentiate caretakers from strangers and react to unfamiliar faces with a concerned or hesitant facial expression and even fear or alarm. Many will cry when picked up and held by a stranger. This "stranger anxiety" begins at about 6–7 months and peaks at 12–18 months. However, it may continue to the ages of 2, 3, or even 4 years.

Babies and toddlers do become attached to several people, but they need to see those people often. Joseph Goldstein and Albert Solnit (1984) suggested that children at this age may demonstrate stranger anxiety with a parent whom they have not seen for several days. They quickly lose their sense of attachment to someone they see only sporadically. Bray (1991) suggested that, for this reason, visitations be no more than 3 days apart. If the visitations with the secondary-residence parent have been frequent since birth, they should continue to occur every couple of days but could be expanded to 4–8 hours in duration (Garrity & Baris, 1994; Hodges, 1991; Skafte, 1985).

Again, overnight stays are not recommended for children this age because they are not able to readily understand the meaning of the absence of the custodial parent (Bray, 1991; Garrity & Baris, 1994; Hodges, 1991; Skafte, 1985). For example, a child this age does not know that a parent who has not been seen for 24 hours still exists. Overnight visits also disrupt the daily routines of caregiving for the child. Logistically, overnight visits are also difficult because of the amount of equipment needed. One may need to purchase or borrow not only car seats but also cribs, baby bathtubs, swings, walkers, portable carriers, and high chairs.

If visitation frequency has been low (only once or twice a week), visits should be brief, from 2 to 4 hours. The toddler needs many regular visitations to build up tolerance for the absence of the primary-residence parent. Also, if the secondary-residence parent has not been a part of the child's life, he or she would have to be phased in gradually with visitations based on the developmental guidelines for early infancy—1 or 2 hours at a time, every other day.

Category 3: Age 18 to 36 Months

Children in this age group undergo a transformation from babyhood to childhood. Toddlers of 18 months are almost all walking, and some are beginning to talk. By 24 months most have a small working vocabulary with which to express themselves, and many are speaking in short sentences. Toilet training usually takes place between 24 and 36 months, with a few children trained at 18 months and almost all children trained by 36 months. Most children are able to feed and dress themselves for the most part by age 3, and a large number are attending preschool programs.

Psychologically, children in this age range still experience anxiety when put in strange situations. Children may understand the difference between day and night. However, the concepts of yesterday, today, and tomorrow are only vaguely understood at the younger ages in this range. These children are also learning what psychologists call *object constancy*—the understanding that although someone is not readily visible, he or she still does exist somewhere. When children in this age group say "bye-bye," they understand that they are being separated from a caregiver, but they also are beginning to understand that the caregiver continues to function in his or her normal setting and that they will be reunited with that person.

With this knowledge in mind, most experts do not recommend overnight visitations until at least the age of 2. Skafte (1985) and Hodges (1991) recommended overnight stays beginning at age 3, but not weekend-long visitations. Teyber (1992) recommended an overnight visitation with the noncustodial parent once every 3–4 days, or once on the weekend, along with a telephone call every other night. Bray (1991) recommended that overnight visitations begin somewhere between age 12 and 36 months. Garrity and Baris (1994) recommended that overnight visitations begin somewhere between 2½ and 5 years. However, they still recommended that the visitation be relatively brief: 24–36 hours. Ideally, a schedule of four such visitations per month with some brief (3-hour) midweek visits would provide a visitation frequency of six visits per month—roughly one every 5 days.

In the real world, however, this may not be feasible. A parent's work schedule may disallow long visitations except on the weekends. If this is the case, it might be possible to work out two to four weekend visitations per month, varying the pattern from Friday afternoon to Saturday afternoon one weekend, followed by a Sunday morning to Monday morning visitation the following weekend, along with some brief, midweek visits.

By age 3, most children understand the concepts of yesterday, today, and tomorrow. Object constancy is generally well established. A child this age can recall a parent whom he or she has not seen for several days or a week. Even a caregiver whom he or she has not seen for weeks will become familiar after a warm-up period. Weekend visitations may be acceptable for some 3-year-old children but may be unduly stressful for others.

However, because a 2-week period is a long absence for children this age, an infrequent visitation pattern of two weekends per month may be stressful for the child in that he or she has to refamiliarize himself or herself with the secondary-residence parent on each visitation. Several shorter visitations per month are preferable to only one or two lengthy ones. If this cannot be arranged, short, midweek visitations should be arranged so that the child has at least one or two contacts per week with the secondary-residence parent.

Generally, vacations are not recommended for children at this age. If the children tolerate weekend visitations well, parents may want to try each having several (two to three) 4-day vacations per year with the child. This guideline should be applied for the primary-residence as well as the secondary-residence parent. In other words, the primary parent should not presume to take the child on a 2-week vacation with no contact during that time with the secondary parent, because it will disrupt the child's familiarity with the secondary-residence parent.

Category 4: Age 4 to 6 Years

Children in this age group have their first experiences with leaving home (if they have not been in day care) and going out into the world. They are actively interested in socializing with other children and begin to form their first friendships. Their communications skills are well developed, and they are beginning to read and write. Most know their full names, age, parents' names, telephone number and address, and school name. Most understand the time concept of "several days." They know the days of the week by the end of this period and the seasons of the year. However, they seldom know what day of the week, the month, or the day of the month it is. They cannot locate "today's date" on a calendar. They know that clocks tell time and may know what time they go to bed, but they cannot tell time on a clock. They may know what street they live on, but they have no concept of the distance in miles between parents' homes, how long it takes to get from one place to the other, or how to go from one home to another (if the parents live close together).

Because children this age cannot locate themselves in space and time accurately, many experts do not recommend joint physical custody, in the sense of alternating homes every couple of days or alternating homes week by week. Most experts feel that children this age need the security and simplicity of having a primary residence that serves as "home base"—a place where they have lived for a long time, a place where they can locate all of their belongings, a place where the routines are consistent from day to day.

Bray (1991) suggested that children ages 3–5 can tolerate overnight visits, or even longer separations, well and recommended that preschoolers and kindergartners see their noncustodial parent at least every 7–10 days. When developing a plan for joint physical custody for 4- or 5-year-old children, many experts recommend a visitation of 3 days and 2 nights (e.g., Friday evening to Sunday evening), occurring at least twice a month (Hodges, 1991; Skafte, 1985). If possible, three such visitations per month are desirable. Ideally, the visitations could be staggered in such a way as to overlap with preschool and kindergarten attendance, so that the secondary-residence parent could develop a meaningful level of involvement with the child's teachers and friends (e.g., a visitation lasting from Sunday morning to drop-off time at school on Tuesday morning).

Such a plan would provide for the child to spend 6 nights per month with the secondary-residence parent. If this is supplemented with two to three brief midweek visitations, the secondary parent might then have contact with the child 8–12 days of the month while still maintaining a home base for the child. Ideally, the child should not go a week without seeing either parent.

By the age of 6, many children can tolerate visitations of 4 days and 3 nights (e.g., from Friday evening to Monday morning). Two lengthy visitations such as this, along with two to four brief midweek visitations, provide for contact with the secondary-residence parent 10–12 days of the month. A home base is still maintained.

Vacations depend again on the child's age and previous history with the secondary-residence parent. Four-year-old children who have had frequent, regular visitations with the secondary parent can usually tolerate week long vacations at holiday times and over the summer. This pattern was recommended by Hodges (1991) and Skafte (1985). By ages 5 and 6 most children can tolerate vacations of 2 weeks, with some telephone contact with the other parent during those periods. Again, to provide the establishment of strong bonds with both parents, these guidelines should apply equally. Neither the primary nor the secondary parent should be separated from the child for more than 2 weeks at a time.

Category 5: Age 7 to 12 Years

During the years from roughly 2nd to 7th grade, children become active and aware participants in the world in which they live. Most 7-year-old children can locate today's date on a calendar and can tell time to the quarter hour. Children in this age group walk freely about their neighborhoods (in safe areas), ride bicycles to the park, and may go back and forth to school on their own. Older children may venture up to a mile or two from home in safe areas. Children know the names of many streets, recognize major landmarks, and can locate where they live on a map.

Skaftee (1985) recommended a visitation plan of alternating weekends with a brief midweek visitation by the noncustodial parent for this age group. However, Hodges (1991) commented that children in this group often find this to be too little time with the noncustodial parent and recommended that children have contact with the noncustodial parent several times a week. Because of their advanced awareness of where they are in space and time, this group may be the one in which true joint physical custody is a feasible option. If the two parents live close together—1 or 2 miles apart—children can walk or ride a bicycle from one home to another. If both parents are in the same school district, children can ride the bus to and from school from either home.

In the 10 to 20 years that courts have been awarding joint physical custody, parents and attorneys have arrived at a number of creative plans that provide for extensive involvement in the child's life by both parents. Keep in mind the lessons of chapter 4—that is, even when there is joint physical custody, most children have a 60–40 split in time between parents, and the parent who has the children 60% of the time is more typically the executive manager of the details of the children's lives.

The simplest plan is one in which the children alternate weeks between the two homes. Rather than alternating on the weekends, many parents prefer to switch weeks on Wednesday afternoons. Thus, the weekends are not disrupted by a transition. An even simpler plan is one in which the child spends, for example, the first 10 days with the mother (with one visit with the father on the 5th night), followed by 20 days with the father (with one visit with the mother on the 10th night). These plans can also work with children whose parents live miles apart and in different school districts, provided that the parents can provide transportation to school and from aftercare. These parents will also have to coordinate after-school and weekend activities with each other and provide transportation to these activities from each home.

Some parents may object to these types of plans because they entail long separations from the children. Children in this age group, however, form strong attachments to school, friends, and after-school activities and thus may tolerate the long separations. Parents who opt for briefer separations may wish to try a series of longer visitations during the month; for example, two visitations of 5 days and 4 nights per month (Thursday afternoon to Monday morning) with a weeknight overnight visit twice a month. These plans were recommended by Hodges (1991) and Teyber (1992). This provides the secondary-residence parent with 10 overnight visits per month plus 2 Monday mornings for contact with the child 12 days per month. The downside of such plans is that the child undergoes eight transitions per month. Transitions are stress points with opportunities for confusion for the child, lost and misplaced belongings, and face-to-face contacts between both parents.

With regard to vacations, most children from ages 8 to 10 can tolerate month-long separations from either parent in the summer, provided that there has been regular, ongoing contact with the noncustodial parent throughout the year. By age 11 or 12, children can tolerate 2-month or even summer-long visitations. Thus, some older children who spend weekends with the noncustodial parent throughout the year and all summer actually live in a 60–40 arrangement. These children's ties to their peer group may be so strong, however, that they object adamantly to long separations from their friends.

Back to the question about how to handle children of different ages who are transitioning. For example, should 3-year-old and 11-year-old siblings both go to their father's home for 2 months in the summer? These issues are complex because they are contingent on the bond between the two children, the pre-existing relationship with the secondary-residence parent, and each child's temperament. A general rule is to consider moving the younger child up by one but no more than two age categories to minimize the stress of separation. The older child can be moved down by one to three age categories without increasing stress or anxiety.

Category 6: Age 13 to 18 Years

During the adolescent years, the bonds of dependency to parents are loosened as the ties to school, after-school activities, and peer groups are intensified. Many children at this age resent a strict visitation schedule as it interferes with their social life and planned activities (Bray, 1991; Hodges, 1991). They feel a much stronger desire to come and go between homes as the need arises. Many are content to see the noncustodial parent for a few hours one evening per week. Some can make the trip themselves once they get a driver's license. Although 14 year olds in most states are able to choose which home will be their primary residence (provided that both are suitable homes), they are not legally free to choose whether to continue visitations. The parents' rights to visitation are established by the courts, and the parent can assert them if the adolescent is noncompliant. However, the parent must weigh this against the developing adolescent's need for autonomy and self-determination. Forcing visitations when the adolescent refuses may deepen the alienation between parent and child.

Many children in adolescence choose to live with their noncustodial parent "to see what it is like." This is particularly true for boys who have not lived with their fathers in the past. It is also true very often for girls to choose to explore living with their fathers (Bray, 1991; Maccoby et al., 1988). The custodial parent would do well to see this for what it is—an attempt to grow up and leave home in stages. It is a logical extension of sleepovers, summer camp, and long summer vacations with grandparents.

VISITATION PROBLEMS

The above guidelines are set out with the proviso that there is low conflict between the two parents. In an ideal world, parents who are divorcing and planning a visitation schedule, or even returning to court to negotiate a new and more suitable visitation plan, would be cooperative and flexible. In reality, this is often far from the case. Visitations are frequently prevented. This problem occupies much time on the court dockets for both superior and juvenile court judges. The Children's Rights Council (1994) estimated the size of the problem of visitation interference, reporting that 6 million children in the United States had their visitations denied by their custodial parents.

How common is this problem? Earlier reports, such as those by Julie Fulton (1979), found that 40% of custodial parents (mostly mothers) reported that they had interfered with the noncustodial parent's visitations at least once. Their reasons had nothing to do with the children's wishes or safety but were solely to "punish" their ex-spouses. Of the 278 Minnesota families Fulton interviewed, 53% of the fathers claimed that their visitations had been blocked by the children's mothers. One quarter said that they had tried legally or informally to change the visitation arrangements but with no success.

Recall Judith Wallerstein and Joan Kelly's (1980a, 1980b) study of more than 100 children of divorce in upper-middle-class California. Wallerstein and Kelly (1980a) found that 20% of the custodial parents (all mothers) saw no purpose in the fathers' visits and had actively tried to sabotage them. They noted anecdotally that the conflict reached pathological, even bizarre, intensity in some cases. One third of the children (usually those older than age 5) were exposed to intense anger and stress at visiting times. Two thirds of the women reported that they were moderately or severely stressed by the father's visits during the first year after separation and so did 80% of the fathers.

Jessica Pearson and Nancy Thoennes's (1988) study, conducted in Denver, Colorado, found a similar figure—that 22% of noncustodial parents reported blocked visitations. Kenneth Kessel (1985) reported that 40% of custodial mothers admitted denying their ex-husbands visitations with the children.

Sanford Braver and his associates at Arizona State University (Braver, Wolchick, Sandler, Fogas, & Zvetina, 1991) reasoned that custodial and noncustodial parents might report very different incidence rates of denial of visitation. Braver et al. interviewed 220 sets of mothers and fathers. Twenty-three percent of the custodial parents (93% were mothers) admitted denying visitations, although 33% of the noncustodial parents (the vast majority were fathers) reported that their visitations had been blocked at some time. On several other measures collected in the study, the parents tended to report their own behavior in a more favorable light than that of the other parent.

More recently, Joyce Arditti (1992), a professor at Virginia Polytechnic Institute and State University, explored a range of issues in an attempt to explain why some noncustodial fathers maintain visitations and others do not. Although 50% of divorced fathers reported that their ex-wives had interfered with their visitations, this was not a strong predictive factor in terms of whether the fathers kept up their visitations. Arditti found that geographical distance paired with the level of hostility during the divorce predicted low visitation rates, along with feelings on the part of fathers that the visits were too short and infrequent.

DECREASES IN VISITATION BY NONCUSTODIAL FATHERS

Although many fathers have their visitations blocked, many simply fade away (or are forced to "retreat from the battle"). Recall the figures given by Furstenberg et al. (1983) on frequency of visitation. They found, in their study of families in Western Pennsylvania, that at 2 years postdivorce only 1 child in 6 saw his or her father as often as once a week on average. Close to half had not seen their fathers in the previous 12 months. (The figures were higher for noncustodial mothers, 31% of whom had had seen their children at least weekly; another 38% had seen them at least monthly.) These rates dropped even lower over time. Among children whose parents had been divorced for 10 years or more, only 1 in 10 saw their fathers weekly, and almost two thirds had not seen their fathers in the previous year. Furstenberg et al. noted that their figures may be lower than those for other parts of the country.

Maccoby and Mnookin (1992), for example, studied a higher income sample of families in the San Francisco area and found that at 3½ years postdivorce about 40% of children living with their mothers saw their fathers for several overnight visits each month. Fully 64% of them had seen their fathers the previous month for at least a few hours. About 39% did not see their father on a regular basis through the year, although only 13% had not seen their father at all the previous year. Children in father-custody homes actually had higher rates of visitation with their mothers: Sixty seven percent had seen their mothers at least once in the previous month, about 18% of them had seen their mothers infrequently during the year, and only 7% had not seen their mother at all during the previous year.

Wallerstein and Kelly (1980b) found similar rates in their study of Marin County, California, families, which began in the late 1970s and extended into the late 1980s (Wallerstein & Blackeslee, 1989). Five years after the divorce, about 45% of the children and teens saw their noncustodial fathers for several overnight visits a month, with another 20% seeing their fathers about once a month. About 17% saw their fathers erratically, and 9% had not seen their fathers at all in the previous year.

Furstenberg et al. (1983) found that frequency of visitation for fathers was linked to income and education level. Fathers who could not maintain child support payments dropped out of the picture more quickly than those who could make payments. Twenty-five percent of the children of fathers who were college graduates had not seen their fathers in the second year after the divorce. This contrasted with 60% of the children of fathers who had dropped out of high school. Furstenberg et al. found that when the father remarried, visitation frequency decreased, and when the mother remarried it dropped still further. When both parents remained single, the percentage of fathers who kept up weekly visitations was at a high of 49%; when both parents remarried, the percentage dropped to just 11%. Part-time parenting is a difficult and ambiguous task that increasingly competes with the reality factors of new adult relationships, new obligations to step-children and children from the next marriage, and often increasing geographical distance that accompanies these changes.

EFFECTS ON CHILDREN OF LIMITED CONTACT WITH NONCUSTODIAL FATHERS

The issue of blocked visitations and absent fathers is very important to the courts in that it constitutes a large portion of postdivorce litigation. In addition, most law and mental health professionals operate from the assumption that there is a direct association between quantity of visitation with the noncustodial parent (particularly the father) and children's adjustment. If children are not seeing their father, then they must be experiencing adverse emotional consequences.

What does the research tell about the importance of continued visitations with the noncustodial father? How do children respond to this problem? At the beginning of the divorce revolution it was assumed that all children suffered from the effects of blocked, irregular, or decreased visitations. This was largely based not only on the poignantly sad vignettes from Wallerstein and Kelly's (1980b) study, but also on clinical experience. However, even anecdotal clinical experience has shown that children's reactions vary enormously. Some children idealize their fathers, even though their visits are brief and sporadic and the father has been unreliable. On the other hand, some children, although they see their fathers often, nevertheless resent them, have open conflict with them, or are caught up in the ongoing conflict between their parents.

Referring back to chapter 4, recall that children in joint custody, as a group, fare no better than children in sole mother custody as a group, even though they presumably see much more of their fathers than do children who spend the majority of time with their mothers. In fact, 15 major studies have concluded that children who have more frequent visitation with, and access to, their fathers do not, as a group, show better adjustment than those who have less or more irregular contact (Ash & Guyer, 1986; Baydar, 1988; Bray & Berger, 1990; Furstenberg, Morgan, & Allison, 1987; Healey, Malley, & Stewart, 1990; Hess & Camara, 1979; Hetherington & Parke, 1979; Johnston, Kline, & Tschann, 1989; Kalter, Kloner, Schreier, & Okla, 1989; King, 1994; Kline, Johnston, & Tschann, 1991; Kurdek &

Berg, 1983; A. M. Thomas & Forehand, 1993; Wallerstein & Corbin, 1989; Zill, 1988).

Recall Hess and Camara's (1979) study, which explored why post-divorce conflict has such a negative effect on children, especially on the parent–child relationship. They studied children from ages 9 to 11 whose parents had divorced and found that neither the frequency nor the duration of visitations had a significant effect on the child's emotional adjustment. It was the quality of the father–child relationship that was important in predicting low levels of acting out and good performance in school. Apparently, a high-quality father–child relationship can occur independent of frequency of visitations. "The child's confidence, or lack of it, in the tie with the father apparently depended less on frequency of scheduling than it did on the quality of interaction that took place when they did meet" (p. 94).

Lawrence Kurdek and Berthold Berg (1983), of Wright State University and the University of Dayton, respectively, evaluated 34 girls and 34 boys with regard to a wide variety of factors related to the divorce. They found that the child's adjustment to the divorce was unrelated to frequency or regularity of visitation or telephone contact with the noncustodial parent. One of the interesting variables was time spent alone with the noncustodial parent, which did predict good adjustment. Apparently, many children react very poorly to visitations when the father brings along his girlfriend and her children. "This finding supports comments that the quality of the interaction between the child and the noncustodial parent is a critical dimension of visitation" (p. 58).

Furstenberg et al. (1987) found that children of divorce were doing no better if they saw their fathers regularly than if they saw them occasionally or not at all. In fact, Furstenberg et al. examined their data by gender to see if perhaps frequency of visitation was more predictive of adjustment in boys than in girls. Again, they found no relationship. In fact, of the 10 statistical measures taken between the two groups with the highest and lowest levels of contact with the noncustodial fathers, 9 were in the wrong direction. "The children with high-contact fathers are doing more poorly than those who hadn't seen their fathers in five years" (p. 699).

Furstenberg et al. (1987) were so chagrined by their results that they suggested that their sample was perhaps not representative or that their measures may have been inappropriate. Nevertheless, they were forced to conclude that "On the basis of our study, we see no strong evidence that children will benefit from the judicial or legislative interventions that have been designed to promote paternal participation, apart from providing economic support" (p. 700). They added that the father's participation in the children's lives may benefit him directly and that it may benefit the mother in terms of shared responsibilities, even if it does not seem to benefit the children.

Marsha Kline of Yale University, along with Janet Johnston and Jeanne Tschann (1991), re-examined the data from the Center for the Family in Transition (Tschann, Johnston, Kline, & Wallerstein, 1989). They studied the range of types of conflict to which children were exposed, both before and after the divorce, and determined that access to the non-custodial parent and the father–child relationship were not significant pre-dictors of children's behavior problems at the 2-year postdivorce mark for girls or for boys. Kline et al. concluded that although children consistently express a strong desire for contact with both parents, "Neither the quality of the father–child relationship nor the amount of access the child has to the father was related to child adjustment, although both of these aspects were significant for the children two years earlier, at the time the parents filed for divorce" (p. 307).

Judith Wallerstein and Shauna Corbin (1989) examined the data from the Center for the Family in Transition with regard to adolescent girls and young adult women to determine if frequency of visitation was asso-ciated with good adjustment at the 10-year mark. The data at the 5-year mark (Wallerstein & Kelly, 1980b) had suggested that children were sig-nificantly benefiting from frequent access to their noncustodial fathers. However, 10 years postdivorce, the frequency of visitations did not predict long-term outcome. Neither did the pattern, length, or reliability of visi-tations.

Joseph Healey of Rhode Island College, along with Janet Malley and Abigail Stewart (1990), conducted a study in which they looked at chil-dren's adjustment with regard to the amount of contact with the father, but they also included several moderator variables, anticipating that the results may be complex. They found that boys and younger children ben-efited from more frequent and regular contact with their fathers, whereas older children, especially girls, had lower self-esteem when the father's con-tact was frequent and regular. The children as a group had high self-esteem when legal conflict was low. In these groups, visits were frequent and reg-ular, and the father–child relationship was close. The category of children who showed the highest levels of behavior problems were those in which legal conflict was high and the visitation frequency had dropped off. Healey noted that increased contact with the father is a two-edged sword—every contact may bring closeness, but it also brings loss for the child when it comes to an end.

James Bray and Sandra Berger (1990) of the Baylor College of Med-icine, summed up their study with "these results support the findings of studies which have found no relationship between the amount of time spent with the non-custodial father and children's behavioral adjustment in stepfamilies" (p. 418). Amanda Thomas of Loyola College, Baltimore, and Rex Forehand of the University of Georgia (1993) stated that "the failure of frequency of visitation to serve as a predictor of adolescent adjustment in this study is of interest" (p. 134). Valerie King of the University of North Carolina at Chapel Hill (1994) concluded, "Thus it seems there is no evidence for the hypothesis that father visitation has beneficial effects for child well-being, at least not for these particular measures of well-being" (p. 87). Johnston et al. (1989), in their study of families with high levels of conflict, concluded that "children with more extensive visitation and those making more frequent switches between parental homes are more likely to be clinically disturbed" (p. 588). Indeed, Nazli Baydar of Princeton University (1988) concluded, "On the contrary, the amount of time spent with the biological father is positively associated with two emotional problems: often cheating or lying and being tense or nervous" (p. 976).

How can this be? All of the above studies hint at the important variable of parental conflict. Recall from chapter 4 that the results on joint custody and children's adjustment are disappointing: Children do not, as a group, fare better in joint legal custody than in sole custody. Mothers and fathers may be favorable to this model, but the operating variable for children is conflict. When conflict is high, children in joint legal and physical custody are exposed to more of it, because of the increased number of transitions and the much greater level of contact between their parents. There are simply many more issues over which to fight. Faced with this situation, children are forced to use emotional reserves and coping skills, which might have been used for the developmental tasks of growing up.

Likewise, when children have increased frequency of visitations with the noncustodial parent—usually, but not always, the father—their fortunes rise and fall with the level of conflict that surrounds them. When conflict is low and children have meaningful time alone with the father, the quality of the relationship is enhanced, and the children benefit accordingly. When conflict is high, the quality of the child's relationship with both parents most likely deteriorates in direct proportion to the level of conflict.

Hetherington and Parke (1979) concluded that the connection between frequency of contact with the noncustodial father and children's adjustment is, at best, complex and multidimensional. When there were four factors in place—agreement in child rearing, a positive attitude toward the other spouse, low conflict between parents, and emotional stability of the father—frequency of contact between the father and child was associated with a more positive adjustment in the child. However, when there were disagreement and inconsistency in attitudes toward the child or when the father was not emotionally stable, frequency of contact with the father was associated with behavior problems in the child and more stress in the mother's relationship with her children.

Joan Kelly (1993) came to a similar conclusion in her review of this issue, which is an important one for the courts and for evaluators who are recommending visitation plans. Kelly stated that the relative importance of frequency of contact with the noncustodial parent must be viewed in the context of seven factors: (a) the child's age, (b) the child's gender, (c) the closeness of the child's relationship with that parent prior to the divorce, (d) the degree of conflict between the parents, (e) the mother's emotional adjustment, (f) the father's emotional adjustment, and (g) the mother's level of hostility toward the father (in mother-custody homes). She concluded that "No one study has yet included all of these variables" (p. 39).

Many of the authors of the studies listed above were reluctant to conclude that the amount of visitation time with the father was unrelated to children's adjustment, because this flies in the face of conventional wisdom and may be used, perhaps, by an angry mother to justify breaking off contact with the father. They offered that perhaps there was a benefit but that it was so subtle that it was not picked up by current measures. Richard Warshak (1996), who has become a fathers' rights advocate, addressed this issue and suggested that clinicians talk to the children. The children, he went on, will tell that the worst thing about their parents' divorce is that they miss their fathers. The children with frequent contact with their fathers feel "lucky" compared with their peers in sole mother custody. He offered the opinion that "the behavior checklists, which have become the darling of divorce outcome studies, fail to measure such emotions" (p. 407).

Perhaps the next wave of research in this area should focus on interviews with children in which they are free to tell their stories.

WHAT THE RESEARCH SHOWS

No empirical studies have yielded information as to how children fare in various access and visitation arrangements at different ages. Therefore, clinicians and evaluators are left to make educated guesses on the basis of the child development literature, the child's relationship with the noncustodial parent, the level of hostility between the parents, and the child's temperament.

Most experts suggest that very young children can adapt to two homes if the number of overall caregivers is small, the routines are similar, and the child sees the noncustodial parent frequently. Most experts do not recommend overnight visitations until children are 2 years old and recommend that weekend visitations should not begin until they are age 3 or 4. Lengthy summer vacations are not usually recommended until children are 4 to 6 years old. Joint physical custody is not usually recommended until ages 7 and 12. Teenagers do best to set their own schedules regarding access and living arrangements.

Visitation problems are common and an ongoing source of litigation for the courts. Studies indicate that whereas 20%–40% of custodial parents admit that they have blocked visitations, one third to one half of noncustodial fathers report that their visitations have been denied. Numerous studies indicate that there is a significant decrease in visitation rates for noncustodial fathers in the years following divorce. These rates are significantly determined not only by the father's income and educational level but also by remarriage and geographical moves.

Although the courts may assume that all children benefit from increased contact with noncustodial fathers, studies indicate that this is not true. Whether children benefit is a complex issue that is determined by the child's relationship with the father and the amount of hostility associated with transitions. Some authors suggest that children do benefit but that measures are not yet sufficiently refined to measure this subjective factor.

GUIDELINES FOR THE CLINICIAN

As shown in chapter 4, joint-custody families do not tend to litigate over unpaid child support in the same numbers as do mother-custody families. However, they do return to court to litigate over visitation problems and arrangements. Visitations may be blocked as disputes arise or as the parents return to court to request that a significant (or sometimes insignificant) change be made in the visitation plan or to reverse primary physical custody altogether. Some seek to end the joint-custody arrangement and consolidate a mother-custody or father-custody position as a way of resolving conflict. If the two parents cannot agree on matters, so this line of reasoning goes, then one parent should assume all control over the children's lives.

When these families go to court, they seldom refer to their own self-interests as the cause of their petition for a change but instead cite "the best interests of the child" as their basis. In some cases the best interests of the children really are the basis for the petition, as in cases in which the current visitation arrangement is clearly stressful or inappropriate for the child. If the issue at hand were economic, the matter could be easily settled by state statutes. However, it is the inclusion of the "best-interests" language and the allegations of distress in the child that necessitate the involvement of mental health professionals in the court process. These experts bring to the family court their knowledge of child development and temperament, parent–child relationships, and childhood psychopathology.

What do the experts recommend to reduce the effects of parental conflict on the child? First, the mental health expert must determine if the one parent is truly mentally unstable, is neglectful, has poor parenting skills, or presents any risk of harm to the child (see Figure 6.1). If this is the case, that parent's visitation time must be sharply curtailed and supervised by someone who can ensure that the child will be safe. A history of mental illness, violent or reckless behavior, or substance abuse is easy to verify, and the courts are generally quick to intervene.

More typically, however, one parent has minor objections to the care that the other parent provides or to the other parent's dating decisions or choice of new spouse. Each attorney may propose to the court that his or her client should get primary custody of the children because the other parent is impossible to work with. If this is the case, should one toss a coin and opt for "heads—the mother gets the children—and tails—the father gets them"? Most experts, along with the courts, feel that such an arbitrary procedure would unfairly deprive one parent of the right to be with the children through no fault of his or her own.

Instead, most experts recommend rearrangements in the visitation plan that shield children from as much of the conflict as possible. For example, a high-stress time for children is the moment of transition, when they sometimes cross from one "enemy zone" to the other. Emotions run very high at these times, even when no words are spoken. Suitcases and car seats are thrown on the sidewalk, legal papers are thrust into faces, doors are slammed, and cars screech out of the driveway. Children see their mother stiffen and look away when she sees their father or see their father glare at their mother and ball his fists. Children are frightened by this display. Many children begin to act out or experience physical symptoms at the time of transition (see chapters 7 and 8, this volume). Recall Wallerstein and Kelly's (1980b) study, discussed earlier in this chapter, in which they reported that one third of children are exposed to intense anger at the time of the visitations in the first year following the divorce. Two thirds of the mothers and 80% of the fathers reported that the visitations were moderately to severely stressful for them also.

This conflict can be avoided in several ways. One is for the parents not to encounter each other. The child can be delivered to a neutral place (the day care center, a grandmother's home, the school, the caregiver's home) by one parent and picked up later by the other. Some children are in counseling because of the stress associated with hostile visitations, and the child therapist's office can be used as a transitioning site. For example, the mother brings the child to the therapist's office and leaves. The father joins the child and therapist during the latter part of the counseling session, then the father leaves with the child at the end of the hour.

Another way is to substitute someone else for the parent at the parent's home or transition site. Allow a trusted neighbor or relative to bring the child out to the other parent while the residential parent is in another part of the house or somewhere else nearby.

Still a third option is to do the transitioning at a public place, such as a store, restaurant, or shopping mall, so that the parents are under pressure to control their emotions and act socially appropriate. A fire station or police station may be more suitable for couples who have been violent, or in some cases, the county child and family services agency, provided that these groups agree to the arrangement.

The second approach to rearranging the visitation plan is to reduce the number of visits. It makes sense that if the visitations are stressful for everyone, then the fewer there are the better. However, care should be taken not to do this at the expense of the noncustodial or secondary-residence parent. Not only does this deprive the child and parent of time together, but it may also represent a moral victory for the primary-residence parent. Care should be taken to maintain approximately the same number of days or nights per month with each parent.

A general rule is to review the developmental guidelines offered previously and move to a visitation plan that involves the longest separations that are recommended for the child's current or next age range. Second, the shortest visitations should be dropped altogether. For example, a 2-year-old child might have two visits per week with the secondary-residence parent, consisting of 1 day and night on one of those visits and 3 hours on the second visitation. The 3-hour visitation could be dropped, and the 24-hour visitation could be expanded to 36 hours. This may not be the ideal for the child developmentally, but it does reduce the transitions from 16 to 8 per month. One selling point is that it expands the secondary-residence parent's time with the child from 108 to 144 hours per month, a 33% increase.

For example, a 5-year-old child might have a visitation plan in which she spends two weekends per month with her father and has a midweek visitation of 3 hours each week. This results in 4 overnight visits per month and a total visitation time of 108 hours per month, but also means 12 transitions. The brief visitations could be dropped and the weekend visitations expanded from Friday to Monday, with dropoff and pickup at preschool. Thus the secondary-residence parent has 6 overnight visits per month and a total of 120 hours of time with the child, but with a reduction to just 4 transitions per month at a neutral place.

Recall the visitation plan mentioned earlier in which an 8-year-old child split her time equally between two hostile parents but had in all 22 transitions per month. This evaluator recommended to the court that the child maintain the joint-custody arrangement but simply alternate weeks with her parents, which would reduce the number of transitions to 4 per month. A good reference in this area is Carla Garrity and Mitchell Baris's (1994) book *Caught in the Middle*. These authors constructed a table for recommended modifications in visitation plans for hostile parents that were based on both the child's age and on the level of hostility that is present at these difficult points.

CASE STUDY UPDATE

Dan and Monica's court battle over custody and visitation lasted for a year. When it was over, Dan had charged $28,000 in legal fees to his credit cards. Monica's father had loaned her $32,000. Their net worth was only $50,000, so the custody battle left them $10,000 in debt.

I determined that Monica was stable and rational, although certainly being separated from 4-year-old Hudson and 2-month-old Rebecca was quite stressful. I also found Dan to be an adequate parent capable of caring for the children. I recommended that both children have two nonconsecutive overnight visitations per week (together) with Dan, with one occurring during the week and one occurring on the weekend. Hudson could be dropped off at preschool on Thursday morning and Monday morning, but unfortunately, because Monica stayed home with the baby, she and Dan would have to face each other when most of the transitions were made. Monica's family was too polarized in the battle to be of much use in reducing conflict at the visitation times. I also recommended that each parent be allowed two vacations with the children during the summer, each not to last more than 1 week in length.

In addition, I recommended that in 1 year—when Rebecca would be 18 months old and Hudson would be 5—the overnight visits be extended to two longer visitations per month lasting 48 hours at a time, plus two shorter visitations per month lasting 24 hours. If the visitations continued to be hostile, the shorter visits could be reduced or dropped and the longer visitations increased to three per month of $2\frac{1}{2}$ days in length. Thus, as the children grew a little older, the number of transitions could be reduced from 16 to 6 per month. By that time, Monica would probably be working, and the dropoffs and pickups could take place at the caregiver's home.

7

UNDERSTANDING THE STRESS RESPONSES OF CHILDREN CAUGHT IN POSTDIVORCE CONFLICT

CASE STUDY

Eight-year-old Megan set to work coloring in her calendar—blue for the days that she spent with her father, red for the days that she spent with her mother. I helped her to block-out the days on a generic calendar, placing a large S on the points of transition from Mom to Dad—red to blue—or from Dad to Mom—blue to red. First, Monday and Tuesday were blue; Wednesday and Thursday were red; then Friday, Saturday, and Sunday were blue. Then the next week the order was reversed—Monday and Tuesday were red; Wednesday and Thursday were blue; and Friday, Saturday, and Sunday were red. "There it is," she said. "All done. Half the time I go to Mom's and half the time I go to Dad's." Megan added up the S's— 12 changes. "How do you know who you are to go home with?" I asked. "By whoever comes into the cafeteria after school," Megan replied. "That's the one I go home with."

I checked my notes. It seemed that we had both gotten confused. "Look, Megan. It says here you go with Dad on Monday, Wednesday, Friday, Saturday, and Sunday one week—except you go home early to Mom's house on Sunday night—and you go home with Mom on Tuesday and

Thursday. Then the next week you switch and go home with Mom on Monday, Wednesday, Friday, Saturday, and Sunday, and you go home with Dad on Tuesday and Thursday." "Oh, yes, now I remember," Megan said with a frown. She redoubled her efforts to get it right and set to work on a new calendar. In a few minutes she had it all completed. "There, it's all done. All the days are even. Half are red and half are blue." We counted thirteen nights with her father, 17 nights with her mother, but 15 days with each, and 20 transitions.

"Don't you think it's a bit confusing?" I asked. "You did get it mixed up the first time. And you really don't know where you go each day. You wait to see who will come in the cafeteria after school." "But it's fair," Megan asserted. I sketched out a calendar in which the first 10 days were blue and the next 20 days were red, with one transition. "This is one way of doing it that some kids like. They spend the first part of the month with their dad and almost three weeks of it with their mom, with one overnight visitation in the middle of each long visitation. Some kids like this because it's not so confusing." "No, no no!" insisted Megan, "It wouldn't be fair to my dad. It has to be split down the middle, half with Mom and half with Dad. I have two Christmases, and two Thanksgivings, and two birthdays. I spend Dad's birthday with him and Mom's birthday with her." Megan continued her litany, on through the two summer vacations, as if to give herself comfort in the knowledge that her leading two separate but equal existences would give her life structure and stability.

"But your parents are going back to the court to talk to the judge," I continued, "because your mom thinks this visitation plan is too confusing. I am told that this judge may flip a coin and say 'heads, you go to your mom's most all the time, and tails, you go to your dad's most all the time.'" "No, no, no," Megan blurted. "That would be terrible! I have to see my mom half the time, or she'll miss me. And I have to see my dad half the time, or it will hurt his feelings. The judge can't do that."

I agreed that splitting Megan's time was clearly very important but that the two had to come up a better plan. I clarified that Megan needed to have a say in the matter and that I was in a position to be her advocate. So we set about filling in a new calendar—one that was blue from one Wednesday afternoon to the next Wednesday afternoon. Then it switched to red from one Wednesday afternoon to the next. "There, how's that," I announced. "Half red, half blue. You will always know where you're going because you will switch on Wednesday." "I like it," said Megan. "It's fair. Only let's make sure." She laboriously put a large D in each blue box and a large M in each red box. Then she counted the D's and M's. She added "Mom's birthday" on the 10th of the month, "Dad's birthday" on the 27th, and "my birthday" on the 16th. "Just to be sure," she said, "that I spend Mom's birthday with Mom, Dad's birthday with Dad, and that I have two birthdays, one with each parent."

When the case was finally heard, I recommended this visitation plan of alternating weeks to the court. I testified that Megan had a strong attachment to both parents and a strong need to please both parents. For her, equilibration, or keeping things absolutely equal, was a way of coping with her parents' conflict and thus keeping her life situation stable, secure, and predictable. The superior court judge, after hearing the evidence, asked me only how soon the new visitation plan should go into effect.

What kind of coping patterns are likely to be seen in a child who is 8-years-old and whose parents have been litigating and arguing through lawyers for several years? Do girls cope in different ways than do boys? How do children's coping styles change with the entry into middle childhood or adolescence? What is *equilibration*? What temperamental traits are more likely to sensitize children to their parents' conflict or to insulate and protect them?

In this chapter I explore in more detail the ways in which children cope with the "divorce wars" in their lives. I move beyond large-group studies and look at the specific ways that children cope with parental conflict, which vary by age, gender, and the frequency of transitions. Evidence points to the fact that children may make efforts to stay out of the conflict when they are young yet will inevitably be pulled into the struggle and begin to ally with one parent. Several patterns are described, and two more case studies are provided. Children do bring their own inherent personalities to the struggle, and I review research on the qualities that have a bearing on how children fare in the struggle—temperament, cognitive style, and problem-solving skills.

CHILDREN COPING WITH CONFLICT

In the late 1980s, psychologist Janet Johnston led a team of researchers in California in a series of studies of 80 families with 100 children who were referred to mental health clinics from four family courts in the San Francisco Bay area (Johnston & Campbell, 1988; Johnston, Campbell, & Mayes, 1985; Johnston, Gonzalez, & Campbell, 1987; Johnston et al., 1989). This was not a random sample of divorcing families but those who were disputing custody and visitation arrangements and had failed to reach agreements through attorney negotiations or mandated mediation. One child who was younger than 12 was selected from each family for the study. Fifty-six percent of the children were in sole-mother-custody homes, 14% were in father-custody homes, and 30% lived in joint-custody arrangements. The families were interviewed again about 3 years later.

These researchers sought to know the particular effects on children of being exposed to joint custody and frequent visitations with disputing parents. What they found is not surprising now, in view of the information in this book's previous chapters. First, they found that these children witnessed a good deal of verbal and physical conflict between their parents. Although the parents stated that they attempted to shield the children from the conflict, this was not the report that the children gave. Second, they observed that the most stressful time for these children was at the point of transition from one parent to the other, which was often, but not always, the time when they observed their parents engaged in conflict. Third, they found that children's coping styles varied with age, gender, and temperament but that several distinct patterns of coping could be described for each age group. Fourth, they found consistent evidence that children who had more frequent transitions from one home to the other in these highly conflicted families had more emotional troubles and behavioral disturbances than those who had less frequent access. Where the conflict was more open, the children had more severe disturbances. What is particularly interesting about this series of studies is that, for the first time, children "caught in the crossfire" began to emerge as individuals struggling to cope with their difficult lives.

PROBLEMS AT VISITATION TIMES

In Johnston and her colleagues' studies of children in highly conflicted divorced families, visitation times were an ongoing time of stress for both children and parents (Johnston & Campbell, 1988; Johnston, Campbell, & Mayes, 1985). Young children had multiple symptoms both before and after visitations. Both parents were quick to blame the other for the child's distress—the custodial parent often insisting that the visitation was too stressful and not necessary, and the noncustodial parent insisting that the custodial parent had in some way set the child up for emotional distress. Among the younger preschool children ages 2–3, separation anxiety was the most common response; these children resisted separating from the primary parent at the start of a visitation and resisted leaving the secondary parent when returning.

The majority of these children also showed much apprehension at the time of visitation, although they manifested it in an agitated, hyperactive manner. Over half of the children had tantrums and problems of angry defiance at visitation times, as well as happy and enthusiastic responses. About half of these children demonstrated stress reactions through regressive behaviors such as wetting, soiling, clinging, and wishing to sleep with the parent when they returned.

The children who were older preschoolers, ages 4 and 5, continued to have high levels of tension and apprehension at visitation times, regressive behaviors, and tantrums, as well as excitement and enthusiasm about the visitation. The biggest difference among children in this older group is that separation anxiety decreased, although it was still a problem for 60% of this group. Difficulty sleeping was a little less of a problem also. This group manifested more quiet withdrawal at visitation times. These children, being older and having better verbal skills, were more able to internalize their fears and worries in preparation for the coming conflict.

Johnston and Campbell (1988) found this same trend with young school-age children 6–8. This group used emotional withdrawal as a predominant method to cope with the stress, and 84% of the children were reported to be unusually tense and apprehensive at the time of the visitation. As might be expected, somatic symptoms increased in this group as they struggled to internalize their anxiety. Johnston and Campbell noted that the increases were not only in symptoms that might be anticipated, such as headaches and stomachaches, but also in actual physical illnesses, such as colds, fever, allergic reactions, diarrhea, vomiting, asthma, and eczema. Regressive behavior decreased in this group, as did tantrums. Resistance to visitations remained at high levels in this group, although it was manifested differently. Whereas the preschoolers demonstrated resistance through crying and clinging, the 6- to 8-year-old children were more likely to cling to the primary parent and engage in whining and verbal protests.

The older school-age children studied by Johnston and Campbell (1988) demonstrated fewer difficulties at visitation times, but their distress was still at higher levels than those of children from nonconflicted divorced homes. Regressive behaviors and tantrums had dropped to very low levels. They were still most likely to be withdrawn, quiet, anxious, and apprehensive, although a little less so than the 6- to 8-year-old children. Nearly half still experienced physical symptoms, and more than half were still resistant to visitations. These older children were much more argumentative in their protest and much more likely to take action to avoid visitations—to hide, run away, or lock themselves in a room and refuse to come out. About the same percentage of children, roughly half, were reported to be happy about the visitations.

EXPOSURE TO CONFLICT

That these children would be exposed to conflict should come as no surprise. Recall Wallerstein and Kelly's (1980a) study, which found that 30% of children (in an unselected sample of divorcing parents) were exposed to intense anger and stress at visitation times. Tension was so high in the first year after the divorce that two thirds of the mothers and 80% of the fathers reported that visitation times were very stressful for them as well.

Respondents in Johnston and Campbell's (1988) sample were referred for the study because of their involvement in the family court system and their litigation over custody and access issues. More than half had been to court repeatedly, and a few had had several full trials. For the sample as a whole, scores given to these families, as measured by the Conflict Tactics Scale (CTS; Straus, 1979), were at the 99th percentile on Verbal Aggression at 1 year postdivorce. Although scores decreased at the 3-year follow-up, the average Verbal Aggression score was still high, at the 90th percentile—in comparison with national norms established by Straus (1979). Eighty-eight percent of the parents in the sample had been physically violent toward each other at least once in the past, and 71% had been aggressive in the previous year. These children heard not only arguing and loud voices but also obscene language and threats of violence. Much of the time they overheard telephone conversations. They observed not only physical confrontations—with shoving, hitting, and slapping—but also saw objects thrown and smashed.

These figures are similar to those reported by Newman, Harrell, and Salem (1995), who found that, among a group of parents who were seen in family court because of conflicts over custody, 80% of the women and 72% of the men reported some experience of abuse at the hands of the spouse at some time during the marital breakdown. This abuse often included verbal threats and intimidation, and two thirds of the women reported physical abuse by their husbands.

What is known about the effect on young children of witnessing angry encounters? Several researchers from the 1960s through the 1980s have studied the impact of marital conflict on groups of children in intact homes. Recall that, in chapter 2, it was found that exposure to marital conflict both before and after the divorce may affect children more so than the actual divorce. What was not known by the mid-1980s was how children of different ages reacted to this conflict. Mark Cummings and his associates, Carolyn Zahn-Waxler and Marian Radke-Yarrow (1984), at the National Institute of Mental Health, explored this question with a group of 24 children whom they studied as toddlers (ages 1–2½ years) and again as early-school-age children (6–7 years). Mothers in these intact, not-divorcing families were taught to rate the children's reactions to naturally occurring episodes of anger in the home. The toddlers observed, on average, a total of about 17 angry incidents during the 18-month rating period. Thirty-eight percent responded with visible distress—crying, unhappy facial expressions, seeking comfort, or putting a blanket over their head. About 26% displayed angry reactions such as hitting, pushing, scolding, or yelling. A small number, about 10%, displayed inappropriate responses, such as smiling, and an even smaller number, 6%, tried to intervene by comforting the parent. Approximately 29% ignored the incident or looked away.

Cummings et al. (1984) found that by school age these children responded differently. (According to mothers' ratings, the children witnessed fewer naturally occurring incidents—about 5 per child.) Only 5% of these children displayed distress during the angry encounters, and virtually none displayed angry reactions. None displayed inappropriate responses of smiling or excitement, and a very large portion, 45%, tried to intervene. These children were resourceful—they comforted parents, sympathized with them, did good deeds to defuse the situation, tried to distract the warring parents, or stepped into the middle of the conflict and attempted to mediate the dispute. Fully 50% of the children took a neutral stance of ignoring or deliberately looking away.

Johnston and Campbell (1988) found similar types of responses at different ages in their sample of families locked in intense postdivorce conflict. Although Johnston and Campbell did not give precise figures on the amount of conflict witnessed by the preschoolers in their sample, they stated that only 2 of their 48 2- to 5-year-old children were actually shielded from the conflict. The predominant response of the preschoolers ages 2 and 3 was one of submissive distress: Roughly three quarters of them cried, clung, froze, or regressed. More than one third of the children, more typically the boys, engaged in angry acting out, as if identifying with the parents' anger.

As the children became a little older, ages 4 and 5, 32% of the group found ways to avoid the conflict. Nearly half the children, especially the girls, made active efforts to deter the fight by distracting their parents or telling them to stop or "make up."

As the children in Johnston and Campbell's (1988) study moved into elementary school age, they continued to be acutely emotionally distressed at witnessing conflict between their parents. The angry displays and tantrums decreased as these children used more internalizing strategies to manage their emotions. More than half tried to avoid the conflict, and a high number reported somatic symptoms such as stomachaches and hyperventilating. Attempts to control the fight reached a peak in this age range as the children acted more to prevent contact between their parents or to intervene in their fights. It is not surprising that it was their intrusion into the conflict that resulted in these children taking sides for the first time.

By late-elementary and middle-school age, the children's acute physical and emotional distress had decreased markedly. A larger number of children had opted not to actively intervene in the conflict. Avoidance efforts remained at high levels. However, perhaps as a by-product of the above changes, nearly half of these children had taken a stand with one parent or another in the conflict. In view of the above course of symptoms over time, it is not difficult to understand how allying with one parent against the other may have been for many of these children a way to ease their emotional distress and confusion. Although many of the younger children experienced the frustration and helplessness of trying to placate both parents and end their fighting, these children had given up and opted out of this middle position.

Janet Johnston, Linda Campbell, and Sharon Mayes (1985) gave precise figures as to the frequency and quantity of conflict to which their sample of 44 school-age children was exposed. By the parents' reports (which may have been underestimations), these children witnessed, in a 12-month period, an average of 11 verbal arguments between their parents, 28 instances of verbal abuse, and 7 episodes of physical aggression of one parent against the other. Again by the parents' report, the children witnessed approximately half of all hostile encounters between the parents. Thus, it is possible that the children witnessed or overheard more encounters than their parents realized.

These figures can be compared with those of families from a random sample of divorces (that were not necessarily hostile) studied by Roberto Gonzalez, along with Krantz and Johnston (1984). These researchers administered the CTS (Straus, 1979) to 60 women with children under age 18 whose names were drawn from the court records of those who had filed for divorce. Comparing only families who had finished the 2-year mark into postdivorce adjustment, Johnston, Campbell, and Mayes (1985) concluded that the rate of verbal aggression in the group sent to them for dispute resolution was four times greater than that of the divorcing sample seen by Gonzalez et al. The rate of physical aggression between the parents was 36 times that of Gonzalez et al.'s sample.

EFFECT OF POSTDIVORCE CONFLICT ON CHILDREN'S ADJUSTMENT

Janet Johnston, Marsha Kline, and Jeanne Tschann (1989) explored the effect of exposure to conflict on these children by obtaining a quantitative measure of adjustment—total score on the Achenbach Child Behavior Checklist (CBCL; Achenbach, 1991)—then dividing their sample in two ways: first by custody type, then by frequency of contact. (Keep in mind that all of the families in this sample had high levels of conflict, thus they could not be divided by high and low levels of conflict.) They used as their cutoff score the 90th percentile to select out children who were determined to be clinically disturbed.

Using this criterion, Johnston et al. (1989) found that 16% of the children were seriously emotionally disturbed. They were just as likely to be in joint custody as in mother custody or father custody. They were just as likely to have two involved parents as to have lost contact with one parent. Demographic factors were also unrelated: Social class, income level, ethnicity, number of children in the family, length of time since the separation, or parent remarriage had no association with level of disturbance.

The factor that stood out was frequency of visitations. Children who had more transitions per week between their two homes were more seriously disturbed with a broad array of symptoms. Furthermore, the higher the parents' Verbal and Physical Aggression scores on the CTS, the more disturbed was the child. Some of the figures also suggested that the impact of the conflict on girls' adjustment was greater than that for boys.

In an earlier article, Janet Johnston, Roberto Gonzalez, and Linda Campbell (1987) explored the relationship between the child's level of emotional disturbance and the degree to which the child was "caught up" in the dispute. Specifically, they asked the parents to rate the frequency with which they did the following: used the child as an active weapon to collect evidence or communicate threats and insults; used the child as a passive weapon by restricting the child's access to the other parent; used the child as a communication channel to send nonthreatening messages such as schedule changes; allowed the child to witness disputes by seeing the parent argue on the telephone with the other parent or denigrate that parent to others; tried to separate or protect the child from the dispute; tried to give appropriate, nonjudgmental explanations to the child about the other parent's behavior or decisions. Children who were more caught up in the struggle had higher levels of emotional disturbance at the 2-year mark than those who were not. Also a sex difference was observed: Girls were more withdrawn and depressed than boys. The older children were more likely to have somatic complaints and to be aggressive.

Johnston et al. (1987) found that the level of children's involvement in the parents' dispute, along with frequency of the children's access to the noncustodial parent, predicted levels of emotional disturbance. It is interesting that length of time since the divorce had only small, indirect effects on child disturbance, as conflict did not seem to diminish with the passage of time for many of these families. Nevertheless, these three factors—the level of aggression between the parents, the degree to which the child was caught up in it, and the frequency of visitations with the noncustodial parent—together strongly predicted high levels of emotional disturbance in children.

COPING STRATEGIES AT DIFFERENT STAGES OF DEVELOPMENT

Early Preschoolers

Johnston and Campbell (1988) observed the children of highly conflicted divorces in play therapy situations and made observational notes as well as speculations as to the psychodynamic basis for the children's behavior. Their primary conclusion about the early preschoolers, the children ages 2–3, was that the majority of them had difficulty separating from parents. However, because the majority of children from intact families or nonconflicted divorced families also would have difficulty separating at this age, comparisons are difficult to make.

Johnston and Campbell (1988) described 17% of the early-preschool group as "sad, resigned, forlorn, empty, or vacant waifs with dampened spirits" (p. 136). They seemed to react to separation with panic or defeat and, when reunited, were regressed and dependent, "like a ragdoll." Another subgroup of the early preschoolers, 30%, were more contained and inhibited. They were described as compliant, shy, and not willing to venture forth from their parents. They needed encouragement and direction to play, but when conflict was brought up in play, they avoided it or denied it altogether. The largest subgroup, 52%, strongly and aggressively refused to separate from parents. They were bossy, demanding, and oppositional. Some used strong verbal statements in their play to make sense of their situation, but their verbal abilities were naturally limited at this age.

Older Preschoolers

The 4- to 5-year-old children in Johnston and Campbell's (1988) study naturally understood much more of what was going on between their parents. They were caught up in trying to understand who was right and who was wrong in a particular encounter, what was real and what was not (i.e., a lie), and whether a parent was emotionally and physically all right. They were aware that they were the focus of the conflict and thus very important, but they also were concerned about their own safety.

Twenty-five percent of the older preschool children had behavior that at times could be described as chaotic, autistic, or bizarre. These children seemed highly agitated and had difficulty making eye contact or sitting still, and their thought content was highly confused and disorganized. They appeared, in fact, to have brief, mildly psychotic episodes. The following case study is an example of this pattern.

> Craig, age 5, was seen by me for a consultation after having seen two other experts. The first, a child abuse specialist, determined that he had been sexually abused by his mother, Cathy. The second, a child psychiatrist, determined that he had not been abused, that instead he had been coached by his grandmother Dolores, who wanted custody of him, to make bizarre statements about his mother. The psychiatrist noted the possibility also of brief psychotic episodes.
>
> Craig had made statements to the child abuse specialist about seeing his mother dancing naked, and he had made statements to the psychiatrist about seeing his mother whirl cats around by their tails before throwing them into the middle of the produce aisle of the grocery store. I also heard bizarre stories that could not be true, about his mother,

his grandmother, and about Craig himself (e.g., "The devil chased me once, chased me with a gun. I tried to kill him. I had big muscles. I could run away. I rocked him like a baby.")

Craig's mood shifted dramatically in play therapy sessions from coherence to incoherence, from calm to extreme anxiety, and from age-appropriate play to extremely regressed play. I noted in my summary report to the social services caseworker that Craig was confused about which was his "bad family" and which was his "good family" and that he had brief psychotic episodes when under stress. One of his statements to me was "I guess everybody is my bad family, and I'll go eat worms and die."

Craig was most disturbed when transitioning from his grandmother to his mother, who were litigating over custody of him. On one occasion Craig, his mother, and his grandmother were all in the waiting room at the same time. Craig was balled in a fetal position on the sofa between them. When aroused and walked down the hall to my office, he began growling like an animal. He groveled on the floor and began speaking in the grandmother's voice: "Mommy poked me in the eye with a sword." On a second occasion, Craig was sitting in the waiting room with his mother and grandmother sitting facing each other. Craig suddenly got up, walked over to a tall, potted plant and, without a word, began to chew the leaves on the plant. After that episode, I no longer scheduled Craig to be in the presence of both caregivers at the same time.

A second, larger subgroup of the older preschool children, 56%, adapted by becoming "pleasers." One way that they avoided conflict and defused their parents' anger was by becoming very appealing and helpful. This was particularly characteristic of the girls, who tried to be sweet and thoughtful as they took on a caretaking stance toward their parents. The boys were more likely to become silly and excited, entertaining their parents with swaggering and provocative antics.

A third subgroup, 28%, was actively trying to make sense of their parents' conflict and to obtain some emotional distance from it. They were able to use their good verbal and intellectual skills, as well as their ability to use fantasy themes in play, to come to their own conclusions as to what was going on. Although they were somewhat more anxious, they were also more mature and more emotionally differentiated or separate from their parents.

School-Age Children

Johnston and Campbell (1988) noted that school-age children (6–12 years), by virtue of their increased cognitive development, are more aware of what is going on between their parents. They are able to see that there are two opposing perspectives that may both have some merit. They have more awareness that they are the focus of an intense struggle—the prize, so to speak—and that they wield some power in this respect. They have an understanding of fairness in interpersonal relationships. They are more able to see both parents as individuals with strong emotions tied up in the battle over winning their loyalty. These changes mark how they cope with the conflict.

On the basis of their observations, Johnston and Campbell delineated four patterns of coping in school-age children and rank ordered them from healthiest and most adaptive to least functional and least adaptive: maneuvering, equilibrating, merging, and diffusing.

By *maneuvering* Johnston and Campbell meant that some children, 20% of their group, maneuvered through the obstacle course of parental disputes by refusing to get too involved in them. They maintained their distance by refusing to choose sides and refusing to carry messages, while actively manipulating the situation to meet their own needs. I have seen children develop passive–aggressive defenses in the midst of these hostile scenarios—a coping style which, under conditions of helplessness, is useful. These children seem to "not hear" when one parent is denigrating the other, claim "I forget" when asked questions about the other parent, and are unresponsive when asked uncomfortable questions about where their loyalties lie, seeming to be selectively deaf.

A few seem to maneuver through the conflict by actively telling each parent information that they feel, correctly, the parent wants to hear. Both parents are relatively happy with this—until the child's therapist brings them together, and they are astonished to find that they have been hearing separate but opposing stories about how each is the favored parent. Johnston and Campbell (1988) noted that the more well-adjusted children appeared to function as mediators and diplomats, whereas the less well-adjusted children appeared to be sneaky and manipulative, exploiting their parents' conflict for personal gain.

Another 23% of Johnston and Campbell's (1988) sample of school-age children were *equilibrators*, as was Megan in the opening case study. Rather than master the situation, as the maneuverers do, they try to cope by mastering their feelings, by keeping everything in balance, internally and externally. They suppress their feelings of guilt and anxiety over their parents' conflict, which results in a high level of psychosomatic illness. They feel worried about and responsible toward both parents. They focus on set rules to keep them equidistant from both parents and to minimize conflict and emotional upset. Although Johnston and Campbell observed this pattern about equally among boys and girls, I have observed this pattern more often among girls, the same girls who were "pleasers" at ages 4 and 5.

The largest subgroup of children in Johnston and Campbell's (1988) study, 43%, seemed to cope with the conflict by *merging*. These children, generally described as good, conforming, and patient outside the home, entered into the battle and merged with their angry parents. They were seldom described as behavior problems. Johnston and Campbell stated that "they learned to please by becoming nonpersons, by making no demands" (p. 165). These children seldom express any feelings that are their own.

During the early-school-age years, these children seem to merge with the parent they are with at the moment, taking on that parent's viewpoint and feeling what that parent feels. It is as if they block off knowledge of or feelings about the other parent at the time. If these children are away from home with one parent and encounter the other parent, they react with shock and confusion at the confrontation of two separate worlds.

Many of the older children, ages 9–12, were seen by Johnston and Campbell (1988) to merge by consolidating a position with one parent against the other. They parroted the parent's statements, often reciting a litany of the other parent's faults and shortcomings and past behaviors. Many of these stories turned out to be "family legends" rather than material that the child had experienced firsthand. More will be said about this group in chapter 8, which covers parental alienation syndrome.

The last and most disturbed subgroup seen by Johnston and Campbell (1988) used a coping mechanism named *diffusion*. These children, less than 20% of the sample and nearly all boys, were severely disturbed. They had not been able to form a coherent self through the years of parental conflict, to problem solve their way through the conflict. They had not found a way to stay out of or enter into the conflict successfully. Some had bizarre thoughts and brief psychotic episodes. Some were self-destructive and suicidal, whereas others had violent outbursts and extreme acting out. The following case study provides an illustration.

> Eight-year-old Angel had the dark complexion and curly black hair of his father, Enrique, a ballet dancer from Argentina. However, he was stocky like his mother Nancy, who had emigrated to the United States from the Dominican Republic at the age of 4 with her family. She met Enrique while he was touring the United States and was instantly smitten with the highly dramatic and romantic figure, although there were rumors that he had beaten former girlfriends. Once married and in the United States, Enrique planned to open a ballet studio. However, he did not adjust well to American life and could not find work. Soon Nancy grew disgruntled with her husband and felt that she had married beneath her.
>
> By the time Angel was 5, the couple was divorced. Enrique took the divorce hard and drifted from one low-wage job to another. He became erratic, volatile, and possessive with Angel. Several times he refused to give him up after a visitation. Once he flew back to Argentina for a year and dropped out of sight. Just as abruptly, he returned to the United States and resumed visitations. Once he learned that Nancy had begun dating again, this time a well-to-do business owner, he be-

came insanely jealous and began to stalk her. He made several false reports of physical abuse of Angel against Nancy and her relatives. He attempted to have Nancy arrested three times, once having her served by the sheriff's office at her medical practice. One night, when returning Angel to her home, Enrique encountered Nancy's new husband. A fight ensued in which Angel was pulled on by both men and dragged down a flight of steps. When Nancy saw the bruises on Angel's arm the next day, she took him to a children's hospital, which filed a report of physical abuse.

Relations deteriorated further between the two parents. Nancy had nothing but contempt for Enrique. She began, in subtle ways, to keep information from him about Angel and to marginalize his role in Angel's life. Enrique responded by filing legal actions against her: for blocking visitations, violating their divorce decree, and alienating Angel from him; finally, he petitioned the court for a change of custody. Nancy dismissed these as flimsy attempts by Enrique's to obtain custody so that he could get access to the substantial child support that she would be forced to pay.

Angel was described by the guardian ad litem as "anxious." She noted that he still slept on the floor of his mother's bedroom and was afraid to be alone. In our office visits, he was alternately anxious and afraid to speak at times, yet explosive at other times. My report read, "At the end of this meeting, mother brought up the observation that Angel has been afraid that she will call the police. She recalled the incident in which father dragged Angel down the steps, leaving bruises on his arm. Angel became suddenly explosive, rose to his feet, stamped and shouted. The volatility of his reaction was a surprise. He stubbornly insisted that father did not hurt him, that he fell down in the bathtub. His anger over her statement, and his defense of his father were quite intense."

In the second meeting, Angel had a brief argument with mother on the way to the office that then erupted into a full temper tantrum when I asked to open a package of markers that he brought with him. Angel escalated to the point of throwing objects around the waiting room, slamming doors, and running down the stairs. He was yelling angry statements throughout, yet also smiling and looking at his mother to see what her reaction would be. Mother reported that he had been pushing limits like this at home and at school with his teacher.

"Angel had to be tackled by his mother and forcibly led back into the office. There I engaged him in an encounter with bataca bats. Angel was finally able to express what was the source of his frustration —the fact that he didn't want the package of markers opened. . . . Angel seems to have an ambivalent relationship with his mother. Throughout this 45-minute encounter, he ran from his mother, then collapsed in her lap, shoved her and shouted at her, then went to her for a reassuring hug. He seems to be pushing away from her, while still being quite dependent on her."

In a later interview, in which Nancy was not present, Angel revealed to me his wish to change his last name to that of his father and to live with his father. He continued to insist that his father did not harm him. He also stated that he was afraid of his mother and felt that she would not listen to him. In my report, I noted that Angel may be in danger in his father's care in that if his father injured him, Angel would not report it to anyone. I also noted that Angel was at risk for serious acting out, such as running away, attacking his mother, and harming himself.

In reviewing the family histories, Johnston and Campbell (1988) noted that the etiologies of the families and children differed quite a bit. The families of the maneuverers and equilibrators had been entrenched in intense conflict for only a few years, and a working alliance between the parents had only recently broken down. The parents of the mergers, however, had never formed a strong working relationship, and often the child had been allied with one parent long before the marriage broke up. The families of the diffusers had been the most chaotic, with poor boundaries throughout the family system. Often the children in these families had caretaker roles with the parents.

Johnston and Campbell (1988) noted that the maneuverers and equilibrators also had the most going for them in terms of resilience factors. They were more likely to be intelligent, attractive, successful in school and in sports, and to have good social skills. The children who were mergers and diffusers, on the other hand, were more likely to have several strikes against them, such as being overweight, having learning disabilities, and being unskilled in relating to peers and teachers.

Johnston and Campbell brought up an important perspective: There are factors that are unique to individual children that they bring to the situation that may shape the way in which they respond to and are affected by ongoing postdivorce conflict. This conclusion comes from several lines of research. We know from the large body of studies on resilience in children that not all children are the same when responding to stressful, even traumatic, life events. Some falter, whereas others manage successfully. Some even triumph over marked adversity. Those who falter tend to have low cognitive abilities, poor social skills, irritable or difficult temperaments, and few special skills or talents. They tend to be boys. Those who succeed tend to have high intelligence, good social skills, pleasing personalities that engage the attention of helpful adults, good internal controls on their emotions and impulses, and special talents that elicit positive interest on the part of adults. They tend to be girls. The areas of research on resilience, first conducted on adults and then extended to children, have focused on temperament, appraisal, and coping mechanisms (see Garmezy, 1987; Masten & Garmezy, 1985; Robins & Rutter, 1990; and Rutter, 1987, for reviews on resilience in childhood).

Temperament has been a factor in predicting outcomes of how children cope with stress since the pioneering studies of Alexander Thomas and Stella Chess (1977). Temperament is one of those concepts that makes sense because it is based on grandmother's wisdom: There are "easy" children, and then there are "difficult" children. Thomas and Chess further delineated difficult temperament as being composed of four factors: negative mood, high activity level, distractibility, and low adaptability. *Negative mood* refers to the tendency in these children to be easily provoked into displays of negative emotion. Difficult children are often fidgety and excessively active, requiring much intervention by adults to get them to "settle down." These children are also described as not adaptable—they do not make transitions easily from one activity to another but react with angry outbursts and negative mood.

Recall the study by Block et al. (1986), cited in chapter 2, in which some children whose parents were destined to later divorce were found to have higher levels of disruptive behavior problems prior to the divorce. The implication was that the ongoing marital conflict to which these children had been exposed (rather than the divorce itself) had resulted in exacerbated acting out in a subgroup of children. One could also hypothesize that it is the children with difficult temperaments who are more negatively affected by marital conflict and ongoing postdivorce conflict.

E. Mavis Hetherington (1991) of the University of Virginia took this as a supposition when reviewing the data from her longitudinal study. She reasoned that children with difficult temperaments are caught up in postdivorce conflict in ways that children with easy temperaments are not. This assumption was based on the work of Michael Rutter, the eminent British psychiatrist and researcher who argued (1987) that difficult children, by virtue of their unpleasant behavior, elicit the anger of their parents more often than do other children. These children seem to act as lightning rods in that they draw the tension of marital disputes onto themselves. Once the target of displaced criticism and anger, they are more likely to respond with acting out, which elicits further angry responses. In addition, they are less pleasing to others and so less likely to elicit sympathy and support and less likely to use them when they are offered. Most are boys, and boys, as a group, tend to not verbalize their anger or seek support from others but to withdraw or act out aggressively.

Hetherington (1991) found that the divorced mothers in her sample, compared with the nondivorced mothers, were more likely to have rated their children as having been difficult infants. This was more pronounced for boys than it was for girls. Like Block et al. (1986), she found that children with difficult temperaments had parents who were more likely to divorce later. (Over the course of her study, many of the parents in the nondivorced, control sample went on to divorce.) Boys with difficult temperaments in single-mother homes were more likely to initiate hostile interchanges with their mothers, to counterattack, and to continue the fights. A few girls with difficult temperaments exhibited more negative behaviors in divorced families than in nondivorced families.

Hetherington studied the fight cycles between these difficult children and their mothers in detail. She found that "spontaneous negative start-ups"—initiating a fight with a child who is behaving in a neutral or positive fashion—were more than twice as likely to happen with mothers and sons in divorced families as in nondivorced families. If the boys were behaving in a negativistic manner, the divorced mothers were more likely to counterattack than were the nondivorced mothers. Once the fight cycle began with divorced mothers and sons, it was likely to continue for a longer span of time. This was especially true of divorced mothers and sons with difficult temperaments. Hetherington noted that these mother–son dyads were more intense and ambivalent than they were hostile. Often they had warm, positive interactions with each other as well.

Hetherington (1991) found little association between temperament in girls and the impact of divorce. Six years after the divorce, mothers and daughters seemed to have very satisfying and trouble-free relationships for the most part. The exception was early-physically-maturing girls. Girls who physically matured early and began involvement in heterosexual activities had very high levels of conflict in divorced (usually single-mother) homes, more so than in nondivorced homes.

Hetherington (1991) also addressed this question: How do factors in the mother, the child's temperament, and the divorce itself combine to predict good and poor outcomes? She found that when mothers had little or no psychopathology and the level of stress was low, mothers did not respond differently overall to children with difficult or easy temperaments. However, the presence of emotional problems such as depression or anxiety in the mother, or of a high level of stress in the home, combined with a child with a difficult temperament, increased the likelihood of the fight cycles described above. Furthermore, the combination of these two factors significantly increased the likelihood that the mother would respond to her difficult child in a negative way following the divorce. The availability of support systems had surprisingly little effect on the situation, in that when the mother's emotional problems were serious and stress levels were high, she could not effectively utilize support to deal with her difficult child. Mothers were able to use help only when one of these conditions was present.

One of the intriguing findings of Hetherington's (1991) study was that girls with easy temperaments, under certain conditions, actually developed more social competence and more adaptive skills when under stress. These conditions were (a) the availability of social support from adults and (b) stress levels that were low or moderate. Hetherington measured stress levels by totaling the presence of 12 factors, which included family conflict, parental divorce, remarriage, second divorce, and second remarriage. Protective factors included such factors as a good relationship with a parent who had the following qualities: good self-esteem, good social skills, and an advanced education. This remarkable effect was true only for girls, however. Hetherington concluded that after divorce, if the stresses are moderate ones and if they are spread out over time, so that the child can deal with and resolve them one at a time, some children are actually strengthened by the experience. Girls with easy temperaments who are helped through hard times by healthy, supportive adults benefit from having had practice at solving problems and become more responsive to and sensitive in dealing with others.

In a more recent study, and in contrast to the above, Stephanie Kasen of Columbia University, along with Patricia Cohen, Judith Brook, and Claudia Hartmark (1996), did not find the same interaction between predivorce temperament and incidence rates of divorce that was found by Block et al. (1986) and by Hetherington (1991). Again, Kasen et al., following a large sample of children over 8 years, some of whose families went on to divorce, were able to categorize the children with difficult temperaments and to follow more than 500 children who remained in intact families: 99 whose mothers divorced but had not remarried and 41 who were living in stepfamilies. There were no significant differences in the temperament clusters of Immaturity, Anxiety, Behavior Problems, or Affective Problems (derived by the authors from the Thomas & Chess, 1977, constructs) between children of intact families and those of families that went on to divorce. This was true for boys and for girls. What the authors did find, however, was that the children with difficult temperaments did have greater adjustment problems postdivorce, especially in remarried families.

Rex Forehand of the University of Georgia, along with Lisa Armistead and Corinne David (1997), reviewed the literature on whether the boys of parents who go on to divorce exhibit more behavior problems prior to the divorce (suggesting that it is not the divorce itself that causes behavior problems in this sample but rather the boys' temperament and response to marital conflict). Forehand et al. found three other studies that supported the findings of Block et al. (1986): Baydar (1988), Cherlin et al. (1991), and Elliott and Richards (1991). Later studies, such as those by Kasen, Cohen, Brook, and Hartmark (1996), Morrison and Cherlin (1995), and Shaw, Emery, and Tuer (1993), did not find a difference in levels of predivorce behavior problems between the boys whose families stayed together and those who later divorced.

Forehand et al. (1997) used an adolescent population to focus on this debate, and they corrected for several previous problems with better selection criteria and a wider range of measures. Like the other recent studies,

Forehand et al. found that adolescents in the to-be-divorced group functioned similarly to those who would remain in intact families but better overall than those whose parents had already divorced. Thus, they concluded that it is the disruption of the family itself, more so than predivorce temperament, that has a deleterious effect on children. Overall, Forehand et al.'s study and Hetherington's (1991) study generally support Rutter's (1987) hypothesis that children with difficult temperaments tend to be those who do most poorly in response to whatever adverse life experiences come their way. The factors that shape children's reactions may be a complex interplay of age, gender, temperament, the levels of parental conflict, and the parent–child relationship.

John Grych and Frank Fincham (1997) of Marquette University, Milwaukee, and the University of Wales, Great Britain, respectively, made the cogent point that children should not be simply viewed as an outcome measure—as passively affected by divorce—but that they should be regarded as agents who have a role in shaping events as well. More sophisticated research studies take into account this notion that children's behaviors may have an impact on parents' adjustment and subsequent behavior, as much as or even more so than the reverse. Difficult, noncompliant, and acting-out children may so stress a marriage that they contribute to the parents' divorce. Such children may intensify postdivorce conflict by their response to the divorce. Behaviors such as challenging a single-parent's already weakened authority, hostile blaming of the parent, school truancy, and aggressive outbursts may intensify parental conflict over which parent is to blame and how to handle such a child. Whereas some children are temperamentally easy and skilled at mobilizing support networks, difficult children may refuse to accept help from others or even may alienate potential allies.

ROLE OF COGNITIVE STYLE

A second line of research has studied how cognitive style affects the way children cope with divorce and postdivorce conflict. Martin Seligman (1990) of the University of Pennsylvania has made it his life's work to study the origins of optimism and pessimism and how these different ways of organizing experiences affect people's health, happiness, and ability to cope with stress and adversity. One of the enduring conclusions from his studies has been that people who are prone to depression seem to explain negative life events as due to internal causes, which are broad based, pervasive, permanent, and impossible to change. Optimists, who seem to shrug off experiences such as rejection and failure, attribute causes of negative events to factors that are external to them and short lived or that are at least circumscribed and easy to change.

Susan Nolen-Hoeksema, along with Martin Seligman and Joan Girgus (1992), conducted a longitudinal study, the Princeton–Penn Longitudinal Study, of how children cope with adversity. This group of researchers followed 400 3rd-grade children until they had finished 7th grade. Nolen-Hoeksema et al. wanted to know this: What predicts depression in children? A pessimistic explanatory style? Or the accumulation of bad life events?

Nolen-Hoeksema et al. (1992) found that the children's explanatory style, whether pessimistic or optimistic, remained fairly constant across the 5 years. Those who were pessimists tended to become more depressed over time. Those who were depressed in the 3rd grade tended to be more depressed more often over time. The more misfortunes happened to the children, the more depressed they became. Children who had more bad life events and a more pessimistic outlook had very high rates of depression. They also were described by others as more helpless when coping with peer problems and in the classroom.

Nolen-Hoeksema et al. (1992) also concluded that age makes a difference. In the younger children, the level of bad events was the best predictor of future depression. In the older children, explanatory style, along with bad events, predicted future depression. It may be that the younger children do not yet have a clear explanatory style because of cognitive immaturity. As to which comes first, depression or explanatory style, the authors concluded that it is hard to say. Clearly, children who are pessimistic react to large numbers of bad events with more depression; likewise, children who are depressed react to bad events with more pessimism about the future. The two factors dovetail to create a sense of helplessness in some children and chronic discouragement about their future prospects for a happy life.

Seligman, in his 1990 book, Learned Optimism, took a close look at 60 children whose parents had divorced by the time the study began. What he found was that the children of divorce, as a group, were significantly more depressed than the children from intact families and that they stayed more depressed throughout the 3 years that they were studied. These symptoms included sadness, acting out in the classroom, lower self-esteem, less enthusiasm, more worrying, and more physical complaints. These children also reported a higher frequency of bad events happening to them than the children of intact families—not just bad experiences that were related to the transitions of the divorce but also events that were seemingly unrelated.

As a comparison, Seligman (1990) and his team also took a look at 75 children whose parents did not divorce but who said that their parents fought a lot. The children of these families looked similar to the children of divorce. They were more depressed than the rest of the group, their depression continued long after the parents stopped fighting, and they reported a higher number of adverse life experiences.

Seligman (1990) theorized that when parents are engaged in intense and prolonged conflict, coupled with divorce, and the possibility of ongoing conflict, children are put at risk for depression. The depression leads to poor school performance and peer problems. A pessimistic explanatory style begins to form (i.e., "Everything bad happens to me"; "Nothing will ever work out for me"; "Everything I do goes wrong"). Ongoing school problems, coupled with pessimism, maintain depression over time. Ongoing postdivorce conflict reinforces the child's belief that bad things will continue to happen to him or her in the future and that he or she is helpless to do anything about it. The course is now set for depression in adolescence and adulthood. Seligman did not address the issue of how it is that some children handle their parents' conflicted divorce with pessimism and some with optimism. He did suggest, however, that children with a pessimistic explanatory style can be taught to view their situations more positively.

ROLES OF APPRAISAL AND COPING

A third line of research on individual factors includes a group of studies on the use of appraisal and coping mechanisms by the children of divorce. This work comes out of the seminal research by Arnold Lazarus and Susan Folkman (1984) on stress, appraisal, and coping. Lazarus and Folkman determined that it is not just a particular stressful life event that causes emotional problems such as anxiety, depression, or health problems but the manner in which a person assesses that event and how he or she copes with it that are crucial in determining the outcome. For example, people can determine that something that is happening to them is meaningful or not meaningful; they may assess it as something that they can or cannot handle, and they may appraise the situation as one in which there is a high likelihood of a good outcome or a low possibility of success. Likewise, people may cope with the event actively (e.g., "talked to a friend") or passively (e.g., "got my mind off of it and thought about something else"). They may use an external strategy (e.g., "I confronted the person with my anger") or an internal strategy (e.g., "I prayed and tried to think about the future, when it would all be behind me"). Past research on adolescents and adults has consistently shown that active coping, where change can occur, leads to good health and good adjustment. Internal coping (praying, viewing the situation in a more positive light, getting one's mind on other things) has proved to be effective when active coping is not feasible. Studies consistently have shown that avoidance coping (i.e., sleeping, denial, overeating, wishing it would all go away) is associated with a wide range of emotional and health problems and maladaptive behaviors in children and adolescents, as well as in adults (see Ellis, 1995, chapter 4, for a review).

Helen Radovanovic (1993) of the Clarke Institute of Psychiatry in Ontario, Canada, investigated the association between children's use of coping skills through their parents' postdivorce conflict and their overall adjustment. She hypothesized that the children who were more flexible and had a wider range of responses, particularly seeking social support and redefining the problem in a more positive way, would be functioning at a higher level than those who did not. The children, all between the ages of 7 and 12, came from 52 families referred by the family courts for clinical assessment. The parents had been separated or divorced for 3 years on average and were still locked in disputes over custody and access to the children. Mothers reported 25 incidents of verbal or physical aggression between the parents the previous year, and the fathers reported an average of 40 incidents.

Three times as many children in Radovanovic's (1993) court-referred sample had significantly high levels of emotional disturbance (30%) as did children in the normative sample. It should come as no surprise that the amount of conflict between the parents was related to the degree of behavior problems shown by the children and as reported by the parents. Radovanovic found modest correlations between the number of coping responses the children reported for each event of aggression between their parents and the children's good behavioral adjustment at home. She also found modest correlations with the children's ability to cognitively "reframe" the event, but not with the seeking of social support. On a discouraging note, Radovanovic also found a strong correlation between the length of the parents' separation and the children's low estimates of self-worth and competence. Apparently, the longer the parents battled and the more they battled, the worse these children felt about themselves, no matter how well they tried to cope with the situation.

Irwin Sandler and his associates at Arizona State University have conducted a series of studies over many years in which they examined the ways in which children of divorce appraise their life situations and cope with their life circumstances, to determine if what we have learned about adults applies to children as well. Sandler's findings are complex and will be summarized only briefly. Sheets, Sandler, and West (1996) found that children who appraised the divorce with self-critical feelings and fears of being abandoned were more prone to depression following the divorce. Similarly, Sandler, Wolchik, Braver, and Fogas (1991) found that children who appraised the situation with the expectation that they would lose many material possessions, that there would be "a change for the worse," and that they had a loss of control over their lives were more prone to anxiety following the divorce.

In a more recent study, Sandler's group looked at locus of control to predict children's response to divorce (Kim, Sandler, & Tein, 1997). Contrary to what they expected, having an internal locus of control did not give children an advantage in responding to stress. They theorized that this is because the events following divorce in children's lives are those over which they have no control, so internality is not advantageous. However, an unknown locus of control, or not knowing what degree of control they did or did not have over the coming events, did predict higher levels of stressful reactions to divorce. They concluded that understanding why events occur is the factor that may ameliorate stress in children following a divorce. Children who have the ability to understand why bad events occur may be able to make sense out of their world and predict future bad events. Likewise, children who can understand why good events occur may be able to reassure themselves that more positive events will happen in the future. Recall from chapter 5 that children who were highly involved in custody disputes did not appear to experience negative consequences from this process, as one might expect. This may be because they were kept informed, understood the nature of events taking place around them, and felt some degree of control over the outcome.

Last, Sandler's group has investigated coping skills in children in response to divorce. In two studies (Lengua & Sandler, 1996; Sandler, Tein, & West, 1994), this group found that avoidance coping was associated with higher levels of depression, anxiety, and conduct problems in children of divorce. The authors noted that for children of divorce, stressors may be chronic and ongoing long after the divorce, and avoidance may be particularly problematic. These children may fail to problem solve situations that are somewhat under their control or fail to use cognitive reframing strategies to deal with emotions about situations that they cannot change. Emotional and behavioral symptoms in some children dovetail with avoidant responses in a complex way, such that it is not known clearly which comes first. Sometimes avoidant strategies may be beneficial, such as when "not thinking about it" is used to quell inner turmoil or when behavioral avoidance is used to stay out of parental squabbles. The key here is flexibility.

Lengua and Sandler (1996) also found modest associations between active coping skills and lower rates of depression, anxiety, and conduct problems. Children encounter multiple stressors following a divorce—such as losses of the home, friends through a move, time with parents, and social status—that tax their coping skills. Children who can reappraise their situation more positively—for example, by seeing good qualities in the mother's new boyfriend—adapt to unwanted situations successfully. Likewise, children who use active coping—to make new friends, for example —are bound to fare better than those who do not. Finally, Lengua and Sandler found that children who have approach flexibility, who are able to adjust their coping style to the demands of the situation, and who have a strong task orientation (e.g., who can focus on schoolwork) had the lowest levels of anxiety, depression, and conduct problems.

The fact that these associations were only modest is not surprising in view of the studies cited above. Predicting an individual child's response to a difficult divorce may depend not just on the child's coping skills but also, as Hetherington (1991) found, on whether the stressors are spread out over time and whether healthy, well-adjusted adults are there to support the child's efforts.

All of these studies indicate that there are wide individual differences among children in terms of how they cope with postdivorce conflict. Many will do surprisingly well. These are the maneuverers of Johnston and Campbell's (1988) study. They are likely to be resilient children with good intellectual skills, children who can "read" their parents' moods, and have an acute sense of timing and appropriateness. They have a healthy detachment from their parents. They are pleasant and charming with others. They are likely to be described as "easy" children. They are never a behavior problem in the classroom or with caregivers. They are highly adaptable and flexible and make smooth transitions from one situation to another. They are likely to be optimists and have positive expectations about the future. When they are faced with problems, they actively try to think what to do, ask for help, or try to think about the problem in a new way so that they do not feel so bad about it. They have good social skills and make attachments to people outside the home who can be supportive and nurturing. They focus on specific tasks, such as homework, sports, or music lessons, as a way to cope with stress.

Children who do not fare well are less intelligent and thus are less adaptable and flexible in their thinking and less able to "size up" situations and problem solve objectively and creatively. They are more likely to have poor emotional control and to react to conflict with angry outbursts and defiance. This behavior is likely to invite the displacement of parental anger onto them, to alienate friends, and even to alienate adults who might have been supportive. Alone and angry, these children withdraw from activities and become pessimistic about themselves and their life situations. School failure and lack of friends both set the stage for a cycle of depression, further isolation, and angry acting out.

WHAT THE RESEARCH SHOWS

In this chapter I reviewed research on the particular reactions of small groups of children caught up in postdivorce conflict. These children witness a significant amount of conflict both before and after the divorce. Younger preschoolers tend to react with separation anxiety and tantrums. Older preschoolers show less separation anxiety but more withdrawal, apprehension, and tantrums. Early-school-age children continue to react with tension and apprehension but begin to experience somatic symptoms and demonstrate active resistance to the visitations with verbal protests. Older school-age children resist visitations more vehemently. They appear to minimize distress by allying with one parent against the other. The degree of emotional disturbance in children in these highly conflicted situations appears to be determined by three factors: (a) the degree of hostility, (b) the frequency of visitations, and (c) the extent to which the child is actively "caught up" in the conflict. These findings hold more for girls than for boys.

Many developmental psychologists suggest that children should not be viewed as outcome measures but as active agents in their responses to the situations. Common patterns among preschoolers are depressive reactions; oppositional reactions; chaotic, autistic reactions; pleasing; and distancing. Common patterns among school-age children are maneuvering, equilibrating, merging, and diffusing. The coping pattern chosen by a child depends on his or her emotional resilience and the level of family disorganization.

Coping patterns are also determined by temperament. Boys with difficult temperaments are especially at risk for poor adjustment in highly conflicted postdivorce situations; so are early physically maturing adolescent girls who act out heterosexually. Girls with easy temperaments seem to handle the conflict best. Children of divorce and children whose parents have high levels of conflict are more prone to depression and to pessimistic explanatory styles and feelings of powerlessness and helplessness.

Studies of coping styles in children have yielded only mildly significant results, in that children are genuinely powerless to have any strong impact on their life situations. However, these studies show that children who use active coping interventions (such as making new friends) tend to do better than those who use avoidance mechanisms. Also, children who cope successfully tend to reframe the event in positive terms, as opposed to those who see the divorce only in terms of loss and a permanent change for the worse. Finally, those with a strong task orientation, who shift away from thoughts about the divorce and focus on schoolwork, for example, seem to cope more successfully.

GUIDELINES FOR THE CLINICIAN

Disruptive or distressed behavior at visitation times is a common presenting complaint. The parent may say "My child has stomachaches before going on a visitation" or "My child does not want to go on the visitation" or "When my child comes back from a visitation, he or she is wild for several days." In my experience, the parent who has this complaint is almost always focused on the other parent as the source of the problem. This focus typically arises in the following manner, for example, "Do you suppose my child is being abused on the visitation?" or "I think my ex-spouse must let the children stay up too late at night and eat too much junk food" or "I'm sure my ex-spouse is trying to turn the children against me, and if so, I'm going to go to court and have his visitations stopped."

In ruling out possible causes of visitation problems, the examiner is warned to be extremely cautious, to entertain a large number of hypotheses and eliminate each one systematically, starting with the most likely and innocuous possibilities and proceeding toward the most unlikely and inflammatory explanations. The clinician must not allow himself or herself to be drawn into an alliance with the parent to go on a hunting expedition looking only for confirmation of sexual abuse.

A good rule is to obtain permission from the parent from the outset to interview anyone, especially the other parent, who may have information to share about the child's behavior. The motives of the parent who will not permit this should be suspect. The examiner should interview the parent thoroughly to determine if there are underlying hurt and anger from the divorce and a need for revenge. The best-case scenario in which to undertake such an evaluation is the following: (a) the parent is not hostile but anxious and concerned, (b) the parent does not appear to have any overt psychopathology, (c) there was an amicable divorce, and (d) the parent is eager to meet and talk with the other parent about the problem.

Given that the clinician has weeded out the unsuitable cases, here is a working model of factors to consider, in order:

Factors Within the Situation

1. Is there high tension, overt conflict at the time of the transition?
2. Are the transitions very frequent?
3. Is the child triangulated in the parents' battle?
4. Are the homes extremely different?
5. Is there no communication or coordination between the parents?

Factors Within the Child

6. Does the child have an irritable, disruptive temperament? An anxious temperament? A distractible, inattentive temperament?
7. Does the child have separation anxiety, especially if he or she is young?
8. Is the child strongly allied with one parent, especially if the child is older?
9. Is the child maneuvering—that is, expressing distress over separating from, for example, the mother to go to the father, then expressing distress over separating from the father to return to the mother, thus pleasing both parents?

10. Is the child equilibrating—that is, experiencing withdrawal, anxiety, and somatic symptoms out of a need to please both parents?
11. Is the child depressed, coping with the divorce with a negative, pessimistic explanatory style?
12. Does the child have poor coping skills? Is he or she coping with the transitions by using angry ventilation and avoidance rather than proactive approaches and internalization?
13. Is the visitation plan simply unsuited to the child's age, developmentally? (see chapter 6, this volume).

Factors in the Residential Parent

14. Does the residential parent have poor parenting skills?
15. Does the residential parent have a poor relationship with the child?
16. Is the residential parent hostile toward the other parent? Does he or she feel betrayed or abandoned by the other parent? Is he or she secretly pleased at the child's resistance?
17. Is the residential parent anxious or withdrawn at the time of the visitation, unable to separate from the child?
18. Does the residential parent have a history of seeking to reduce the time, importance, and involvement of the nonresidential parent in the child's life?

Factors in the Nonresidential Parent

19. Does the nonresidential parent have a poor bond with the child?
20. Does the nonresidential parent provide a home situation that is lonely and unstimulating?
21. Does the nonresidential parent spend time with the child, or does he or she leave the child in the care of unrelated people?
22. Is the nonresidential parent hostile toward the primary parent? Denigrate the other parent? Express an interest in reversing custody? Engage the child in an alliance?
23. Could someone in the home, other than the parent, be abusing or neglecting the child?
24. Could the nonresidential parent be abusing or neglecting the child?

This list is by no means definitive. However, it does provide a guide with which to proceed in a highly ethical and professional manner. The consideration of tension at the time of visitation is strategically placed first in the list, and pursuing the possibility of abuse, particularly sexual abuse, is last. The checklist may be used as a handout for parents to enlighten them as to all the possible explanations for stress at visitation times. It may also be used to develop a treatment plan. Problems related to factors within the child may be addressed through treatment approaches: play therapy, educational group therapy for children, and family therapy. Problems in the other three categories may or may not be amenable to treatment interventions. Court-ordered mediation may be more successful. Determinations of neglect or abuse would naturally be referred to child protective services and, ultimately, to the courts.

CASE STUDY UPDATE

The father and stepmother of Megan were contacted 2 years after I made recommendations to the court regarding her visitation schedule. The juvenile court judge did alter the visitation plan but awarded Megan's father the following visitation: each Wednesday night overnight, and alternate weekends, extending from Thursday night to Sunday mornings. This gave the father 12 nights per month and reduced the number of visitations to 8 per month. The father reported that although there were several small changes in the visitation plan, the parents were getting along considerably better. He was not sure, though, to what to attribute his success. He stated that Megan's mother was required to negotiate changes with him instead of announcing them to him. This gave him considerable bargaining power. Also, my report cast the mother in an unfavorable light, and the fact that it was in writing, he felt, had made an impact on her. Although the court action had cost him $25,000, he was glad he went through with it. He had formed a much stronger relationship with Megan and was able to play a major part in her life. He stated that he recommended that parents in his situation submit to regular therapeutic mediation or postdivorce counseling with a neutral third party to attempt to settle their differences.

8

PARENTAL ALIENATION SYNDROME: A NEW CHALLENGE FOR FAMILY COURTS

CASE STUDY

Don had not seen his daughters for 5 months. Jackie, his former wife and the girls' mother, had successfully blocked, evaded, or otherwise sabotaged his visitations during that time. The family was ordered by the court to undergo psychological evaluations after Don had petitioned the court for expanded visitation or custody of his two daughters, Renata, age 15, and Dorene, age 12. He was pursuing his current court action with the encouragement of his second wife, Lila, and the financial support of her mother.

Don and Jackie were married when they were teenagers, after Jackie had become pregnant. The couple's 5-year marriage broke up over allegations of affairs on Don's part, which he denied. Don, in fact, alleged that Jackie was entertaining men in the home. When they divorced, Renata was 5, and Dorene was 2. Although it was she who had filed for the divorce, Jackie firmly maintained to her friends and to professionals that Don had abandoned her with two babies to care for and no job skills.

In the 10½ years following the divorce, the two parents continued to experience extreme conflict. Jackie filed 10 contempt charges against Don for failure to pay child support. Don was self-employed, and his work was seasonal and irregular. He fell behind in support payments from time to time but always caught up on payments when work was good. Some of the contempt citations were for amounts as little as $28.00.

Jackie filed three reports of child abuse alleged to have occurred against the youngest child, Dorene, by Lila. All charges were investigated and found to be unsubstantiated. The couple appeared in juvenile court on three occasions because of the charges of abuse and had been court ordered into family counseling with a child psychiatrist. After 9 months of treatment, they stopped, with no reported improvement.

Over the years, Don, a rather passive man, had had his visitations blocked in a number of ways. At times, he gave up in despair and did not pursue visitations for up to 2–3 months at a time. He had attempted to watch his daughters' softball games but gave up after Jackie screamed at him to "go away and stop harassing us" in front of his daughters. His MMPI–2 profile suggested that he was a rather anxious individual with a tendency to somaticize.

Jackie was a particularly hostile individual who had been castigated from the bench by two judges for her campaign of revenge against Don. She was extremely hostile towards me and was difficult to interview because she resisted the evaluation. Jackie was clearly proud of her daughters, who were honor-roll students and first-rate athletes. She took all the credit for her daughters' successes and viewed Don as a "lowlife" who had nothing to offer Renata and Dorene.

Jackie described Lila as a "witch" who was bent on converting her daughters to Satanism. She told the girls that their father was not normal and that his house was possessed by the devil. (Apparently this was based on Lila's statement that she felt the presence of her grandfather in an old chifforobe that he had owned all his life and that now belonged to her.) Jackie was convinced that Lila had deliberately pushed Dorene down a flight of stairs when she was 22 months old, injuring her.

When the children had gone on previous visitations to Don and Lila's home, Jackie had written on pieces of paper and hidden in their clothes her own telephone number, the number 911, and the emergency child protective services (CPS) number "in case your father and stepmother hurt you." When the children returned from visitations to the father, Jackie stripped them and examined them for bruises and injuries and washed their clothes immediately to "decontaminate" them.

Jackie's MMPI–2 profile showed elevations on K and Pa, indicating defensiveness and projection of blame. She had remarried and divorced a second time in the intervening years. She had married a third time and maintained that the third marriage was very happy, although at the time of the final court hearing Jackie appeared with a cast on her arm, allegedly sustained because of abuse from her third husband, from whom she had just separated.

Jackie's wish was for Don to pay his child support and "leave them alone forever." In fact, she announced with pride to her daughters that she had made out her will in such a way that if she died, they were to "go to" her parents so that they would never "be given" to their father.

When Renata and Dorene were observed with Jackie, they sat closely, with their arms around each other and around their mother. They gave an angry report of grievances against their father that took the form of a litany, and many of the items were trivial. For example, they complained, as a sign of their father's lack of love for them, that he took them to a Chinese restaurant for dinner where the bill was only $28.00. They asserted that Jackie ruled their lives with an iron hand, telling them what they could wear in the morning and with what friends they could associate but that this was a sign of her complete devotion to them.

When the daughters were in the waiting room and about to be interviewed with their father, Renata would cry continuously, and Dorene would hold her and console her with an angry scowl on her face. During the first meeting with Don, Renata's crying progressed to wailing, and Dorene glared more intensely. Renata's thoughts became loose and disorganized as she protested to Don that Lila "will turn us into devil-worshippers" if they were forced by the court to have visitations with them. Both girls staunchly maintained that Lila was a Satanist.

Dorene insisted that she, at the age of 22 months, remembered Lila pushing her down a flight of stairs. She continued to insist on this memory, although it was pointed out to her that she could not possibly remember an event at that age.

When asked how they would feel if the judge awarded custody of them to their father, Renata became irrational and vaguely suicidal. She wailed, "I would die. It would kill me as a person. My mom is all I've ever known. I'd die without her. She'd die trying to get us back."

In the second meeting with Don, Renata still cried, and Dorene still glared and comforted Renata, but the two were much calmer. They appeared to enjoy getting answers from their father to questions such as "Why did you not come to our softball games?" and "Why did you stop seeing us for so long?"

Scenes such as the above are now commonplace to clinicians who work with children and families who are litigating over custody and visitation issues. The courts are faced with these questions:

- Are the children's fears of the targeted parent real or imagined?
- Is the child competent to give an opinion as to whether to proceed with visitations?
- Has the child been "brainwashed" by a malicious parent?
- If the fears are groundless, should the children be ordered to

continue visitations, even though they would suffer apparent emotional distress as a result?

- Can the child ever establish a bond with the targeted parent while still living in the home of the alienating parent?

These are not simple questions, inasmuch as the courts are charged with protecting the safety of minor children. While doing so, the courts must secure the legal rights of both the alienating as well as the targeted parent.

Many such cases are referred to clinicians to resolve in the hope that clinicians can shed light on some of these issues. The clinicians must answer the following questions: Who is the patient? Is it the child? The child and the targeted parent as a family unit? The alienating parent? Or is it the alienating parent and the child? What are the goals of treatment? The potential answers to these questions are especially conflicting in that the goal of the alienating parent may be to sever all ties with the targeted parent. The goals of the targeted parent may be to re-establish a harmonious visitation pattern with the child or to reverse custody. The therapist may determine that the goal of treatment is to de-enmesh the alienating parent and child. The goals of the court may be to simply head off further litigation and thus reduce the court's burdened load of domestic cases. The clinician cannot align himself or herself with all agendas and is thus likely to be the target of hostility from one or several sources.

In this chapter I review what is known about children who are extremely allied with one parent, resisting visitations bitterly and reacting with extreme distress to contact with the targeted parent. In the opening section I show how and when the term *parental alienation syndrome* (PAS) arose, then follow with a summary of the research to date. Although there have been no well-controlled, empirical studies on this topic, many clinicians who have first-hand experience with this problem have described common characteristics of this group. Because this disorder has been described as a *folie à deux* relationship, I review what is known about *folie à deux* and draw parallels with PAS. These studies and others are integrated into an overall formulation of the development and maintenance of PAS. The chapter concludes with a discussion of treatment approaches. These cases have been known by clinicians to be intractable to traditional forms of treatment, and clinicians take widely opposing and controversial viewpoints as to how the courts and psychotherapists should intervene.

CONCEPTUALIZATION OF PAS

As the wave of custody disputes began to move through the courts, child psychiatrist Richard Gardner (1987) described a pattern of behavior seen with increasing frequency in children involved in protracted custody disputes—a pattern of hostility, alienation, and cognitive distortion, usually directed toward their noncustodial parent. He coined the term *parental alienation syndrome (PAS)* to describe this symptom profile and elaborated with case examples. Gardner went on to say that in about 90% of the hundreds of cases of PAS he had seen to that time, the children were in mother-custody homes and were severely alienated from their fathers. The situation was the reverse in the remaining 10% of the cases. He later developed the description and treatment of this syndrome into the book *Parental Alienation Syndrome* (Gardner, 1992a).

Gardner's term has now come to be the standard used to describe this phenomenon, although sometimes it describes the children's behavior and at other times the parent's behavior as well. This point may be subtle, but it is an important one, because it contributes to confusion in this field. A *syndrome*, such as posttraumatic stress disorder (PTSD), for example, refers to a set of symptoms experienced by a victim of extreme trauma. It does not refer to characteristics of the perpetrator of the trauma or to the relationship between the perpetrator and the victim. However, in recent articles, Michael Bone and Michael Walsh (1999) gave four criteria for PAS—two that describe the actions of the alienating parent, one that describes the history of the relationship between the alienated parent and child, and one that describes the child's behavior in regard to the first three elements. Gardner (1999), in a recent article, provided a schema with which to determine PAS that is based almost entirely on the characteristics of the alienating parent.

Although the term PAS is widely used, it is not universally respected. It is not recognized by the American Psychiatric Association because no research has established the specific criteria for a diagnosis of this syndrome. Furthermore, there are no data establishing incidence rates, the course of the syndrome over time, sex differences, or prognosis—information that is available for PTSD, for example. Custodial mothers are the group most often blamed for this disorder in children, and their behavior is often referred to as "brainwashing." For these reasons, feminists take issue with the term PAS because they perceive it as imparting a bias against women.

All these objections aside, PAS has found acceptance by clinicians as it is consistently seen in cases of protracted, hostile custody and visitation disputes. Gardner (1992a) described elements of this syndrome by presenting case material. These children are first and foremost obsessed with professing hatred of the targeted parent. They speak of their hatred in a highly emotionally charged manner, without embarrassment or guilt. Even clothing or toys that come from the targeted parent's home may be viewed as "contaminated." The justifications that the children make for their hatred are typically baseless and trivial events that would be forgotten by most children. Third, these children have a lack of ambivalence about both parents. The alienating parent is all good, and the targeted parent is all bad. Evidence of once having had positive experiences with the all-bad parent are dismissed as having been forgotten or having been coerced. Gardner went on to assert that these children try to protect the alienating parent from criticism by asserting that these opinions are completely their own. These children will take the alienating parent's side in a conflict, even distorting the evidence to maintain their position. In doing so, their story often has the sound of a "borrowed scenario"—they use the exact wording and phrasing used by the alienating parent. A sixth trait of these children is their lack of guilt over their mistreatment and rejection of the targeted parent and their complete lack of gratitude for gifts, time and attention, and financial support. Last, Gardner noted that the hatred of these children for the targeted parent often extends to the parent's extended family—aunts, uncles, stepbrothers and stepsisters, even the grandparents. The reason given is often that these hated people are trying to influence the child to have a better relationship with the targeted parent.

Gardner (1992a) went on to state that in many cases the alienating parent is actively programming the child, or "brainwashing" him or her, to hate the other parent. Gardner gave examples of one parent actively denigrating the other parent to the child, reconstructing the events of the divorce in such a way as to put all the blame on the other parent, and destroying all reminders of the absent parent. The alienating parent often blocks visitations, insists on fewer visitations, and refuses to put telephone calls through or lets the answering machine get them. This parent may denigrate the targeted parent by insisting he park on the street, not come up the steps, and not arrive a minute too early or too late; by not notifying the targeted parent of school events; or by not forwarding report cards, school photographs, and so on. The alienating parent will schedule events that conflict with visitation times and refuse to be flexible in rearranging visitation times. These parents will trivialize the importance of any contact with the targeted parent and insist that the other parent's attempts to have a relationship with the children constitute "harassment."

However, in other cases the alienation process may be subconscious or completely unconscious. These parents will hint that there are terrible secrets they could tell about the targeted parent without naming them. They will maintain a position of neutrality about the visitations, insisting that the child should make the decision about whether to have a relationship with the other parent. Some will subtly suggest to the children that they may be in danger on the visitation, by comments such as "I hope you'll be okay." Others undermine the visitation by implying that they will be unduly sad or lonely while the child is away, thus making the child feel guilty. Gardner also included as unconscious programming those parents who move to a distant city or state for no other reason than to minimize the hated parent's role in the children's lives and to make any contact a hardship on the targeted parent.

Gardner (1992a) attributed the development of the PAS phenomenon to the changes in the courts' handling of custody cases that have occurred since the late 1970s. Prior to that time, the tender-years presumption, in which the mother was automatically awarded custody at least of young children, prevailed. Since the late 1970s this principle has been regarded as sexist and out of date. Fathers are now to be considered on an equal footing with mothers when it comes to custody of the children. Custodial decisions are now based on fitness, attachment, and suitability rather than on gender.

Gardner (1992a) asserted that this shift has brought about intense litigation between mothers and fathers for custody at the time of the divorce, as well as ongoing petitions for a change of custody over the subsequent years after the divorce. According to him, it has also contributed to the perception by many mothers that their bond with their children is threatened by fathers and by the courts and therefore more precarious. As he sees it, mothers have been more likely to alienate their children from fathers as an effort to secure their traditionally primary role as parent to their children. Gardner sees this process as one in which the alienating parent—which is the mother in 90% of cases, according to him—sets about brainwashing the child, overtly and intentionally, if not subconsciously as well.

Although these social changes may be contributing factors, it is nevertheless clear that many couples ride out the pain and loss of the divorce relatively smoothly, whereas others become entrenched and polarized in deeply hostile custody and visitation disputes, to the detriment of all involved. Gardner does not consider the role that may be played by family dynamics, parental psychopathology, situational factors, or temperament traits that may predispose some children to the development of PAS while leaving others unscathed.

Gardner (1992a) made brief mention of the fact that the custodial parent engages the child in a *folie à deux* relationship in PAS. He sees a similarity between the two disorders in that in each one a more influential person induces a form of psychiatric disturbance in a more suggestible person. Like the induced individuals, children are suggestible and often seek to ingratiate themselves to the parent.

Gardner further explicated PAS by delineating its three degrees of severity. In mild cases, the mother (primarily) has a healthy emotional bond with the children. She may have hostile feelings toward the father but realizes that these are destructive to the children and chooses not to litigate or to marginalize him in the children's lives. The children may be ambivalent about visitation but are allowed to express some affection for the other parent in their mother's presence. They may voice some opposition to the father merely to strengthen their mother's position in a dispute.

In moderate cases, the alienating parent is less likely to be paranoid and can differentiate between allegations that are preposterous and those that are possible. The children in this category are still hostile, although less fanatical than those in the severe category, and often become comfortable with the targeted parent once they are alone with him or her.

It is the most entrenched cases to which Gardner refers as *severe alienation syndrome*. In this form of PAS the alienating parent is paranoid and fanatical. He or she believes firmly that occurrences of abuse have occurred, although no evidence can be found and despite the fact that the allegations may be outrageous. The children are similarly fanatical. They may become panic-stricken and hysterical over the possibility of visitation with the targeted parent. Their agitation and hostility may be so severe as to make the visitation unfeasible and may not abate, even with prolonged contact with the targeted parent.

RESEARCH ON PAS AND CHILDREN WHO REFUSE VISITATION

John Dunne and Marsha Hedrick (1994), both practitioners in Seattle, Washington, attempted a cursory analysis of cases of PAS that they had seen in their practices. Using Gardner's books and delineating 14 characteristics, they selected 16 families that met Gardner's criteria. In 14 cases the mother had primary custody of the children and was the alienating parent. In 2 cases the alienating parents were the noncustodial mother and the noncustodial father. There were 26 children in these families, 21 of whom met the criteria for PAS. Twelve were female, and 9 were male. Thus mother–daughter dyads were most common, followed by mother–son dyads. Dunne and Hedrick found these children to be of a wide variety of ages and for the alienation to have begun over a broad span of time, from immediately after the separation to many years later.

Janet Johnston and Linda Campbell (1988) have studiously avoided any reference to a syndrome in their description of the problem. Instead they refer to the problem broadly as one of "children who refuse visitation." This may include a wide range of behavior in which the child complains about the nonresidential parent and resists spending time with him or her. In extreme cases, the child may refuse to visit the other parent.

Johnston and Campbell (1988) prefer to use the term *parent–child alignment* to describe cases in which the child makes an overt or covert preference for one parent and denigrates and rejects the other. In severe cases, in which the child is allied with a parent who is engaged in all-out warfare against the other parent, they refer to the formation of "an unholy alliance." They describe families and children with characteristics that are similar to those described by Gardner. Some parents in Johnston and Campbell's study, particularly those with paranoid personalities, were seen as having polarized their views of the ex-spouse, and sometimes their views of the ex-spouse's new partner, perceiving them as "evil" or as "the devil." Occasionally these delusions escalated to psychotic proportions.

The Center for the Family in Transition, in Corte Madera, California, has followed this phenomenon since the early Wallerstein and Kelly (1980b) study, in which 20% of the children of "normal" divorces were conflicted about visitations and another 11% were refusing to go on visitations. Wallerstein and Kelly noted that the subgroup of "refusers" was primarily composed of the older children; most were between the ages of 9 and 12. The reasons they gave were varied. Some were angry and were retaliating against the father for his past lack of involvement. Others found the visitations to the father's home empty, lonely, boring, and alienating. Some were anxious because the father made little effort to nurture or soothe them or to make accommodations for their ages and interests. Still another subgroup was clearly allying with one parent against the other. Twice as many of these children allied with the mother as did with the father. In this study, mother–son alignments were the most common. Whereas alignments with the noncustodial fathers faded quickly, the alignments with custodial mothers were remarkably stable over the 18-month follow-up period. However, at the 5-year follow-up, almost all of the alignments had faded (the majority of the children were then ages 14–17), and the children had resumed a relationship with both parents.

Robert Racusin, Stuart Copans, and Peter Mills (1994), of Dartmouth Medical School, conducted a more recent analysis of children who refuse visitation. These child psychiatrists reviewed the records of 100 children seen at their outpatient clinic and found 12 who were refusing to go on visitations to a noncustodial parent. The reasons they gave for not visiting a father were the father was mean to the mother, the child was angry at the father, the child was afraid of the father's anger, and the father was uninterested in the child, in that order. The reasons given for not visiting mothers were overwhelmingly that the child was afraid of the mother's anger. These 12 children were equally likely to be boys as girls, whereas the nonrefusing clinic population consisted largely of boys. These children were overwhelmingly the oldest in the family as well.

The children were found to be functioning at a lower level on the Child Global Assessment Scale (CGAS; Shaffer et al., 1985) and to be more often placed in a special education program. The custodial parents of the refusers were more likely to have a history of problems with substance abuse, suicidal behavior, psychotic symptoms, and violence toward their spouse. However, the noncustodial parents of refusers had higher rates of substance abuse than did the control group. Racusin et al. suggested that it may be the oldest daughter in the family who is particularly at risk for this problem, in that she is likely to identify with her mother and feel a strong need to take a protective stance toward both younger siblings and a mother who may be depressed or mentally ill.

Janet Johnston (1993) reviewed data on a large sample of children who refused visitation—data that were gathered from two studies. One group—100 children from 80 lower- to middle-income families—were seen from 1982 to 1984 (Johnston & Campbell, 1988). The other sample —75 children from 60 upper-income families—were seen from 1989 to 1990 (Johnston, 1992). All the families had been involved in severe conflict, physical violence, or both, over visitation issues and had been court ordered into mediation. Recall from chapter 7 that the children's reactions followed several trends that were clearly a function of their ages. The younger children experienced the greatest distress at times of visitation, with overt symptoms of resistance dropping from 74% of the toddler group to 56% of the 9- to 12-year-old group. The second, later sample showed a similar trend, with 100% of the preschool group showing signs of distress and resistance, dropping to 57% of the 9- to 12-year-old group. Likewise, the tendency for the children to take sides showed a dramatic increase in the first sample. None of the preschoolers took sides, but siding with one parent increased to 21% of the early-school-age children and 46% of the 9- to 12-year-olds.

Johnston (1993) reviewed the data from both samples and determined that 69 of the entire sample of 155 children from highly conflicted families, or roughly 45%, had formed an alignment with one parent. The figures for the older group—39 of the 51 children ages 9 to 12 years, or 76%, had formed an alignment. The figures from the combined studies are shown in Table 8.1.

In viewing how this process takes place, Johnston (1993) reviewed the data, both hypothetical and empirical, for six factors. First, she reasoned that younger children experience the most distress at visitation times, because separation anxiety is a salient issue for children age 4 and younger. Although Johnson did not find that degree of emotional disturbance in the parent predicted degree of distress and resistance in younger children, she

TABLE 8.1
Percentages of Children in Alignments With Alienating Parents

Degree of alignment	Age (years)			
	2–3	4–5	6–8	9–12
Mild	9	24	33	39
Strong	0	2	10	37
Total N	23	42	39	51

Note. From J. Johnston, "Children of Divorce Who Refuse Visitation," in C. Depner and J. Bray (Eds.), Nonresidential Parenting: New Vistas in Family Living, pp. 109–135. ©1993 by Sage Publications, Inc. Reprinted by Permission of Sage Publications, Inc.

did find that the parents of the most resistant young children were the most skeptical of and ambivalent about the value of the visitations to the child. Thus, they often did little to soothe the child or reassure the child that he or she would be safe and well cared for.

Second, the child's cognitive understanding of the parental dispute was a factor in predicting resistance and the formation of alignments. Recall from chapter 7 that loyalty conflicts are at their peak among 6- to 8-year-old children. The experience of maintaining loyalties to both warring parties, while being developmentally able to see both points of view, created a level of cognitive dissonance that was unbearable for the children. Forming an intense alignment was a way for preadolescent children to decrease this dissonance and honor their maturity, in that they were "old enough to take a stand."

Third, although she cited no particular figures, Johnston observed that the children who formed alignments had been in postdivorce situations in which intense conflict had gone unabated for several years. A fourth factor Johnston (1993) reviewed is that of the degree of emotional disturbance of both the child and parent. She noted that in cases of strong alignments, the child's reality distortion and denigration of the targeted parent took on a bizarre quality. It is these cases that she considers to be most similar to Gardner's cases of severe PAS. In these cases the children were rated as more emotionally disturbed, as measured by the Achenbach Child Behavior Checklist (Achenbach, 1991), the Teacher–Child Rating Scale (Hightower et al., 1986), and the clinical rating scales derived by Johnston. In addition, the alienating parents in these dyads were also seen as more disturbed, in that they had higher ratings on the Derogatis Brief Symptom Inventory (Derogatis & Spencer, 1982). Johnston drew on object-relations theory and attachment theory to suggest that these parents (primarily mothers), out of their own pain and loss following the divorce, are not able to be responsive to their children and allow separation and individuation but instead use the children to reflect their own emotional injuries.

A fifth factor is the degree to which the child has witnessed open hostility and physical violence between the two warring parents. While again citing no figures, Johnston (1993) observed that children who formed strong alignments had witnessed a considerable degree of actual and threats of violence between their parents. Some appeared to experience flashbacks of violent encounters that they had heard or witnessed when they were very young and were still fearful, even though the violence had ceased. Last, Johnston considered the degree to which the targeted parent had responded to the child's rejection with counter-rejection. In many cases, the child's rejection of the targeted parent is likely to be seen as an affront and to elicit reactions of outrage, threats to take the alienating parent back to court, and even verbal abuse and perhaps physical assault on the alienating parent. Some denigrated parents relentlessly pursue the child with frequent telephone calls and letters and attempts to make surprise visits at the child's school and sports events. Johnston concluded that these actions only intensify the child's alignment with the alienating parent.

Although Gardner attributes the appearance of PAS primarily to changes in custody laws and secondarily to programming on the part of a hostile parent, Johnston and Campbell (1988) went considerably further to construct a complex theory that takes into account events that occur from the intrapsychic level to society at large. They conceptualized the process on three levels. At the external–social level, the dispute may be fueled by significant others (such as relatives, attorneys, and therapists) who form coalitions with the disputing parties, splitting the couple into two warring camps. Attorneys, in their effort to be a zealous advocate for their client, seek affidavits from all who might further their client's cause. The child therapist, equally zealous about protecting the safety of a child who might possibly be abused and who at least appears to be genuinely terrified of the targeted parent, allies with the alienating parent as well. Soon sexual abuse evaluators may be sought out, and they may be too quick to believe vague accusations of abuse and thus join the coalition. Seeing a groundswell of activity, the child's grandparents may come forward with financing for attorney fees and more evaluations.

At the interactional or interpersonal level, the dispute can be either a continuation of a conflicted marital relationship or the product of a traumatic separation between the parents. Johnston and Campbell (1988) found that often the separation in these keenly bitter divorces was viewed as particularly traumatic for one of the parties. It initiated a dramatic negative reconstruction of how she or he viewed her or his spouse, as well as attempts to salvage her or his self-esteem. These were separations in which the injured party perceived himself or herself to have been abandoned suddenly, to have been left after secret plotting and planning, to have been deserted for someone else, or to have been left after a single incident of physical abuse. These separations involved unusual degrees of humiliation, abandonment, betrayal, demoralization, defeat, guilt, extreme fear, and complete helplessness.

At the intrapsychic level, according to Johnston and Campbell (1988), these couples appeared to be less able to manage and integrate the feelings of helplessness, anger, loss, and narcissistic injury evoked by the divorce. Sixty-four percent were found to have personality disorders, and 27% were found to have personality disorder traits. Men were most often diagnosed as compulsive, paranoid, antisocial, avoidant, schizoid, and passive–aggressive. Women were most often diagnosed as dependent, histrionic, and borderline.

The injured parent in these hostile divorces, according to Johnston and Campbell (1988), projected all of the blame for the divorce onto the other person in an attempt to salvage his or her own dignity and self-worth. These individuals developed a progressively more polarized view of the other person as all bad—evil, crazy, abusive, alcoholic "monsters"—even when there was little or no basis for this perception in reality. They entered into court disputes to prove the other party was "bad" or "wrong" and to vindicate themselves as the "good" and virtuous party. As outside relatives and professionals came to the aid of these parties, affirming and validating their polarized viewpoints, the impasse became more entrenched.

Johnston and Campbell (1988) went on to assert that these parents inexorably draw the child into the struggle as an ally—not out of concern for the child but out of a need to use the child to replace the lost spouse, to bolster their own self-worth, to enlarge their coalition, and to punish the "bad" parent. It is interesting that Johnston and Campbell noted that although these individuals seemed disturbed in their relationships with their ex-spouses, they appeared to function normally in all other spheres of daily living.

Johnston and Campbell (1988) reasoned that these children, in order to secure their tie to the troubled parent, increasingly become a mirror for the parent's emotions, needs, and viewpoints. In these "unholy alliances," the children may take on the identity of a "raging, paranoid, or sullen parent." They may parrot the complaints of the aggrieved parent and repeat stories word for word. Many of these stories appear to be "family legends" rather than events that they have witnessed. Johnston and Campbell reasoned that these children fear that abandoning or disappointing the mother may result in them being abandoned or destroyed in some way by the mother. In addition, these children take on a parentified role and may feel that it is their constant vigilance and protection that keep the parent functioning.

It is interesting that Johnston and Campbell (1988) observed that children who had allied themselves with a parent appeared to be more organized, more intact, and less anxious than those who had not formed alliances. However, they had to use a good deal of denial, distortion, and splitting to maintain the alliance. Johnston and Campbell found that, once formed, these alliances were extremely resistant to change and often continued through the early adolescent years.

Johnston (1994b) added to this formulation the proposal that some children are more at risk for PAS because of failed separation or failed individuation in the preschool years. She observed that children whose parents launched into bitter divorces in the child's early years formed anxious, insecure attachments to both parents and thus were more prone to forming these extreme alignments. Janet Johnston and Vivienne Roseby (1997) developed this theory in their book *In the Name of the Child*, in which they draw the picture of a child whose mother expresses anxiety, panic, and rage when the child separates and transitions to the father's care. The child thus experiences a sense of abandonment during these transitions and is unable to self-soothe and manage anxious feelings. The child's senses of self and object constancy are impaired, and he comes to see the people in his world as all bad or all good.

FOLIE À DEUX

Both Richard Gardner and Janet Johnston mention the similarity between severely alienated or aligned children and the phenomenon of *folie à deux*. Little known and very rarely seen, this quaint term is now referred to in the *Diagnostic and Statistical Manual of Mental Disorders* (DSM–IV; American Psychiatric Association, 1994) as *shared psychotic disorder*. A brief review of what is known about *folie à deux* reveals striking similarities to PAS. Essentially, the core feature of *folie à deux* is that a delusion develops in one person who is involved in a close relationship with another person who already has a delusional disorder. The primary individual is dominant in the relationship and gradually imposes his or her delusional system on the more passive and initially healthy second person. These individuals are usually related by blood ties or by marriage and have lived together for a long time, often in isolation. The most common dyads are husband to wife, sister to sister, and parent to children.

Alexander Gralnick (1942) noted that mother–child combinations were more common in cases of *folie à deux* than were father–child dyads and that mother–daughter pairs were more common than mother–son pairs. He also noted that the secondary person was "weaker" in some way, such as depressed, unstable, shy, asocial, suspicious, nervous, or younger. Furthermore, the delusions were almost always persecutory in nature.

Deutsch (1938) and Oberndorf (1934) suggested that this disorder could be explained simply by the dynamics of family life. They suggested that children identify with parents and may take on their delusional system out of sympathy and concern for a distressed parent. Children may also feel a sense of shock or strain when witnessing the parent's psychotic episode and may take on the same delusional system in an attempt to rescue him or her or be a caretaker to him or her for many years.

Kenneth Dewhurst and John Todd (1956) incorporated elements of learning theory into their interpretation of *folie à deux*. They noted that both individuals almost always live in relative isolation from the larger community. Their enmeshment and suspiciousness becomes a self-fulfilling prophecy over time, resulting in further isolation. The secondary person is thus cut off from the counterbalancing influences of contact with others who may have a better grasp on reality.

Sam Soni and Arnold Rockley (1974) of Prestwich Hospital, Manchester, England, cited personality traits as a causative factor of *folie à deux*.

They noted that the secondary individual is always described by traits such as seclusiveness, suggestibility, or excessive dependency. This seems to be a requirement for the development of the disorder in that those who react with hostility, refusal, isolation, repression, or rejection would be disinclined to accept the primary person's delusions. They viewed the secondary person as by necessity a rather anxious individual who seeks to reduce his or her anxiety by identifying with the primary person.

Michael Sacks (1988) of Cornell Medical College also commented on the isolation of the family members and how this isolation increases the dependency of the family members on the dominant individual. He stated that a process similar to brainwashing occurs. When the secondary individual is observed in the hospital setting, there is an automatic quality to the recounting of the delusions, and the evidence unfolds as a litany. He offered the possibility that the primary person is stressed or angered by the dependency needs of the secondary person and so directs his or her anger onto others to deflect it away from the dependent individual. The secondary person, unable to tolerate the primary person's resentment, adopts his or her delusions out of fear of the anger. Alternatively, the secondary person may adopt his or her delusions out of fear of loss of the relationship. Because he or she is so intensely attached and dependent on the primary person, the fear of loss is greater than the fear of taking on the delusions.

Alistair Munro (1986) broadened the picture even more by suggesting that the majority of individuals with *folie à deux* are not psychotic but are simply "impressionable people who adopt untrue beliefs as the result of a long and over-close association with a deluded person" (p. 233). He suggested that the current terminology be replaced with *shared delusional experience*. Simon Brooks (1987) of the Nova Scotia Hospital, Dartmouth, N.S., and Dippel, Kemper, and Berger (1991) of the University of Freiburg, Germany, suggested that more than two people can become involved in a *folie à deux* and agreed that they do not have to be psychotic for this to happen. Dippel, Kemper, and Berger cited a case in which six people in an extended family all developed persecutory delusions solely due to the dominant personality and persuasiveness of the mother, who was herself not psychotic.

Finally, Rick Mentjoux, Cornelis van Houten, and Cornelis Koolman (1993) of the Netherlands updated the literature with a review of all published cases over the previous 20 years. Their review covers 76 published studies and 107 *folie à deux* "recipients" or inductees. Like previous authors, Mentjoux, van Houten, and Koolman noted a preponderance of females, both as primary and as secondary participants. They also noted that a preponderance of cases are marked by the complementary roles of dominant and submissive participants. They introduced the idea that the secondary individual is not fully individuated and therefore more at risk for the development of delusions. They also cited enmeshment as a factor, describing families at risk as those with poor boundaries.

Brooks (1987), Munro (1986), and Soni and Rockley (1974) all addressed the issue of treatment of *folie à deux* and agreed that separation from the primary individual is the central focus of treatment for the secondary individual and that a return to normalcy is relatively rapid following the complete separation of the two people. Mentjoux et al. (1993) noted in their review that simple separation from the primary individual was curative for 85% of the cases in which a child was induced by a parent. However, when the individuals were two adults, only 55% improved with separation. They concluded that children in these cases are not likely to be as disturbed as adults who are secondary individuals. The children may have been induced simply by virtue of their young age, their dependency, and their cognitive immaturity. An adult who has been induced, on the other hand, is more likely to have had a lower premorbid level of functioning.

FORMULATION OF PAS

Many lines of thinking converge when putting together a comprehensive picture of the development of PAS. Certainly, societal changes in which marital commitments are easily broken and the fact that the issue of custody is up for review every 2 years sets the stage for strong feelings of anxiety and insecurity, as well as distrust and betrayal, before, during, and after the divorce.

From here it can be surmised that parents' personality factors are predictive of who copes well with anxiety and betrayal and who does not. Richard Gardner (1987, 1992a) cited no test data on these parents but described individuals who are hostile, defensive, lack insight, and project blame onto others. Carla Garrity and Mitchell Baris (1994), two custody evaluators in Colorado, described similar individuals and suggested that the alienating parent typically has a personality disorder. They proposed that the alienating parent is one who uses denial to cope with emotional pain, lacks a capacity for intimacy, is overly suspicious and distrustful, has a strong sense of entitlement, and has little anxiety or self-insight. Garrity and Baris also cited situational events as causative but added to this the observation that the family, prior to the divorce, was a "closed system."

Anita Lampel (1996), a private practitioner in San Bernardino, California, collected data on 24 children whom she evaluated as part of a series of custody evaluations during 1989 and 1990. Her sample included 10 boys and 14 girls ranging in age from 7 to 14. In this initial study, she found that 10 of the children were strongly "aligned" with the mother in that they rated their attachment to their mother as strong and positive and their attachment to their father as negative. Eleven children gave positive ratings of attachment to both parents, and 3 children rated their attachment to both parents as neutral.

In Phase 2 of her study, Lampel (1996) further surveyed 20 more families evaluated between 1991 and 1993. Of these 20 children, 10 were aligned and 10 were nonaligned (had positive ratings of their attachment to each parent). In the group of 10 children who were aligned, 6 preferred the father and 4 preferred the mother. Analysis of responses to projective pictures suggested that both groups showed an inability to solve problems and cope with their feelings. Both groups were less likely than groups of children from nondivorcing families to portray others as offering help, emotional support, or material resources. Both aligned and nonaligned children described adults as not adequate in setting limits. Aligned children showed a trend toward more aggressive responses in the projective material yet also appeared to be more self-confident.

When the Minnesota Multiphasic Personality Inventory (MMPI) profiles of the aligned and nonaligned parents were compared, Lampel noted that the parents of aligned children had higher L and K scores, suggesting that they were more defensive, engaged in more denial about their motives and emotions, and showed little awareness of the consequences of their behavior on others. However, such parents were also better at problem solving and were more capable, outgoing, and self-confident. Lampel concluded that aligned children—in the context of a closed family system in which both parents are in conflict and are inflexible—identify with one parent over the other not because of the manipulation of that parent, but out of a natural desire to bond with the parent who may have better social skills and provide a greater comfort level.

Is there a pattern of psychopathology in the targeted parent in PAS cases, or is the targeted parent simply an innocent victim? Virtually no information is available on the targeted parent in cases of PAS. Richard Gardner, along with Carla Garrity and Mitchell Baris (1994), have not noted any common personality traits among the targeted parents; neither have I. Johnston and Campbell (1988) described a group of passive, avoidant spouses who, in their secretiveness, exacerbated paranoid delusions in their former spouses who already had a paranoid personality. Johnston (1994b) described the targeted parent as often inept and not empathic with the child. She viewed the targeted parent as contributing to the alignment by a mix of counterhostility and dogged pursuit of the child.

Mary Lund (1995), a mediator and evaluator in Santa Monica, California, views the targeted parent, usually the father, as contributing to the alignment through his ineptitude at parenting. She noted that many newly divorced fathers do not know how to address the children's needs and refuse to accept the mother's advice. She noted several cases in which a child was aligned with an indulgent, clinging mother while alienated from a rigid, controlling father. This contrast in parenting styles may be problematic in intact marriages, but in a hostile divorce it rapidly contributes to a pattern of alienation.

Nicholas (1997), a California clinician, conducted a survey of 21 custody evaluators to determine if other clinicians were seeing a consistent pattern in the parents of children with PAS. He found that children's symptoms of PAS correlated with two factors in the targeted parent: (a) a pattern of withdrawing or temporarily giving up on the child and (b) a pattern of becoming irritated with and angry towards the child out of frustration at failed attempts to have contact with the child. These behaviors may not necessarily be causative of PAS but may in fact be normal responses to an abnormal situation.

Johnston and Campbell's (1988) formulation of the alienating parent as one who perceives himself or herself to have experienced a severe emotional wound, one from which he or she cannot recover and which must be assuaged by a campaign of retaliation, is a compelling hypothesis. Several lines of research suggest that it is the oldest child, most typically a daughter, and one who is overly accommodating, not oppositional, and strongly identified with the mother, who is a prime candidate for PAS.

As in *folie à deux*, there are many possible mechanisms by which this unusual degree of enmeshment and the taking on of the parent's persecutory belief system occurs. First, there is the obvious factor that the alienating parent and child may naturally be more strongly bonded to each other if the alienating parent has been the primary caretaker.

After the bitter divorce, the child may identify with the alienating parent out of concern and sympathy for a parent who is hurt, unhappy, and perceived to be suffering because of trauma induced by the absent parent. The child may feel a need to rescue the suffering parent and care for that parent so that she or he will, in turn, be able to care for the child. As the alienating parent–child dyad intensifies in its isolation from the targeted parent, the child becomes increasingly dependent on the alienating parent and therefore anxious about separations. The child experiences more intense fears of loss of the alienating parent as well as fear of rejection by the alienating parent because the child perceives himself or herself to have only one true parent.

As the hostility between the two parents goes unabated for several years, so does the child's anxiety about this conflict. The child may witness verbal and physical confrontations between the parents, be present when police are called, be forced to "hide" when the targeted parent is coming for a visitation, and so on. The child may feel inexorably drawn into the conflict and forced to take a side to reduce his or her ambivalence and confusion. He or she may ally more tightly with the alienating parent out of fear of that parent's anger. The child may fear that the alienating parent will retaliate, reject, or abandon him or her if he or she goes to "the enemy side." By identifying with the alienating parent's anger, the child deflects that hostility away from himself or herself and onto the targeted parent.

As the postdivorce conflict continues, the two parents' worlds become more polarized. Shuttling back and forth between these two worlds creates more cognitive dissonance for the child and makes the process of identity formation progressively more difficult as the child matures. Forming an extreme alliance with one parent may reduce this dissonance as well allow the child to form a more integrated and coherent identity.

Last, the child may take on the alienating parent's belief system to feel a sense of importance as an ally against the "evil" targeted parent. Boys in particular are able to assuage the loss of the father by taking on a role as mother's consort and protector.

Compounded in this picture may be the targeted parent's inept efforts at parenting; his or her weak bond with the child; or his or her failure to make a home for the child that is warm, supportive, and welcoming. In still other cases, the child who may consider a break with the alienating parent cannot do so because of the targeted parent's response to continued rejection by the child—a response that has been hostile, threatening, controlling, and retaliatory.

Continued litigation, delays in the courts, failed attempts at psychotherapy, and institutional support for the alienating parent continue to isolate the child from the noncustodial parent, intensifying and encapsulating the child's distorted belief system about the hated parent.

TREATMENT OF PAS

Richard Gardner (1987, 1992a) suggested that in mild cases of PAS a frank talk with the alienating parent, with explanations as to how this pattern is harmful to children, along with court orders establishing regular visitation, may be all that is needed to rectify the problem. For moderate cases, most writers in this area suggest some form of outside intervention. Gardner suggested several avenues of psychotherapy aimed at three goals: (a) deprogramming the child, (b) confronting the alienating parent, and (c) helping the targeted parent develop a stronger bond with the child and develop a "thick skin" in the face of rejection. Gardner is adamant that attempts at insight therapy with the alienating parent and child will be fruitless.

John Dunne and Marsha Hedrick (1994), of Seattle, gave figures that support the intractability of PAS cases. Of the 16 cases (involving 21 children) they described in their article, 3 resulted in an immediate change of custody by the court system. In all 3, this was successful "in eradicating the alienation." In the other 13 cases, all the usual treatment methods were tried: assignment of a guardian ad litem, individual therapy for the parents, couples therapy for the parents, child play therapy, and parent–child therapy. In 2 of the cases the children were rated as somewhat improved. However, in 11 of the cases there was no improvement, and in 2 cases the children were rated as worse than prior to initiation of treatment.

Clinicians who work with more severe cases of PAS would likely agree that these cases are nearly impossible to treat and would not be surprised by the above figures. The alienating parent and the enmeshed child resist all efforts to separate them, and they view intrusions on their belief system as evidence that others are out to harm them. The similarity of PAS to *folie à deux* suggests that removal of the child from the custody of the alienating parent and immediate placement with the targeted parent may be the best intervention. Gardner strongly recommends this intervention for the most severe cases.

Glenn Cartwright (1993), of McGill University in Montréal, Québec, supports the swift intervention of the courts by taking sanctions against the alienating parent and changing the child's residence if necessary. He stated that efforts at mediation and negotiation, the obligatory psychological evaluations, and recommendations for child and family therapy inevitably all come to failure to find a resolution. They also prolong the alienation of the child from the targeted parent and are often perceived by the alienating parent as covert approval of his or her actions. Cartwright stated that "The manipulation of time becomes the prime weapon in the hands of the alienator, who uses it to structure, occupy, and usurp the child's time in order to prevent 'contaminating' contact with the lost parent" (p. 209).

Lund (1995) agreed, arguing that early negotiation or mediation through the courts can be a powerful tool in averting the development of a full-blown case of PAS. She noted that once contact is stopped between a parent and child for a period of time, it is extremely difficult to reinstate it.

Garrity and Baris (1994), however, recommended against a sudden reversal of custody because it is too traumatic for the child. They observed that children with PAS are so intensely loyal to the alienating parent that they do not thrive, unfold, and blossom—as the court and mental health professionals hope they will—but instead become shut down and emotionally constricted. Garrity and Baris suggested that in intractable cases the child should be left in the custody of the alienating parent, in the hopes that when the child grows into adolescence or young adulthood he or she will seek out the targeted parent through his or her own initiative.

Johnston (1994b) also opposes a sudden custody reversal, viewing it as a "parent-ectomy" to the child. She cited one case in which a child hung himself rather than be moved to the custody of his alienated father. Johnston and Roseby are so adamant on this issue that they restated it more emphatically in their book *In the Name of the Child* (1997). They charged the courts in these cases with "losing sight of the delicate interweaving of the child's developmental needs" when weighing out "each parent's preemptory needs and legal rights" (p. 218). They stated that imposing changes of custody on children who are not equipped to handle them compounds the children's sense of helplessness in these cases: "In so doing, we collude in the process of rendering children unseen and unheard in custody disputes that are fought fraudulently 'in the name of the child'" (p. 218).

Deirdre Rand (1997), of Mill Valley, California, referred to PAS in an unpublished study conducted in Colorado. In that study, Kopetski (1991) reviewed 84 cases of PAS among 413 court-ordered custody evaluations done by a state agency, the Family and Children's Evaluation Team. The team was disheartened to find that in 15 of these families the alienating parent was successful in blocking the children's contact with the targeted parent. The alienating parent was supported in this effort by a therapist who felt that the child should not be separated from an enmeshed relationship with the parent, even though this was evidently not a healthy relationship. Kopetski clearly supported a transfer of custody in these cases to the healthier parent. Thus, many experts in the field take issue with researchers such as Johnston and Roseby (1997) and Garrity and Baris (1994) and clearly support rapid and immediate changes of custody.

Because a transfer of custody is so traumatic, it is a step the courts are unlikely to take, even when it might serve the child's needs best in the long term. In the current cultural climate, the mother–child bond is still viewed with a sanctity second only to patriotism, and the courts are loath to sever that bond. In addition, the targeted parent has often been uninvolved or sporadically involved, often passive, and has failed to develop a strong bond with the child—factors that also add to the court's reluctance to make a transfer of custody.

Psychotherapeutic approaches short of parent-ectomy have yet to be developed. Although joint therapy sessions between the child and the alienated parent may be therapeutic, such progress is often undermined by the sabotage of the alienating parent. Garrity and Baris (1994), and I, agree that attempts at insight therapy with the alienating parent in these moderate to severe cases are often useless.

Garrity and Baris (1994) proposed a new system of intervention that uses a parenting coordinator. This individual communicates with the therapist and parents, sets policy and guidelines for the visitations, and testifies in court. He or she also proposes a separate therapist for the child who does not communicate with the parents and does not testify in court. Such individuals further recommend psychotherapy for the targeted parent. Such a plan may be expensive and would have to be developed by the courts. Lund (1995) also advocated a case management approach for cases of PAS. The case manager is similar to a mediator or guardian ad litem in that he or she would oversee and coordinate the work of several therapists and serve as a conduit of correct information from one party to another. Nancy Palmer (1988), an attorney in Florida, suggested that the court not only appoint a guardian ad litem in cases of alienation but also be sharp, swift, and willing to transfer custody if necessary.

Rand (1997), while not advocating a particular model, described several cases in which a team of experts work in unison to bring about effective results. She suggested that judges have specialized training in PAS. In addition, a special master may be appointed to coordinate the efforts of others. The special master may then refer the family to a PAS mental health expert to conduct evaluations and treatment. The PAS expert may report the alienating parent to a CPS agency for emotional abuse of the child. The CPS worker, if properly trained, will recognize the harmfulness of the alienation process and report back to the court. The special master, the PAS expert, and the CPS worker operate together to bring threat of legal sanctions against the alienating parent and thus gain her or his cooperation.

Johnston and Campbell (1988) developed two treatment models that combine mediation with psychotherapy. One model involved individual and joint sessions with the mediator (an average of 27 hours) plus 4–6 hours of play therapy for the child. The other model involved 17 hours of group mediation plus 8 hours of group therapy for the children. Both approaches were successful, with 20% of the families reported to be free of serious conflict 2–5 years later and 40% to be "improved."

For those children who remain with the alienating parent and lose contact with the targeted parent, the losses are enormous. Cartwright (1993) pointed out that the lost relationship with the targeted parent is only one part of the picture. The child also loses, in many cases, that parent's economic support, as well the emotional and economic resources of the paternal grandparents, aunts and uncles, cousins, and friends of the alienated parent. One can only speculate as to the long-range outcomes. Do adolescents over the age of 14 (in many states, the age at which children are free to make a choice of parental custody) outgrow PAS and begin to see their parents realistically? Or does the distortion in perception of the alienated parent continue into adulthood? What proportion of alienated young adults are able to reconstruct a relationship with the alienated parent?

Cartwright (1993) pointed out that the difficulties in re-establishing a long-abandoned relationship are legion. The adolescent or young adult must be prepared for the "backlash" of the alienating parent if he or she seeks out contact with the long-targeted parent. This young adult must also learn how to forgive the bitter, alienating parent. The targeted parent may not be open to re-establishing a relationship after rejection, or he or she may have simply moved on and left no forwarding address or even have died. If a relationship is possible, good memories of the lost parent and a positive history must be reconstructed.

If clear and concise guidelines for the measurement of PAS in children can be established, researchers can begin to conduct longitudinal studies to answer these questions.

WHAT THE RESEARCH SHOWS

The term *PAS* was coined by Richard Gardner in the 1980s to describe children and their parents who are locked in an intense alliance against the targeted parent. Although the term has not gained formal acceptance by the American Psychiatric Association, it has come to be accepted by clinicians working with families involved in postdivorce conflict. Definitions of PAS have been unclear, because clinicians still confuse the child's symptoms with the parent's behavior and the qualities of the relationship between the child and the alienating parent.

Gardner views the cause of the problem as the changes in the legal basis for awarding custody in the 1970s, which resulted in mothers feeling threatened with the loss of their children. He divides cases into mild, moderate, and severe. Johnston and Campbell (1988) take a much more comprehensive approach, viewing the problem as due to the parent's psychopathology and inability to cope with narcissistic injury on the one hand, and the formation of coalitions with the alienating parent with well-meaning outsiders on the other. They view the more severe cases as due to greater psychopathology in the parent and the witnessing of interparental violence on the part of the child. Clinicians in the field describe PAS as more common among mothers and daughters, though mother–son dyads are also common. The children tend to be the oldest in the family and to have accommodating personalities. Parallels are drawn with *folie à deux*, which also is often characterized by mother–daughter and mother–son dyads. It tends to occur in close, family relationships in which a dominant and disturbed individual is enmeshed with a more passive, dependent, and impressionable individual. The two are often isolated from the community and come to adopt the same disturbed belief system out of fear and distress.

The following formulation of PAS is offered: A divorce occurs that is characterized by extreme levels of humiliation and narcissistic injury. The custodial parent, usually the mother, is unable to integrate the loss. A child in the family, most typically the oldest daughter but often the son, becomes enmeshed with the parent out of concern for the parent, fear of loss of the parent, a need to rescue the parent, and a sense of importance. This child is accommodating and has experienced extreme role strain and anxiety during the parents' conflict, and he or she develops an alliance to reduce ambivalence. Years of rejection, anger, abandonment, court actions, or some combination of these on the part of the targeted parent intensify the enmeshment with the alienating parent.

Treatment of these cases with individual and family therapy has met with dismal failure. Clinicians tend to take polarized views on the subject: Some advocate for swift and severe legal sanctions for the alienating parent and immediate removal of custody to the targeted parent; others take the position that intervention by the court is harmful to alienated children and that they should be allowed to sever all ties with the targeted parent. One program, in which highly conflicted parents were in group treatment, has met with some success. More recent approaches have emphasized the use of a case manager or special master, appointed by the court, to continually monitor these cases, making treatment recommendations and suggesting legal sanctions. Longitudinal studies are needed to answer questions about the long-term outcome of PAS and to determine which interventions are advantageous to which types of cases.

GUIDELINES FOR THE CLINICIAN

The following definition of PAS is offered in the format of a *DSM–IV* diagnosis. This level of parental alienation incorporates features of moderate and severe cases described by Gardner.

PAS is defined as a variant and milder form of *folie à deux*. The essential feature of this disorder is a persistent resistance to contact with the targeted parent and a persecutory belief system held by a child toward that parent. This delusional system develops as a result of an enmeshed relationship with a parent who already has a distorted belief system of having been and continuing to be persecuted by the ex-spouse. The distortions of the parent and child are identical. The content of the beliefs is usually within the realm of possibility and often is based on common past experiences of the parent and child.

Associated Features

Typically, the child is known to be particularly compliant and is highly dependent on the alienating parent. The child is usually between the ages of 8 and 14.

In the years following the divorce, the alienating parent has both subtly and overtly engaged in behaviors directed toward discouraging the formation of a positive bond between the children and the targeted parent. Gifts, cards, and telephone calls may have been denigrated or refused. The alienating parent may insist that all traces of the targeted parent be removed from the house. Visitations may be blocked, postponed, rescheduled, or refused for trivial reasons. The alienating parent may forbid the children to discuss the targeted parent or may encourage the child to express only negative comments about the targeted parent. The alienating parent may move to another state to further diminish the targeted parent's role in the children's lives.

Usually, the two parents have taken numerous court actions with increasing degrees of bitterness and hostility. Typically, these allegations center around blocked visitations, failure to make child support payments, allegations of physical or sexual abuse, and children refusing visitations. The continued court actions further the alienating parent's belief that he or she is being persecuted, and a delusional belief may arise in which the judge is purportedly collaborating with the attorneys, caseworkers, therapists, and the targeted parent.

Visitations by the noncustodial parent are often sporadic, infrequent, and irregular, thus intensifying the enmeshment and isolation of the custodial parent–child dyad. The child is thus cut off from the counterbalancing effects of the targeted parent by seeing that parent infrequently. These separations may be due to the blocking of the visitations by the custodial parent, either directly or indirectly. They may also be due to the failure on the part of the targeted parent to seek visitations out of a sense of despair, helplessness, fear of retaliation, or reluctance to exacerbate the stress on the child. The irregular visitation pattern also intensifies the child's alienation from the targeted parent.

Other associated features of PAS are impairment, sex ratio, and course. Impairment is generally less severe than for shared psychotic disorder, and both alienating parent and child may function well in other areas of daily living. The sex ratio of PAS is more common among mothers and daughters. The course of PAS shows that the persecutory belief systems are long standing and rigid and are resistant to being altered by the legal system, family members, or psychotherapists. Cases may persist into late adolescence and early adulthood.

Usually, if the relationship with the alienating parent is interrupted for a lengthy period of time, the delusional beliefs will diminish or disappear. Parents and children with this disorder rarely seek treatment, because their symptoms are ego syntonic. Secondary cases are brought to light when the alienating parent makes an allegation of abuse by the targeted parent or when the targeted parent petitions the courts to establish regular access to the child or a change of custody.

Criteria

To be given this diagnosis, a child or adolescent would have to meet 9 of the following 12 criteria:

1. *The child maintains a delusion of being persecuted by a parent who is viewed in exceptionally negative terms.* This delusion is plausible but appears to have no basis in reality. For example, efforts by the targeted parent to forge a bond with the child are converted by the child into "harassment" and "punishment." Trivial events are magnified and distorted so that they are reinterpreted as evidence of abuse or neglect or of the targeted parent's bad character.

2. *The child uses the mechanism of splitting to reduce ambiguity.* The alienating parent is viewed as all good, and any negative traits are denied. Likewise, the targeted parent is viewed as all bad, and any positive traits are denied. For example, a controlling, alienating parent is described as "caring so much about me that she wants to be a part of everything I do." Mild physical abuse by the alienating parent is flatly denied, even when there are witnesses. Yet the targeted parent is described as "trying to control me" when he or she makes plans for the visitation weekends. If the targeted parent does not make plans, in order to wait until the child gets to the targeted parent's home so that the child can make his or her own choices, that parent is described as "not caring enough about my visit to make any plans for us."

3. *The child denies any positive feelings for the targeted parent.* Any evidence to the contrary, such as gifts and cards from the child to the parent; photographs of the two together smiling; or recollections by the targeted parent of happy times together are met with denial, minimization, or rationalization. For example, a Fathers' Day card sent to a father and signed "I love you" is explained as "I didn't mean it. I only did it to get you to leave me alone."

4. *The attribution of negative qualities to the targeted parent may take on a quality of distortion or bizarreness that borders on loss of touch with reality.* For example, one teenage girl took an antispasmodic drug for her stomach when going on visitations to her father's home. When she couldn't find her medication, she asserted that she "just knew he went through my purse and found it and flushed it down the toilet just so I would suffer." The father, himself a pediatrician, was astonished, stating he would never go through her purse; never get rid of any person's medication, much less his own daughter's; and would certainly never want her to suffer. When other such allegations were demonstrated to be logistically

impossible, the girl became disoriented, confused, and ambiguous.

5. *The child offers as evidence of the targeted parent's bad character recollections of events that occurred out of the child's presence or before the child could have remembered them.* For example, the child may insist she saw the father physically assault the mother, though she was only 18 months old and asleep when the alleged event took place. The child experiences no cognitive dissonance when presented with the impossibility of witnessing and recalling these events.

6. *The child's hatred and sense of persecution by the targeted parent have the quality of a litany.* The phrasing is dramatic, rehearsed, and more adult sounding than the child's natural language. The child and the alienating parent often use the exact same phrases. Gardner refers to this as borrowed scenarios. For example, one girl stated flatly, "My father used to be a father to me, then he dumped me for his new girlfriend." The mother of the girl stated at another time, "We were working toward a reconciliation after the divorce when he dumped me for his new girlfriend."

7. *The child, when faced with contact with the targeted parent, displays a reaction of extreme anxiety, including panic attacks, stomachaches, vomiting, hysterical crying, falling to the floor, clinging, hyperventilating, clutching transitional objects, and wailing.* The child will insist on not being alone with the targeted parent "for protection." The targeted parent reports that once the transition has been made, and the child is no longer in sight of the alienating parent, these symptoms lessen or disappear altogether.

8. *The child has a dependent and enmeshed relationship with the alienating parent.* The child may sleep with the parent; request that the parent accompany him or her to the toilet; and defer to the alienating parent in regard to minor decisions such as those about clothes, friends, and activities. The child often experiences separation anxiety when faced with other age-appropriate separations from the alienating parent as well.

9. *The child is highly compliant, cooperative, and adaptable with all adults other than the targeted parent.* The child has no history of oppositional or disruptive behavior at home or at school. Behavior checklists completed by the teacher typically show no elevations on any scales.

10. *The child views the alienating parent as a victim—as having been persecuted by the targeted parent and having suffered greatly be-*

cause of that parent's actions. The child maintains a parental attitude of concern, sympathy, and protectiveness toward the alienating parent. For example, the child may continually refer to the father's abandonment of the family, though it was the mother who asked the father to move out and who filed for divorce.

11. *The child maintains a complete lack of concern about or compassion for the targeted parent but instead holds an attitude of exploitation toward the targeted parent.* The child objectifies the targeted parent as an "evil thing." He or she may expect the targeted parent to make telephone calls that are refused, send gifts that are not acknowledged, and make timely child support payments with no expectation of visitation. The child shows a guiltless lack of concern for the targeted parent when telephone calls go unanswered, visitation attempts are thwarted, and efforts by the targeted parent to attend the child's school and athletic activities are rejected.

12. *The child's belief system is particularly rigid, fixed, and resistant to traditional methods of intervention.* Evidence of the incorrectness of the child's belief system is completely denied. Attempts by the courts to establish a bond with the targeted parent are resisted and are included in the persecutory belief system. Efforts at supportive counseling are viewed as "harassment."

CASE STUDY UPDATE

I found no unfitness on the part of Jackie, nor any better fitness on the part of Don, that warranted a change of custody. I did conclude that Renata and Dorene were suffering from PAS and would benefit from expanded visitations with Don and Lila. The visitations would have to be structured in such a way as to provide for "deprogramming" for the girls. Therefore, I recommended to the court that Renata and Dorene spend the first 2 weeks out of every 8-week segment with Don and Lila and 4 consecutive weeks with them in the summer. During the 6-week segments with their mother, they would have alternate Saturday or Sunday visitations with Don and Lila. They would thus have 16 full weeks and 14 weekends per year with Don and Lila. During these visits, Jackie would be barred from contacting the girls. However, the girls would be allowed brief and infrequent calls to their mother.

To provide for a mediator, I recommended that when Renata and Dorene were with their father they attend weekly family counseling sessions. The counselor would provide regular progress reports to Jackie about how the girls were doing. The family counselor would be the one to be called, not Jackie, if the girls became frightened or felt they were in a crisis. If, over time, the counselor felt the long visitations were not in the girls' best interests or that the long periods of maternal custody were destructive for them, he or she would send a letter to the respective attorneys with recommendations as to a change in the custody and visitation plan. Finally, I recommended that if Jackie made threats to injure Don and Lila, made continued telephone calls to Renata and Dorene when they were with their father, refused to give them up for their visitations, or interfered with the visitations in any way, that full custody revert to Don immediately.

The judge in the case did not follow my recommendations but ordered Don to continue with the standard visitation plan of alternating weekends. I attempted to locate the family 6 years later, but they had moved away. However, the pediatrician father of the adolescent girl who refused visitation, believing that her father had hidden her stomach medication, was located 5 years after I testified in his visitation dispute. He stated that the superior court judge would not enforce his visitation, and he eventually stopped seeing his daughter for several years. However, he did not break contact with her; he continued to call her and to send cards and gifts. His second wife sent his daughter presents anonymously, signed only "your secret pal." He attended his daughter's high school football games so he could sit high in the stands and see her perform as a cheerleader, without her knowing that he was there.

She refused to allow him to attend her graduation. Afterward, however, her attitude changed entirely. She enrolled in college and began to pursue weekend visits with him. She began to argue with her mother and seldom went home to see her. Following this turnabout, the mother had become more cooperative with the father and more solicitous toward her daughter.

This father said that he now has a loving bond with his daughter, and he felt that the court battles were worth it. Although he felt that his litigation was costly for him and made his daughter's life more stressful in some ways—it split her loyalties and made her feel she had to align herself with her mother more—he felt that it served as a reality test for her. It let her know that he was not a bad person. Also, he felt that it let her know that he cared about her and that he had not abandoned her. When she was ready to separate from her mother, she knew that she had an ally in her father. He felt that his efforts were helped by the fact that he had a strong bond with his daughter prior to the divorce. His advice to other targeted parents was "you need to pursue every avenue you can to have a relationship with your child."

9

PSYCHOPATHOLOGY OF PARENTS LOCKED IN POSTDIVORCE DISPUTES OVER CUSTODY AND ACCESS ISSUES

CASE STUDY

Kevin stood in the waiting room, although there were chairs available. He looked around with disdain, as if thinking that to sit with the other patients would lower his social status. Kevin was extremely attractive and well dressed, although the tension in his face was obvious, and the manner in which he continually struck the fist of one hand into the palm of the other was intimidating. Kevin's wife, Anne, did sit, but with uneasiness as she, too, felt the tension and was helpless to assuage his barely contained rage.

Anne had been seen by myself previous to this visit because she had been having panic attacks and chest pains. It seems that Anne lived with a good deal of chronic tension, which she at first attributed to her job. However, she gradually began to describe her tension in relation to her marriage to Kevin. He had come and gone as he pleased from his job with a law firm, with early and late meetings, after-work handball games at the club, and unexplained blocks of time when he was absent. Anne was left to manage her job as a nurse, care for their small son, and run the home with no support from Kevin.

Kevin had asked Anne to abort a pregnancy, which he had at first planned with her, and then he asked for a divorce. Anne soon discovered that he was having an affair. The separation occurred after a year in which Kevin was in and out of the home several times. When he was home, he became enraged easily over small events that were not to his liking, and he became physically abusive and threatening. I saw them for three visits of couples therapy and found it fruitless. Kevin was focused on Anne's faults and on blaming her for the failure of the marriage, and he stated that he would not be open to making any changes in his own behavior. The couple went to another therapist, whom Kevin chose, which had the same end result.

The divorce took many months because Kevin at first would not concede on child support and custody issues. He hid many of his financial assets from Anne and her attorney. Kevin engaged an attorney who was a wealthy business associate of his father's. This attorney was willing to work for no payment from Kevin as a favor for Kevin's father's continued business. Anne, on the other hand, could not pay all of her legal expenses on her salary as a pediatric nurse and ended up $25,000 in debt.

Anne was relieved when the divorce was over, hoping to rebuild her life. However, her troubles were just beginning. Kevin continued to harass her with threatening telephone calls and frequent certified mail and facsimiles from his attorney over minor issues. He sat in his car outside her home and watched her. He sat in his car outside their son's day care center and watched her dropoffs and pickups. He became enraged at the visitation times and slammed the car seat into the car, roughly strapped the child in, and sped out of the driveway. He took Anne back to court several times on trivial issues, charging her with interference with custody and alienating his child from him.

Anne was forced to retain a new attorney, because the one to whom she was in debt (from a prestigious law firm) had withdrawn from representing her. Her new attorney had lower fees, and she used him sparingly, but she soon became mired again in debt. Two years after the divorce, Kevin remarried, and Anne hoped that Kevin would move on with his life. But, again, that was not to be the case. As soon as he was legally able, he filed for a change of custody. Anne mustered up the money to hire still a third attorney, as the second one had withdrawn, too. This attorney was very young and could not afford a secretary or a facsimile machine. He did learn that Kevin had received a bonus of $100,000, which he had managed to hide in the divorce, but the attorney did not feel that he could secure a portion of it. Kevin, on the other hand, continued to be represented at no cost by his father's friend.

As the day of the custody hearing grew near, Anne continued to show the effects of prolonged stress. Ever deeper in debt, she had decided to represent herself. She was back on her medication for cardiac arrhythmia and panic attacks. Her second marriage, only a year old, had begun to flounder under the continual financial and emotional pressure of her involvement with Kevin (and her second husband's difficulties with his ex-wife as well).

Throughout Anne continued to ask, "Why is he so angry with me? I don't understand. He seems bent on destroying me. He was the one who made me abort our baby. He had the affair. He asked for the divorce. He hid money from me, and I'll never get out of debt. Why does he have such rage at me?"

In those 25% of divorcing couples who have children in which post-divorce conflict is the prevailing theme (Maccoby & Mnookin, 1992), this question is often asked. It has been asked by clinicians who work with these couples; the couple's attorneys; and the subsequent mediators, social workers, and judges who come into contact with them. Where does this rigid, unreasonable, and relentless anger come from?

In this chapter I review what is known about such parents. First, I look at some of the prevailing theories of clinicians with extensive field experience with these couples and then review the sparse empirical literature. Although the studies are not extensive, they do support clinical impressions that these individuals have common cognitive distortions that are features of personality disorders. Remarriage is often the impetus for a rise in postdivorce conflict. I look at the rates of remarriage as well as the high failure rates of remarriages, along with some of the common pathways in which remarriage reignites interparental conflict. Finally, I review the literature on the subgroup of highly disturbed parents who abduct children. Common patterns are described on the basis of several large-scale studies of this dramatic problem.

THEORIES OF PARENTAL PSYCHOPATHOLOGY IN DIVORCE DISPUTES

Wallerstein and Kelly

Virtually no studies to date have examined the psychopathology of adults caught up in severe postdivorce conflict. However, many writers have commented anecdotally on these individuals. Judith Wallerstein and Joan Kelly (1980b), authors of perhaps the first major study of families in divorce, the California Children of Divorce Project, conducted a series of interviews with a large pool of families undergoing divorce from 1971 to 1977. Although Wallerstein and Kelly did not use precise, psychometric tests—and they have been faulted for this—they presented impressions based on their clinical interviews. For example, they found that four-fifths of the men and an even higher proportion of the women came through the divorce with strong residual anger.

Wallerstein and Kelly (1980b) went on to report that more than half of the mothers and nearly half of the fathers were extremely critical and abusive toward their former spouses, with most of the hostile statements being made in front of the children. Fathers were called "liars," "bastards," "unreliable," "disgusting," and "crazy" and were accused of "sleeping around with cheap women." Mothers were called "whores," "unfit," "drunken bitches," "greedy and grasping," and "crazy."

Wallerstein and Kelly (1980b) determined that at the upper end of the spectrum, one fifth of the women and slightly fewer men exhibited hatred that was so intense that no amount of reasoning could deter them from their goals. They dubbed them the *embittered–chaotic father or mother* and concluded that the rage these people exhibited served two purposes. One was to ward off a devastating depression. These people seemed to feel mortally wounded and that their self-esteem was shattered. The second was to organize themselves, as they felt shocked and stunned and were reeling from a sense of disequilibrium.

Wallerstein and Kelly (1980b) noted that many of these individuals had functioned at a high level prior to the divorce and continued to function well in their job settings. Yet these authors observed well-respected business and professional men who began spying, tried to break into the family home, made obscene telephone calls, assaulted their ex-wives, vandalized the home, and tried to hide (or "childnap") their children. Likewise, they observed mothers, who had otherwise made a good home for the children, whose capacity to handle the day-to-day care of their children deteriorated. They made open demands on their children to align with them, in complete insensitivity to the children's plight.

Johnston and Campbell

Janet Johnston and Linda Campbell (1988), directors of the Center for the Family in Transition in Corte Madera, California, focused on 80 families in which there had been a high degree of postdivorce conflict. Each parent was rated as to a diagnosis by two clinicians. The most notable finding, although surely no surprise, was that 64% of the parents received a diagnosis of personality disorder. Another 27% were found to have personality disorder traits. Men most often received the following diagnoses: compulsive personality disorder and paranoid, antisocial, avoidant, schizoid, and passive–aggressive personality disorder. Women most often received diagnoses of dependent, histrionic, or borderline personality disorder. Interrater reliability for the presence of a personality disorder was high, ranging from .88 to .96. These gender differences are not surprising in that they reflect gender differences in personality disorders of the patient population at large. About one fourth of the parents were found to warrant a diagnosis of substance abuse, and 15% were diagnosed as having intermittent explosive disorder.

In an earlier article, Johnston, Campbell, and Tall (1985) articulated how individuals with personality disorders incorporate the divorce into their existing cognitive frameworks. Disputing parents with borderline personality traits seemed to have a need to fight, to keep things stirred up. Arguing seemed to be their reason for being, and they seemed to provoke a battle as soon as an agreement was reached. Obsessive parents agonized over making the smallest decision and fretted over the minute details of the parenting plan. They delayed settlements and stood by rigid, inflexible positions, refusing to consider alternatives. Johnston, Campbell, and Tall also described a small number of parents who were actively psychotic and had paranoid delusions.

What Johnston and Campbell (1988) found intriguing, however, was the fact that the vast majority of parents in their sample were rated on the Global Assessment of Functioning Scale (Axis V; *DSM-IV*; American Psychiatric Association, 1994) as having had moderate to superior levels of functioning prior to the current problems. Also, their problematic behavior was confined to the conflicts with the ex-spouse over the children. It was situational and relational. Because this does not fit the strict definition of a personality disorder, Johnston and Campbell referred to these individuals as *psychologically vulnerable*. By this they meant that particular factors in the postdivorce situation appeared to reawaken unresolved problems and traumas from the past in people who otherwise were functioning more or less normally.

Johnston and Campbell (1988) conceptualized the core problem in all of the parents in their sample as one of *narcissistic vulnerability*. Divorce —with its implications of failure, loss, rejection, and unworthiness—represents a tremendous blow to one's self-esteem. Narcissistically vulnerable individuals depend on others to validate their inflated (although fragile) positive images of themselves and to be the blank screen onto which they project all the bad parts of themselves. For these people, initiating and winning a custody dispute can serve as a way to save face, to compensate for humiliation and an injured self-image.

Johnston and Campbell (1988) went further and delineated three levels of narcissistic woundedness in disputing parents. They rated 45% of the parents in their sample as mildly narcissistically disturbed. These parents felt cheated and betrayed, and they let their spouses and others know about their anger through a litany of complaints. They turned to friends and family for confirmation of their mistreatment and for reassurances that they were attractive, worthy, feminine (masculine), and so on. They held exaggerated views of their own virtues and made demands in the divorce settlement that were seen as far out of the range of reality. They demanded reparations through the courts, apologies, pledges "to do better," higher-than-normal financial compensation, complete control of the children, and so on. Johnston and Campbell noted that these parents at the mildly narcissistic level rarely get involved in entrenched legal disputes unless family and friends come to their aid to form a coalition or unless their ex-spouses are even more narcissistic and keep up verbal and emotional assaults on them.

Johnston and Campbell (1988) further described 37% of the parents in their sample as moderately narcissistically vulnerable. These parents were characterized by a grandiose sense of self and an air of entitlement. They could see no faults in themselves, only good qualities. They constructed a negative image of the ex-spouse as a defense against seeing any negative traits in themselves.

If the moderately narcissistic individual was the one to leave the marriage, he or she felt no guilt or compassion for the other but felt entitled to leave and to get rid of the spouse. Such individuals further felt entitled to bend the rules of the visitation and divorce agreement to suit their needs at the moment. Requests to cooperate and to consider the other parent's needs were viewed with annoyance.

Moderately narcissistic individuals who were left felt an overwhelming blow to their sense of grandiosity and intense feelings of shame and humiliation. These parents often looked to the courts to counteract their sense of humiliation through a legal victory. If they won, the judge was idealized as having seen the truth. If they lost, they vilified the judge, fired their attorney, sought new representation, and started anew.

Children are, for these parents, narcissistic extensions of themselves. They have a limited ability to see their children as separate from themselves and to understand and empathize with their situation. The children's problems are denied or, if they cannot be denied, are blamed on the other parent.

Johnson and Campbell (1988) reserved the category of severely narcissistically vulnerable for individuals who have formed paranoid delusions around the faults of their ex-spouses. These individuals not only see their ex-spouse as deficient but also construct a monstrous scenario in which the other person is a drug addict, a child molester, or a sociopath. They have a history of being socially isolated and secretive. Faced with the humiliation of the divorce, they begin to review the events of the marriage and the children's lives, forcing each piece into a complicated picture of systematic criminal or immoral behavior on the part of the ex-spouse. Trivial events take on great significance. Inconsequential remarks by the children or others are assumed to have hidden meanings. They perceive the children to be in danger when with the other parent and seek to curtail all contact with that parent. Many "shop around" for mental health professionals who will verify their belief system.

Johnson and Campbell (1988) also suggested that individuals in this seriously disturbed group tend to be married to individuals who are dependent, passive, and unsure of themselves. Faced with the relentless attacks of the paranoid spouse, they begin to withdraw and to be secretive about their actions. This secretiveness is then further incorporated into the paranoid person's delusional system as clear evidence that something is going on.

Johnston and Campbell (1988) took their theory still further by suggesting psychodynamic mechanisms through which these individuals have come to be so vulnerable. Their elegantly crafted hypothesis centers around the reactivation of earlier trauma and the failure to separate and individuate from parents. As examples of earlier loss, they give the following: miscarriages, abortions, previous children who have died, being able to have only one child, a childhood history of divorce, remarriage, parental death, and "not being wanted." Johnston and Campbell also attributed narcissistic vulnerability to what they refer to as failures in the parent's relationship with his or her parents. As examples they cite having a parent who was unsupportful, neglectful, or abandoning; having a parent who was alcoholic or had a mental illness; having lived with a succession of caretakers; having lived in foster homes; having had several fathers; having been neglected or abused; or having parents who were and still are extremely overindulgent, overprotective, and controlling and who encourage the dependency of their grown children. The trauma of the divorce is thought to restimulate these earlier losses and exacerbate underlying issues that were never worked through.

In her latest work, Janet Johnston, along with Vivienne Roseby (1997), revisited this issue of parental psychopathology. They cited emerging evidence that individuals with histories of early loss and trauma are more prone to intense postdivorce conflict, although the studies they cite are unpublished. The study by Luke McClenney, Janet Johnston, and Judith Wallerstein (1994) is both methodologically and conceptually flawed. For example, they combined the death of a parent and the perception of a lack of love in the marriage into one independent variable. Correlations with the dependent variable of adjustment, 2 years, postdivorce, were small and inconsistent. Even McClenney et al. offered the possibility that postdivorce psychopathology may have been shaped by psychopathology that existed prior to the divorce and even prior to the marriage. Miriam Bar (1997) also conducted an unpublished study on the association between childhood trauma and postdivorce psychopathology. She found that the "normal" divorce group had a significantly lower history of childhood trauma (defined as loss of or separation from parents, alcoholic parents, or violent parents) than did parents who had highly conflicted divorces. However, Bar noted that there were demographic differences between the "normal" divorce group, the "high-conflict" divorce group, and the "abduction" group that could have accounted for some or all of the between-groups variation in the outcome measures.

Johnston and Roseby (1997) took issue with mental health professionals who attribute postdivorce conflict to the presence of personality disorders in the parents. Rightfully so, they made the case that labels such as *borderline personality* and *narcissistic personality* have no place in reports submitted to the court because they reinforce the humiliation and degradation that the parent may already be experiencing and may be used by opposing counsel to gain further legal advantage over the other parent.

Garrity and Baris

Carla Garrity and Mitchell Baris (1994) took a similar route in their book *Caught in the Middle*. They view the families who are seen in custody battles as closed systems prior to the divorce. They limit their contact with the outside world and focus on strong ties to religious groups or home schooling. Mistrustful of outsiders, once they begin to divorce they become mistrustful of each other. Garrity and Baris went on to speculate that these individuals have a core difficulty with denial of emotions that results in a lowered capacity for intimacy. Unable to experience their own emotions as children, they become unable to understand and experience the emotions of others or to see the effect of their behavior on others. They have little capacity for self-reflection and insight into their own motivations.

Some of these individuals are thought to perceive the world as a dangerous place and are thus consumed with scanning it for evidence of harmful intent. They must be on their guard to prevent others from humiliating and demeaning them. Still others have a strong sense of narcissistic entitlement. They view the divorce as an enormous insult to their self-image. Some may have pursued the divorce out of a need for punishment or revenge and were completely unprepared for the overwhelming sense of loss that they felt and that triggered unresolved earlier losses. Unable to soothe and comfort themselves, they turn to the children for nurturance and support, to maintain their self-esteem, and to ward off depression. Without giving any data, Garrity and Baris stated that "Their response is traceable to very early experiences. Most of them lacked good, solid models of parenting from their own childhoods" (p. 107). Garrity and Baris gave as examples (a) growing up in an abusive home or a home that lacked protection from painful experiences and (b) families with unclear boundaries.

Cognitive Theories

Although the above-mentioned theories make some sense, the reader can see that any group of divorcing parents—even any group of intact couples—would be able to cite some or many of these factors in their own background. Yet not all, or even most of them, are locked in entrenched divorce and custody battles. This is the danger of psychodynamic theories—that one can describe a behavior as it occurs now, attend to the client's complaint about unhappy events in childhood, understand how the two may be logically associated, and then suppose that a cause-and-effect relationship exists between the two. On the other hand, it is entirely possible that having a personality disorder, or at least several traits of a personality disorder, may be the mediating variable that links adjustment problems both in childhood, and following a divorce, as well as in conjunction with other life crises.

Cognitive theorists such as Aaron Beck and Arthur Freeman (Beck & Freeman, 1990) have established that individuals with personality disorders have cognitive distortions that result in an overselectivity for certain cues, both in their environment and in their past history, to the exclusion of other cues. These cues are matched with internal cognitive schemas. Paranoid personalities are focused on finding evidence of secrets and conspiracies to shame or humiliate them. Schemas such individuals hold in relationships are similar to these: "People often say one thing and mean something else" and "people will take advantage of me if I give them the chance."

Beck and Freeman (1990) lent support to Marsha Linehan's (1987) hypothesis that the core problem with the borderline personality is a dysfunction in emotion regulation that is physiologically based. The combination of unusually intense emotions, impulsive behavior, and self-disparaging attitudes provokes frequent crises in these individuals' lives and predisposes them to dependent yet unstable relationships. Borderline personalities may be focused on scanning for evidence of lack of emotional support and nurturance from others. They hold schemas such as "It's not safe to trust people, they hurt you and let you down," "No one will ever love me deeply enough because I'm no good," and "It is unbearable not to get what I need from someone else."

Narcissists scan their environment for feedback that they are special and admired. They hold schemas such as "Other people should satisfy my needs," "It's intolerable if I'm not accorded my due respect or don't get what I'm entitled to," and "People have no right to criticize me."

Beck and Freeman (1990) reviewed the psychoanalytic theories for the personality disorders, many of which focus on early losses and maternal deprivation, and concluded that the evidence simply is not there. With regard to narcissists, for example, they noted that there is a strong gender difference, that it is largely a disorder of men—a fact that suggests cultural factors. They also concluded that "It is important to note that there is no empirical evidence that clearly links nurturant deprivation in childhood with characteristics of adult narcissism" (p. 236).

PERSONALITY TRAITS OF PARENTS INVOLVED IN
POSTDIVORCE CONFLICT

What are perhaps more useful to consider are some of the cardinal features of all the parents who are seen in hostile custody disputes. Most notable perhaps is their projection of blame. These individuals are black–white thinkers. They are right, and the other parent is wrong. They are virtuous; the other parent has no redeeming qualities. They are blameless; the other parent is completely at fault. As a corollary of this, they are lacking in introspection. As a rule, one will not see individuals in these cases who are prone to self-doubt, excessive guilt, brooding, and regrets over past mistakes. They have made no mistakes; their spouse made them all.

In the last 5–10 years, a growing body of data has been accumulating on the MMPI–2 scores of adults involved in custody disputes. Much of this research supports the observation that these parents are highly invested in projection of blame. Marc Ackerman (1995) asserted that "research has demonstrated that the average K scale of individuals involved in custody evaluations is 62 on the MMPI" (p. 110) yet cited no source for this figure. Allen Posthuma of Vancouver, British Columbia, and James Harper of the Fielding Institute in Santa Barbara, California, also reported on a large sample of litigants in custody cases (188 families)—data that the two accumulated over a long span of time in clinical practice (Posthuma & Harper, 1998). The elevation for this group on the K scale was a T score of 54—only a slight elevation above the mean of 50. This was in contrast to the results of an unpublished study by Moreland and Greenberg (cited by Posthuma & Harper), who found a mean of 62 on K for a sample of 201 custody litigants. Moreland and Greenberg found means of 55 for women and 57 for men on the MMPI–2, in a later sample.

Jeffrey Siegel (1996), a private practitioner in Dallas, Texas, examined the MMPI–2 profiles of 34 women and 46 men undergoing divorce and child custody litigation. He found that the women's mean T scores for the L and K scales were 60 and 64. The comparable means for the men were 58 and 61, respectively. These scores were clearly elevated above the norm and suggest a strong pattern of defensiveness and denial of personal problems. Siegel and Langford (1998) expanded this study to compare the MMPI–2 validity scales of two groups of mothers undergoing custody evaluations—those who engaged in behaviors that alienated the children from the other parent and those who did not. Their results supported their hypothesis, in that the alienating mothers had a higher K scale score (T = 67) than the nonalienating group (T = 60), suggesting that they had demonstrably higher levels of defensiveness and projection of blame. This figure is similar to the mean of 66 on the K scale of the preferred parents of aligned children reported in Lampel's (1996) study.

Kay Bathurst, Allen Gottfried, and Adele Gottfried (1997), of the California State University system, summarized a 6-year study in which they collected MMPI–2 data from parents involved in custody disputes. On the basis of early information in the study, they hypothesized that they would find elevations on the *L* and *K* scales, relative to the *F* scale, suggesting that parents underreport symptoms and view themselves in an overly virtuous light. Bathurst et al. also expected, on the basis of an unpublished study by Caldwell (1995), to find elevations on Scales 3 (Hysteria), 4 (Psychopathy), and 6 (Paranoia). Caldwell had suggested that these elevations would be seen on the basis of the common clinical observations that these parents deny the negative aspects of their own personality, that they readily disclose feelings of hostility and suspiciousness, and that they have high levels of family discord. Bathurst et al. also expected to see higher than normal elevations on the *O–H* (Over-Controlled Hostility) scale.

Bathurst et al. (1997) collected data from 508 parents undergoing custody evaluations in the southern California area. As predicted, the *L* scale was mildly elevated, at a mean of 55, and the *K* scale was moderately elevated, at a mean of 60. The *O–H* scale also was moderately elevated, with a mean of 60. Scales 3, 4, and 6 were elevated, but only slightly above 50. The authors reported that 36/63 was the most common grouping of scales showing elevations. Despite this, however, the group of child custody litigants, as a whole, were not significantly different from a "normal" sample on the MMPI–2 clinical scales. Bathurst et al. concluded that the MMPI–2 profiles of their sample indicate problems with mistrust, hostility, defensiveness, and family turmoil that are associated with going through a divorce. They suggested that these findings might not generalize beyond this conservative interpretation. In other words, these traits may be the outcome of the divorce conflict, not necessarily a precipitating factor.

Kenneth Pope, James Butcher, and Joyce Seelen (2000) incorporated the above data into an even larger study of parents undergoing custody evaluations, as part of an ongoing data collection project begun by Butcher (1997). This sample included a total of 1,799 people (881 men and 918 women). For the group as a whole, the means for the *L* and *K* scales were both a modestly elevated 56.5. Although the majority of the MMPI–2 profiles were in the normal range, 20% of the men and 23.5% of the women had well-defined elevations on the clinical scales. The most common elevated profile was a 6/9 for men and a 6/4 for women.

What can be concluded from these studies is that parents undergoing custody disputes do tend to show a pattern of defensiveness on the MMPI–2, with elevations on the *L* scale in the range of 55–60 (which is nonsignificant) and elevations on the *K* scale in the range of 54–64 (also in the nonsignificant range). Parents involved in the most entrenched disputes, in which children were displaying symptoms of PAS, showed higher *K* elevations, in the range of 66–67 (just above significance). The most common elevation was on Scale 6, which is understandable in that parents in custody disputes often are the subjects of scorn by others and do justifiably feel that others are plotting against them. Scales 3, 4, and 9 may also be elevated, because they involve traits of narcissism, resentment toward others, denial of wrongdoing, and high levels of family conflict.

In addition to defensiveness and projection of blame, parents involved in protracted custody disputes have been known for the rigidity of their thinking. Professionals who attempt to reason with them—therapists, attorneys, social workers, judges—find them exasperating, because they do not seem able to take in information, consider it carefully, and integrate it into their existing belief system. Evidence that does not support their position or that clearly contradicts it is simply rejected. Even when they are warned that their behavior is destructive to themselves or their children, they are compelled to repeat it. Irrational and even distorted beliefs are clung to persistently. They are often impervious to therapeutic interventions.

A third feature of these parents that has been noted in the literature is that they are lacking in the ability to empathize with others or to see another person's point of view. They are particularly egocentric in that they are capable of imagining the impact of events only on themselves. They are noted for their inability to separate their own needs and emotions from those of their children. Questions such as "Why do you suppose your daughter loves her father so much?" "Why is your husband pursuing custody of the children so aggressively?" "What does he feel he has to offer the children?" and "What are your former wife's strengths as a parent?" are met with blank looks.

It is easy to see how these three core traits are certainly interrelated. People who project blame onto others are black–white thinkers, just as black–white thinkers are rigid and inflexible in their cognitive style. Naturally, people with constricted cognitive styles are able to see only one perspective, and that is their own, all of which leads to the observation that these are core traits of many of the personality disorders.

Carl Hoppe and Lynne Kenney (1994) conducted an analysis of 180 Rorschach protocols of parents undergoing custody evaluations—data that were gathered over a period of 5 years of clinical practice. Their study is weakened by the fact that the raters were not blind as to the group that generated the protocols. Also, the norms in the scoring manual that was used were adapted as the control-group norms. Nevertheless, Hoppe and Kenney's analysis did yield several dramatic deviations from the norm in this group. They concluded that these parents demonstrated significant "cognitive simplicity"—they failed to see subtleties in the situation or to see the material from several points of view. Their responses also suggested that they had poor impulse control and were often swept up by their emotions. These individuals were described as not bringing much skill or depth to relationships but were rather needy and demanding, and they had unrealistic expectations from their partners. They had poor problem-solving skills and approached life in a trial-and-error manner. They tended to avoid highly emotionally charged situations and reacted to such situations with denial, projection of blame, and defensiveness. Last, Hoppe and Kenney characterized these individuals by pathological narcissism—a maladaptive stance against internal feelings of inadequacy.

Marion Ehrenberg of the University of Victoria, in Victoria, British Columbia, and his colleagues (Ehrenberg, Hunter, & Elterman, 1996) conducted an elegant study in which they hypothesized that a set of core traits would characterize ex-couples who were unable to form workable parenting plans. Following the work of object-relations theorists, Ehrenberg et al. suggested that individuals who become overwhelmed under stress in interpersonal situations demonstrate several characteristics: They have difficulty taking another person's perspective, they have poor interpersonal skills, and they are more self-serving. This self-centered perspective keeps them from being flooded by their own strong emotions. As marital conflict increases and they become more vulnerable, they have difficulty empathizing with their children's needs or seeing their children's point of view. They tend to overvalue their importance to their children and undervalue the importance of the other parent.

Ehrenberg et al. (1996) further proposed that individuals with narcissistic personality traits are prone to highly conflicted relationships because they are highly dependent on admiration and attention from their partner. They often develop relationships with others who have similar narcissistic needs, but they become rapidly disillusioned with these relationships. Under the stress of the marital breakup, these needy couples feel particularly deprived of soothing and admiration, and they turn to the children, as well as others, to meet these needs. A good reference on this type of couple is Joan Lachkar's (1986) article "Narcissistic Borderline Couples."

Ehrenberg et al. (1996) interviewed 16 couples with good communication skills and 16 couples with chronic conflict and made the following hypotheses: (a) the agreeable couples would be less narcissistic, (b) they would be more able to take another person's perspective, (c) they would be more comfortable with tension in interpersonal situations, (d) they would be less self-oriented, (e) they would be more empathic, and (f) they would be more child oriented in their parenting decisions. Ehrenberg et al. used seven measures: the Narcissistic Personality Inventory, the Interpersonal Reactivity Index (three subscales only—Perspective Taking, Empathic Concern, and Personal Distress), the Selfism Scale (which measures self-orientation), the Adult–Adolescent Parenting Inventory (which measures empathy-related parenting and child-rearing attitudes), and Self-

Important Parenting Beliefs. Of these measures, the results were in the predicted direction on five of them: The conflicted couples were more narcissistic, more stressed by interpersonal tension, more self-oriented, less empathic, and less child oriented. They did not, however, differ significantly in perspective taking or parental self-importance.

Ehrenberg et al. (1996) constructed two paths by which couples reach such entrenched positions. One path is anchored in a history of narcissistic personality traits. The other appears to be more reactive—some individuals may be acutely distressed and develop a self-orientation to protect against a sense of extreme vulnerability. The authors suggested that these two paths may be intertwined, in that narcissistic individuals may be prone to being more vulnerable and vice versa.

REMARRIAGE AS A TRIGGER FOR PARENTAL PSYCHOPATHOLOGY

Demographers such as Paul Glick (1989a, 1989b), following the trends in rates of marriage, divorce, and remarriage, have concluded that Americans, when they divorce, are rejecting not marriage in general, only that particular marriage. In fact, Andrew Cherlin (1981) noted that 62% of women and a higher proportion of men remarry within 5 years of the divorce. Nazli Baydar (1988) reanalyzed data from the National Survey of Children and found similar figures—30% of divorced mothers remarried within 3 years, 50% remarried within 5 years, and 60% remarried within 8 years. In general, younger women and women with fewer children are more likely to remarry. In Wallerstein and Blakeslee's (1989) study, the group of men who were under 40 at the time of the divorce were most likely to remarry. Women who divorced past the age of 40 were the least likely to remarry.

Given these figures, it is not surprising that a large number of children will grow up in homes with a stepparent. Glick (1989a) estimated that 40% of families today are likely to become stepfamilies by the time the youngest child reaches maturity. Demographers have also concluded that remarriages do not tend to fare any better than first marriages. Furstenberg (1987) found that the rate of divorce for second marriages, 56%, was slightly higher than that for first marriages, 49%. Glick (1984) estimated the redivorce rate to be 61% for men and 54% for women in their 30s in the 1980s. It has been noted that second marriages for women with children are especially at risk. These remarriages are almost twice as likely to end in divorce as those of remarried husbands (Tzeng & Mare, 1995). This may be due to conflicts over the woman's children from her first marriage. Demographers and researchers have also noted that these second marriages tend to be shorter. Baydar (1988) found that 42% of these second marriages ended within 5 years. Thus, a large proportion of children who experienced remarriage also experienced a second divorce.

Of the adolescent children interviewed 10 years after a divorce by Wallerstein and Blakeslee (1989), half reported they had experienced the second divorce of one of their parents. Wallerstein and Blakeslee also noted that only 1 out of 8 of the adolescents felt that both parents had made successful second marriages.

Wallerstein and Blakeslee (1989) concluded that there were winners and losers in the postdivorce-and-remarriage life course. These authors reinterviewed 47 women and 36 women from 52 of the original sample of families first seen in the mid-1970s for divorce counseling at the Center for the Family in Transition in Corte Madera, California. Wallerstein and Blakeslee rated these men and women on four dimensions: nature and quality of interpersonal relationships, general contentment with life, freedom from loneliness and emotional distress, and financial status and stability. They concluded that, for the most part, divorce and remarriage do not live up to expectations. Almost half of the women and two thirds of the men concluded that the quality of their lives was no worse, yet no better, than before the divorce. Only 10% of the parents reported that both were better off now that they were divorced. In fact, 20% reported that both parents were worse off 10 years later than they had been during the marriage.

Wallerstein and Blakeslee (1989) found that, after divorce, psychological growth among women was greater than that for men. Younger women, particularly those with higher education, were able to move on with their lives far more successfully than women who were older at the time of the divorce. The authors described these women as having high self-esteem, a clearer sense of reality and of self-concept, and better judgment in decision making. The older group—women who were 40 or older at the time of the divorce—fared more poorly. Besides being less likely to remarry, they also were more likely to be living in economic and social conditions that were below those of what they had experienced when they were married. Many felt lonely and rejected; half reported deteriorating health.

Wallerstein and Blakeslee (1989) concluded that the men in the study demonstrated surprisingly few psychological changes and had stable lives. Because so much of a man's roles in life are defined by employment, when a man's job remained unchanged his roles and work contacts remained stable as well. However, age continued to play an important role. Well-established men who had divorced in their 20s to early 40s were the winners. At the 10-year mark, half of the men in their 40s reported being happily remarried. Half of the men who had divorced in their 40s had not remarried. Only one third of this group, now in their 50s, were happily remarried. Wallerstein and Blakeslee concluded that remarriage provided something of a buffer against the anxieties of aging and of aging alone and that lack of a marriage in midlife puts both men and women at risk.

Constance Ahrons, professor of sociology at the University of Southern California and director of the Binuclear Family Study (Ahrons & Rodgers, 1987), concluded that "remarried couples overwhelmingly report that they are unprepared for the complexities of remarried life" (p. 163). William Hodges (1991), after surveying the large body of studies on remarriage, also concluded that most parents are surprised at the difficulty of the adjustment to remarriage (p. 219).

In exploring the sources of strain in remarriages, most writers in the field emphasize the conflicting roles and altered relationships in stepfamilies. Hodges (1991) pointed out that in nuclear families, couples have an opportunity to form a strong bond as a couple before the arrival of children. In addition, when children arrive, both parents ideally have an equal stake in parenting and a roughly equal bond with the children. In a stepfamily, however, couples form a bond in which children are present from the start. The parent–child bond is built on the exclusion of the stepparent from the beginning. It is unlikely that the parent and stepparent will ever have equal status with the child or equal control over the child's life. Ahrons and Rodgers (1987) pointed out that, in view of the fact that so many parents remarry quickly, few children and ex-spouses have adequate time to grieve the loss of the previous nuclear family structure and adjust to new roles. The length of time between the divorce and the first remarriage will predict the severity of stress among previous family members as all are compelled to make dramatic adjustments in a short span of time.

For parents in highly conflicted divorces, remarriage tends to increase tensions that already existed at high levels. It is interesting that Wallerstein and Blakeslee (1989) commented that insight into the cause of the breakdown of the marriage was rare in their sample of men and women alike. They saw little evidence that men or women understood how they had contributed to the failure of the marriage. Of their sample of 83 parents, they reported that very few men and no women accepted blame for the divorce. Keep in mind that this observation was made of a relatively random sample of divorcing parents. These were not parents in highly conflicted divorces. Therefore, one would anticipate insight to be lacking at even greater levels in highly conflicted divorces. Parents who continue to project blame onto the other parent and to maintain fixed scenarios as to how they were abused, mistreated, betrayed, or otherwise deeply wounded by the other parent react to the remarriage of the other parent in such a way as to integrate the remarriage into existing rigid belief systems.

The Ahrons Binuclear Study (Ahrons & Wallisch, 1987) found that the coparenting relationship tended to deteriorate following remarriage. This was most likely to be true in the case in which the mother had custody of the children and the father had remarried. Conflict around coparenting was lowest in cases where neither parent had remarried. The nonremarried couples tended to spend more time with each other and have an amicable relationship.

Ahrons and Rodgers (1987) concluded that remarriage tends to cause a deterioration in coparenting in that it unbalances the system. When the father is the first to remarry, many mothers are likely to perceive the remarriage as a further narcissistic blow, yet another abandonment. This fear is very real in the sense that remarried fathers are less likely to continue to offer services to their former spouses, such as home repairs and maintenance of the yard. If the father's new wife works, his standard of living is likely to rise, further adding to the disparity between the father's standard of living and that of the single-parent mother. In addition, the prospect of the father having new children to support is perceived as a threat to the single-parent mother's continued dependence on her former husband for financial support of her children.

Ahrons and Wallisch (1987) found that stepmothers felt much role strain as well. As a group they were the most dissatisfied with their position in the family. They were less satisfied about their relationship to the stepchildren, felt their relationship to their husband was negatively affected by their husband's children, and were less involved with his children.

A stepmother who does not have children may be perceived as a competitor for the role of mother in the children's lives. Ahrons and Wallisch (1987) noted that, of all combinations postdivorce, mothers and stepmothers had the most hostile (yet at times the most positive) relationships. (Fathers and stepfathers, for example, had the least conflicted relationships.) Given the primacy of mothers in children's lives, these women seemed to feel they had the most at stake. Many stepmothers who had not had children clung to the idealized notion that this new family would be no different than an intact, nuclear family. They quickly became discouraged when they realized that the children would not accept them as a substitute for their mothers. Still other stepmothers discouraged fathers' relationships with their children, viewing them as an outside threat to the marriage. They interpreted the father's wish to see his children more often as giving in to the manipulations of his ex-wife. Ahrons and Rodgers (1987) reported that when the mother remarries, although this creates some new problems, it balances the system greatly and appears to reduce some of the anger and resentment on the part of the mother.

John Santrock of the University of Texas and coauthor Karen Sitterle (1987) made similar observations in their study of remarried custodial fathers and remarried custodial mothers. These stepmothers made consistent efforts to establish a good relationship with their stepchildren, often sharing the bulk of child-rearing activities with their husbands. (As a group, they tended to be far more active in the children's lives than were the stepfathers.) However, the children continued to reject them, viewing them as detached, unsupportive, and uninvolved in their lives. Many of these stepmothers had begun to detach as well. Santrock and Sitterle observed that the children in father-custody families continued to perceive their noncustodial mothers as warm and nurturant and were strongly loyal to them. They concluded that the presence of the stepmother in these father-custody families threatened the child's attachment to the natural mother or enhanced the child's feelings of loss of the mother. They also observed that simple father-custody families (in which the stepmother brought no children into the family) fared best. Complex remarried father-custody homes—in which the stepmother brought children into the re-marriage—were marked by more conflict. This escalated to even greater levels when the stepmother had several children and the new couple had a child together.

Johnston and Roseby (1997) noted that new stepmothers often intensify postdivorce conflict by rallying to the father's cause, agitating to save the children from a "neglectful" mother. This scenario is equally likely when a stepfather joins the family and allies himself against the vilified natural father of the children to consolidate his position. Fathers who may have felt humiliated by the loss of contact with their children and loss of control over decision making in the children's lives may feel further threatened and marginalized by the presence of a stepfather who takes a strong role as father to the children. Ahrons and Rodgers (1987) pointed out that the introduction of any new stepparent will involve the taking over of some roles and responsibilities that once were accorded the natural parent. This is likely to exacerbate tensions among all parties involved and must be done gradually and with sensitivity.

Given these findings, one can speculate that highly conflicted post-divorce families who remarry quickly are at high risk for intensifying tensions, especially if it is the father and he remarries soon after the divorce. The potential for conflict is further heightened by two factors: the step-parent's taking on a strong parental role with the stepchildren and the stepparent's inclusion of children from previous marriages.

PARENTAL ABDUCTIONS OF CHILDREN IN CUSTODY DISPUTES

The most serious cases of interparental conflict lead to parent abduction, a phenomenon that was rarely seen before the divorce revolution. These cases extend from the simplest—a child who is not returned by a parent until the next day—to the dramatic cases, which make headline news. For example, in a recent case (Williams, 1999) Philadelphia millionaire Bipin Shah offered a $2 million award to the individual or group who recovered his daughters, who had gone into hiding, though no one had accused Shah of harming the girls. He also filed a $100 million lawsuit against Faye Yager of Atlanta, Georgia, who is said to have spearheaded the group Children of the Underground, a network of safe houses for mothers and children seeking to escape custody and visitation orders (currently, this suit is still pending). Shah regained custody of his daughters, now 7 and 9, in April 1999, having located them in Lucerne, Switzerland. His search had cost $3.2 million, had taken him from Finland to South Africa, and had involved networking with more than 125 bounty hunters.

The earliest work on the topic of parental abductions of children was authored by criminologist Michael Agopian (1981). Agopian studied 91 cases of parental abduction (of 130 children) screened by the district attorney's office in Los Angeles in one year in the late 1970s. He noted that the majority of parents who abducted children were White (68%), male (71%), younger than their mid-30s (73%), and employed (70%). In 70% of the cases, only one child was abducted, and the child was as likely to be a boy as a girl. One third of the children were between ages 3–5, one quarter were 6–8, and one quarter were 9–11. The abducting parent, usually the father, was likely to have a criminal record. In these more serious cases, which came to the attention of the district attorney's office, less than half the children were found and returned.

Psychiatrists Diane Schetky and Lee Haller (1983), at Yale University and Georgetown University, respectively, reported on three detailed case studies of parental abductions. They commented on "ego impairment" in the abducting parents: Two had borderline personality disorder, and one had some form of psychosis. Much like all parents entrenched in postdivorce conflict, they were viewed as having trouble differentiating their own needs from those of the children. They were seen as engaging in denial of wrongdoing in the marriage and blaming the former spouse for all of their difficulties. Still enmeshed with their former spouse, they appeared to be acting out of spite and revenge.

Not all demographic studies indicate that the majority of parental abductors are male. Inger Sagatun and Lin Barrett (1990) obtained information on 43 cases of parental abduction from a family court services agency in California from 1983 to 1987 and found different figures. In their study, 25 of the abductors, or 59%, were women. These mothers were more likely to have been awarded custody of the children, and the length of the abduction was likely to be longer when the mother was the abductor.

Base Rates of Abduction

How common is the phenomenon of parental abduction of children? Ellen Goodman (1976), writing at the peak of the divorce revolution, put the figure at 25,000–100,000 per year. David Finkelhor of the University of New Hampshire, along with Gerald Hotaling and Andrea Sedlak (1991), conducted a national survey of 35,000 households to derive base rates for parental abduction. Narrowing their focus to the 10,544 households with children, Finkelhor et al. identified a total of 142 children from 104 households as having been abducted at least briefly by a family member in the previous year. Given that there were about 65 million children in the nation at that time, they estimated that about 163,200 children had been abducted by a family member in violation of a court order, had been abducted for at least one night, and were being concealed. In 12% of these cases, the child was taken out of state. In about 18% of the cases, serious force was used. In only about 3%, or about 5,000, of these cases was the child never returned. In fact, in the majority of cases, the respondents in the survey knew where the children were at all times. Finkelhor et al. suggested that what is referred to as *missing children* might be more accurately labeled *children who were not where they were supposed to be* for a brief period of time.

The National Center for Missing and Exploited Children (see Janvier, McCormick, & Donaldson, 1990) reported that an even smaller number of children are kidnapped by a parent each year—1,400 children in the United States among which 100 children are taken abroad. Given such a disparity in estimates of the size of the problem, it may be that Finkelhor et al.'s (1991) study may include cases that were never reported to law enforcement agencies or centers for missing children because the child's whereabouts were known to the searching parent.

Clinicians who work with highly conflicted families may want to keep in mind the risk factors. Finkelhor et al. (1991) determined that the peak age for children to be abducted was 2–3 years. The perpetrators tended to be men (75%) in their 30s. The most high-risk time for the most serious abductions was the period right after the separation and before the divorce was final. It is interesting to note that there were regional trends. Parental abduction appeared to occur disproportionately in the southern states, with over 50% of the cases occurring there. Finkelhor et al. speculated that more traditional court rulings in the South favoring mothers may make fathers more discouraged about obtaining due process in custody proceedings.

Peggy Plass, David Finkelhor, and Gerald Hotaling (1997) expanded Finkelhor et al.'s (1991) survey by including a control group in a later study. Further refining risk factors, they found that the abductors were highly likely to be White and to have a history of domestic violence. If the parents of the child had not been married, the risk of abduction was much lower. The risk of abduction rose with educational level. However, in the most serious cases, lower educational level was associated with increased risk.

Common Patterns in Abductions

How do abductions occur? The above surveys noted that most abductions occurred when a noncustodial father refused to return children after a visitation. He may have simply kept them longer than the divorce decree allowed, or he may have kept them for longer periods of time while pursuing a change of custody through the courts. Thus, the custodial mother knew of the children's whereabouts. Only a few are sudden, violent abductions in which the child is concealed or taken to another country. In a minority of abductions the custodial parent, usually the mother, conceals the child in the belief that she is protecting the child from abuse by the father or his family.

Many of the demographic features thus change with the locale in which the survey is conducted and the method by which parents of abducted children are located. For example, a Canadian study conducted by Cole and Bradford (1992) revealed that 55% of the abductors were born outside of North America. This is because of the high immigrant population in Ottawa, Ontario. Cole and Bradford evaluated 20 abductors at the Ottawa Family Court Clinic over a 6-year period. This group was still largely male (80%) and in their mid-30s. It is notable that in 60% of the cases access to the child was being denied to the abductor. This was substantially higher than the 15% figure reported for the control group of families in custody–access disputes that did not involve abduction. Cole and Bradford found high rates of behavioral disorders in the group of abductors: Sixty-five percent of them (compared with only 30% of the control group) had previous psychiatric treatment. Fully 40% of the abductors had involvement with the legal system, whereas this was true for only 5% of the control group. These researchers diagnosed 90% of the abductors with a psychiatric disorder: 45% with a personality disorder, 35% with a substance abuse disorder, 5% with an affective (mood) disorder, and 5% with a psychotic disorder. Although these figures are high, they were also somewhat high in the control group: Twenty-five percent had a personality disorder, 15% had a substance abuse disorder, and 20% had an affective disorder.

Rosemary Janvier, along with her colleagues McCormick and Donaldson (1990), recruited participants by mailing surveys to parents who had contacted one or more of the many missing-children's organizations in the country. Janvier et al. were able to obtain responses from 65 parents of 101 missing children. Only 15 of the children had been recovered, so these were serious cases. The perpetrators were male in only 55% of this sample. Fully 40% of these kidnappings were international. In these cases a parent, typically a father, who had no previous record of psychiatric problems or criminal history, took a male child back to his country of origin shortly before a divorce was finalized. The more serious offenses in which the mother was the perpetrator were likely to occur in the United States and involved a mother taking a child, boy or girl, underground, fearing abuse by the father. Children were recovered in only 7% of the domestic cases, whereas 19% of the international cases resulted in the return of the child. Janvier et al. found the attempts to recover children from international abductions to be particularly costly, with the majority of parents spending $10,000–$50,000 for the return of their children.

Children's Adjustment to Abduction

Many researchers have been surprised at the low rates of behavior disorders in children who have been abducted. Rex Forehand of the University of Georgia and his coauthors Nicholas Long, Carolyn Zogg, and Elizabeth Parish (1989) concluded that "these findings indicate that parental abduction has a less severe impact than the earlier clinical descriptions of psychiatrically referred children" (p. 315). Their study of 17 children—obtained, again, through missing-children's organizations—revealed that although there was an increase in child behavior problems, the effects were limited in severity and short lived. Five of the 17 children had elected to stay with the abducting parent, with the permission of the searching parent. These findings were similar to those of Hegar and Greif (1993), mentioned below, who were able to conduct follow-up interviews with 69 parents whose children were kidnapped by a parent and later located and returned. Behavior at home was rated to be satisfactory by 85% of the parents. Eighty-nine percent had satisfactory school grades, and 90% had satisfactory behavior in school. A surprising 23% of the children had elected to continue living with the abductor and were allowed to do so. Greif and Hegar concluded that many of the abductions were attempts to "normalize" family relationships, much in the same way that other families do so through the courts.

The observation of low rates of disturbance in children was a surprising finding in Cole and Bradford's (1992) study as well. Fully 84% of the abducted children were asymptomatic, compared with 73% of the control group. The authors concluded that children seen in clinics who are the subject of custody disputes are likely to have somewhat elevated levels of behavior problems already, because of parental hostility and conflict over transitions. Parental abduction does not appear to increase levels of behavior problems to any significant degree over those existing levels.

A Typology of Child Abductions

Greif and Hegar (1992; Hegar & Greif, 1993) have conducted the most extensive study to date of parent abductors, the children, and the parents who are searching. With the assistance of 15 organizations for the recovery of missing children, these authors were able to obtain lengthy completed questionnaires from 371 parents throughout the United States and Canada, who recounted the abduction of 519 children. Over half the children had not been returned, so these were, by self-selection, serious cases. Even prior to the abduction, these were homes marked by hostility, tension, and chaos. Fifty-two percent of the families had occurrences of family violence prior to the abduction. Substance abuse and psychiatric problems were often blamed for the divorce. The abductor had threatened to take the children in nearly half the cases, and 21% of the children were taken to a foreign country. Similar to Janvier et al.'s (1990) study, the portion of abductors who were male was 55%, as compared with 45% for female abductors. (The proportion of female abductors appears to rise in studies that recruit participants from organizations for the return of missing children. In Forehand et al.'s [1989] study, 59% of the abductors were male, and 41% were female.)

Greif and Hegar (1993) identified five patterns of parental abduction that accounted for 82% of their respondents. The first and largest group, Abduction by a Violent Visitor, were cases in which, typically, the mother had filed for divorce after battering by the father and fled with the children. The father either tracked them down and kidnapped the children or waited and took the children some months later while having the children on visitation. His goal was to hurt the mother, express his anger, and gain control in possibly forcing a reconciliation. These marriages were likely to have been ended because of violence, substance abuse, or maltreatment of the children and were marked by a history of previous threats to take the children.

Pattern 2, Abduction by a Nonviolent Visitor, described cases in which the noncustodial parent, somewhat more often the mother, took the children because her visitations were being blocked or the custodial father was moving away. Her goal was simply to have more contact with the children. Pattern 3, Abduction by a Nonviolent Shared Custodian, was also characterized by a nonviolent history on the part of the abductor. Here, though, custody was shared or the couple was not yet divorced, and the mother fled with the children because of the father's history of battering or abuse of the children.

Pattern 4, Abduction by a Violent Shared Custodian, is similar to Pattern 1. In these cases, in which the abductor is more typically male, there has been a history of spouse abuse, and particularly battles over money, although custody has been shared. The abductor seems to be motivated by a fear of loss of contact with the children or a need to have more control over his or her life.

Pattern 5, Abduction by a Sole Custodian, is similar to Patterns 2 and 3. In these cases, the abductor is nearly always female. There has not been a history of violence. The mother may object to the father's new wife and simply feel that the children are hers and that it is her choice to move with them wherever she chooses. In some of these cases, the abductor's motives could not be understood, or her motives reflected "an emotionally troubled state of mind."

Intervention Programs to Prevent Abductions

In addressing what has become a national problem, several of the above-mentioned authors have made recommendations to reduce the risk of abductions. Janvier et al. (1990) recommended that threats be taken seriously from the outset and that the court put in place restraining orders and supervised visitations for parents who threaten to abduct children. They also recommended tougher laws enforcing criminal penalties for child abductions. Greif and Hegar (1993) noted that domestic violence cases that lead to divorce appear to be particularly high-risk cases and recommended that parents who have been violent not receive custody of children. Although this may not prevent abductions, it may give the custodial parent the legal right to begin a nationwide search immediately after the children are taken. Appointment of a guardian to the children in such chaotic divorces may also facilitate prompt legal action when children are suddenly missing. Greif and Hegar also advocated the adjudication of custody in such a way as to be inclusive and respectful of each parent's relationship with the children. Finally, Greif and Hegar urged the courts to offer more mediation and counseling services to angry, desperate parents and to be more accessible and available to parents who perceive an imminent crisis. It is hoped that courts that are perceived as responsive may deter desperate parents from taking the law into their own hands.

In what may be a model program for the prevention of child abductions, Janet Johnston and Linda Girdner (1998) drew up profiles of parents at high risk for child abduction and directed them into a treatment program directly aimed at preventing interference with custody. The 50 families were recruited from family court counselors throughout the San Francisco Bay area. The program consisted of either 10 hours or 40 hours of psychoeducational counseling, including provision of information on the laws regarding child abduction and custody violations.

The risk profiles Johnston and Girdner (1998) drew up were similar to those of other studies. In Profile 1, the most common, the parent was unemployed, had no home or financial ties to the area, had threatened to abduct the child, and had relatives or an underground network that had pledged to help. Profile 2 consisted of parents, usually mothers, who were convinced that the father was neglecting, molesting, or abusing the child. Profile 3 included parents who were paranoid and delusional, a highly dangerous group, although also only 4% of the sample. Another small group was Profile 4, the sociopathic group. These were usually men who had a history of domestic violence and previous arrests and who had abducted the child to get revenge on the mother. Profile 5 included couples in which one or both parents were from other countries. As the marriage was ending, the parent felt particularly isolated in the United States and felt a need to return to his or her native country to restore a sense of self-identity. These parents were particularly noted for their deprecation of American culture. Profile 6 included parents who were particularly poor and uneducated and had little understanding of or access to the judicial system. Many had not been married to the father and had assumed that he had no rights to have contact with the child. These parents, usually mothers, simply moved the child to another state to stay with relatives.

In this psychoeducational counseling program, as high-risk families were identified they were directed into treatment immediately, and they received heightened attention from the court. At follow-up 9 months later, only 10% of the families had reoccurrences of child abduction, and virtually none had been violent toward each other. This is in comparison with 44% of the sample who had already been cited for interfering with custody. It appears that child abductions are, for some populations, an act of desperation by parents who feel disenfranchised with the legal system. Immediate intervention and court hearings may give such parents a sense of control and substantially reduce the incidence of violence and abductions.

WHAT THE RESEARCH SHOWS

Clinicians have observed common personality traits in individuals locked in protracted custody disputes. These parents have been described as excessively hostile, narcissistically wounded, and extremely demanding and unreasonable. They engage in high levels of defensiveness and projection of blame as well as rigid, black-and-white thinking. They have difficulty seeing a situation from several viewpoints and have only a limited capacity for understanding the feelings and needs of others. They are described as insensitive to their children and are said to view them as narcissistic extensions of themselves. The limited empirical research that is available largely supports these clinical observations. What has been somewhat controversial is the secondary observation that although these parents seem disturbed with regard to the divorce and custody dispute, they typically have high levels of functioning before the divorce and in non-divorce–related spheres of living. Thus, it is difficult to conclude that their disturbed behavior warrants a diagnosis of personality disorder. Some theorists suggest a particular developmental origin for this constellation of traits, although cognitive theories of personality traits based on temperament may be more viable.

Large-scale studies indicate that most divorced parents remarry and that they do so quickly, within 5 years of the divorce. Many families underestimate the high level of conflict that is generated by remarriage, a factor that contributes to the high divorce rate of second marriages. Writers in the field of remarriage have concluded that the situations that trigger or reignite the highest levels of conflict are these: when the father remarries before the custodial mother, when the remarriage occurs soon after the divorce, when stepparents bring children from previous marriages into the remarriage, and when stepparents take a strong parental role with the stepchildren.

Child abductions by parents are often dramatic and grab the attention of the news media. Estimates of the size of the problem vary widely, because the severity of abductions ranges from cases in which a child is not returned home on time to those in which a child has been taken underground and never seen again. Studies of child abductors suggest there are many subgroups and that these groups vary with recruitment method. In general, more than half of the abductors are young men with a history of personality disorders, domestic violence, or involvement with the courts. They are most at risk for abduction at the time of the divorce when they feel disenfranchised by the mother and the court system. A subset of these are men from foreign countries who disparage American culture and wish to return their children to their homeland. The most common group of female abductors are those who are convinced that the father is abusing or molesting the children and who conceal the children or flee the state. It is surprising that the studies of the children who are abducted by a parent show little ill effect from the turmoil. Recommendations for prevention have involved more intense involvement of the court with mediation, counseling, and education, in the hope that these desperate parents will not feel the justice system has ignored their concerns.

GUIDELINES FOR THE CLINICIAN

A conservative approach to understanding the dynamics of parents who are embroiled in intense conflict is to start from the generally accepted premise that the majority of these individuals can be said to have mild personality disorders or at least traits of personality disorders that may become exacerbated under stress. I propose that not all personality disorders are represented among populations of embattled postdivorce parents. For example, passive–dependent, avoidant, and schizoid personality disorders are almost never seen in custody battles. Likewise, sociopathic individuals rarely have the deep attachment to their children or feel passionately about retaining custody of them. These individuals must be healthy enough to have formed strong bonds with others yet be narcissistically vulnerable and prone to angry retaliation. A more productive way to approach family therapy–mediation with these parents is to conceptualize the nature of the personality disorder, understand the nature of the perceived threat, and approach the individual through treatment and through mediation with a goal of reducing the level of perceived threat.

For example, parents in the histrionic and narcissistic group have strong needs to be recognized, to be held in high esteem, and to be the center of attention. These individuals perceive the events of the divorce as "a loss of face," a deflation of self-image, a wounding, and a degradation. Small disappointments are perceived as major threats to the person's pride or ego. Kevin in the case study at the beginning of this chapter is an example, and Dan, described in chapter 5, also is narcissistic, but to a lesser degree.

The mediator–therapist may want to take special care to be deferential to this individual, to seek out his or her opinion or notify him or her in advance of any developments (e.g., "Excuse me, I don't mean to interrupt, but I must say something here"). Similarly, one may want to advise the ex-spouse to be likewise as deferential as possible, to refrain from using insulting words, dismissing the person in a flippant manner, hanging up the telephone on him or her, and so on. One may want to build up such an individual by commenting on his or her specific assets and strengths as a parent and as a person: For example, "Your notes are very thorough. I'm sure that thoroughness is one of the qualities that has made you so successful in your work." One may want to empathize with his or her situation (e.g., "It is tragic that someone of your character has to go through such a degrading process"). Another tactic is to reframe events in a narcissistic manner to gain the individual's cooperation. For example,

> She may be taking you back to court not to humiliate you but because she is so emotionally involved with you, she can't let go. She needs to stay connected with you. The best thing you could do for her is to settle out of court so that she can let go.

Hostile–dependent, borderline, and histrionic personalities have intense needs for affection, nurturance, succorance, reassurance, and emotional support. These individuals often come into a marriage with unrealistic expectations that their partner is all-giving and all-caring and will provide for their emotional needs endlessly. These needy individuals react to the divorce as an abandonment, a withdrawal of needed supplies without which they cannot survive. They feel deeply betrayed, duped, used, manipulated. Janice of chapter 3's case study is a good example, as is Jennifer in chapter 5 and, to a lesser degree, Terry in chapter 2 and Monica in chapter 6.

The therapist–mediator could reduce such individuals' feelings of threat by assuring them of their attractiveness, worthiness, and lovableness.

For example, "Why would you want to keep on fighting with him? I'm sure there is someone out there who could love you more completely and faithfully." This individual should be encouraged to look to other people—friends, family, church members—for reassurances of their self-worth. The ex-spouse who continues to assert this person's unworthiness is likely to provoke more anger and aggression. A better approach, if one is advising this ex-spouse, is to have this person express regret or remorse about the hurt they have caused, for example, "I know that you feel I have hurt you terribly. I'm not sure I understand yet why you feel this way, but I am very sorry for any hurt that I may have caused you."

The clinician may also want to point out the supplies and resources of emotional gratification that the person still has but of which he or she may have lost sight, for example,

> I know you feel alone right now, but you must remind yourself that you have the children's love, your family has stood by you, and the neighbors all gave affidavits as to how you were the primary parent. It is your ex-spouse who is more alone now than you are.

Rhoda Feinberg and James Greene (1997) suggested that the attorney who works with a parent who has a histrionic personality understand that these individuals operate on emotions and not on logic and intellectual data. They are prone to making dramatic presentations to the attorney of how they have been wronged and victimized. They are also prone to frequent crisis calls over how they have been wronged in a terrible fashion by their former spouse. Feinberg and Greene observed that these clients tend not to follow through with requests for records, papers, and information. They advised attorneys to acknowledge their client's emotional needs but to always check out with corroborating documents and witnesses the information such clients provide. They cautioned the attorney that parents with borderline personalities are likely to seek out new relationships rapidly and should be cautioned about the dangers of doing so. These clients are prone to impulsive and extreme moods. For them, an attorney who is stable, calm, and practical can be a point of stability.

Feinberg and Greene (1997) suggested that the attorney working with a client with a narcissistic personality minimize the win–lose language of the court process, as it is has implications for feelings of humiliation and defeat. They also advised the attorney to help the client who has unrealistic and grandiose ideas of victory to establish more realistic and modest expectations. Clients with narcissistic personality may see themselves as the attorney's only client, or the most special client, and the attorney must also counter these unrealistic perceptions.

People with paranoid, passive–aggressive, and obsessive traits have intense needs for control in relationships and to regulate the degree of closeness and vulnerability. They have an aversion to appearing weak, exposed, or manipulated. For them, the divorce and the loss of children represents a stripping away of their sense of control over their lives and what is important to them. Turning over decisions to mental health professionals, mediators, attorneys, and judges means in some ways being controlled by someone else, being helpless, being unsure about the future—all of which are threatening. A good example is Ted in chapter 5, who was difficult to interview because he went into such detail and insisted in telling lengthy stories and controlling the interviews. Jackie, described in chapter 8, combines elements of paranoid and obsessive personality disorder.

Therapists—mediators would do well to direct their efforts toward providing these individuals with as much control over what is going on as is practical—to allow them to set an agenda; encourage them to make lists of issues to review; take notes; and keep a diary of major events, dates, places, and so on. It is best to be deferential and polite, always including this person in any communications with other parties, making sure he or she is never left out. Another caveat is to give these individuals control over clearly defined areas of turf, be they ever so small or so seemingly trivial. These individuals are inflexible and rigid, and they do not react well to last-minute changes in appointment times, in the topic, who is to be there, and so on. They also need to have future visits clearly planned in advance and a timeline laid out as to what will happen and when.

Feinberg and Greene (1997) suggested that the attorney working with an obsessive client help him or her move his or her focus away from schedules, rules, and procedures and to see instead the "big picture." The attorney may be frustrated with the individual's inability to see other points of view, even after repeated explanations. However, the attorney must still underscore the different viewpoints of not only the other party but also the judge and law-making bodies. The attorney working with such a client must also be mindful of firmly taking control of the case.

With the paranoid client, Feinberg and Greene (1997) pointed out that the attorney must be careful to probe for more information, because these individuals are reluctant to give a full and detailed accounting of an event until they trust the attorney. The attorney can build trust slowly with these clients by being exceptionally open and forthcoming and admitting mistakes. Feinberg and Greene cautioned attorneys to never go into a situation for which the paranoid client is not prepared. Always tell him or her ahead of time what personal information may be disclosed, to whom, and for what reason.

Johnston and Roseby (1997) made the cogent point that attorneys and the courts have roles to play here as well in terms of exacerbating or being sensitive to parental psychopathology. Attorneys, in their zeal to be advocates for their clients, often ally with an enraged spouse in a campaign to humiliate, punish, and otherwise destroy the other spouse. This often occurs as an emotional destruction, through the inflammatory language of the legal filings, harassing and embarrassing questions at the time of the deposition, or simply as a wearing-down process through endless delays. It may also occur as a wearing down of the other party financially as the months and months of legal filings take their toll. Johnston and Roseby also gave examples of how judges, in their often sharp rebukes from the bench, further degrade and humiliate parents who are already in a fragile emotional state. The court is seen as a semidivine authority on morality by many individuals, and extreme curtailments of contact with the children, along with critical attacks, have provoked some parents to violence or suicide.

The clinician working with blended and remarried families involved in hostile disputes can also be an ally who directs the families in how not to exacerbate existing tensions. Stepparents must be introduced slowly. They should sidestep existing alliances wherever possible. Careful efforts should be made not to take over the other parent's existing roles and responsibilities. The children should never call the stepparent "Dad" or "Mom," no matter how innocent the intent, as long as the biological parent is an active part of the child's life. In some cases, for example, where one parent essentially disappears from a small child's life, and the child bonds with a stepparent, the remarried family may function much like an intact family. But for the most part stepparents must give up any fantasy of having a "normal" family and realize that this family is fragile, complex, and prone to crises. They must support the primacy of both parents in the children's lives, wherever possible, and stay on the sidelines as marginal players. If they have a role to play in this warfare, it is much like that of the Red Cross—ferrying the wounded out of combat zones and providing comfort and relief behind the lines while not taking sides.

Clinicians who are treating divorced parents should note the risk factors for parental abduction. The most common scenario is one in which the wife has left a husband who was volatile, demanding, abusive, and prone to substance abuse, as Greif and Hegar (1992) noted. However, I have worked in the past with left-behind mothers and have noted these additional risk factors: the father has little education, little or no job stability, no investments in remaining in the area—such as owning his own home or business—and has supportive parents who themselves have financial assets. In these cases, the paternal grandparents often encourage an abduction with offers of financial and legal support to the father. If these factors exist, the mother should be strongly enjoined to take up the matter with her attorney and seek protective orders right away.

Mothers who abduct children are much more difficult to predict. However, mothers may first disclose a desire to flee the state with the children or go underground to their therapist. The therapist has several ethical as well as clinical obligations in these cases. The therapist must be careful not to support any decision that may be perceived by the courts as illegal. The therapist should strongly encourage the mother to review her decision with her attorney first. Such a move—although the mother may perceive it, correctly or incorrectly, as an effort to protect the children—may be seen by the courts as contempt for the divorce decree, and it may result in arrest of the mother and reversal of custody of the children. Such an outcome could be disastrous for the whole family.

CASE STUDY UPDATE

Anne was seen intermittently over the course of 5 years' time since she first presented with panic attacks. She and Kevin continued to have battles over the telephone and in person over every aspect of sharing their son's time and controlling decision making in her life. She opened one session with "You know, Kevin is as angry today as he was 5 years ago. I still just don't understand it. I asked him this last time why he was angry at me. His version of what happened is that it was I who chose to file for divorce. He says he tried to hang in there. Can you believe that?"

I asked Anne what she had learned in the 3 years since they had divorced. She replied, "If I had to do it all over again, I would stay with Kevin. I wouldn't have divorced him. We would live in the house and raise our son and we would have separate lives." Astonished at her answer —given that very few people regret their divorces—I asked for an explanation. She explained that she had no idea, going into the divorce, just how financially and emotionally stressful it would be. She had thought that Kevin would get over his anger, "but he still screams and yells." She was especially unprepared for the sense of loss she felt in being unable to see her child on so many weekends and holidays. When she was divorcing from Kevin, she never thought deeply about the pain of being separated from her son so often and for so much of the time. She had thought that it would be a little bit sad but that she would get over it in time. In reality, she continued to feel sad every time she was away from him. She still cried sometimes on her weekends without him, even though it had been 3½ years since she and Kevin began a structured visitation arrangement. Looking back on her reasons for divorce, she said that she thought at the time that Kevin might hit her in front of their son, and she was worried about what kind of role model that would be. But now she wondered if that was a good enough reason to end the marriage, given what had transpired and what still lay ahead. She knew that there would be more litigation into the future and that Kevin would continue to do everything he could to get custody of their son.

I asked Anne what advice she would give to a person who might find himself or herself in a similar situation with a narcissistic ex-spouse who was ruthless and enraged. "Stand your ground with appropriate limits and boundaries. Hold him to the letter of the divorce agreement. Don't let him bully you into capitulating. Don't give in on everything," she asserted. "But I've learned also that I have to give a little too, or we'll get stuck in conflict. I have learned that I have to baby his ego some. I make every effort to keep him informed, to consult with him on decisions, however small. I have learned to let a lot go, not to argue with him. I keep reminding myself that I have primary custody, that I have the last say on a lot of things, so I can give in on some other things and not feel I've lost the battle."

Anne and I continued to ponder how long Kevin would remain injured and enraged. When he remarried and moved into a luxurious home, we both thought that his newly enhanced self-image would ease his hurt, but it did not. We mused over whether his having another child (Kevin's second wife had no other children and was not planning children with Kevin) would ease his need for revenge. But we had learned to not try to predict the future.

10

EVALUATION OF SEXUAL ABUSE ALLEGATIONS IN CHILD CUSTODY CASES

CASE STUDY 1

Jay and Marva and their 5-year-old daughter Janna were seen in the context of a custody evaluation. Marva had left the home 6 months earlier, asserting that she was protecting Janna from further sexual abuse by her father. Jay, via his attorney, requested a psychological evaluation of Marva because of her lengthy history of psychiatric treatment and suicidal threats. Marva counterfiled for a psychological evaluation of Jay, alleging he was a child molester. The court appointed me to evaluate all the parties simultaneously.

Marva and Jay had been married for 7 years at the time of the separation. Marva had a child from her former marriage, Jennifer, who was 14. Marva had entered treatment 4 years prior to the evaluation for "stress and depression" due to her unfulfilling marriage to Jay and to "the effects of abuse in my previous marriage." Marva continued in treatment with four therapists over 4 years, changing therapists whenever her managed care coverage changed to a new plan. These therapists had given her the following assemblage of diagnoses: bipolar disorder, dependent personality, obsessive–compulsive personality, clinical depression, and posttraumatic stress disorder (PTSD). She had been treated with various antidepressants.

Over the course of the 4 years, Marva had come to identify more personally and intensively with abuse victims. She began to recall and identify instances of abuse by her parents. She read books on domestic violence victims. She felt abused by her employer and filed a sexual harassment suit. She felt abused by the children in the day care center where she worked. Marva submitted to me a 50-page document, typed, single spaced, that detailed instances of her abuse by Jay, describing the most trivial of his behaviors as examples of "mental abuse."

Jay was a passive man who felt helpless and confused when confronted with Marva's anger. Understanding how neglected Marva felt when he traveled, he took a lower paying job so he would be home early every night. "I tried to meet her needs," he said in the evaluation, "but her needs were so great, I couldn't see how anybody could meet her needs." Jay responded to Marva's angry attacks by further withdrawing from her, watching television, and drinking excessively in the evenings. Marva responded to his withdrawal by becoming more frustrated, angry, and furious with Jay for not trying to make her happy.

Marva continued to explore her feelings of abuse by Jay in her sessions with her therapist. One day she discovered a rash on Janna's vaginal area. She asked Janna if Jay had touched her there, and Janna replied, "no." When Marva told her therapist about this discovery, the therapist advised Marva to take Janna to the children's hospital for a sexual abuse evaluation. Marva did so and made a report of sexual abuse to the child protective services (CPS) agency. Janna was examined and interviewed, and sexual abuse was not substantiated. However, Marva's report to the therapist failed to include this information: The therapist advised Marva to flee the home immediately with Janna and Jennifer and stay in a motel.

When Marva disclosed to her attorney what she had done, he was furious. She had acted impulsively, without consulting him. The only way to "rehabilitate" her with the court was to stick by the story adamantly, so that she did not come across as a manipulative mother. Marva, Janna, and Jennifer moved from one motel to the other for months, until the temporary hearing was held. At that hearing, the judge ordered that Jay remain in the home and Marva have temporary custody of Janna. Marva was incensed that she had to go on living in motels. She fired her attorney. She felt abused by the attorney, the judge, and the judicial system.

At the time of the evaluation, Marva continued to portray herself as a victim of an abusive man—a man who had abused her and her daughter. She brought in the evidence to prove it—a photograph of Jay's pajamas on which lay a plastic sticker that belonged to Janna. "I have this in a safe deposit box at the bank," boasted Marva, "and at the custody trial, I will be vindicated and everyone will know what kind of man Jay is."

Frank and Donna also were seen in the context of a custody dispute. They had been married for 15 years at the time of their separation. They had two children: Adam, age 10, and Annie, age 4. Like Marva, Donna had fled with the children, making allegations of sexual abuse. However, she had hid from Frank, and he had not seen his children for 3 months. Both Donna and Frank had college educations but had achieved little in their work lives. Both worked at low-wage jobs, and their custody battle was being funded by the respective grandparents.

Donna was described as an unusual woman by the people in the community who had contact with her. Wearing outlandish, mismatched clothes, Donna was often loud, and her emotions were strangely out of synch with the content of her conversation. She talked to Adam's teacher about her ability to commune with spirits and to foresee the future. She rambled on at the pediatrician's office about "alternative" cures for common childhood illnesses, while failing to follow through on the pediatrician's recommendations. The sitter for the children had quit after Donna had made accusations that she was stealing or hiding things from her in the house.

Donna and Frank had been in treatment with a family therapist for over a year, with no improvement. Donna was angry at Frank for his passivity and his lack of involvement in the household. She disliked his drinking in the evenings. She resented his not taking charge of the discipline of Adam. Frank was excessively meek and passive and was uninvolved. Finding Donna to be completely intimidating and unreasonable, he retreated to a back room of the house when she came home, to drink beer and watch television. The therapist was at a loss to intervene in this system. Donna was completely unreasonable. Frank rarely spoke in the sessions. The therapist did express concern about Adam. Several times Donna had become verbally abusive toward Adam and had hit him.

At the time of the evaluation, Adam was completely alienated from his father. Living in hiding with his mother, Adam had taken on her manner and her forms of speech. He came to the first interview talking in a loud, expansive, and inappropriate manner about how he was a cowboy and a great chef, and how he would be rich and famous one day. He knew, too, that the FBI was following his mom in the car. Like his mother, he knew that his father was the Olympic Park Bomber (the individual responsible for the bomb at Centennial Olympic Park in July 1996), even though the FBI had refused to investigate Donna's report to them. He bragged about growing up in a bug-infested apartment in a neighborhood of crack dealers. Over two meetings, Adam made a list of extreme and implausible allegations, which included witnessing bloody altercations between his parents, his father taking him to bars to pick up women, and his father kicking him down the stairs and into a crawlspace full of rats and roaches. He stated that his father had molested him during the ages of 3 and 4, that his father had asked him for advice on how to pick up women, and that he had once witnessed his father trying to murder a man in an alley behind a liquor store. When the examiner challenged his stories, Adam insisted they were true. However, as the examiner continued to go over them in detail, Adam's speech became rambling and disjointed, and he had trouble maintaining eye contact. He became disoriented and said, "These things I have to remember, these things in my head are making me sick." Several times he stated that he wanted to kill his father.

Adam's teacher expressed concern about him because he was in a behavior-disordered curriculum at school—he was rejected by his peers; had no social skills; was prone to episodes of rage; and had violently attacked other students several times, showing no remorse. "This is the kind of kid who comes to school with a weapon," the teacher said, "and shoots down a crowd of people."

Adam was introduced to his father in the second interview. He had to be brought into the room by his grandparents. His posture was rigid, and his gaze was fixed. He wore a T-shirt that depicted a man tearing his hair out and screaming "I can't take it any more!" However, by the second meeting with his father, Adam wore a T-shirt that Frank had given him. The two joked comfortably about their favorite foods and movies they would like to see. Adam acted "normal" as long as the conversation did not veer into the bizarre allegations.

In the 1970s the divorce rate surged along with contentious battles over custody of children—a phenomenon that was perhaps heightened by the legislation granting fathers a more fair and impartial consideration for custody of their children. Parallel to this, several nationally publicized cases of sexual abuse in day care centers—the McMartin case in California; the Jordan, Minnesota case; and the Little Rascals Nursery case in North Carolina—contributed to a national obsession with the sexual abuse of young children. Sexual abuse cases are without parallel in mental health and in law. The sexual abuse of a young child takes place in secrecy. The child may show no symptoms whatsoever after an incident of sexual abuse. Yet there is a public perception that one incident of sexual abutse has devastating, long-range consequences for the child (for review, see Rind, Tromovitch, & Bauserman, 1998). There is no test for the occurrence of sexual abuse. The only witness (other than the perpetrator) is a child, whose verbal statement may be primitive, lacking in detail, contradictory, and easily subject to outside influence. The child may have been abused but have motives for not reporting it. On the other hand, he or she may not have been abused but have reason to make a false report of sexual abuse. If one turns to circumstantial evidence, one can only look to a pattern of altered behavior that may be observed by others. Yet there is no clear behavioral pattern that is typical only of sexual abuse and that cannot be explained by any other causative factor. Also, reports of a child's behavior are highly subject to the viewer's own bias at the time.

Given the increasing divorce rate and the national hysteria over child sexual abuse that reached a peak in the 1980s, it was to be expected that reports of sexual abuse allegations were likely to arise in contentious court battles over custody of children. Since these allegations first arose in the late 1970s, the opinions of mental health and legal experts have changed enormously. In the beginning, most allegations were taken at face value under the catchphrase "believe the children" (Sgroi, Porter, & Blick, 1982). However, by the mid-1980s many clinicians were seeing cases of false or unsubstantiated sexual abuse allegations. As of this writing, in the late 1990s, the pendulum has swung in the other direction, and many social workers, court officials, and mental health evaluators assume that a sexual abuse allegation arising during a custody conflict is naturally false. This prompted Canadian psychologist Susan Penfold (1995) to note that "mothers who raise concerns about sexual abuse during child custody disputes may do so at their peril" (p. 339).

In this chapter I briefly review the extensive reports on evaluating children for sexual abuse when the allegations arise in the context of a custody dispute. I first look at base rates to get a sense of how often these cases arise and what proportion of them are concluded to be false or unsubstantiated. Evaluating the allegation must be done carefully and thoroughly, and an outline is proposed for that task. First, the evaluator must examine the overall context and what is known about situational factors in true-accusation cases and in false-accusation cases. Then the evaluator must draw a profile of the accuser and the accused, comparing these with known true cases and false cases. Last, there are data to be gathered from and about the child. Because the child is the primary focus in most evaluations, this source of data will be reviewed in close detail in seven subsections.

CO-OCCURRENCE OF SEXUAL ABUSE ALLEGATIONS WITH CUSTODY AND ACCESS DISPUTES

How frequently are sexual abuse allegations made during custody disputes? The figures on this vary enormously from one study to another. Nancy Thoennes and Patricia Tjaden (1990), researchers in Denver, Colorado, obtained a 2-year grant from the National Center of Child Abuse and Neglect to investigate the incidence of sexual abuse allegations that arise in custody and visitation disputes nationwide. They contacted court administrators, judges, custody mediators, and child protection workers throughout the country to collect data on a large body of child custody cases. Of the nearly 9,000 cases they located, only 169, or 1.5%, involved sexual abuse allegations. The range from one region to another was 1%–8%. This is a small number—surprisingly small, perhaps, to clinicians who do evaluations in disputed cases. It may be likely that the bulk of these cases involved disputes over child support, delayed or missed visitations, geographic moves out of state, objections to live-in companions, and so on.

Similarly, Julia McIntosh and Ronald Prinz (1993) of the University of South Carolina found low base rates of sexual abuse allegations in their population as well. They examined all family court cases involving divorcing families with children, as well as postdivorce cases pertaining to child custody or access that were completed for one county in Columbia, South Carolina, in 1987. This resulted in 603 cases reviewed—588 divorces and 15 postdivorce disputes. Only 85 of these cases were contested custody or access cases. There were 5 cases of alleged sexual abuse. This resulted in an allegation rate of 6% of the contested cases.

Reported rates of sexual abuse may vary with the nature of the case that is seen. For example, it may be that the majority of the cases cited above were uncontested cases or cases that settled out of court with minimum intervention. Melvin Guyer and Peter Ash (1986) of the University of Michigan, who specialize in court-ordered evaluations, noted a marked increase in the number of sexual abuse allegations in their cases. Over a 5-year period, in which they saw 400 cases, 33% involved sexual abuse allegations.

Hollida Wakefield and Ralph Underwager (1991) of Northfield, Minnesota, specialize in evaluating children for sexual abuse. These clinicians saw 500 cases over 6 years and found 40% of the cases to be linked to custody and divorce conflicts. Thus, although the vast majority of couples divorcing with children or returning to court with conflict over custody and access are not alleging abuse, the cases that are referred to custody evaluators and sexual abuse specialists are likely to be cases in which the two are linked.

What percentage of these cases turn out to be based on false allegations? These cases are characterized by the high rates of conclusions that the allegations could not be substantiated or were clearly false. Studies of children evaluated for sexual abuse in hospital emergency rooms usually yield a low rate of unfounded cases. For example, an early study by Joseph Peters (1976) concluded that only 4 out of 64 cases were "improbable." A later and more extensive study of 576 sexual abuse cases in Denver, conducted by Jones and McGraw (1987), found that only 7.8% were clearly fictitious, although 24% were deemed unfounded because of a lack of information, and 17% were considered "unsubstantiated suspicions." In the majority of these cases, the false allegation was made by the adult, not the child.

The earliest red flag as to the high incidence of false reports in child custody cases was raised by Elissa Benedek, a psychiatrist with the University of Michigan, and Diane Schetky, a psychiatrist at Yale University (1985). These clinicians concluded that sexual abuse had not occurred in 10 of their 18 cases. Arthur Green, noted for his classic article on false sexual abuse allegations in child custody cases (1986), found 4 false allegations among the 11 cases he had seen. Green's article stirred controversy in the mental health field because he proposed a list of characteristics that would distinguish true from untrue allegations of sexual abuse. A large group of psychiatrists and psychologists made a formal response with a lengthy attack on Green's thesis, stating that it "contained many unsubstantiated claims that could mislead clinicians and legal decision makers" (Hanson, 1988, p. 258).

Subsequent studies, done on a larger scale, have also found relatively high base rates of false allegations. Of the 160 cases studied by Thoennes and Tjaden (1990), no abuse was believed to have occurred in 33% of the cases. In an additional 17% of the cases, no determination could be reached one way or the other. Of the 500 cases mentioned above, seen by Wakefield and Underwager (1991), 75% resulted in no finding of abuse. This was measured by the result that the charges were dropped, the charges were never filed, the person was acquitted in criminal court, or the juvenile court found no abuse in the family. Wakefield and Underwager also cited an unpublished paper by Dwyer (1986) of the Human Sexuality Program of the University of Minnesota. Dwyer concluded that 77% of the sexual abuse allegations cases coming to his center that were linked to divorces were "hoax" cases.

These data are difficult to interpret, because cases may be unfounded or unsubstantiated for a variety of reasons. There is typically no outside witness and no physical evidence in most cases of fondling or genital manipulation with children. The only witness may be a young child who is developmentally unable to give an adequate account of what happened. Therefore, "unsubstantiated" does not imply that an allegation was false but that no conclusion can be drawn one way or another because of a lack of information. Similarly, cases may be dropped or not pursued by prosecutors, not because they are false but because of a lack of evidence, uncooperative witnesses, the tainting of the child's report because of multiple interviews, and so on.

From these studies, we can see that from the perspective of custody evaluators and mediators, attorneys, and family law judges the possibility that a sexual abuse allegation that arises during a custody or access dispute is false or unsubstantiated is high, perhaps as high as 50%. However, it must also be kept in mind that the chances that the charge will be substantiated may also be as high as 50%. Therefore, the courts and evaluators must be alert to the context in which the two types of cases arise and the characteristics of true cases and false cases. The following is an outline designed to aid the evaluator as well as to guide the attorney who is reviewing such an evaluation.

THE CONTEXT

Kathleen Faller (1991), of the University of Michigan School of Social Work, reviewed several types of true allegations that arise in connection with divorce and custody disputes. As in many other samples, the majority (70%) of the allegations were made against fathers, with the next highest figure against stepfathers (14%). Among Faller's 136 cases of suspected sexual abuse reported to the University of Michigan Project on Child Abuse and Neglect, only 23% were established as false or unfounded. Of the 125 cases in which true claims of sexual abuse were made (and which arose in the context of a custody dispute), Faller described three categories.

One scenario is that in which the discovery of sexual abuse resulted in one parent filing for separation and subsequent divorce to protect the child. These cases were straightforward in that there had been no plans to divorce prior to making the allegation. In 11 of the cases, the child disclosed the abuse to the mother, who then filed for divorce. The mother disclosed the abuse only when visitation plans were being developed. In 16 of the cases, the child disclosed the abuse to the mother or an outside person, and the mother expressed concern about visitations right away.

A second scenario is one in which the parents separate and the child feels safer, and able to reveal long-standing victimization, once the perpetrator is out of the home. Also in this category were cases in which the mother may have had suspicions about sexual abuse during the marriage but chose not to reveal them because she felt it advantageous to stay in the marriage. Twenty-six cases fell into this category of "delayed" reporting.

A third scenario is one in which a marital breakup occurs, and sexual abuse begins in the context of the father's emotional regression and neediness. There may have been indications of boundary violations during the marriage, such as sexualized kissing, bathing or sleeping with the child, or having erections while wrestling with the child, but the presence of the other parent imposed some limitations on any further boundary violations. Once the parents separated, further and more serious boundary violations occurred, often associated with depression, loneliness, and drinking. The largest portion—52 of the cases—fell into the parental regression category.

In what context do false allegations of sexual abuse arise? Allegations that are determined to be false or unsubstantiated are not by any means all hoaxes. Many parents are led to believe sexual abuse out of their misperceptions of the situation: a lack of knowledge of normal, childhood sexual exploration; a misinterpretation of displays of affection between the child and noncustodial parent; and overinterpretations of fuzzy boundary situations such as sleeping or bathing with the child. Some allegations arise because of heightened separation anxiety during visitations and children's disturbed behavior arising out of parental conflict over visitation (see chapter 7). Some arise out of parental psychopathology, which will be explored in depth later. A very small minority may be directly due to parental coaching.

The important situational factors to understand about false allegations are that they occur in the context of extreme marital discord and family dysfunction that has been occurring for some time; in the context in which one parent has vilified the other parent to an extreme degree and thus believes the other parent is capable of harming the child; and in the context in which the making of a claim of sexual abuse gives the accuser a clear strategic benefit in accomplishing a legal, financial, or emotional goal (i.e., reversal of custody and awarding of child support, denial of contact, public humiliation, justification for abduction). Robert Sheridan (1990) proposed that false allegations enable the mother to diminish her felt sense of guilt for the divorce by shifting blame to the father, stigmatizing him and thus elevating her in terms of others' perceptions. Last, the allegations nearly always arise on the part of the accusing parent (not the child) and are vigorously pursued by the accuser.

Benedek and Schetky (1985) analyzed 10 cases of false allegations. Among the cases they found these common characteristics: the mothers had a higher incidence of emotional disorders; the parent, not the child, made the first disclosure; and the allegations were made after the separation or divorce, not during the marriage.

Thoennes and Tjaden (1990) interviewed CPS workers about the believability of allegations of sexual abuse that arose in custody disputes. From those interviews they reported on several factors that seem to be important—at least to CPS workers.

- *Age.* In cases of very young children (younger than age 3), a great majority of the cases were determined to be false or unfounded. In children older than age 7, two thirds of the cases were determined to be substantiated.
- *Frequency of alleged abuse.* Cases in which a single act of sexual abuse was alleged were much less likely to be substantiated than cases in which multiple acts of abuse were alleged. Similarly, cases in which sexual abuse reports had been made multiple times in the past were more often substantiated than those in which the index case was the first report.
- *Anger level.* The higher the anger level between the parents,

the less likely the CPS workers were to believe that the allegations were true.

- *Time since the divorce.* It is interesting that allegations that arose within 2 years of the divorce were less likely to be substantiated than those that occurred more than 2 years after the divorce. Thoennes and Tajden speculated that the children in these cases may be older and thus more able to give an adequate disclosure and that the parents in these cases may be perceived as less angry than newly divorced parents.

THE ACCUSER

Clinicians who work in the area of sexual abuse allegation agree on the hallmark features of accusers who make allegations of sexual abuse that are later determined to be valid. Generally, (a) they have been slow to report the possibility of abuse; (b) they are shocked, upset, and anxious at the discovery of possible abuse; (c) they express remorse for not protecting the child adequately and for not preventing the abuse; (d) they are willing to consider other possible explanations for the child's behavior or symptoms; (e) they agonize over whether to believe the child or the CPS worker or to believe the accused (husband or boyfriend); (f) they are concerned about the impact of the evaluation process on the child; (g) they are not resistant to the child being interviewed alone; (h) if the sexual abuse cannot be substantiated, they are content to let the investigation go, as long as the child's contact with the accused is supervised; (i) the accuser displays remarkably little hostility toward the accused; and (j) the accuser experiences a sense of shame and humiliation about the possibility that sexual abuse has occurred and is reluctant to let anyone know about it.

The accuser in most false-allegation cases is usually, but not always, the mother of a very young child. Sometimes it is the father who accuses the mother's boyfriend or new husband of abusing a young child. At times, adolescent sons from the other parent's previous marriage are accused of sexual abuse of a young child. Accusers are noted for being quick to assume that sexual abuse has occurred; for their hostility toward the accused; and for their lack of empathy for the stress that may be experienced by the child, much less the many negative consequences that may occur to the accused individual. They refuse to consider alternative explanations for out-of-the-ordinary behaviors, pursue evaluations relentlessly, and look for second and third opinions if the first opinion fails to substantiate sexual abuse. They have no sense of shame about the investigation and are eager to tell everyone, even acquaintances and complete strangers, about the investigation. Many researchers have delineated groups of individual accusers who are often seen in false-allegation cases. The following is a compilation.

The Accuser Is a Mother Who Has a Personality Disorder

Various writers in this area have referred to the mother involved in a custody or access dispute who makes a false allegation of sexual abuse as an individual who meets the criteria for a diagnosis of hysterical, borderline, passive–aggressive, or paranoid personality disorder (Benedek & Schetky, 1985; Blush & Ross, 1987; Bresee, Stearns, Bess, & Packer, 1986; Elterman & Ehrenberg, 1991; Green, 1986; Klajner-Diamond et al., 1987; Mikkelsen, Gutheil, & Emens, 1992; Wakefield & Underwager, 1991). Such mothers are described as having a history of multiple episodes of psychiatric treatment and a pattern of unstable, unhappy relationships. They present in interviews as moody, volatile, impulsive, and prone to overreact to minor disappointments and slights. Blush and Ross (1987) gave a particularly apt description of the hysterical personality seen in such cases:

> The female emotionally presents herself as a fearful person who believes she has been a victim of manipulation, coercion, and physical, social, or sexual abuse in the marriage. She has tended to see herself as a powerless victim of the other parent's past as well as present behaviors. She also has tended to see the man as being a source of physical threat, economic punitiveness and retribution, or an individual who simply has not understood the physical and psychological needs of her children. (p. 6)

For an individual such as the one described above, believing in the possibility of sexual abuse fits into a cognitive schema in which the accuser is a victim of a malicious husband, the child is an extension of the accuser, and the child is therefore a victim also. The accuser thus feels justified in pursuing legal action against the accused, and the accuser expects to gain a great deal of sympathy, attention, and emotional support from helping professionals and from the court. This type of case is typified by Case Study 1 at the beginning of this chapter.

Wakefield and Underwager (1990) reviewed their extensive files to determine what portion of their cases merited a diagnosis of personality disorder. They selected 72 cases of falsely accusing parents (4 of whom were men) and 103 falsely accused parents (4 of whom were women). Seventy-four percent of the falsely accusing parents were judged to have a personality disorder—histrionic, borderline, passive–aggressive, or paranoid—and 24% were judged to have no diagnosis. In comparison, 70% of the group of mostly men who were falsely accused were judged to have no diagnosis. Similarly, among a group of 67 parents who were involved in custody disputes that were equally bitter, but in which no allegations of sexual abuse had been made, 66% were assessed as normal.

The Accuser May Not Have a Personality Disorder but Is Obsessed With Hatred and Hostility Toward the Former Spouse

Blush and Ross (1987) referred to these individuals as "justified vindicators." In these cases, the accuser is likely to have overreacted to displays of affection between the accused and the child, such as kissing, or to the accused parent's having bathed the child and washed his or her genitals. He or she may have overinterpreted behavioral reactions on the part of the child, such as a nightmare, or, in some cases, to have outright fabricated what he or she feels to be symptoms of sexual abuse.

The accuser is known to be a dominant and intimidating individual to mental health professionals and to the courts. He or she is on a mission to humiliate and degrade the accused parent and may threaten legal action against those who are unsympathetic to his or her cause. Attorneys and mental health professionals who do not agree with his or her strategy are replaced. This accuser's focus is on the demand that criminal action be taken against the accused. Concern for the child's well-being or the impact of the evaluation process on the child are secondary issues.

The Accuser Has Paranoid Schizophrenia or a Psychotic Disorder

Although this is rare, many clinician–researchers note the possibility of a psychotic disorder in the presentation of these cases (Benedek & Schetky, 1985; Blush & Ross, 1987; Elterman & Ehrenberg, 1991; Green, 1986; Klajner-Diamond et al., 1987). Klajner-Diamond et al. (1987) referred to Munchausen syndrome-by-proxy cases as one example that fits into this category. Green (1986) referred to cases of *folie à deux*. What these cases have in common is that the mother is not seeking attention, or particularly hostile, as above, but is delusional. In these cases the mother is deeply enmeshed with the child and has boundary problems, being unsure of which symptoms are felt by the child and which are felt by herself, unclear about how the disclosure arose—if it was she or the child who had made the statement, and so on. These mothers have a past history of paranoid delusions when under stress, of social isolation, and of unusual preoccupations. They are frightened and confused and view the child's sexual abuse as part of a conspiracy of some sort, for example, satanic rituals, the father's involvement in a child pornography ring, and abuse of all the children in the family. Green stated that these women often have a history of having accused the spouse of sexual misconduct toward other family members as well. In these cases the accuser's belief system is outside the realm of possibility, and the child may have come to believe the delusion as well. This case is typified by Case Study 2 in its opening paragraphs.

The Accuser Is Overly Anxious and Overprotective

Benedek and Schetky (1985), Bresee et al. (1986), Klajner-Diamond et al. (1987), and Wakefield and Underwager (1991) describe the accuser —again, most typically the mother—as highly anxious and perhaps over-reacting to minor signs and symptoms of distress in the child. This person may have been sexually abused as a child or raped as an adult and is therefore highly sensitized to behavioral cues that might be linked in her mind to sexual trauma. She may be a parent who has seen numerous presentations in the national media about child sexual abuse and has become hypervigilant to signs of sexual abuse in young children. She may overinterpret normal childhood behaviors, such as masturbation, playing "doctor" with other children, being curious about the mother's breasts, and having the Barbie and Ken dolls lie on top of each other and kiss. Some mothers in this group have been primary caretakers of very young children in cases where the father has had little to no involvement with the children. The mother may have initiated the divorce because the father was distant, un-involved, neglectful, or prone to excessive drinking. Permitting the child to leave her care and be alone with the father sets the stage for tremendous anxiety about the child's safety and well-being. In these cases, it is under-standable that this parent might overinterpret signs of distress in the child on return from a visitation.

THE ACCUSED

Given the wide range of situations in which incest may occur, there is no definitive profile of a father, stepfather, or live-in boyfriend who is a "child molester." Neither is there any physical or psychometric test that offers a definitive, scientifically valid assessment of an individual's predisposition to abuse a particular child. However, there are indicators that most clinicians would agree constitute danger signs that lend concern to a sexual abuse allegation. Attorney Patricia Bresee and others (1986) in San Mateo, California, offered these: (a) impulse control problems, (b) difficulty directing emotional reactions, (c) excessive self-centeredness, (d) strong dependency needs, and (e) poor judgment. Arthur Green (1986), a professor of psychiatry at Presbyterian Hospital in New York, suggested that some fathers may regress into a pattern of incestuous behavior in the throes of depression following the divorce. The excessive use of alcohol, in combination with some of these factors, potentiates the possibility of sexual abuse. What most experts agree is that parents who sexually abuse children are marked by antisocial personality features, a focus on immediate gratification of impulses, and a pattern of reckless behavior in the past.

Blush and Ross (1987) asserted that the father who is falsely accused of sexual abuse is often a passive, dependent, inadequate man. Far from reckless and self-centered, he often acts as a caretaker to the accuser during the courtship and the early years of the marriage. They further described such an individual as socially naïve about adult relationships. He earns the love of the accuser by yielding to her wants and demands. It is because of his passivity that he often finds himself married to a more dominant woman—either by virtue of her histrionic personality or her vindictiveness and her controlling nature. His ineptness with the sexual aspect of the relationship is used to portray him as a sexual deviant. Often it is his passivity in the face of allegations that make him an easy target. His helpless and ineffective response may make him look guilty to an investigator. Blush and Ross did not offer figures on what portion of the accused men in their sample fit this profile, but they did raise interesting points. Both of the men in the case studies that opened this chapter were characterized as unusually passive.

THE CHILD

Since the late 1970s, the rate of reports of possible child sexual abuse has skyrocketed at most CPS agencies around the country. For example, John Eckenrode and his colleagues at Cornell University (Eckenrode, Powers, Doris, Munsch, & Bolger, 1988) found that reports of child abuse and neglect in New York increased from 30,000 in 1974 to 84,000 in 1984. Approximately 2,000 of these were child sexual abuse reports. During this time, CPS workers in the state reported that more than half of the reports were substantiated in 1974, but only 35% were substantiated in 1984. Accordingly, the task of substantiating child sexual abuse has become a growing subspecialty with private clinicians and with case workers. Much research in the past decade has examined the accuracy of children's recall, the suggestibility of children's testimony, and the effectiveness of different interview and assessment techniques. This is beyond the scope of this chapter, and the reader is referred to some of the excellent texts in the field, such as Kathryn Kuehnle's (1996) *Assessing Allegations of Child Sexual Abuse*, Aaron Hoorwitz's (1992) *The Clinical Detective*, David Finkelhor's (1984) *Child Sexual Abuse*, and Stephen J. Ceci and Helene Hembrooke's (1998) *Expert Witnesses in Child Abuse Cases*. This section provides an overview of factors to be considered in the context of custody and access disputes.

As in custody evaluations, the clinician must keep in mind that a verbal disclosure of possible sexual abuse from a child is one small piece of information that must be examined in its own right and must "fit" with numerous other, equally important variables. When approaching the child, the examiner must again look at multiple lines of data: (a) physical evidence, (b) the child's mental state, (c) the child's behavior, (d) behavioral checklists, (e) the child's verbal statements, (f) the child's responses to projective tests, and (g) consistency among sources.

Physical Evidence

Physical evidence is often rare in sexual abuse allegations. However, if physical evidence exists, it is a highly confirmative factor. Bruising, stretching, or tears of the vagina or anus may be found by the pediatrician on examination of the child. However, these injuries may have occurred through accidents, not necessarily through sexual abuse.

Occasionally, tests confirm the presence of a sexually transmitted disease. Although this confirms that the child had sexual contact with someone, it does not confirm that the child had sexual contact with the alleged perpetrator or when the sexual contact occurred. The examiner should review the child's day-to-day schedule in the mother's home, the father's home, and at day care to determine what individuals had access to the child, were alone with the child, and provided physical care to the child.

Child's Mental State

The child's mental state is relevant in a number of ways. First, the child may have a thought disorder or may be enmeshed with a parent who has a thought disorder and thus be unable to sort out reality. The example of 5-year old-Craig (see chapter 7), who claimed to have seen his mother dancing naked yet also claimed she disemboweled cats in the grocery store, is a case in point. I recently evaluated a boy who had been accused of sexually abusing his half-sister during her parents' custody dispute. The sexual abuse investigator failed to note that the girl had a developmental delay, had encopresis and enuresis, and spoke to invisible gypsies whom she said followed her around. Although a diagnosis of childhood schizophrenia does not rule out sexual abuse, it does prompt the evaluator to question whether a disturbed child may be making numerous bizarre statements, some of which may sound like sexual abuse. Such statements may have been selected by the accusing parent for use as a weapon in a custody proceeding.

Second, in true cases of sexual abuse the evaluator is likely to see that the child is in some mental distress when recounting the details of the abuse, although this might not be true in all cases. This caveat is important, because there are no absolute emotional reaction indicators of child sexual abuse. Many young children who have been involved in episodes of genital fondling may have found the activity innocuous and experience no distress. Children who were sexually abused and who experienced the event as distressing will have difficulty recounting the episode, whereas children who are making false allegations may recount episodes of traumatic abuse with no upset.

Child's Behavior

Behavioral symptoms have long been offered by many evaluators as indicators or markers for sexual abuse, although none are absolute or well validated. Wakefield and Underwager (1991) stated that "Nearly every problem behavior ever detected in children has been offered by someone as a sign of possible child sexual abuse" (p. 459). This is because children exhibit a number of generalized stress responses to all manner of stressors, including sexual abuse. Some of those offered by Bresee et al. (1986) are abrupt changes in personality, regression in developmental skills, compulsive masturbation, emergence of new fears or phobias, overly controlling behavior, overly submissive behavior, clinging to parents, social withdrawal, school refusal, sleep disturbances, and crying. Angela Browne and David Finkelhor of the Family Violence Research Program of the University of New Hampshire (1986) also included internalizing symptoms, such as fearful, inhibited, depressed, or overcontrolled behaviors; externalizing symptoms, such as aggressive, antisocial, or undercontrolled behaviors; changes in eating habits; toileting problems; psychosomatic symptoms, such as headaches and stomachaches, gastrointestinal disturbances; excessive sexual curiosity; frequent exposure of the genitals; fear; anger and hostility; guilt and shame; running away; delinquency; school truancy; major depression; and self-destructive behavior. In an update of Brown and Finkelhor's (1986) study, Kathleen Kendall-Tackett, Linda Williams, and David Finkelhor (1993) reviewed all of the behavioral indicators from the previous study, adding PTSD symptoms, such as nightmares; suicidal feelings; neurotic symptoms; cruel behavior; sexualized behavior, such as sexualized play with dolls, putting objects into anuses or vaginas, requesting sexual stimulation from adults or other children, and age-inappropriate sexual knowledge; promiscuity; hyperactivity; and substance abuse.

Kendall-Tackett et al. (1993) noted that across all studies the percentage of a group of sexual abuse victims who exhibited a particular symptom, although higher than that of nonclinical groups, was relatively low —between 20% and 30%. This is partly because children at different developmental ages exhibit different kinds of symptoms. For example, Kendall-Tackett et al., after conducting an exhaustive review of numerous studies, concluded that the following symptoms were the most common:

- *For preschoolers*—anxiety, nightmares, general PTSD, internalizing, externalizing, and inappropriate sexual behavior

- *For school-age children*—fear, neurotic and general mental illness, aggression, nightmares, school problems, hyperactivity, and regressive behavior
- *For adolescents*—depression, withdrawal, suicidal or self-injurious behaviors, somatic complaints, illegal acts, running away, and substance abuse.

Although this outline narrows the scope of symptoms, the above profiles are also not unlike general indexes of stress for children of different ages.

Kendall-Tackett et al. (1993) concluded that sexually abused children do not appear to have behavioral symptoms that are different from other children seen in mental health clinics, with the exception perhaps of sexualized behavior and PTSD symptoms. Here, also, however, these markers are not reliable: Only 32% of the abuse victims across a wide range of studies exhibited PTSD symptoms, and 28% displayed sexualized behavior. The evaluator must keep in mind that sexualized behaviors may have been brought about by exposure to sexual information, not necessarily by sexual abuse. Also, they do not reveal in which home the child was exposed to sexual contact or information. Add to this Kendall-Tackett et al.'s conclusion that about one third of all sexually abused children display no behavioral symptoms whatsoever. Therefore, the potential to make errors of false positives (concluding that sexual abuse occurred when it did not) and false negatives (concluding incorrectly that sexual abuse did not occur) is high.

The evaluator may note reports of behavioral changes, but it is important to give more weight to the reports of collateral contacts than to the report of the parent making the allegation. The evaluator must rule out other possible causes—a difficult task, given that children in the midst of custody and divorce conflicts are subjected to numerous changes in living arrangements and psychosocial stressors.

Behavioral Checklists

Many behavioral checklists are routinely used in evaluations of sexually abused children, with partial success. General measures, such as the Child Behavior Checklist (CBC; Achenbach, 1991), Burks Behavior Rating Scales (Burks, 1977), the Conners Rating Scales (Conners, 1990), and the Louisville Behavior Checklist (Miller, 1984), can be used. Such general measures have the advantage of embedded items that may indicate sexual abuse and may protect somewhat against rater bias. However, Kuehnle (1996) concluded that these measures do not carry enough specificity with regard to symptoms of sexual abuse. For example, Tong, Oates, and McDowell (1987) found that 36% of sexually abused children obtained profiles that were entirely normal on the CBC.

Several measures that are specific to behaviors associated with child sexual abuse have been developed and hold some promise. For example, William Friedrich and his colleagues at the Mayo Clinic in Rochester, Minnesota (1992), developed the 25-item Child Sexual Behavior Inventory (CSBI), which purports to discriminate between children who have and who have not been sexually abused. However, in Friedrich et al.'s study, which comprised groups of children from several areas of the United States and Canada, not only sexual abuse status but also several other factors correlated with higher scores on the CSBI: family chaos and disruption, low family income, low maternal education, and level of family nudity in the home.

The Children's Impact of Traumatic Events Scale–Revised (CITES–R) was developed by Vicky Wolfe and her colleagues in Western Ontario (Wolfe, Gentile, & Wolfe, 1989; Wolfe, Wolfe, Gentile & LaRose, 1987) to measure the internal, cognitive changes that occur in children who have been sexually abused. The nine subscales are Betrayal, Guilt, Helplesssness, Intrusive Thoughts, Sexualization, Stigmatization, Internal Attributions, Global Attributions, and Stable Attributions. Although the CITES–R is a good tool to use when formulating a treatment plan, it cannot be used with children who have not been sexually abused, because all questions are centered around the index event. Children who are fabricating can answer "yes" to the questions, and there is no validity scale.

The Children's Attributions and Perceptions Scale, by Anthony Mannarino and his colleagues at the Medical College of Pennsylvania (Mannarino, Cohen, & Berman, 1994), is similar to the CITES–R in that it taps internal states and cognitions. The 18 items make up four subscales: Feeling Different From Peers, Personal Attributions for Negative Events, Perceived Credibility, and Interpersonal Trust. Mannarino et al. reported group means that were higher among girls who had been sexually abused than among girls who had not, but these means differed by only a few points. They did not report on the ability of a cutoff score to predict membership in the sexually abused group. John Briere's Trauma Symptom Checklist for Children (1996) is perhaps the most comprehensive, incorporating elements of all three of the above measures, but it has not been used to discriminate groups of abused and nonabused children.

Users of these scales must be cautioned to obtain ratings from more than one source. Kuehnle (1996) noted that the parent who makes an allegation of sexual abuse is likely to give much higher ratings than collateral contacts such as the teacher and caregiver. She noted that although these scales may be useful, empirical data are weak, and the research indicates that the scales do not reliably discriminate children who have been sexually abused from those who have not.

Child's Verbal Statements

Interviewing children with regard to their reports of sexual abuse has been elevated to the level of a science over the past decade. This has come about at the expense of the many individuals who were arrested and incarcerated in the 1970s and 1980s on the basis of false allegations thought to be true because of the inept interviewing techniques of sexual abuse evaluators (see the amicus brief in the Wee Care day care center case, filed by Bruck & Ceci, 1995; and the major review by Bruck, 1998). Because of the potential of irreparably harming people's lives, as well as of inviting a malpractice lawsuit, the evaluator is cautioned to be well read and trained in this area.

Most evaluators are now in agreement as to several general guidelines. First, the interviews ideally should take place over several meetings, not just one, and the content should proceed from the general to the specific. The examiner should avoid specific questions about sexual abuse, if possible, allowing them to occur spontaneously. Second, the child's general cognitive and verbal skills should be assessed, as well as her or his ability to recall recent and remote events and to answer simple questions accurately and truthfully. Third, the child's ability to distinguish real from nonreal events should be established. Fourth, the child's overall manner of delivery should be noted. Is it made with distress? With hesitation? Matter of factly? With malice toward the alleged perpetrator? The child's language style should be noted as well. Does it contain age-appropriate terms, grammar, and inflection? Or does it contain adult words, rote expressions, and proceed in a litany, as if rehearsed?

Fifth, does the account proceed in a graphic, detailed manner, as if the child is describing an internal, visual picture of the event? Stories such as these are notable in that inessential details are provided in a spontaneous manner (e.g., "there was a blue rug on the bathroom floor with white things on it"). Sixth, the interviewer is strongly cautioned to not ask leading questions, or even yes–no questions, and to not repeat questions. Although most interviewers know this intuitively, at present many are not aware of what a leading question is. For example, "Did it hurt?" or "Were you wearing your pajamas?" are leading questions in that children will tend to answer in the affirmative if they believe that "yes" is the correct answer. Last, the interviewer is advised to note internal inconsistencies or contradictions in the account. Again, the reader is referred to the books cited above for more information. An excellent overview of specific interviewing techniques is *Pretrial Interviewing: The Search for the Truth in Alleged Child Sexual Abuse Cases*, by Natalie Woodbury (1996).

One of the most promising developments in this field is the Criterion-Based Content Analysis/Statement Validity Assessment (CBCA/SVA), a European procedure for analyzing children's verbal reports of abuse. David

Raskin of the University of Arizona and Phillip Esplin of Phoenix, Arizona (1991a, 1991b), provided an excellent overview of this method. They first lay out the phases of the interview: gathering information from other family members, generating alternative hypotheses, and establishing rapport with the child. Then they propose methods by which to gain a baseline assessment of the child's verbal, cognitive, expressive, and memory capacities. Finally, the narrative is elicited from the child through a series of stages that progress from the general to the specific: free recall, cue questions, direct questions, probing questions, and suggestive questions. Once the narrative is ended, it is transcribed and scored for the presence of 18 variables. Finally, situational factors are rated according to a validity checklist.

Michael Lamb, Kathleen Sternberg, Phillip Esplin, and Meir Hovav (1997) recently attempted to validate the CBCA/SVA by rating the narratives of child sexual abuse victims in Israel. Their study was limited to 98 cases in which the truthfulness of the allegation could be established with outside evidence. They used multiple interviewers and raters and focused on a wide variety of cases, but they limited their analysis to the 14 best indicators (as found by Horowitz et al., 1997). It is disappointing that only 6 of the 14 indicators appeared to discriminate the true cases from false cases. In fact, 3 of the indicators were more often present in the implausible accounts than in the validated accounts. Lamb et al. (1997) were forced to conclude that although the CBCA/SVA has promise, it still cannot be relied on as a well-validated psychometric measure.

Child's Response to Projective Tests

Many evaluators use projective materials in a confirmatory manner, to check for the presence of traumatic or highly sexualized content or themes. Early reports, such as that by Benedek and Schetky (1985), recommended observing the child play with dolls and puppets. Bresee et al. (1986) recommended the Draw-A-Person and Draw-A-Family tasks, sentence completion measures, the Children's Apperception Test, the Rorschach, and structured play. Kuehnle's (1996) article is a good resource for a review of the use of all of these materials, along with the Roberts Apperception Test (McArthur & Roberts, 1990) and the Projective Story-Telling Test (Caruso, 1988). She noted that children's artwork is unreliable as a diagnostic tool for sexual abuse: Although many evaluators offer lists of details in figure drawings that purport to indicate sexual abuse, the research shows that a large proportion of children who have not been sexually abused display the same indicators in their figure drawings. Kuehnle suggested that artwork be used as a form of expression for the child. For example, the evaluator might ask the child who is sufficiently capable to "draw what happened to you."

Awad (1987) recommended the use of anatomically correct dolls, although with the caution that the results obtained with their use are not a reliable indication of abuse. Much research has been done since the 1980's on what can and cannot be concluded from children's spontaneous play with anatomically correct dolls, and their use has fallen into disfavor. Evaluators who use the dolls should be well versed in the literature on what nonabused children often do with anatomically correct dolls. For example, most nonsexually abused children undress the dolls with little or no encouragement and manipulate the genitals. A sizable number, 35%, will show initial shyness and avoidance of the dolls' genitalia (Boat & Everson, 1994; Glaser & Collins, 1989).

Many evaluators consider only simulations of vaginal intercourse with anatomically correct dolls as indicative of sexual abuse. Barbara Boat and Mark Everson of the University of North Carolina (1994) observed a large group of randomly selected children interacting with such dolls, both with the examiner in and out of the room. They analyzed the results by age (2, 3, 4, and 5 years) and gender. One clear finding was that 2-year-old children did not at all interact with the dolls in a sexualized way, suggesting that they are not capable at this age of representational play. However, 12%–25% of the boys ages 3 to 5 placed the dolls in a position that suggested vaginal intercourse while the examiner was in the room (7%–9% of the girls did). Four percent to 7% of the boys engaged the dolls in clear vaginal intercourse with genital insertion. A small minority of the nonsexually abused children actually rubbed the dolls against their own body, engaging them in simulated intercourse. The results were even more dramatic when analyzed by race and socioeconomic status. African American boys of lower socioeconomic status, ages 3 to 5, engaged the dolls in suggested intercourse 27% of the time when the examiner was in the room and engaged the dolls in actual vaginal intercourse 20% of the time when the examiner was out of the room.

The use of anatomically correct dolls to prompt children to make accurate recollections of how they were touched by someone also is being called into question. The reader is referred to the dramatic study led by Maggie Bruck at McGill University (Bruck, Ceci, Francoeur, & Renick, 1995), which is being cited in court cases around the country. Bruck and her researchers observed groups of 3-year-old children examined by a physician during their annual physicals. Half were examined in the genital area by being touched lightly; the other half kept their underpants on throughout the physical. On being presented with the anatomically correct dolls and asked to describe where the doctor had touched them, only 47% of the genitally examined children and 50% of the no-genital-exam children gave correct responses. In fact, 5 of the 12 girls who were lightly touched in the genital area actually inserted their finger into the doll's vagina or anus. Five of the children indicated aggressive behavior and struck the dolls (which of course did not occur). When a wooden spoon was on the table, the children picked up the spoon and inserted it into the doll's vagina, indicating that this was done to them also.

As with drawings, the dolls may have better use as a tool of expression for the child (e.g., "Show me and tell me what happened"). Kuehnle (1996) advised clinicians to be well versed in the guidelines of the American Professional Society on the Abuse of Children (1995). This group does not advise using the anatomical dolls as a diagnostic test but does recommend them for the following purposes: (a) icebreaker, (b) anatomical model, (c) demonstration aid, (d) memory stimulus, and (e) diagnostic screen.

Consistency Among Data Sources

Last, the interviewer should consider the overall accuracy and consistency of the various elements of data gathered from the child or from informants about the child. If, perhaps, there is bruising of the genitalia, are the bruises old or recent? Do they correspond in time with the date of the allegation? If there are behavioral changes, do they correspond in time with the supposed dates of the abuse allegation? Do they instead correspond in time with the beginning of some other change in the child's life? For example, in the case of the girl who spoke to gypsies, her behavioral changes were said to have begun 18 months prior to the time of the alleged sexual abuse.

Does the child's mental state correspond with the level of trauma that supposedly occurred? If, for example, sexual contact was alleged to have occurred that was not experienced by the child as traumatic, the child's matter-of-fact statement may be congruent, but it would not be so if the child described horrendous, frightening abuse. Similarly, if the child described particularly traumatic sexual abuse by the father, yet spoke with enthusiasm of an upcoming trip with him or approached the father in the waiting room and snuggled in his lap, these would be incongruent behaviors. Inconsistencies in verbal statements have already been noted. One must consider whether the story is plausible—given the time of day, location in the home, and who was (or was not) in the home at the time, for example. The evaluator is advised to know well the context in which true cases of sexual abuse occur (i.e., how the child is selected, induced to cooperate, the progression of acts that occur, how the child is silenced, etc.) to determine if this index case is a plausible scenario.

WHAT THE RESEARCH SHOWS

The national hysteria over sexual abuse accusations has been occurring simultaneously with the divorce revolution, resulting in the dramatic rise in sexual abuse accusations made during custody and access disputes. Although such accusations of sexual abuse are not common in the majority of court cases regarding custody, in cases that involve protracted custody disputes that are referred to specialized evaluators, these accusations may make up 50% of the evaluator's caseload. These evaluators report the rate of false or unsubstantiated cases to be from 35% to 75% of this sample. Therefore, the task of determining true allegations from false allegations is complex.

The evaluator must first assess the context in which the allegation arose. False allegations tend to occur when there has been a history of high levels of interparental conflict at the time of the divorce or shortly afterward, when the family is dysfunctional and the accuser has emotional problems, when the supposed disclosure is made only to the accuser, and when the accuser stands to gain from the investigation. Typically these accusations involve a very young child and only one alleged act of abuse.

The accusers with false allegations seldom coax children into lying but often sincerely believe that the children are being harmed by the other parent or that parent's new spouse. These individuals tend to fall into four groups: (a) those who are openly hostile and vindictive, (b) those who have borderline or histrionic personality dynamics, (c) those who are overly anxious and protective, and (d) those who are floridly paranoid.

There are no studies of the accused parents in false-allegation cases, but some observers suggest that fathers who are passive and dependent and who have been caretakers to their wives in the marriage are more at risk for being the target of false accusations. The two case studies presented in this chapter fit this profile.

Information to be gathered about the child and from the child falls along seven lines of evidence. Physical evidence is rarely available in these cases, but when it is, it is highly confirmatory. Mental state also is important to assess. False accusation cases are typified by a bizarre or psychotic presentation, or they may involve the recounting of severe trauma with no visible distress. Behavioral indicators have often been relied on heavily by evaluators, but they are unreliable as indicators of sexual abuse. Behavioral indicators seen in children who have been sexually abused are not quantitatively or qualitatively different from children with stress reactions of a nonabusive nature. Even indicators such as sexualized behaviors and PTSD symptoms result in high false positives and high false negatives. Similarly, behavioral checklists have been used to evaluate these children, some of which embed sexual abuse symptoms and some of which focus exclusively on symptoms of sexual abuse. Although such checklists may be useful in formulating a treatment plan and in measuring treatment outcome, they have not been shown to reliably discriminate children who have been abused from those who have not.

The child's statement must be taken carefully, and the evaluator is advised to obtain specialized training in this area. The interviews should occur over several meetings, proceeding gradually from the general to the specific. The evaluator is wise to do some informal assessment of the child's capabilities before starting and should be schooled in the art of avoiding leading questions. The most promising new development in the science of interviewing children is the CBCA/SVA. However, recent results of empirical research with the CBCA/SVA have been disappointing.

Last, the evaluator may use projective techniques, such as storytelling, anatomical dolls, and figure drawings. Experts maintain that these measures are notoriously unreliable in confirming or disconfirming sexual abuse in children. Recent and innovative research in this area has demonstrated how commonly young children make false reports with these materials. Similarly, new research has demonstrated how frequently children's behavior with anatomical dolls can lead the evaluator to erroneous conclusions. Given how infrequently the above measures yield accurate conclusions, the evaluator's strongest measure is the consistency among all the data points that are gathered. The evaluator in these cases should look for consistency not only among and within the seven sources of information from the child but also within the four elements of the case—the context, the accuser, the accused, and the child.

GUIDELINES FOR THE CLINICIAN

Sexual abuse cases that arise in custody and access disputes are exceedingly complex. The clinician is cautioned to think like an evaluator and not like a clinician for several reasons. These cases, to be handled well, will entail the gathering of data from several sources. Although the American Psychological Association (APA) has not established guidelines regarding sexual abuse allegations in custody disputes, one would do well to return to the guidelines for custody evaluations (APA, 1994). One must gather multiple types of information from multiple sources. Before the clinician draws a conclusion, he or she must cross-validate information, making sure that multiple lines of evidence support each other in a consistent fashion. Multiple lines of evidence are (a) interviews with the parents and siblings; (b) interviews with collateral witnesses, such as the teacher, caregiver, and pediatrician; (c) police reports; (d) reports of CPS workers; (e) observations of the child alone and with parents, if appropriate; (f) the child's drawings, spontaneous play, and responses to projective material; (g) medical reports; and (h) the interview with the child.

Blush and Ross (1987) made the cogent argument that a necessary beginning strategy for professionals in this area is to regard themselves as clinician–investigators and not as clinician–therapists. The clinician who takes the stance that he or she is simply there to support the victim (the child) and help the victim work through the impact of the alleged abuse clearly defines himself or herself as a clinician–therapist. There are many inherent risks involved in taking on this role. The clinician–therapist communicates to the child–parent pair that he or she is aligned with them. Once this alignment takes place, this reinforces to the parent and child that the abuse allegation is felt to be valid and that the clinician is "on their side."

One then risks the possibility that the accuser will feel betrayed when the clinician begins to seek more information to corroborate the report. Yet one must seek to corroborate the report. The accused parent who is not interviewed as part of an ongoing treatment plan may feel betrayed and that the therapist has aligned himself or herself with the accuser from the outset. The sympathetic clinician also risks becoming what Johnston and Campbell (1988) referred to as a *conspiracy of well-meaning professionals,* who inadvertently become part of a coalition to alienate a child from the other parent in cases of false allegations (pp. 44–51). Compounding this is the possibility that the clinician–therapist may then be called to testify in court about the possibility that the allegation might not be true. In some cases, this may result in legal action being taken against the accuser, a step that may further intensify the accuser's sense of betrayal by the clinician–therapist.

Blush and Ross (1987) noted that most clinicians are trained to be therapists, not investigators. Sexual abuse allegations in the course of child custody cases make unique demands on the clinician to conduct a thorough and impartial evaluation yet to provide emotional support and treatment as well. Few clinicians can nimbly and ethically wear both hats. Approaching the case with objectivity, skepticism, and open-mindedness, gathering data from all relevant sources before concluding that abuse has occurred or that treatment is necessary or indicated, is a better course to follow.

Gary Melton and Susan Limber of the University of Nebraska (1989) addressed some of the dual-role issues in their seminal article for *American Psychologist.* They noted that in the past psychologists have been involved in child sexual abuse cases only as clinicians who evaluated a child for treatment and formulated treatment plans. In the 1980s, new roles developed for psychologists as investigators and evidence gatherers for the prosecution (and occasionally for the defense) in criminal proceedings. Melton and Limber pointed out the weighty responsibility that involvement in such cases carries—the welfare of the child, the privacy of the family, and the personal liberty and civil rights of the accused—and strongly admonished evaluators to be careful of the limitations of their role. One must realize that when testifying about research, one is testifying about group data, which may say little to nothing about the particular case in question. One must never offer opinions as to the truth or falseness of the allegation —that is for the "trier of fact" to conclude. Testimony should be limited to hard data whenever possible. Even when testifying about hard data, the evaluator should understand and explain for the court the limitations of each measure used and the likelihood of false negatives and false positives.

In a series of studies, Thomas Horner, Melvin Guyer, and Neil Kalter of the University of Michigan pointed out the lack of scientific validity in evaluators' conclusions about the truthfulness of child sexual abuse accusations (Horner & Guyer, 1991; Horner, Guyer, & Kalter, 1991, 1993). These researchers presented a case study of a hypothetical 3-year-old child who was allegedly sexually abused and the subject of a visitation dispute between her parents. Following this, the clinicians were asked to estimate the probability that the child had been sexually abused. The average estimated probability was .43 for the clinical psychologists, .63 for the social workers, and .42 for other health care professionals. However, within these groups the range was extreme—from 5% to 90% for the psychologists and social workers and from 1% to 100% for the other health care workers. After a period of discussion the clinicians were asked to make another estimated probability. All groups lowered their estimates by 10 to 20 percentage points, moving in the conservative direction. However, there were still holdouts who stubbornly clung to their positions; thus the range continued to be from 1% to 100% for the group as a whole. The authors concluded that "These findings lend strong support for the view that individual experts can provide courts little if any assurance that they are able to provide even crudely reasonable (i.e., objective) estimate[s] of likelihood that child sexual abuse has occurred or will occur" (Horner et al., 1991).

Catherine Brooks, a law professor in Omaha, Nebraska, and Madelyn Milchman, a psychologist in Upper Montclair, New Jersey (1991), reviewed a case in which a 3-year-old boy was evaluated for sexual abuse in the midst of a custody dispute by four professionals, whose work was reviewed by still two others, all of whom disagreed as to the findings. Three years later the case was still in litigation in two states in family court and in criminal court. Brooks and Milchman concluded that professionals often disagree in matters of expert opinion and asserted that the court should simply hear out each person's testimony and weigh it on its individual merits as to its thoroughness and scientific validity.

At the outset of this chapter, mention was made of evaluators and court officials who take the stance that any allegation of sexual abuse arising in a custody dispute must be false. Those are the 1% found in the studies above. Equally important are the "outliers" in the above study—those who went against group consensus and gave an estimate of 100% that sexual abuse had occurred. Gardner (1992b) warned against the "self-styled validators" who go about sexual abuse investigations expecting to confirm their predetermined conclusions that sexual abuse has occurred. I once encountered one evaluator in a custody case who concluded that a 4-year-old boy had been sexually abused by his father because he enjoyed play acting that he was a fireman putting out fires by urinating on them. Another clinician concluded that a girl had been sexually abused because she used bugs and spiders in her sand-play stories. Such loosely drawn conclusions need no further comment.

The following are a few further pointers:

- Keep clients aware of what is going on as the evaluation drags on, for example, to whom you are talking and why. The length of the evaluation is often unexpected and makes the parents and child anxious (Bricklin, 1995; Melton & Limber, 1989). Melton and Limber (1989) asserted that the length of time in which children live in a state of ambiguity over the outcome of their case is more stressful than testifying.
- Be honest with the client and court about the limits of your role and your expertise from the outset. Prepare the client for the possibility that you may be unable to conclude anything one way or the other (Bricklin, 1995; Melton & Limber, 1989). Educate the client as well as the court as to the limitations that make substantiation difficult or impossible, for example, the young age or limited verbal skills of the child, the occurrence of previous multiple interviews contaminating the child's narrative, the child's alignment with the accusing parent, and the time that has elapsed since the alleged event occurred.
- Be prepared to follow a case for a length of time, because some allegations are able to be substantiated or unsubstantiated only after multiple interviews and protracted case management (Awad & McDonough, 1991). I was involved in a sexual abuse allegation–custody dispute case that lasted for 3 years, until permission was finally obtained from the court to interview the child and the alleged perpetrator (the adolescent half-sister) together—at which point the allegations fell apart and the case was discovered to be unsubstantiated.
- Minimize the influence of your own personal experiences and attitudes. Susan Penfold (1995) advised clinician–evaluators to be aware of their biases and to cite their limitations when presenting information. It is a good idea to review one's evaluation findings, testimony, or both, with a colleague, before going forward.

CASE STUDY 1 UPDATE

In my report to the court, I recommended that Jay have primary custody of Janna. I was particularly concerned that Marva would block

Jay's access to Janna in the future, that she might continue to make false accusations of sexual abuse, and that she was a risk for leaving the state with Janna. After the report was submitted, Marva's new boyfriend gave her a large sum of money with which to continue her legal battle. Her attorney launched a new round of petitions and requests for depositions. Faced with the continued litigation, Jay agreed to reach an out-of-court settlement with Marva in which they agreed to joint legal and physical custody of Janna. One parent would have Janna two thirds of the time to the other parent's one third, and this would alternate between the parents from one year to the next. Whichever parent chose to leave the state automatically surrendered primary custody to the other parent.

Several months after the case was settled, I interviewed Jay by telephone. He told me that Marva and her new boyfriend had broken up and that she was left with a debt of $20,000 in legal bills. Unable to work full-time and care for Janna, she had let Jay have Janna the two thirds time for the first year. Jay reported that Janna was doing well and that Marva was more cooperative. His advice to other fathers who might be accused of sexual abuse was to "remain calm, don't explode, don't do anything out of anger, just let it work its way through the courts."

CASE STUDY 2 UPDATE

In the case of Frank and Donna, I also recommended that Frank have primary custody of Adam. I was of the opinion that Adam had a *folie à deux* delusional system with Donna and that his functioning was deteriorating. At the hearing, the judge was so influenced by the report that she ordered Donna out of the house and gave Frank custody of Adam "immediately." Two months later, Donna was still odd and strangely disjointed in her manner, but she had not had the psychotic break that was feared. Adam was at first angry but rapidly accepted the court's decision and was making a good adjustment.

Frank was contacted 1 year later. Adam had continued to make a good adjustment. He had begun to read 1 year previously and was reading nearly at his grade level. He had been mainstreamed into most of his classes. Frank had met someone new, and Adam had taken to her quite well. However, when Frank began his new relationship, Donna deteriorated. She had been hospitalized twice for her delusions and was diagnosed as having bipolar disorder. She had been unable to work consistently and was about to move to California to live with her mother.

11

ETHICAL PROBLEMS AND PITFALLS

CASE STUDY 1: GOING BEYOND THE DATA

A father called with concern about his 5-year-old daughter, who returned from visitations to her mother with acute emotional distress, nightmares, and stomach upset. He was considering stopping the visitations and asked the psychologist to evaluate the child and give him an opinion as to whether that was advisable.

The psychologist interviewed the father and, in obtaining the history, learned that he and his daughter's mother had never married. The father had considered marrying the mother when he learned she was pregnant but became alarmed when he saw a hostile and violent side to her. When he broke off the engagement, the mother continued her hostilities, stalking him, threatening him, and damaging his car. The mother at first kept the baby, but when the baby was 18 months old, in a fit of anger one afternoon, she gave the child to the father, seemingly to punish him. The father obtained legal custody, and the mother's visitations proceeded regularly with little problem for the next several years.

When the child was 5, the father sought to raise the mother's child support payments, as she had had a substantial salary increase. The mother's hostility again intensified. The father played for the therapist an audiotaped telephone conversation of the mother threatening "I'm going to tell [the child] that you are no good, that you wanted her murdered before

295

she was born!" The psychologist heard the child moaning in the background.

The psychologist evaluated the child and determined that the child was distressed by contact with the mother. She related a fear of her mother and said that her mother screamed at her and that she had nightmares in which her mother was a monster.

Seeking to obtain a full picture of the situation, the psychologist wrote the mother a letter asking her to participate in the evaluation. When the mother failed to respond, the psychologist wrote again, advising the mother that, on the basis of what he had heard so far, he would have to advise the father not to send the child on the visitations.

The psychologist also advised the father that he should get an attorney and consult with him or her about the legalities of stopping the visitations. The father refused. The psychologist warned the father that he could be held in contempt of court. The mother still failed to respond to the letter. However, she did negotiate a settlement with the father, and the visitations resumed.

The father returned 2 years later with a similar problem. The child was acutely distressed before and after visitations, although she was now angry at her mother as much as she was afraid of her. The mother had remarried and had a new baby and reportedly had become obsessed with hygiene. The father and child reported that the mother insisted on cutting the child's fingernails very short. If the child refused, she spent the entire weekend in her room. The mother had once cut the nails until they bled.

The psychologist again wrote the mother a letter seeking her input. The mother did call, after a long delay, and did speak on the telephone with the psychologist. She digressed into a rambling, incoherent, hostile attack on the father and would not discuss the child. The psychologist concluded that the mother was unstable and posed a reasonable danger to the child. The father asked the psychologist if he should send the child on the next visitation, and the psychologist replied "no." The father now had an attorney, and the psychologist reaffirmed that the father should discuss the matter with his attorney, which he did. He immediately filed a petition for a modification of visitation.

The mother took the father to court on the issue of the blocked visitations. The psychologist was not at that hearing. The father defended his actions, asserting that he had stopped the visitations on the advice of the psychologist. The judge in the matter (Judge 1) stated that she had a low opinion of mental health professionals and took issue with the psychologist for overstepping his bounds. She held the father in contempt and jailed him for 2 days. She suggested that the psychologist should be held in contempt as well. (The modification case was subsequently heard in a different county by Judge 2. This judge restricted the mother's visitation to a 4-hour visitation and ordered her to get psychiatric treatment.)

The mother took Judge 1's advice. She had a history of filing *pro se* lawsuits (i.e., lawsuits filed without an attorney), having been taught how to do so by an unemployed paralegal. She filed a $5 million suit against the psychologist for "interfering with custody." The malpractice company determined that this was a criminal charge, not a professional issue, and refused to cover the psychologist's legal fees, which were substantial.

The psychologist retained his own attorney and sought the consultation of another psychologist. The case was finally heard 1 year later. The attorney sought to dismiss the case because it was filed in the wrong county, was baseless, and violated the psychologist's right to free speech. The judge who heard the case (Judge 1) dismissed the case, but not without writing a 10-page stinging indictment of the psychologist's actions.

The licensing board reviewed the case 2 years after it was dismissed. After reading Judge 1's opinion, it proposed to suspend the psychologist's license and require him to be supervised for 1 year. The psychologist, on the advice of his attorney and consultant, refused to accept the verdict and requested a hearing before an administrative law judge. The psychologist was apprehensive because being on trial would be extremely stressful and would involve even more substantial legal fees, which were still not covered by the malpractice policy. The psychologist waited. Two years later— now 5 years after the initial complaint—the board dropped the charges "with concern."

Lessons

Mental health professionals should never get involved in a case unless they are working with a known and trusted attorney. Individuals without attorneys may take actions that they feel are justified, and therefore correct, without consideration as to how they may be perceived by the court—for example, refusing to pay child support, blocking a visitation, making frivolous accusations of child abuse, and fleeing with the child. They may assert that they are obtaining legal advice from the mental health professional or are acting only on the professional's directive. Attorneys not only advise parents, but they also act to "put the brakes on" parents who may be emotionally distraught and are not acting in their own best interests.

Eric Harris and colleagues (Harris, Bennett, & Remar, 1997), of the American Psychological Association (APA) Insurance Trust, suggested that psychologists not become involved in a custody or access dispute unless they have been appointed by the court. Glassman (1998) also advised not becoming involved in a custody case unless one is court appointed, in that this offers the psychologist "limited or quasi-judicial immunity against the subsequent filing of a malpractice suit" (p. 122). However, Harris went on to add that court appointment is no guarantee that one will not be sued.

The second lesson to be learned from this case is to be respectful of the courts and to understand that in the arena of the courtroom, the judge is all powerful and is answerable to virtually no one. Schutz et al. (1989) asserted that most judges are bound by strict judicial guidelines as to their rulings, fearing the embarrassment of being overturned by appeal to a higher court. This is not so with civil courts. Value judgments about the relative merits of parenting strengths are not the sort of judicial material that is governed by strict guidelines; thus, these cases are not subject to the same threats of appeal. "The best interests rule can mean whatever the judge hearing the case wants it to mean, within reason" (Schutz et al., 1989, p. 4). They concluded that judges are free to dismiss the psychologist's report no matter how scientific or competent it might be. Blau (1997) agreed that, in family law, the judge has wide latitude to invoke rulings based not only on case law but also on personal biases about marriage, children, and the family.

Mental health professionals should never assume that they cannot be sued if they do not violate any major ethical canon. It takes only $25 in many jurisdictions to file a suit with the court clerk. The suit can be entirely baseless. It will still have to be defended, even if it has no merit. More than likely the professional will also have to acknowledge the presence of the suit—even if it is not settled against him or her—for many years, on applications for malpractice insurance, hospital privileges, managed care panels, professional organizations, and so on.

Mental health professionals are not to make recommendations or suggest actions that are within the jurisdiction of the court. Psychologists are barred from recommending custody when they have evaluated only one party (APA, 1994). Similarly, psychologists should not recommend a visitation arrangement without having access to interviews with both parties. Harris et al. (1997) noted that the principle is the same, although it is not specifically spelled out in the APA guidelines. They suggested that psychologists use statements such as "The child is distressed after visitations" and avoid the word *should*. They went further and gave the example of the parent who calls with a seemingly innocent request that the clinician see a child who is distressed after visitations and "write a little note to the judge asking that he not be made to go on the visitations any more." This should not be done.

Never assume that the malpractice company will provide a defense. The company is charged with minimizing costs; its task is to find loopholes under which the insured is not covered. In the event of having to go to trial, the company will more than likely settle the case with a payment rather than go to the expense of a costly defense (Bennett, Bryant, VandenBos, & Greenwood, 1990). The company is a business and is not concerned with the effect of a negative settlement on one's career.

Finally, in the words of Harris et al. (1997), "The licensing board is not your friend. The board protects the public against you, not you, the provider." One would do well to heed these words. Many boards are composed of individuals who are single minded and have unlimited powers. They answer to no one. In the above case study, the board took issue with the psychologist, citing him for a violation of the state ethics code that requires that psychologists not advise a patient to break the law (advising the father to withhold a visitation was viewed as advising him to break the law). The psychologist was prepared to argue that he also had a duty to protect the health and safety of his client, who was a minor and who was perceived to be in reasonable danger. Advising the father to proceed with the visitation as usual would have put the psychologist in conflict with his ethical code.

In Georgia, for example, the licensing board for psychologists has no due-process procedures. Psychologists do not have the right to be notified that a complaint has been filed, to know who filed it, to know the basis of the complaint, or to appear before the board to defend themselves. J. Thomas (1998) cited the case of a Georgia psychologist and custody evaluator who was suddenly notified that a complaint against him had been found to be legitimate and that a penalty had been assessed—unaware that it was based on a complaint filed against him 8 years previously and about which he had no knowledge.

CASE STUDY 2: MANAGING PRIVILEGED COMMUNICATION

A father sought the services of a family therapist, complaining of stress both at home and at work. In the first few individual sessions, he disclosed that he had a problem with heavy drinking, which he associated with owning a bar and restaurant and working late into the early morning with his staff. He also revealed much conflict at home, as his wife complained of his being away from home at night and not spending time with the family. The therapist elected to see the couple together for several sessions. These were acrimonious meetings, during which each parent hurled accusations at the other. He complained that she failed to discipline her older children from a previous marriage and that they were becoming delinquents and school dropouts and that her relatives, whom he had employed, had stolen money from the restaurant. Several meetings took place that the husband failed to attend because he had to fill in suddenly at the restaurant. The wife did attend and focused her complaints on that he was neglectful and mentally abusive.

The couple eventually separated, filed for divorce, and dropped out of treatment. The mother left the home to live with another man, leaving their young son with the father in the marital home. The mother then called the family therapist with this request: "I have a new therapist now, and he's going to help me get custody of my son. He told me to tell you that you should send me copies of my records, and if you don't, I should report you to the licensing board. I want to use them against my husband to show the court what a bad father he is."

The therapist politely explained to her that he could not send the records, because both husband and wife had the right to confidentiality of the records and would have to release them simultaneously. The woman then consulted with her therapist. She called again requesting copies of just the meetings that she had attended alone, "to show the court how he mentally abused and harassed me," and reasserted her threat to make a licensing board complaint if she did not receive them. The therapist responded that he was not sure if the rights to these records were jointly owned by the couple or only by her. He requested time to consult with an attorney and offered a second option—to consult with the husband about whether he would authorize a release of these records to his former wife. She agreed to the second option. The husband was contacted and the situation explained. The husband consulted his attorney and then offered to have a first look at all of the records, after which he would decide whether to allow his former wife to see them. First he required the wife's release for him to view the records with his attorney.

The wife was then contacted again and presented with the situation. She agreed to consult her attorney. She did not call the therapist back and then filed a complaint with the licensing board. The detective from the board served the therapist with notice of the complaint, subpoenaed the records, and began an investigation into the therapist's activities.

Lessons

This case illustrates, first, why the risk of lawsuits and complaints is so high in the child and family forensic area. Parents with personality disorders are more likely to be involved in these cases. In the course of a marital deterioration with the potential loss of the children, behavioral patterns worsen. These parents are particularly hostile. They may ally themselves with well-meaning therapists who champion their cause, even against another therapist. They have access to an attorney and have already filed legal petitions against others. Some may be determined to sue or file a complaint, no matter what the clinician does.

Second, the above case foretells the pitfalls of dual roles. Section 7 of the *Guidelines for Child Custody Evaluations in Divorce Proceedings* (APA, 1994) clearly spells out the role boundary problems between custody evaluator and family therapist. If the husband or wife in the above case were to call on the psychologist to conduct a custody evaluation on the parties during the course of treatment, this would be a clear role violation. However, transitioning from family therapist to custody evaluator later is clearly a bad idea as well (Glassman, 1998). Likewise, transitioning from evaluator to family therapist also is ill advised. The APA guidelines suggest that therapeutic contact with the child or parents involved in a custody dispute, following the evaluation, is not advisable and should be "undertaken with caution" (p. 678). Although the evaluator may have spent many hours with the family and established a rapport with the child, the potential exists for the family to return to court many more times. In the process the court may require the evaluator to reinterview the parties and update the court on the success of the current visitation plan, a parent's mental status, and so on.

The case study also illustrates difficulties with confidentiality. Who owns the privilege? (The therapist owns the records.) Clearly, the couple both own the rights to view the records of the joint sessions, although the family therapist should attempt to discourage the couple from using the records to cause harm to each other. To do so would be to betray the trust the two had in the privacy of the therapeutic process when they began treatment. If the therapist had released the records to one party without the permission of both parties, he would clearly violate the ethics code (Harris et al., 1997; Remar, 1998). One alternative to this dilemma may be to give couples informed consent at the beginning of marital therapy (e.g., "In the event you should divorce and be involved in a conflict over custody of your child[ren], you may not ask me to testify on your behalf, recommend you for custody, or ask for copies of my records. Your records will remained protected from a custody conflict"; Remar, 1998).

CASE STUDY 3: HAVING CLEAR AND ETHICAL GOALS

A man called a family evaluator with the following opening: "My attorney said to call you. My ex-wife is saying bad things about me to my son. When I go to pick up my son, he's angry and won't get in the car. She's an evil person. She's trying to turn him against me. Can you help me?" The evaluator asked, "What is it you would like me to do?" The man responded, "Well, I don't know. Can you make her stop saying these things?"

A woman called a family evaluator with the following opening: "A friend of mine said to call you. I divorced my ex-husband a year ago and moved here to get away from him. He was abusive and harassing me. I felt that he was a bad influence on my son. I felt that here we could start a new life together. Now he's wanting visitation. My son has seen him once. Now he has to go for a 2-week summer vacation, and he doesn't want to go. I don't think that he should have to go if he doesn't want to. Do you? Can you help me?"

Another woman called with this request: "I've got a hearing next Tuesday, and my ex-boyfriend is saying I've got to send my 2-year-old son on a week-long visitation to his house. It'll kill him. He hardly knows his father. We were never married. He abandoned me when I was pregnant. He's fathered three illegitimate children, none of whom he supports. He's hardly ever seen my son. He just sees him now and then to try to put the make on me. He's only doing this because I took him to court for child support when my son turned 2. Can you go to court next week and tell the judge what a bum he is and that my son shouldn't go?"

Lessons

Parents who call with these sorts of requests are dangerous. These parents are highly emotional and even desperate and often angry. They may know what they want, but what they want may be something that is inappropriate, unethical, not feasible, or even illegal. These parents are not concerned with whether the mental health professional may be sued for malpractice or endure licensing board complaints. It is up to the evaluator to protect himself or herself from entering into situations in which his or her ethics are compromised. The evaluator should always proceed cautiously and defensively, looking out for his or her own best interests. The evaluator is best advised to stop the parent presenting a long, twisted narrative and ask for the name of the representing attorney.

Beware of the attorney who sends a client on such a "fishing expedition." This attorney may be too busy to do a thorough job or has not been paid in awhile and so does not want to go the extra mile of finding an appropriate referral. Again, keep in mind that the attorney is not concerned about whether the evaluator may suffer professionally as a result of involvement in the case. The attorney is doing his or her job by pursuing only his or her client's interests.

Thorough, careful attorneys will consider what it is that they want and call a family evaluator with the credentials to do a credible job. They will call well in advance of a court date and explain the outlines of the case. They will ask the evaluator if he or she is available, if he or she is willing to take the case, what time frame will be needed, and what fees will be involved. Good attorneys will frame the request clearly and concisely. The best family law attorneys are cognizant of the ethical codes of mental health professionals and will not knowingly ask them to conduct a case in such a way as to jeopardize their reputation. These attorneys are concerned about the embarrassment of asking questions on the witness stand that a professional cannot ethically answer. They would like to be viewed as competent and to be recommended to clients and colleagues.

In speaking to the attorney, the evaluator will need to first clarify what type of legal proceeding is anticipated:

1. Is this a custody evaluation occurring at the time of the divorce?

2. Is this a petition to reverse custody, occurring long after the divorce?
3. Is this a petition to modify a visitation plan?
4. Is this a petition to temporarily stop or supervise the visitations?
5. Is this a petition to terminate parental rights?

Next, the evaluator must clarify the scope of the work: Is the evaluator

1. to render an opinion as to who is the better parent to be the primary custodian for the child at this time? (a custody evaluation)
2. to give an opinion as to the fitness of the individual to parent the child at this time? (a parental fitness evaluation)
3. to give an opinion as to the best visitation plan for the child, based on age, temperament, bondedness with the nonresidential parent, level of interparental conflict, and so on? (a visitation plan evaluation)
4. to give an expert opinion as to the child's mental state before and after the visitation and present an explanation as to why this is? (a visitation distress evaluation)
5. to give the court an opinion as to whether the situational variables and the child's symptoms and behavior are congruent with those of children who have been sexually abused? (a child sexual abuse evaluation)
6. to give the court an opinion as to whether the child's symptoms and behavior, along with the parent's behavior and situational variables, are consistent with extreme alignment with one parent and irrational fear of and anger toward the other parent? (a parental alienation syndrome evaluation)
7. to give the court an opinion as to whether the adolescent (usually age 14 in most states) is sufficiently mature, objective, and emotionally stable to make an informed choice as to custody? (a competency-to-choose-custody evaluation)
8. to give an expert opinion as to the likely effect on the child of a sudden change in living arrangements (i.e., parent moving the child to a distant state, sudden reintroduction of a parent whom the child has not known)? (a move-away or a move-back case. Such evaluations are now required by statute in California. See Halon [1994] for a discussion of five factors to review in move-away cases.)
9. to give the court an expert opinion as to the advisability of separating the children in this case? (a split-custody case)
10. to give an expert opinion as to the parent's level of risk for

harming the child when alone with the child? (a risk assessment)

11. to give an opinion as to the quality of work rendered by another evaluator? (a second opinion)

12. to give an expert opinion on a purely hypothetical and scholarly issue, independent of interviewing any of the parties involved (a so-called "nonwitness expert" opinion)?

Finally, the evaluator must frame limitations concisely for the attorney and for the client on what he or she can do and, even more important, what he or she cannot do. For example,

1. If the evaluator is asked to do a custody evaluation, either during a divorce or postdivorce, he or she must inform the parties that he or she can render an opinion about who should have primary custody only if he or she has been appointed by the court to do so and have access to all parties and all data.

2. If the evaluator's work is a parental fitness evaluation, and he or she has access to only one parent (although access is available to all of the children, the collateral contacts, and the documents), he or she cannot make any opinion to the court as to issues of custody.

3. If the evaluator's work is to make a recommendation about visitation, he or she must try to have access to all parties. Without access, he or she must qualify the remarks as "limited" because of a lack of information. He or she must confine the remarks to how the child appears to be coping with the current visitation plan, with qualifications and limitations. Or, he or she can testify as to what is generally recommended in the published literature for "most children" in the current situation given the data that are available.

4. The evaluator must inform the attorney that he or she cannot make statements about the possible diagnosis of a parent whom he or she has never interviewed—no matter how much information has been gathered in a secondary manner.

5. Predicting risk is an inexact science, with low rates of accuracy. As such, risk assessments must be made with many qualifiers and caveats about limitations. The evaluator must give some sense of the level of risk that might be incurred under what conditions, with recommendations as to what safeguards should be in place to lower the risk.

6. When asked to provide a second opinion, the evaluator cannot disagree with the conclusions or findings of the first evaluator. Rather, the second evaluator can only comment as

to procedural flaws, key omissions, failure to meet the standards set by professional associations, improper test usage, sloppy record keeping, and so on. In other words, the second evaluator can disagree only with the soundness of the methodology used, not the end result.

7. The evaluator who is called on to answer questions about a theoretical issue must stick with the scientific data that have been accumulated in published professional books and journals. He or she should not give personal opinions or make his or her remarks on the basis of "vast clinical experience." Blau (1997) stated that the Daubert rule (expert opinions are admissible only if they are based on a relative degree of scientific certitude and are widely recognized and accepted by professionals and scholars in that field) has become the gold standard for psychologists' testimony in criminal and civil courts and that it has not yet drifted down to family court, but it is coming. Second, the "nonwitness expert" (Saks, 1990) must make clear that he or she is not giving an opinion as to a particular child or parent but only as to base rates or probabilities about groups of people who are similar to this child or this parent. One cannot make a one-to-one generalization from the group to which a person belongs to the behavior of any given individual in the group.

CASE STUDY 4: CLARIFYING ROLES AND CONFIDENTIALITY

A woman called a family therapist—evaluator with a request for counseling for her two daughters, ages 4 and 6. She had just moved from New York to a large, southeastern city to get away from her ex-husband. She gave the account that her daughters had been sexually molested by their father and that they had all been involved in several court actions in New York. The court had ordered her to have the girls undergo counseling once they got to their new home.

The therapist—evaluator asked if this was a court-ordered evaluation or if it was counseling. The mother replied that it was court-ordered counseling. She had contacted her managed care plan, which had authorized visits. The therapist reviewed legal papers and contacted the child psychiatrist who had been the latest in a series of mental health professionals to have been involved with this family. The psychiatrist explained that the mother had made accusations that the father had sexually abused the children but, because of the children's ages and their unwillingness to speak to adults, the charges had never been substantiated. He had seen the girls in his office with their father on one visit, however, and they were clearly terrified of him. The mother, although she presents well, had made several bizarre allegations in the case. The psychiatrist felt that he needed more time to conduct his evaluation, but the mother had insisted on leaving the state. Therefore, at the hastily arranged hearing it was agreed that the mother could leave New York, but once she got to her destination she had to involve the girls in counseling for a period of time, after which the therapist would make a report to the New York courts as to whether he or she felt the girls had been sexually abused.

The therapist explained the problem of role confusion to the psychiatrist, who dismissed it as a trivial point. The psychologist obtained all the records in the case, spoke with the attorneys and the guardian ad litem, had five sessions with the girls and two with their mother, and had lengthy telephone interviews with the father and the psychiatrist. She came to the conclusion that it was highly unlikely that the girls had been sexually abused but that they had been alienated from their father by an angry, disturbed mother.

When the therapist was to make a report to the New York courts, she met with the mother to review her findings and to obtain a release of confidentiality. She explained to the mother that because the court order said "counseling," the girls had been given a diagnosis, and charges had been filed with their health plan. Because of these factors, the mother, as sole custodian, had the sole right to release those records to the courts in New York. She was also within her rights to suppress them and order that they not be released. The mother smiled and specified that they should not be released.

When the psychologist informed the attorneys, the psychiatrist, and the courts in New York that the mother had chosen not to allow the psychologist to make a report to the court, they were outraged. The mother had signed the consent order permitting the release of a report. However, the psychologist pointed out, the consent order also specified that the girls be in "counseling," which allowed the mother to invoke legal privilege. The psychiatrist and the father's attorney ordered the psychologist to release her findings. The psychologist refused. The psychiatrist made disparaging remarks about the local court system not comprehending that the APA standards are national ones. The psychologist recommended to the guardian ad litem that a new consent order be drawn up, specifying that the children were to be evaluated and that the parents waive their rights to confidentiality of the children's records. The guardian agreed with this solution and took the matter to the solicitor. The family was not heard from again.

Lessons

The family forensic area is rife with problem cases that involve unclear directives. Attorneys may explain to clients that their custody evaluation will be billed as "counseling" and covered by their health insurance plan. It should not and will not be. Judges may order families in conflict to have "counseling" and then return to court, at which time the counselor is to report on their progress and even recommend one party for custody. This in direct violation of the family's right to privacy and of the confidentiality of the therapeutic process. A parent who asks a mental health professional to provide psychotherapy for a child with visitation distress often intends to call that professional later as an expert witness.

The difference between providing counseling and conducting an evaluation for the purpose of providing an opinion at a court hearing is subtle and not well understood by parents or attorneys. The therapist–evaluator, however, does well to take the time to clearly explain the differences: (a) the individual acting in a therapeutic role charges his or her clinical rate, (b) the child's symptoms must meet the criteria for a clinical diagnosis, (c) the treatment must be medically necessary (if charges are submitted to a health care plan), and (d) a treatment plan with goals must be established. The records are sealed and available only to the parents (and their health care plan), and the therapist will be reluctant to testify in court because doing so would violate the child's right to privacy. In addition to having the above explained, as in any treatment the client should read and review his or her rights and waivers as to confidentiality and sign a consent-to-treatment form.

The evaluator should be fully cognizant of an impending legal proceeding and direct his or her goals toward that end. No diagnosis is rendered, there is no treatment plan, and the fees are paid directly by the client (parent or attorney). The 1994 APA *Guidelines for Child Custody Evaluations in Divorce Proceedings* state that

> A psychologist conducting a child custody evaluation ensures that the participants, including children to the extent feasible, are aware of the limits of confidentiality. . . . The psychologist informs participants that in consenting to the evaluation, they are consenting to disclosure of the evaluation's findings in the context of the forthcoming litigation and in any other proceedings deemed necessary by the courts. (p. 679)

Participants in a family forensic evaluation should also be informed that the evaluator is not obligated to provide treatment—thus he or she cannot be held liable if the evaluation is stressful and causes psychiatric symptoms and if he or she does not intervene to treat those symptoms. (The evaluator would refer the client to an appropriate clinician for any necessary treatment.) As in custody evaluations, the client involved in any form of family forensic evaluation should read and sign a contract that covers these issues, as well as fees and terms of payment.

The evaluator should make it clear to the participant that he or she waives his or her rights to confidentiality, but in a limited fashion. The report, once released, will go to the judge, the attorneys, and the guardian ad litem in the case. The material will not be released to anyone else. In court, however, the file itself may be read in its entirety by the attorneys, and portions may be entered into the court record. Once the report is released, an attorney may give his or her client a copy. The client may make copies for distribution to friends and neighbors. The client may be admonished to not do so, but there is no statute forbidding this.

The therapist in the above case likely should have clarified her role before interviewing the children. The court's intent was to have the psychologist complete the psychiatrist's evaluation with a subsequent report to the court. The order should have been redrafted to reflect this intent. This case is a reminder to request a copy of the consent order early in any court-ordered evaluation, to read it carefully, and to consult with the attorneys before beginning work.

CASE STUDY 5: AVOIDING THE PITFALLS AND PERILS OF AVERAGE WORK

After several years of a stormy marriage, which produced one 6-year-old son, a mother decided to call it quits. Complaining of her husband's angry tirades and irrational behavior, she filed for divorce and asked for custody of their son. She also expressed the intent to move back to her home state of Maine. The father was devastated and felt that he was losing everything. Both parents were ordered by the court to undergo a custody evaluation by Dr. White.

Dr. White had difficulty right away with the father. She sought to obtain copies of the records of past treatment, which included several courses of medication prescribed by psychiatrists and a brief hospitalization. The father, who was an attorney with his own practice, used every legal means to block this request. The mother, although described as a histrionic personality, was accommodating about yielding the records of her past treatment. The father continued to be domineering and difficult to interview, whereas the mother was charming and pleasant. Dr. White conducted numerous interviews with all three members of the family. She also interviewed the three psychiatrists who treated the father, the one psychiatrist who treated the mother, and the child's therapist. She administered the MMPI–2, the Wechsler Adult Intelligence Scale, the Wechsler Intelligence Scale for Children–3, the Family Relations Test, the Millon Clinical Multiaxial Inventory, and the Perception of Relations Test. In her summation, Dr. White went into detail about her formulation of the father's psychiatric problems. She summarized, "In view of these matters, I am recommending that the mother have primary custody of the 6-year-old child." She sent copies of her report to the judge and the respective attorneys.

The father was outraged. In reading the report, he noted that his wife had made many statements that were fabrications. He personally called collateral witnesses who contradicted his wife. He then obtained affidavits from them. Also, he found factual errors in Dr. White's report. He wrote Dr. White demanding a meeting to review these issues. Dr. White refused, explaining that all of these issues would be explored under cross-examination at the final hearing.

The father hired a second evaluator, Dr. Black, to review Dr. White's report for weaknesses and to testify in court to rebut Dr. White's findings. Dr. Black found many problems with Dr. White's evaluation. Although it violated no ethical canons, the report was not of top quality. Dr. Black felt uncomfortable in this role, because Dr. White was well respected in the community. The father was highly litigious and thus likely to file a lawsuit against Dr. White. He had already filed suit against one of the psychiatrists for releasing records to Dr. White without his permission. However, Dr. Black felt that a forensic report should set the standards for high quality for two reasons: (a) because it would be subject to very close scrutiny in the courtroom and (b) because the stakes are high in forensic cases. In this case, the child's future was at stake, as well as the well-being of the distraught father. In addition, Dr. Black felt that a close examination of the report would be instructive to the juvenile court judge in the case, giving him information that could inform his opinions in similar cases in the future. Dr. Black went ahead with a limited review of whether Dr. White's report adhered to the highest standards of the profession.

Lessons

Such requests to evaluate another mental health professional's report are infrequent, and there is no strong consensus as to the best procedure. Philip Stahl (1996), a clinician in Dublin, California, recommended a more involved procedure in which the reviewer obtains the court's permission to review the entire file of the evaluator—test scores, interview notes, telephone conversations, and so on. In this ideal case, the reviewer would be court appointed, would have the permission of both parents, and would be paid by both parents. It is interesting that Stahl strongly recommended that the reviewer have at least 5 years' experience as a custody evaluator as well as experience as a supervisor, teacher, or consultant to other mental health professionals.

Dr. Black's criticism of Dr. White's report is instructive. First, whereas Dr. White held it against the father that he refused to surrender his medical records, Dr. Black disagreed. The father had sought treatment in the past with the understanding that his records would never be used against him in a court of law, especially to deprive him of contact with his son. If he had known that the records could potentially be used against him, and if this were to become common practice, he and many other individuals would be reluctant to seek treatment.

Although many custody evaluation contracts specify that the parents surrender their rights to their previous medical or psychiatric records, experts are divided as to whether this is advisable. Carl Malmquist of the University of Minnesota (1994) explored this problem in his comprehensive review. He noted that many attorneys in custody cases subpoena a parent's past treatment records as part of a "fishing expedition" to find embarrassing information. Many courts seek access to the records, and the greater the protest by the parent, the more the judge holds that against the parent. Because the relevant issue in custody evaluations is not whether the parent has a past history of psychiatric treatment but whether the parent's symptoms affect his or her ability to be a parent to the child, Malmquist raised the question of whether there is a compelling need to review past records.

Malmquist (1994) stated that courts have adopted opinions on both ends of the continuum as to whether the records should be requested and reviewed. In some jurisdictions (Delaware, Kansas, Kentucky, Nebraska, Louisiana), the parent entering a custody evaluation automatically waives the privilege. These states have held that when a parent asserts his or her demand for custody, he or she automatically places his mental condition at issue. Other states have taken a more middle-of-the-road position. Some have ruled that the judge may review the records in chambers to determine their relevance to the custody proceeding. Some have ruled that it should be left to the discretion of the trial judge as to whether the psychotherapist–patient privilege should be overridden because the information about past treatment is crucial to the custody evaluation, and the interests of the child are greater than the parent's need for privacy. Still others have sought to appoint an outside psychiatrist to conduct an independent evaluation of the parent's current mental condition, thus protecting the confidentiality of the records.

Malmquist (1994) concluded that there is no current consensus in the judicial community about the release of psychiatric records in custody cases. Individuals both requesting and releasing records in these cases are open to risk of lawsuits and complaints. He recommended the following as guidelines: (a) an allegation that one parent is mentally disturbed should never, in and of itself, be sufficient to request an open review of the records; (b) the records that are sought should bear directly on an issue that is before the court; (c) the standard that should be used is evidence of "parental unfitness"; and (d) in some cases, the parties should agree to appoint an independent psychiatric evaluator to render an opinion as to the parent's current fitness.

Dr. Black testified that Dr. White was unnecessarily intrusive into the couple's privacy. Dr. Black gave the court a synopsis of the above literature. He stated that Dr. White should have developed a list of specific questions for the respective psychiatrists that centered around both parties' ability to parent the child, reviewed those questions with each parent, and then asked the psychiatrists only for answers to those questions.

Dr. White appeared to have based her recommendation for custody largely on the father's extensive psychiatric history. This may seem reasonable to clinicians in the field but is clearly off course. The 1994 APA *Guidelines for Child Custody Evaluations in Divorce Proceedings* state that "Psychopathology may be relevant to such an assessment, insofar as it has impact on the child or the ability to parent, but it is not the primary focus" (p. 678). Dr. Black cited Dr. White for failing to establish a direct connection between the father's psychiatric history and his ability to parent his child.

In Dr. Black's testimony, this point stirred up quite a controversy. The opposing counsel and the guardian ad litem were in disbelief that the father's psychiatric history, as a stand-alone issue, should not be used to deny him custody of his son. Dr. Black was firm in articulating this point to the court—that Dr. White should have first determined, from interviews with collateral witnesses, that the father's mood, demeanor, and behavior with his son were in some way deviant or deleterious to his son. On the basis of having first established a basis for requesting previous psychiatric records, Dr. White should then have established a direct link between the father's psychiatric history and his competency to parent his son. Dr. Black, under intense cross-examination, was again firm in stating to the court that revealing in the custody evaluation report the father's private statements to his psychiatrist years ago, as well as the mother's medications, were an unnecessary violation of the family's privacy and rights to confidentiality.

Next, Dr. Black cited Dr. White for failure to lay out a scope of work in her evaluation or to organize her findings in a reasonable manner. This is not required by the APA guidelines but is suggested by Section I, Part 3: "The focus of the evaluation is on parenting capacity, the psychological and developmental needs of the child, and the resulting fit" (p. 678). Such an organizing principle, at the least, conveys to the court that the evaluator was focused on collecting data relevant to specific questions or issues and thus was focused in his or her endeavor. Dr. Black proposed several ways in which Dr. White might have laid out her investigation. Dr. Black was challenged on this issue by opposing counsel. Under cross-examination, he cited as examples three possible methods given by Skafte (1985), the three-part outline suggested by the APA guidelines, and the legal statutes in that state by which judges are to decide custody.

Dr. White concluded her long report by simply stating "In view of these matters, I recommend. . ." Dr. Black questioned, "In view of *what* matters?" Having had no overarching goals from the outset, Dr. White had no organized conclusions at the close of her evaluation. Dr. Black, in his testimony, gave several examples of ways to organize one's conclusion section. He cited Richard Gardner (1989), who uses four topics in his summations. He also mentioned Schutz, Dixon, Lindenberger, and Ruther (1989), who listed 10 factors to consider when making a custody recommendation (pp. 184–185). Last, he cited Marc Ackerman (1995), who listed 37 appropriate and 25 inappropriate parent behaviors and suggested the evaluator rate the parents on each (pp. 142–155).

Dr. Black went on to argue that Dr. White had failed to explain exactly how she derived her conclusions and recommendations. The APA guidelines state, "Recommendations are based on articulated assumptions, data, interpretations, and inferences based upon established professional and scientific standards" (p. 679). The Forensic Specialty Guidelines (APA, Division 41, 1991) state that "Forensic psychologists . . . actively disclose which information from which source was used in formulating a particular written product or oral testimony" (p. 665). Paul Schenck, a custody evaluator in Atlanta, Georgia (1999), advised making one's reports lengthy so that judges can trace how a clinician arrived at his or her conclusions. "If they agree with my conclusions, the report provides a detailed, logical basis for doing so. If they disagree, everyone will know more clearly the points where the judge and I differed" (p. 228).

Some writers have been more specific along the lines of citing one's basis for conclusions. Weithorn and Grisso (1987) stated, "We suggest that any clinical opinion or inference should be supported by two or more data sources" (p. 178). Following this example, the 1994 APA guidelines state that "Important facts and opinions are documented from at least two sources wherever their reliability is questionable" (p. 679). William Halikias, a clinician in Vermont (1994), applied this rule to all child and family forensic evaluations:

> Although it is appealing to believe that all the data were integrated into the conclusions, it is usually more accurate to admit that two or three pieces of information combine to form a specific judgment. The psychologist should be able to specify what information determined which conclusions. (p. 960)

Dr. Black cited these sources in his testimony.

One of the issues that incensed the father was that Dr. White did not attempt to corroborate his wife's statements about herself and him, many of which proved to be untrue. (The father established the untruth of some statements through affidavits that he later submitted to the court.) Perhaps it was the wife's pleasant manner that made her statements seem believable. However, Dr. White should have cross-validated her statements with collateral witnesses or documents.

Gardner (1989) recommended that every allegation that a parent makes about the other parent be marked in the margins of one's notes, so that the evaluator can address these issues with the other parent or look for evidence from other sources (pp. 127–128). This is a good technique to use with the parent's strong statements about his or her own parental involvement as well. As shown in chapter 9, parents who are involved in struggles over custody of and access to their children tend to see themselves in a distorted way. They magnify their own virtues while magnifying the other parent's deficits, thus distorting reality to fit one's own needs at the time. Dr. Black did read the affidavits and interview the witnesses whom Dr. White refused to interview. Dr. Black stated in his testimony that these witnesses did not corroborate the mother's accounts and that Dr. White had erred in taking her statements at face value.

In his report to the court, Dr. Black quoted from the *Specialty Guidelines for Forensic Psychologists* (APA, Division 41, 1991):

> While many forms of data used by forensic psychologists are hearsay, forensic psychologists attempt to corroborate critical data that form the basis for their professional product. When using hearsay data that have not been corroborated, but are nevertheless utilized, forensic psychologists have an affirmative responsibility to acknowledge the uncorroborated status of those data and the reasons for relying upon such data. (p. 662)

The APA specialty guidelines further state that "If information is gathered from third parties that is significant and may be used as a basis for conclusions, psychologists corroborate it by at least one other source wherever possible and appropriate and document this in the report" (p. 679).

Although conceding that it may be a minor point, Dr. Black questioned Dr. White's administration of intelligence tests to the child and the parents. The father had a law degree, which should suggest above-average intelligence. The mother worked as a bookkeeper; thus, one could assume she had at least average mental abilities. The child had had no academic problems. What was the rationale for intelligence tests? The use of any tests in custody evaluations should proceed with caution. As was stated in chapter 5, such tests should be used only when the results are directly relevant to the specific issues to be addressed by the evaluation. Dr. Black also testified that the Millon Clinical Multiaxial Inventory-II was inappropriate for use in custody evaluations because it was normed on clinical samples. Also, the Family Relations Test and the Perception of Relations Test were challenged on the basis of weak empirical validity. Dr. Black testified that these tests did not rise to the level required by forensic evaluations.

Dr. White did not have a feedback session with both parents to review her findings and recommendations. Although this is not specified in the

1994 APA guidelines, it is highly recommended by experts in the field. Gardner (1989) recommended that the evaluator meet with the parents at the conclusion of the evaluation to allow the parents to comment on his or her procedures, to correct factual errors, and to give input as to areas of information that may have been overlooked. Gardner was candid in stating that he is not omniscient and has made mistakes. Occasionally, when these omissions were pointed out in the final meeting, he has altered his recommendations.

Halikias (1994) recommended a feedback session in all child and family forensic evaluations:

> Whenever possible, the evaluator does well to have a feedback conference before a court hearing. In this way, participants have the opportunity informally to discuss and challenge the evaluator's findings, and there is always a possibility that based on this conference, participants will choose to settle their conflict rather than proceed to a legal hearing. (p. 961)

If the parents settle out of court, this may save the court up to 2 or 3 days of bench time. Schenck (1999) offers the parents a copy of the preliminary report and does not send out the final report until all corrections are made. Had Dr. White followed these guidelines, the father may have had a forum in which to address his concerns about false information, collateral contacts not having been interviewed, inaccurate details, and so on. Such a forum may have diminished the father's wrath at Dr. White. Dr. Black argued in his testimony that in refusing to have such a meeting, Dr. White had possibly denied the family a humane and sympathetic forum in which to express their concerns, had passed up an opportunity to improve the quality of her report, and had forgone a chance to settle out of court and thus save the court some bench time.

Dr. Black faulted Dr. White for not correcting the errors when the father brought them to her attention and requested a meeting. As Schenck (1999) pointed out, if an attorney finds factual errors in a report, he will use it to cast doubt on the integrity of the evaluation. "The appearance of sloppy work can severely weaken the judge's willingness to rely on the report as a firm foundation for custody decisions" (p. 225). Schutz et al. (1989) echoed this theme: "The accuracy of all factual material should be carefully checked, since inaccuracy in even minor details may leave the impression of carelessness and a lack of expertise" (p. 95).

Finally, Dr. Black noted in his testimony that Dr. White failed to include a "limitations" section in her report. Lois Weithorn, a psychologist at the University of Virginia (1987), noted that complaints against evaluators are common in custody evaluations because the stakes are so high —the potential loss of a child—but also because psychologists, in particular, often fail to appreciate the limitations of their work. The court may entrust a level of scientific certainty to the evaluation—a level of certitude that is simply not supported by the data. It is always wise, therefore, for the evaluator to note weaknesses and omissions in the report and to state clearly for the court what is not known at this time and what cannot be known.

For example, Dr. White failed to interview the child's teacher, to review his report cards, and to determine if he had any particular academic needs. She failed to inquire as to which parent was supporting the boy's homework and meeting with his teacher on a regular basis. The parents' strengths and weaknesses in this area were not noted. This was a limitation of Dr. White's evaluation. She also failed to inquire as to how each parent would provide the other parent access to the child, how much access each parent would provide, and under what conditions. This was another limitation. Dr. White also failed to state that there is no body of literature that demonstrates a link between the father's psychiatric history—obsessive-compulsive disorder—with good or poor parenting. Neither did she state that there is no scientific basis for concluding that the mother's presentation—histrionic personality—is linked with good or poor parenting. This was another limitation. The 1994 APA guidelines clearly state that "The psychologist strives to acknowledge to the court any limitations in methods or data used" (p. 679).

CASE STUDY 6: DEALING WITH NONCUSTODIAL PARENTS

Early in her practice, a psychologist and family therapist was consulted by a father of a 10-year-old boy. The boy had routinely slept with his mother since the divorce, several years previous, and was refusing overnight visitations with his father because he could not go to sleep without his mother. The therapist saw the boy and the father and attempted to involve the mother in treatment. Instead, she received a letter from the mother's attorney advising her that the father did not have the legal right to pursue treatment for the boy. The attorney threatened further legal action if the therapist continued to see the boy. The therapist ended her involvement in the case.

Some years later, the therapist was contacted by a father who was going through a divorce. The father was concerned that the custodial mother was involving his son and daughter, ages 8 and 6, in her affair with a man. The involvement included spending the night in a motel together and going on trips with the children to purchase marijuana. The therapist felt confident that she was not violating any standing court order, because the father was not yet divorced. Nevertheless, the therapist received a threatening letter from the mother's attorney notifying her that the couple had had a temporary hearing at which the mother had been granted primary physical custody of the children. Only the mother had the right to pursue treatment for the children. The mother's attorney further threatened to file a complaint against the therapist. The therapist contacted the father's attorney, who had referred him to the therapist, and questioned the attorney as to why she would make an inappropriate referral. The attorney justified the referral on the basis that the father had temporary joint legal custody. The mother's attorney was consulted. He clarified that the father had the right to seek treatment but only after first consulting the mother, which he had not done. The therapist terminated her involvement in the case.

In addition, the therapist was contacted by a father who asked the therapist to see his daughter and give him an opinion as to whether the current visitation plan was best for his daughter or whether a modification —one in which there were fewer transitions—might be better. The father was clear that he had joint legal custody and had the right to pursue treatment without obtaining the mother's permission. After two visits, the child's mother called the therapist and objected to the meeting. Sounding threatening, she clarified that the father did have the right to seek treatment for the child but had to notify her afterward, which he had failed to do. The therapist met with the mother to give her feedback as to her findings and ended her involvement in the case.

Some years later, a father going through a divorce contacted the therapist with a request to see his son for one visit to get a second opinion on some issues that had come up in the custody evaluation. The father had temporary joint legal custody. The therapist read the temporary divorce decree. It was vaguely worded and did not seem to require that notification be given to the mother. The therapist asked an attorney to review the decree. The attorney concurred that it did not bar the father from independently seeking a professional opinion about his son's state of mind. The therapist saw the son for one visit. The mother sent the therapist a letter threatening to make a complaint to the licensing board. She stated that she did not care that the wording was vague or that an attorney had interpreted the decree and found no bar to the father's actions—*her* interpretation was that the father could not take the child to anyone, for any purpose, without her permission. The therapist ended her involvement in the case.

Lessons

Seeing a child at the request of the parent who does not have primary physical custody is risky. The noncustodial parent may have a genuine concern about the child's well-being. He or she may have tried to discuss the issue with the primary custodial parent and been rebuffed. The primary parent may even be neglectful in not seeking treatment or a consultation about the child. The intent of the law concerning joint legal custody may be that both parents have legitimate rights to seek treatment, counseling, or a professional opinion about the child. Yet the fact is that the primary custodial parent may view such an action as a threat to his or her authority and take legal action against the mental health professional.

Virtually nothing has been written about ethical procedures to follow in such cases. William Bernet, a psychiatry professor at Vanderbilt University (1993), concluded that there is disagreement among mental health professionals as to how to handle this problem. Existing state laws and the higher courts have not provided clear guidelines either. Bernet suggested that attorneys further muddy the waters by giving parents contradictory advice depending on who their client is—the primary custodial parent or the noncustodial parent. He suggested that, in general, parents are well advised to think through every possible situation ahead of time and provide guidelines in the divorce decree that spell out what the noncustodial parent can and cannot do. Bernet suggested that psychiatrists should not see children for a psychiatric evaluation at the request of the noncustodial parent because it encourages that parent to "shop around"—to take the child for repeated evaluations until he or she has the opinion that he or she is looking for in order to go forward with an agenda to file for a reversal of custody. Bernet did not address the issue of the noncustodial parent who has legitimate concerns about the child's well-being.

The ethical problems revolving around the noncustodial parent's rights are multifaceted. For example, does the noncustodial parent have the right to review the child's records and progress in treatment? Should the therapist–evaluator attempt to involve the noncustodial parent in treatment? What if the primary custodial parent forbids the therapist to have contact with the noncustodial parent? Attorney Robert Remar (1991), at the request of the Georgia Psychological Association, reviewed state law with respect to these issues and wrote a series of guidelines for the state association. Remar suggested that when parents are legally separated or divorced and a standing court order exists, the therapist or evaluator is well advised to obtain a copy and review the language. In general, most states have consistently moved toward joint legal custody, thus broadening the rights of the noncustodial parent. However, some decrees may contain language requiring the noncustodial parent to "consult" with the primary parent, to "notify" the other parent 3 days before the visit, and so on.

Even when one follows the decree, however, the primary custodial parent may feel challenged and retaliate. It is perhaps a better policy to obtain agreement from the noncustodial parent to notify the custodial parent immediately of plans for an office visit. In many cases, the primary custodial parent will act to bar the visit. Ideally, if this occurs, the attorney for the noncustodial parent will take the issue to court and ask for a guardian ad litem to be appointed. In these cases, the therapist may then turn to the guardian ad litem for permission to interview a child. Relying on the guardian ad litem as a gatekeeper serves as protection to some degree.

The issue of the custodial parent who forbids the therapist to have contact with the noncustodial parent is even more challenging. This parent may have an agenda to marginalize the noncustodial parent's involvement and influence in the child's life. The therapist–evaluator would do well to decline to support such an agenda. Not only is it in all likelihood not in the child's best interests, but it also further opens one to the risk of complaints. If the therapist then refuses telephone calls from the noncustodial parent or refuses to disclose information about the child to the noncustodial parent, he or she may be subject to a lawsuit for denying the noncustodial parent his or her legal rights.

WHAT THE RESEARCH SHOWS

Malpractice suits and licensing board complaints against clinicians who do child and family forensic evaluations have risen in recent years. Although there are no national records of complaints filed against psychologists for ethical violations or malpractice, the APA does keep a record of cases that are referred to it from the state associations. *American Psychologist* (APA, 1997) reported that, for 1996, 73 new cases of ethical violations or malpractice were opened. The largest category (27 cases) were those in which members had been subject to the loss of their license, mostly for sexual misconduct with a client. However, the second highest category (10 cases) were complaints about inappropriate professional practice in the area of child custody. In 1997, 46 new cases were opened (APA, 1998b). Sexual misconduct was again the highest category of case opened and followed by child custody cases.

Richard Gardner (1989) began his master text on child and family forensic work with his explanation of why, as of 1988, he no longer did child custody evaluations. By that time, after two lawsuits, four complaints to the medical board, and numerous threats against him, he had had enough. He could not go through further litigation and also worried about his personal safety. One Atlanta child custody evaluator recently remarked, "I've weathered four complaints about me to the licensing board in 16 years. Though, all in all, that's a pretty good record, I've had enough. I'm quitting." (personal communication, 1999) Ben Schutz, one of the authors of *Solomon's Sword* (Schutz et al., 1989), reported that of the four authors he is the only one whose practice still focuses mainly on this type of work. He offered the explanation that it is a risky business and that it is very "corrosive" (i.e., it is stressful to continually put oneself in the line of fire between two warring parties).

Yet there is also much to be said for this type of work. For academically trained psychologists, forensic work offers an opportunity to use all the tools of one's training: theories of psychopathology, developmental psychology, psychological testing, research on marital and family dynamics, and diagnostic and investigative interviewing. The research background of psychologists grounds them in a science of taking a neutral position; putting aside preconceived notions as far as possible; and approaching a situation with many hypotheses, ruling them out one by one. It is a training that lends itself to the rules of the courtroom, more so than training purely as a clinician.

Schutz (personal communication, April 12, 1999) stated that he has stayed in the field and thrived in it because it is intellectually challenging. "These cases are like mysteries," says Schutz, who also writes mysteries. "There are complex issues to explore. You gather information in a systematic way and you slowly and meticulously put the pieces of the puzzle together." Schutz also offered that, like other forensic work, there is much at stake in these cases. For the clinician who may feel frustrated that he or she has so little power to intervene in a child's troubled family environment, testifying in such a case can make a positive and dramatic intervention in a child's life. Schutz went on to point out that although these cases are adversarial, they also can be therapeutic if handled well. "Sometimes you can design a system of support services that enable the children to get the most and the best they can from both parents." In fact, a recent call to Richard Gardner's office revealed that he had left the field of custody evaluations for "only six or eight months" (personal communication, April 19, 1999) and that he has been back at it for the past 10 years.

In short, this work can be challenging and gratifying as well as professionally dangerous. As in clinical cases, one is well advised to accept cases carefully, being sure to understand the scope of work that is required and that it is ethical and appropriate. Be clear in regard to goals and methods, and be sure that each element of the plan is directed toward a specifiable goal. Extremely hostile and reckless clients can derail a career. One can always withdraw from a case if threatened personally or professionally. Send appropriate letters to the attorneys and the judge in the matter, refund the unused retainer, and refer the client to another professional. Freely consult other colleagues, and note this in the record. Psychologists who are APA members and are insured with its Insurance Trust-sanctioned malpractice plan should keep handy the number of their free legal consultation service: 1–800–477–1200. For those who are not so insured, keep close by the telephone number of the attorney who serves as counsel to the state professional organization. Do not hesitate to call for legal advice if faced with an adverse action.

12

WHERE DO WE GO FROM HERE?

The past 30 years have seen nothing short of a revolution in attitudes toward marriage, child rearing, and divorce. Between 1969, beginning with California, and ending in 1985, with South Dakota, all 50 states enacted "no-fault" divorce laws—laws that permitted individuals to leave marriages simply on the basis that they chose not to be married any more. Hailed as a progressive step, it was anticipated that some small portion of miserable couples could begin to rebuild their lives with better prospects for the future. Surely no one anticipated that the divorce rate would increase by 30% and that millions of children would be subjected to not just one upheaval in their lives but to several as their parents went through a series of failed marriages and divorces, multiple geographical moves, and several changes of custody.

Divorce has become an industry in the United States. Most bookstores now display a shelf on divorce, with everything from directions on how to do your own divorce, how to negotiate a custody and visitation plan with your ex-spouse, how to counsel your children and ameliorate their emotional troubles, and to how to get on with your life and start over. These books are written by the new breed of specialists in divorce—attorneys and mental health professionals with specialized skills that did not exist 20–30 years ago. In 1996, *Divorce* magazine was launched, hoping to capitalize on the fraction of the population—2.4 million adults—who are newly divorced each year ("Magazine Wedded," 1996). Given that

Americans are a consumer society eager to try out new products, a calendar for children was brought out so that children could keep track of which parent they will be with on which day ("My Two Homes," 1997). Even new forms of courts have been developed to handle the overload of divorce and postdivorce litigation that is clogging the judicial system.

In 1995, the backlash began. The news media began to release reports of longitudinal studies on the children of divorce—reports that painted a bleak picture. The National Center for Health Statistics reported that children in single-parent families were two to three times more likely to have behavioral problems than children whose parents remained married. They were more likely to drop out of school, get pregnant in the teen-age years, and be arrested (Milk, 1995). (Note that these figures are on children from single-parent families, a population that overlaps, but is not the same as, children of divorce.)

In April 1995, the Council on Families in America issued a major report on children who grow up in single-parent families. The study was conducted by professors Sara McLanahan of Princeton University and Gary Sandefur of the University of Wisconsin and was published as the 1994 book *Growing Up With a Single Parent*. Journalist Leslie Milk (1995) quoted these findings from the study:

> The weakening of marriage has had devastating consequences for the well-being of children . . . By far the most important causal factor is the remarkable collapse of marriage, leading to growing family instability and decreasing parental investment in children . . . [In conclusion], America's divorce revolution has failed. (p. 603)

The report was featured on a segment of ABC's news program *Day One* with Diane Sawyer ("Marriage and Divorce," 1995), who interviewed professors Jean Bethke-Elshtain (social and political ethics) and David Popenoe (sociology), both of Rutgers University. These experts pointed to a series of long-term studies that indicated that children of divorced and unwed mothers are more than twice as likely to drop out of school and to receive psychiatric treatment as the children of intact families. Teen-age girls in these families are twice as likely to become pregnant. Poverty rates are three times as high for African American children in single-parent homes. For White children the figures are even more startling—the poverty rates are five times as high in these families. In the interview with Sawyer, Bethke-Elshtain and Popenoe derided people who contemplate divorce because they are not in love with their spouse any more. "Romance," they said, "is not the point of marriage. It never was. Marriage is society's way of providing security for its children." Popenoe went on to say that marriage should be taken seriously, because it provides the best system for raising children. Bethke-Elshtain was more caustic:

> We're seeing more multiple divorces, all kinds of configurations. And I think it's a kind of consumer. It's sort of like the shopping mall theory

of human relationships. We'll just go on to a better one and, in the meantime, there are these kids kind of tagging along, so to ease our conscience, we say . . . "Don't worry about the kids. They know we love them."

Whereas it was popular in the 1970s to view divorce with acceptance, sadness, and even humor, *divorce-bashing* is now the buzzword of the day. The backlash intensified with the 1996 publication of Maggie Gallagher's book *The Abolition of Marriage* and Barbara Dafoe Whitehead's book *The Divorce Culture*. Whitehead wrote,

> If recent social history were written through the eyes of children, 1974 (when the divorce rate began affecting more than a million children annually) might be described as The Great Crash, a moment when divorce became the leading cause of broken families and unexpectedly plunged children into a trough of family instability, increased economic vulnerability, and traumatic loss. (p. 84)

Writing for *USA Today*, journalist Deirdre Donahue (1997) noted that Whitehead's book began as an article for *Atlantic Monthly* in 1993 titled "Dan Quayle Was Right" (about single-parent families). Whitehead's article pointed a finger at White, middle-class America and said that this was where the problem was in families today. This hit a nerve with readers. The magazine had the largest response to that article of any it has published. Whitehead targeted her attack not at divorced parents per se but at the new American attitude that views divorce as an entitlement, as one of the basic rights, along with the pursuit of freedom and happiness. There will always be a need, Whitehead argued, for divorce in cases of violence and mental illness, for example, but the seeking of divorce for entirely personal reasons—unhappiness, estrangement, personal growth, "because I fell out of love," and so on—should be viewed with a measure of scorn. These divorces are sought purely for the parent's fulfillment, with little regard for the children's well-being.

Donahue (1997) noted that Whitehead's book received positive reviews from many experts in the field, among them Bill Galston, President Clinton's former deputy assistant for domestic policy. He stated that the divorce culture is a White, middle-class problem and that "People don't want to hear that their quest for personal fulfillment may come at the expense of their children" (p. 02D). Atlanta divorce attorney John Wilson III (personal communication, April 1999), echoed this sentiment, questioning whether, as a nation, Americans have become so consumed with the pursuit of personal fulfillment that we have lost the resolve to make and keep commitments and uphold responsibilities. In her review, Donahue observed that Whitehead's (1996) thesis is controversial and that many reviewers with divorce-friendly philosophies have attacked it as too negative. However, the book is well researched, and Whitehead's methodology is sound.

In April and May of 1996, the backlash continued as National Public Radio aired a six-part series on the current status of divorce in America ("The History of," 1996). In Part 1, Margot Adler interviewed David Blankenhorn, President of the Institute of American Values, and Barbara Whitehead. In the interview Blankenhorn stated that the reasons Americans are divorcing in higher numbers is not because of longer life spans or higher affluence, as some people suggest, but because we think about marriage differently, and the laws make divorce easy. He suggested that in the United States individual freedom and the parents' own self-interests win out over children's needs. Whitehead echoed this sentiment. As a historian, she suggested that the family was once protected from this kind of egocentric pursuit of gratification. Instead, marriage has begun to look like the American job—short term and subject to abrupt termination.

KEEPING MARRIAGES TOGETHER

As part of the backlash against divorce, many individuals from widely differing backgrounds have begun to come forward with proposals to alter how we go about marriage and divorce. One major focus has been to strengthen marriages and keep parents in them. This thrust has come from the mainline Protestant churches across the country. Milk (1995) described how Michael McManus, a Washington-based syndicated columnist and former *Time* magazine correspondent, realized his own marriage was in trouble when he went on a weekend retreat for couples sponsored by a Presbyterian church. Discovering the importance of building a good marriage, McManus developed his own program, Marriage Savers. Said McManus, "We're preventing bad marriages. If it is the job of a church to bond couples for life, it has to provide more help before and after" (cited in Gleick, 1995, p. 49). McManus's programs begin with premarital counseling and test— PREPARE (Premarital Personal and Relationship Evaluation). McManus claimed that this 9-point questionnaire can predict divorce with 80% accuracy. He also claimed that his program saves 90% of the marriages of couples who participate in it each year. That number stood at 5,000 per year in 1996. "Too many churches are just wedding factories or blessing machines," says McManus. "It is time the church took a strong interest in preserving marriage and preventing divorce" (cited in Milk, 1995, p. G103).

Hanna Rosin (1996) referred to McManus as the "Johnny Appleseed of the pro-marriage movement" (p. B4). McManus and his staff are working with churches across the country to adopt a "community support policy" toward marriage within church congregations. Reporter Renee Montagne with National Public Radio ("The History of," 1996) interviewed members of the Big Valley Grace Community Church in Modesto, California, during the events surrounding an upcoming wedding. This was the church in which McManus began his program in the mid-1980s. Big Valley adopted the Community Marriage Policy, in which all couples who were married in the church were required to undergo 4 months of premarital counseling. Although this may seem lengthy, McManus reasoned that if the Catholics have long accepted the required 6 months' premarital counseling then surely the Protestants could tolerate a similar limit. The group leaders in the church take pride in the fact that they often steer away from marriage those couples who seem unsuitable.

Another example of the backlash against divorce is the Denver Metro Community Marriage Policy ("Denver Metro," 1999). In this program, church members sign a document agreeing to encourage long courtships and sexual abstinence before marriage and to require engaged couples to undergo lengthy individual and group premarital counseling. They also pledge to support the couple through the marriage, encourage the couple to attend marriage enrichment weekends, and create a "marriage ministry of mentoring couples" to work with couples whose marriage is in trouble.

In her report for NPR, reporter Montagne noted that when McManus began his program he was successful in getting 95 pastors in Modesto to sign similar pacts with their churches. As a result, divorce has declined by 50% in Modesto over the past 10 years. At the time the interview was aired, ministers in 46 cities and towns had signed the Community Marriage Policy. The largest city to sign up was Austin, Texas, with 252 pastors and 210 churches. Clearly, this appears to be a positive step in the divorce revolution for those who are actively involved in a mainline Protestant church that subscribes to this program.

Many of these church programs also focus around the adoption of what George Washington University sociologist Amitai Etzioni calls *supervows*—marital contracts that go beyond the civil marriage contract to make a more permanent union. Sometimes called *covenant marriages*, these couples agree that if either should decide to divorce, they will wait for a long period of time, during which they will undergo lengthy secular and religious counseling. These are typically contracts signed by couples within the church, although they may be secular as well. Louisiana took a bold step in August 1997 by offering the covenant marriage as an alternative form of marriage license ("A Covenant," 1997; "Helping Marriages," 1997). Although both the covenant marriage and the traditional marriage are legal, the covenant marriage has several requirements intended to strengthen it. Couples must undergo premarital counseling and read a handbook on marriage. They sign an affidavit stating that they understand that the covenant marriage is for life. According to law in Louisiana, the covenant marriage can be dissolved only in extreme circumstances—adultery, abuse, abandonment, or conviction of a felony. Couples who seek divorce must undergo counseling before a divorce will be granted by the courts. When the law was passed in 1997, the Catholic and Episcopal churches were considering whether to make the signing of a covenant marriage affidavit mandatory in addition to a church wedding.

A popular church-based program for troubled marriages is Retrouvaille, the French term for *rediscovery*. Founded in Quebec in the 1960s, Retrouvaille has many similarities to Alcoholics Anonymous meetings. The program centers around an intensive weekend-long session at a hotel, followed by six follow-up sessions. In these meetings, a trained group of married peers in the church, who have themselves rebuilt their broken marriages, barrage the troubled couple with personal stories, unconditional acceptance, and group support. Although it operates under the auspices of the Catholic Church, it receives no church funding and is open to non-Catholics as well. The group reports that of those couples who were contacted 2 years after participating in a Retrouvaille program, 82% were still together ("Church Based," 1995).

NEW TRENDS IN DIVORCE LAW

Before couples come to the courthouse to petition for divorce, the states are hoping to have laws in place to deter them. Journalist Hanna Rosin (1996) wrote that the idea of repealing no-fault divorce came to David Blankenhorn of the Institute for American Values like an epiphany, "a bolt of lightning" (p. B4). Blankenhorn decided that the enemy of the American family was the no-fault divorce reform of the 1970s. His realization sparked a flurry of legislation. As of 1996, 18 states had proposed legislation to repeal no-fault divorce laws. Many are still only in the beginning stages or have been voted down and are in the process of being reintroduced.

State Rep. Jesse Dalman (R-MI) introduced a package of bills in 1996 that would return the courts to a fault standard in divorce. "No-fault divorce does not mean no-impact divorce. There's a big impact, and there's a big impact on the children, and it's a fantasy to think otherwise" ("The History of," 1996). Part of Dalman's package would make getting married more expensive and difficult unless couples had had premarital counseling. The main thrust of the bill is this: If one of the parties does not wish to be divorced, the spouse who is filing for divorce must prove the other spouse unfit. Thus, Americans would return to the categories of fault of the 1960s and earlier, the "five As": abandonment, abuse, addiction, adultery, and alcoholism. Dalman's bill would also require divorcing couples with children to attend an educational course. They would also be required to submit a parenting plan to the court detailing how they proposed to handle the areas that are most subject to conflict between divorced parents: discipline, visitation, education, and the children's emotional needs.

Tyson (1996) observed that although some efforts to repeal no-fault divorce laws had failed (e.g., Iowa and Michigan), many states were meeting with success in introducing bills that would slow down the process of divorce or make it more difficult. Iowa introduced a bill that required predivorce counseling and a longer waiting period for divorce. Michigan and Minnesota now mandate premarital counseling. Finally, bills were introduced in Colorado, Washington, West Virginia, and Minnesota that would enable couples to enter into covenant marriages.

In Georgia, Rep. Brian Joyce introduced a bill that would divide divorces into different categories. Divorces in which minor children were involved would be treated differently (Stanton, 1996). In Idaho, Rep. Tom Dorr, after speaking at length with his constituents, concluded that the people of Idaho wanted to put the brakes on divorce. He proposed a waiting period of 1 year when one spouse objected to the divorce or when young children were involved. In Iowa, Governor Terry Branstad has been pushing for a law requiring community forums on the importance of the family and requiring divorcing parents to attend re-education classes on the impact of divorce on children before they receive permission from the court to end their marriage.

Milk (1995) interviewed Washington divorce lawyer Marna Tucker with regard to suggestions proposed by divorce lawyers on this subject. Tucker recommended the court adopt rehabilitative alimony and extend child support through the college years. She recommended parenting seminars and mandatory mediation, trends already in place in many states. She also proposed making divorce more difficult when children are involved, such as extending the waiting period to 6 months or even 1 year. During this time, 6 months of counseling would be mandated for all family members. Parents who denigrate each other in front of the child would be subject to steep fines.

CHANGES IN THE COURT PROCESS

Frank Furstenberg and Andrew Cherlin (1991), in the closing chapter of their book, take a long and pessimistic look at divorce in America today. They, too, take issue with the no-fault divorce movement—yet they see no going back. Americans have always prized individual freedom and self-fulfillment, and this is highly unlikely to change. In fact, the *Wall Street Journal* recently cited a Yankelovich poll that revealed that although 65% of Americans believe that no-fault divorce laws have been bad for families, only 59% felt the government ought to get involved in making divorce more difficult ("A Covenant for," 1997). Americans have made divorce easier to obtain than in virtually any country in Western Europe. When one partner is opposed to the divorce, English law requires a 5-year waiting period. French law is even more restrictive: The courts can require a 6-year waiting period—or even deny the divorce altogether if it would pose a hardship for a mother and young children.

Furstenberg and Cherlin (1991) concluded that the passage of laws will not strengthen divorce. People cannot be compelled to stay in marriages that they find unfulfilling. Only a dramatic change in public sentiment could bring about such a change in how marriage is viewed. Americans would have to, as a culture, strengthen "values such as responsibility to others, a greater sense of social obligation, and a devaluation of self-fulfillment" (p. 104). Furstenberg and Cherlin concluded that mass education has had only a small effect on the problem. They summed up the state of marriage and divorce in the United States by stating that it would take a social upheaval on the scale of the Great Depression or a nationwide religious movement to renew a commitment to family ties. This change does not appear to be taking place.

Strengthening Laws and Standards

Instead, Furstenberg and Cherlin (1991) suggested, Americans should do more through the courts to aid the children of divorce. They see two avenues of approach. One is to strengthen laws regarding child support. Laws that require that child support payments be automatically deducted from the parent's paycheck would guarantee the payments while minimizing conflict between the parents. A second approach is to reduce conflict, given the wealth of studies that show the detrimental effects of parental conflict on children. These authors suggest that the courts adopt a primary-caregiver standard when deciding custody of children. Thus, the parent who has provided the most care for the children would be given a strong advantage in custody negotiations over the parent who has not done so. In this way, the authors hope, the parents, knowing who has provided the most care, might settle out of court quickly.

It is interesting that Joan Kelly (1994), an expert in the field since the publication of *Surviving the Break-Up* (Wallerstein & Kelly, 1980b), argued against the use of a primary-caregiver standard. She proposed that the court continue to make rulings on the basis of the "best interests of the child" standard. She argued that the best-interests standard is a better benchmark, because it allows the parties involved to consider the quality of the child's relationship with each parent, which may be more important than quantity of time spent caring for the child. In her seminal article, Kelly (1994) outlined several proposals for better resolving custodial disputes in the court. These are primarily parent education programs, mandatory mediation, and special masters programs.

Parental Programs

Parent education programs have sprung up around the country in response to the burgeoning number of divorce and custody cases seen in family and juvenile courts. Although these programs began in the 1970s, they began to proliferate in the 1990s. The best resource on this new field is the January 1996 issue of *Family and Conciliation Courts*, which is devoted primarily to this topic. Karen Blaisure and Margie Geasler (1996), professors at Western Michigan University, conducted a nationwide survey in September 1994 that revealed 541 parent education programs in 44 states throughout the country at that time. They found that some were court mandated, and some were voluntary. Most were run by officers and employees of the court, whereas others were run by community mental health centers or by private practitioners who had a contract with the local courts. The majority of the programs were one session in length, lasting either 2 hours or 4 hours. There were virtually no attempts to do follow-up interviews with the participants. However, exit surveys were revealing. In one such survey in Utah, 56% of the parents resented having to attend the program, yet 92% thought the program was worthwhile at the conclusion of the session. Readers who may wish to conduct such a program are referred to the Appendix of Blaisure and Geasler's article for a list of the 13 programs used throughout the country.

Salem, Schepard, and Schlissel (1996), attorneys and members of the Association of Family and Conciliation Courts, noted that this steady expansion of parent education programs has made the teaching of them a distinct field of practice. As the programs expand and diversify, according to these authors, the developers have the responsibility to continually evaluate and improve them by conducting research. Some of the research areas that were in development in 1996 were the impact of parent education on mediation, the use of video demonstrations, the impact of program attendance on relitigation rates, and the impact of attendance at the programs on parent behavior change and parenting skills. Salem et al. also suggested that the experts in this field need to develop training standards and qualifications for these new experts. They pointed out that by supporting these educational programs the courts are truly innovative—they make the social statement that the role of the courts is not to serve simply as an arena for family warfare but to extend into the community to help families address their problems.

As parent education programs proliferate, a trend toward making the programs mandatory appears to be emerging. In 1995, *Time* magazine (Gleick, 1995) reported that Utah and Connecticut had made such classes mandatory for all divorcing parents entering family court. Six states (Texas, Colorado, South Carolina, Washington, Montana, and Arizona) were considering mandating the courses statewide. In Maryland, Virginia, New Jersey, and Florida, the courses were optional or mandatory, depending on the judge and the jurisdiction. (Blaisure & Geasler [1996] found that there were 396 court jurisdictions around the country in which parent education programs were mandated.) Eileen Biondi (1996) categorized the programs around the country at that time into four groups: those mandated statewide, those mandated districtwide, those that could be mandated at the discretion of the local court, and those that were voluntary. As stated before, Connecticut was the first to make the program statewide, in January 1994, followed by Utah in July. Biondi went on to describe programs in eight states, which are mandated on a districtwide basis, and 17 that are subject to local court rulings. With the programs being well received by both judges and parents alike, the trend is clearly toward broader mandates.

The proliferation of parent education programs reached a groundswell in the early 1990s, culminating in 1994 in the First International Congress on Parent Education Programs. At this conference, participants were asked by researchers Braver, Salem, Pearson, and DeLuse (1996) to complete a questionnaire on the content of their home programs. Responses were received from 102 programs in existence at the time. These were new programs—80% had been in operation less than 4 years. In fact, one third of them were less than 1 year old. Nearly all the mandated programs were one session in length, whereas the voluntary programs were typically longer —from two to six meetings in length. These programs were informational in focus; they did not teach skills per se. The most consistently covered topics were the effects of divorce on children and the benefits of parental cooperation and conflict resolution. Some of the programs focused on the demonstration of conflict resolution skills and the handling of parenting problems. Only a few programs covered the effects of divorce on the parents. Even fewer covered the legal issues that might arise, such as the legal rights of parents, setting child support guidelines, and filing legal paperwork. This is unfortunate in view of the high number of parents who do not have legal representation in these cases. Joe Glenn (1998) described a program in Jackson County, Missouri, that includes 4 hours of group instruction and play therapy for children while their parents are in the adult meetings. He reported that the responses to the children's participation have been especially positive.

Do parent education programs work? Are they successful in reducing conflict? What are the relitigation rates? Jack Arbuthnot and Donald Gordon of Ohio University have been involved in several studies addressing these questions. In the first study, Arbuthnot and Gordon (1996) followed a parent education group, whose members were taught skills in conflict management, by surveying the participants immediately after the class and 6 months later. They also followed a group of parents who did not take the parent education class. The parents who finished the course reported that they engaged in fewer hostile behaviors that placed their children in the center of conflict than did the comparison group. They also reported that they were more willing to let their children spend time with the other parent. However, they did not indicate that they argued with the other parent any less; neither were they inclined to encourage a relationship with the child's other parent. The "treatment" group also did not indicate that their children were showing better adjustment and fewer emotional problems. Arbuthnot, Kramer, and Gordon (1997) re-evaluated these parents again 2 years after the class. They reported that the parents who had attended the course, compared with those who had not, relitigated half as often. A closer examination of the data revealed that parents who had mastered the skills taught in the class relitigated at lower rates than those who had attended but had not mastered the skills.

Kramer, Arbuthnot, Gordon, and Rousis (1998) sought to determine which aspect of the parent education program was most important by following one group of parents who attended a skills-based class and one group who attended an information-giving course. The results indicated that the parents in the skills-based class reported better parental communication. Neither program appeared to be advantageous over the other in terms of lowering domestic violence, lowering parental conflict, or lowering the level of child behavior problems. Overall, the parents with the best functioning, in terms of greater knowledge about divorce and better communication skills, reported less parental conflict—regardless of which group they had attended. One weakness of these studies is that the outcome data consisted of parents' self-reports on a survey. Chapter 9 showed that parents in highly conflicted divorces are not able to view their shortcomings accurately and tend to project blame, so the survey data may not reflect what the parent is actually doing and saying to the other parent.

Last, Gray, Verdieck, Smith, and Freed (1997) reviewed the results of the first year of a psychoeducational program for divorcing parents— 152 of whom were court mandated and 123 of whom were not. Interviewing these families 6 months later, Gray et al. found positive results for the group in terms of reduced interparental conflict, children's adjustment to the divorce (as reported by the parents), and the parents' ability to settle the legal issues of the divorce without drawing the children into the conflict.

Some people in the divorce education arena have raised the issue that the "one size fits all" educational class may not be suitable to large numbers of disputing parents who feel that they have a different set of problems with which to deal. For instance, wives of batterers have special concerns about violent altercations, about face-to-face confrontations with the ex-husband at times of visitation dropoffs, and even about being in the same class with the batterer. Similarly, gay and lesbian parents who have adopted a child and then separated feel unlike heterosexual families. Mothers who have custody of their children, yet never married, have different concerns as well. For example, they may not understand that the father of the child has legal rights to visitation. Johnston and Girdner (1998) found that almost half of their sample of parents who carried out child abductions had never married the other parent. Johnston and Roseby (1997) described a highly specialized group education program in California, the Pre-Contempt/Contemnor's Group Diversion Counseling Program in Los Angeles County. This program was made for families who chronically litigate over visitation and access disputes. In addition to the standard format of divorce education groups, it includes information on custody and visitation court laws and the consequences of not complying with court orders.

In summary, divorce education programs may be useful to the courts because they reduce the potential conflict between some parents, which can mean enormous savings for the courts in terms of bench time. It may be, however, that it is those parents who are best able to learn the material and to master the conflict-resolution skills who can use the programs most effectively.

Mediation

Mediation, as shown in chapter 3, is another effective tool that is becoming widely used by the courts. In California, all cases involving juveniles that are contested go automatically into mediation. In Georgia, however, mediation may or may not be mandatory, depending on the judge and the jurisdiction. Some portion of parents can use mediation and settle out of court—but again, the parents with more entrenched bitterness and more serious psychopathology may not benefit from mandatory mediation.

Atlanta family law attorney Randy Kessler (personal communication, April 12, 1999) sees mediation as here to stay but anticipates that mediators will become more specialized in the future. For example, mediators may subspecialize in the mediation of the financial aspects of the settlement. Some mediators may have a background in social work as well as law and subspecialize in mediating sexual abuse allegations. Kessler also foresees mediators who may specialize in disputes over the dissolution of gay and lesbian relationships. Divorces that involve children, and in which one partner is gay and one is straight, may be particularly complex. Kessler would like to see judges use mediators more judiciously and with more focus on specialization.

Parenting Plans

Another trend that has occurred in this field is the emphasis on parenting plans. Many experts in this field have observed that when there is vague language in a divorce decree, when areas of decision making are to be negotiated, or when areas are omitted or unanticipated, there is bound to be litigation, especially if the divorce is a highly conflicted one. Attorneys and courts have responded by encouraging parents to craft a detailed, precise plan of custody, access, and decision making that leaves no room for ambiguity. Robert Tompkins, of the Superior Court of Connecticut, stated that such a plan should go far beyond the usual custody order (Tompkins, 1995). In addition to spelling out the allotment of the child's time with regard to the school year, the summer, vacations, holidays, birthdays, and other events, the parenting plan also should address decision making in several domains of parental responsibilities, such as education, religion, and health care. It should address areas such as child care, if the child is young, and decision making in regard to after-school activities. It may address issues such as who pays for the child's clothing, who stays home with the child when she or he is sick, who can have the child's hair cut, or when a teenager can drive. It will also specify how the parents will resolve conflicts—through mediation with an attorney, through therapeutic mediation with a mental health professional, through an arbitrator, and so on.

Garrity and Baris (1994) suggested that the parenting plan include many of the same areas of conflict as those listed by Tompkins (1995). They also suggested that the attorneys and other parties involved in the case include the specific arrangements that will be made for picking up and dropping off the child (where, when, under what conditions, how long a parent is to wait), rules for telephone calls (who can make them, how often, duration, if the other parent can listen in), the coordination of clothing and toys back and forth between the two homes (whether the child who goes from Parent A to Parent B wears the same clothing at Parent B's house, whether Parent B is to wash the clothes, whether the child is to wear only the clothes of Parent B at Parent B's house), and so on. Flexibility in scheduling is another highly conflicted area that can be anticipated with a parenting plan. For example, a father who travels out of town on an erratic schedule may need a provision for alternate times. Last, the parenting plan should anticipate strategies for handling the possibility that a child may refuse a visitation.

No research to date has examined the effectiveness of parenting plans on, for example, reducing rates of litigation. However, Tompkins (1995) cited an unpublished study that found that 60% of the family attorneys surveyed who used parenting plans found that the plans reduced levels of parental conflict. Forty percent said that they were not helpful. Tompkins concluded that parenting plans may make the difference for that middle 50% of divorcing parents who have mild to moderate levels of conflict (as opposed to no conflict or severe conflict) who can benefit from a wide array of interventions. Kessler (personal communication, April 12, 1999) pointed out that the divorce decree or custody order—or parenting plan, for that matter—should not be considered an end in the process. It is the beginning, a blueprint for the future relationship and events that may arise. The clearer and more exhaustive it is, the less potential there is for disagreement in the future.

Specialized Courts, New Roles for Attorneys

Parents who are divorcing in an urban area with many resources may have availed themselves of all the above-mentioned resources by the time they get to court—they may have attended a 3-hour educational program, attended a brief session of mediation, and drawn up a detailed parenting plan. Ideally, they would then be in agreement as to their plans for sharing custody, access, and decision making and thus have settled out of court. Embattled couples who do not reach agreement and still go to court may be able to benefit from new programs in the court system.

In the judicial system, the trend has been toward more specialized courts that can process long-standing cases of repeated litigation, more swiftly and with more expertise thanks to the use of professionals who are highly trained in this field. In Atlanta, Georgia, the family division of Superior Court of Fulton County has launched a trial program, Family Court, whose motto is "One family, one judge." Rather than send cases of family violence, divorce, child support, paternity, and custody conflicts to be heard by several different judges in different courts, all cases can be seen by one judge, who will come to know the family over a period of time. Juvenile crime and child molestation cases can also be seen in Family Court if they are related cases.

This model, patterned after existing Family Court models in Washington and California, is a 3-year project funded with state and county monies, and it is part of a pilot project nationwide in which courts in four other jurisdictions are participating. The goals of the program are to coordinate related cases in a family with case management and more efficient resolution. Staff attorney Emily McBurney, who has worked in New York, Massachusetts, and Washington, DC, stated that although many states have a family court, few have adopted some of the innovations of this program. "This is the most humane system I've worked for," she stated, "because so much effort is put into mitigating the pain that these families go through" (personal communication, March 21, 1999). The thrust of the program is to be as nonadversarial as possible. Every case is kept moving through the system so that none languish. Because the judge hears only family cases, these families are not put on the back burner for a high-profile murder trial. These families get the special attention they need; many are low income and without attorney representation, so the legal center helps them with booklets, reading material, forms, and filing papers.

The families meet with the judge or a judge's designee within 30 days of filing for an informal conference on the status of the case. Many settle at that informal meeting. Others are sent to mediation and settle their case there. If they do not settle, the family gets a 60-day conference and a 120-day conference, if necessary, to try to settle out of court. Few cases actually go to court, according to McBurney. The advantages to the family are clear: They get attention, assistance, and more control over the court process. The program is less costly for them and far less hostile.

An essential part of Family Court is the court psychologist. Barbara Rubin began this position in June 1998 and reports that her role is evolving over time (personal communication, February 22, 1999). In addition to conducting custody evaluations for low-income families, Rubin is available to provide consultation to the judges and to the parents. She investigates sexual abuse allegations, gives input in visitation disputes, and provides focused, short-term couples counseling. On several occasions she has been called in to provide crisis intervention for parents who become distraught at trial.

Connecticut has developed the Regional Family Trial Docket as a specialized court to handle only complex, embittered, long-standing custody feuds. Christina Burnham (1997) gave the history of this program in a special issue of *Family Advocate* focusing on new developments in family court for 2000. In the past 2 years, the Regional Family Trial Docket has resolved 189 very difficult cases. In so doing, the court has removed a large number of complex cases from the Superior Court docket. However, because the cases are so long, they usually take 6–7 days to resolve. Initially the court used the volunteer services of a team of two gender-balanced attorneys, referred to as *special masters*. These attorneys have highly specialized skills in domestic relations and custody conflicts. After the first year of the program, the teams were reconstituted as a gender-balanced team consisting of one attorney and one mental health professional. The Connecticut Association of Marriage and Family Therapists and the Connecticut Psychological Association have donated the services of more than 100 practitioners who each give 2 days a year to the program, at no charge.

Still another specialized court is the Expedited Visitation Services program administered by the Superior Court of Maricopa County, Arizona. This court focuses only on visitation disputes. Cheryl Lee, John Shaughnessy, and Joel Bankes (1995), attorneys associated with the Arizona courts, described the program as a mediation–arbitration model of dispute resolution. In this program, special masters serve six roles for the court: They investigate the reasons why visitation has been blocked; they conduct mediation sessions with the parents and help the parents understand that the visitation must take place; refer parents to outside agencies if needed; make recommendations to the court; and supervise the case for 6 months.

The special masters in this program have an advanced degree in any human services area who have subsequent training in mediation. The director of the program is a psychologist. Lee et al. (1995) did not indicate whether the special masters in this program are volunteers, paid staff, or private contractors. It is interesting that Lee et al. found that the children in their study perceived more conflict between their parents as the visitations were enforced and they saw the noncustodial parent more often. However, as the visitations took place on a regular basis over a span of time in the program, the level of conflict tapered off. Lee et al. felt that the impact of the conflict on the children in the program was offset by better overall adjustment and less depression and acting out over the course of the study.

The court programs just described were developed to staunch the flood of postdivorce custody and access disputes that at times overload the court docket and create unnecessarily long delays. If a family does not have access to one of these special programs and does not want to wait, another alternative is outside arbitration. Hanley Gurwin, an attorney in Michigan, writing for the special edition of *Family Advocate* cited above, claimed that "If the 80's was the decade of mediation, the 90's is the decade of arbitration" (1997, p. 29). The landmark case for this trend was *Dick v. Dick* (210 Mich. Ct. App. 576), in which the court declared that custody issues, like financial and property settlements, could be settled through arbitration and that the agreements could be binding. In 1997 Michigan, Pennsylvania, Missouri, and Texas were all using the services of a private attorney or retired judge to arbitrate child custody cases. This innovation offers many advantages to the parents in the case: They can mutually choose the arbitrator, and they can meet at a convenient time and in a private setting. Also, the proceeding is less formal than a trial. Although it is costly, it does give the parents a good deal of control over the legal process, something they are not likely to get in court. The American Academy of Matrimonial Lawyers has trained more than 300 attorneys in arbitration since 1990, and Gurwin expects that number to grow in the coming years.

Still another alternative to litigation is the Collaborative Law Program. Begun in Minnesota by an attorney who was determined to find a method for keeping postdivorce conflict cases out of court, the program has spread to California, Georgia, and Ohio (Attorney Diane Woods, personal communication, November 15, 1999). The program is essentially this: The two parties and their attorneys sign a contract to meet together for as many meetings as it takes to arrive at a mutually agreed-on settlement and to not litigate. No mediator or arbitrator is present, just the two parents and their respective attorneys. If the attempt at collaboration fails, the attorneys are dismissed. The parents must seek new counsel to go forward with litigation. Thus, the pressure to collaborate and to settle from the outset is high. The American Bar Association just began to conduct training in collaborative law in the summer of 1999. Attorneys Diane Woods, Lynn Russell, and Ansley Barton in the Atlanta area have been instrumental in getting this program off the ground in Georgia. The Collaborative Law Institute, as it is called in Atlanta, trained 40 attorneys in the spring of 1999 and is scheduled to train more attorneys in the spring of 2000.

NEW ROLES FOR MENTAL HEALTH PROFESSIONALS

The exponential rise in postdivorce conflict has seen new programs, new courts, and new roles for attorneys, such as those of mediator, special master, and arbitrator. Along those lines, mental health professionals working in close contact with attorneys and the courts have moved into new roles as well, in some ways blurring the line between attorney and clinician.

Legal Therapist Counselor

Some large law firms have begun to employ legal therapist counselors (LTCs) to be part of the matrimonial law team. Attorney Ronni Burrows and assistant counsel Elaine Buzzinotti (1997) of Pittsburgh, Pennsylvania, described LTCs as experienced mental health professionals with more than a master's degree who provide psychoeducational, but not clinical, services to clients. Understanding that clients going through divorce and postdivorce litigation are often emotionally distraught and confused, the LTC begins by providing books and articles on divorce and reviewing treatment options. He or she conducts a brief assessment of the client's emotional state, helps the client prepare a list of questions for the attorney, and explains some of the upcoming legal processes. The LTC reviews the custody evaluation with the client, especially if the report is confusing or unfavorable. The LTC accompanies the attorney and the client to all hearings to provide emotional support and clarification to the client. Also, perhaps most important to the attorney, the LTC fields all of the emotional crisis calls that are frequent in these cases. Some attorneys absorb the costs of the LTC as part of their hourly billing, whereas others charge a separate hourly fee for the LTC.

In 1995 the Legal Therapy Institute and Duquesne University in Pittsburgh began the Certification Program for Legal Therapist Counselor, which involves intensive coursework and a 40-hour practicum in a law firm.

Private Consultant

Another emerging role is that of private consultant to families contemplating divorce. In this situation, parents may come in singly or together, requesting information and suggestions on an appropriate visitation schedule for a child, the advisability of a move, ways in which to handle difficult transitions at visitation times, and so on. These are strictly advice-giving meetings and are not intended as psychotherapy. The records are confidential, unless both parents request that the consultant write a summary to be forwarded to both attorneys. For divorcing or divorced parents with low to moderate conflicts, a private consultant may be all that is needed to settle the matter out of court.

Mediator

A third role is that of *mediator*. Many psychologists around the country are pursuing formal training in mediation, attracted to the possibility of offering highly specialized services that are not regulated by managed care plans.

Formal mediation is highly structured and may be done with attorneys present, with a well-developed agenda and ground rules, and written proposals drawn up at the conclusion of several sessions. I have done *informal mediation* with parents who are at an impasse and wish an outside opinion. This is particularly effective method with parents who have a relatively amicable relationship and wish to preserve their goodwill toward each other by excluding attorneys and court petitions. If the informal mediator has seen the child or family in treatment in the past, the mediator may have a rapport with each family that a formal mediator may not have. In this role, however, the informal mediator should make clear that there is no diagnosis rendered, charges are paid out of pocket, there is no treatment plan, and so on. Records of the meetings should be kept confidential and shared only with the parents. Many parents find this to be the arena of dispute resolution that is the most sensitive to their needs and over which they have the most control.

Johnston and Roseby (1997) developed a form of *therapeutic mediation* in the course of the large body of research conducted by Johnston and others on highly conflicted divorced families. In therapeutic mediation, the families are referred by the courts in an effort to resolve their continued litigation, although the mediation–counseling is confidential. In the initial phases of the study, Johnston and her colleagues (Johnston & Campbell, 1988; Johnston & Roseby, 1997) saw parents individually and together briefly for 25–35 sessions. Johnston et al. also tried a group therapeutic mediation approach in which they saw a group of parents for 7 multihour sessions (about 17 hours in all). Since then, they have shortened the therapeutic mediation program to 3–5 multihour sessions, or about 10 total hours of mediation. In this series of sessions, the mediators–counselors make a rapid assessment of the couple's impasse (see chapter 8), followed by a strategic reframing and redirection toward better methods of handling their dispute. This form of mediation is considered therapeutic because the mediators–counselors focus on resolving the emotional injury that is at the heart of the impasse.

Special Master, Counselor, and Parent Coordinator

In the paragraphs above, I referred to the special master. This role is widely known in some regions of the country and yet virtually unknown in others. The special master is also known as *wiseperson* in New Mexico, a *custody commissioner* in Hawaii, and a *coparenting counselor* or *medarb* in Colorado. Joan Kelly, a psychologist and executive director of the Northern California Mediation Center, defined the *special master* as "a hybrid court officer who has the authority to make certain decisions related to parenting and visiting that the parents cannot make themselves" (1994, p. 136). She referred to special masters as being mainly mental health professionals with training in several relevant areas: divorce conflict, custody evaluations, parenting issues, child development, and mediation.

Special masters are generally appointed by a judge when there is a history of repeated litigation and the court wishes to bring the matter to a close through the services of a highly specialized expert in the field. The special master attempts to mediate the dispute; then, if the parents cannot reach agreement, the special master drafts recommendations, which are sent to the judge for approval.

Matthew Sullivan (1997), a forensic psychologist in California, stated that a special master may be an attorney or a mental health professional. He listed the following goals of special masters: to reduce conflict and keep cases out of court, to monitor a serious family situation, to teach conflict resolution skills, to provide a readily available resource to families in crisis, and to enhance the safety and stability of the family. Typically, the special master is appointed to follow a family for 1–2 years. Sullivan emphasized that the special master is empowered to make court orders that are binding. Low-level and mid-level decisions may be decided by the special master during regular consultations, but high-level decisions (such as a major change in time sharing or a geographic move) can be recommended by the special master and then reviewed and approved by a judge. Garrity and Baris (1994) used the term *parenting coordinator* and conceptualized this role along much of the same lines as the special master.

One program that has been well received throughout the metro Atlanta, Georgia, area is the Cooperative Parenting Program, developed by a practice group: Family Solutions, Inc. Begun by Susan Boyan and Anne Marie Timini in 1995 to serve the growing need for out-of-court settlement of postdivorce disputes, these counselors have developed over time a two-pronged approach. One component of the program, the Cooperative Parenting Group Format, consists of eight weekly group sessions with approximately 10 couples, who meet for 2½ hours. This program is strictly didactic and is designed for couples with mild to moderate levels of conflict. Referrals come from other parents, therapists, and attorneys. Participation is voluntary. In these meetings, which can be attended by one or both parents, the focus is on skill development, small- and large-group discussion, parent interaction, and weekly homework assignments.

The Cooperative Parenting Co-Parent format is the second arm of the program and is more tailored to couples with high levels of intractable postdivorce conflict. Here, individual divorced couples are court mandated into 14–16 sessions of 1½ hours in length with a parenting coordinator. This program could best be described as mediation–education in that couples are expected to learn better conflict resolution skills as well as to hammer out a detailed parenting plan by the end of the series. The parenting coordinator is empowered by the court order in many cases to force couples to come to agreement—even, if need be, to write a temporary alteration in the court order. Attorneys are invited to sit in and observe. If one party discontinues, the meetings are discontinued, and the court is notified. At the end of the sessions, a final plan is drafted and sent to the court with recommendations. Both parents agree to return to the parenting coordinator in the future before seeking legal action.

Anne Marie Timini, codeveloper of the Cooperative Parenting Program, sees these programs as the direction in which the resolution of postdivorce conflict is heading. "More and more, I see these cases being settled, not in the courtroom, but in someone's private office" (personal communication, March 23, 1999). She views the parenting coordinator as a new type of specialist, whose credentials, training, and legal authority have yet to be fully spelled out: "This field is really in its infancy."

Arbitrator

As with attorneys, mental health professionals have also begun to move into the role of arbitrator in those custody cases that are particularly complex and long standing. Here, though, the lines among mediator, special master, and arbitrator blur even more. In fact, Janet Johnston and Linda Girdner (1998) used the terms *special master, coparenting coordinator,* and *arbitrator* interchangeably. Theoretically, the arbitrator is given the decision-making power to resolve a dispute, and the decision can be binding on the two parents.

Robert Zibbell (1995), a private psychologist in Framingham, Massachusetts, recounted the case of an embittered couple who had returned to court for several years over the details of visitations, vacations, and scheduling changes. The family had refused to continue to work with the guardian ad litem in the case. The attorneys consulted with each other and agreed on an arbitrator. In Phase 1, the attorneys drew up an arbitration contract that dictated the ground rules regarding payment, access to records, and the appeals process. (For example, if one parent were dissatisfied with the arbitral award, he or she would have to bear the burden of a review process.) In Phase 2, the arbitrator completed the interviews and read the relevant documents, much as one would in a child custody evaluation. In Phase 3, a proposal was drafted and sent to the parents and their attorneys for review. Then the arbitrator held a final interview with each parent (they had refused to sit in the same room) to provide them with an opportunity to give feedback. In the last phase, the final decision was drawn up, sent to the attorneys, and agreed to by the parents. The case did not go on to court.

Zibbell (1995) noted some striking advantages for the litigating couple. Although the procedure may have been costly, they were able to save "significant expense" over what a trial would have cost. As with mediation, the couple was allowed to have much more control over the process. They could choose the arbitrator, and they received a timely hearing rather than waiting for several months for their case to come up on the court docket and having to keep rescheduling because of petitions, motions, and continuances. They were more comfortable in the office setting than in the courtroom, could give feedback to the arbitrator, and did not have to sit in the same room together. Although this last factor is a simple one, it is important, because often face-to-face confrontations between warring parties elicit emotional reactions that derail the work of developing compromises.

Johnston and Roseby (1997) delineated two models of arbitration conducted by mental health professionals. In the nontherapeutic model, the arbitrator is chosen by the parties' attorneys to resolve a particular dispute, and the parents are bound by the arbitrator's award. In the second model, the arbitrator may also serve clinical functions, such as parenting counselor or the child's therapist. In this model confidentiality and boundary problems are bound to arise.

Richard Gardner (1989), known to be a maverick in the child custody area, suggested over 10 years ago that mental health professionals become arbitrators. In fact, he suggested abolishing the court system altogether in custody and access disputes. Instead, he proposed that the couple go through a three-stage process. The first would be mediation, which has already been described. In the second phase, if the couple could not mediate successfully, they would go to an arbitration panel composed of two mental health professionals and one attorney. They would plead their case to this panel, and the decision would be binding. If one parent were still dissatisfied, he or she could take the case to an appeals panel, also composed of two mental health professionals and one attorney. In Gardner's world, mental health professionals would have more voting power than attorneys, and there would be no courtroom dramas.

Johnston and Roseby (1997) also questioned the place of the court in family decisions. They noted that divorce, custody, and access disputes are exceptionally draining to attorneys, mental health professionals, and judges alike. Many cases require years of professional help to resolve, and some are impossible to bring to a positive conclusion. Judges have no more expertise in this area than the slew of professionals and programs listed above, and their rulings are seldom the end of the difficulties for the family. Johnston and Roseby called for a new role for the courts—to provide not an arena for the airing of disputes but the leadership to bring together the resources of the community to help highly conflicted families, something akin to triage and referral. Johnston and Roseby proposed a five-phase model that would exist in parallel to the court system.

First, families would attend parenting and divorce education programs. Next, they would go to consultation and mediation programs. Third, if they had not been able to resolve their dispute, they would be referred to therapeutic mediation or for a custody evaluation. If the parents were still disputing, they would go on to the special master/parenting coordinator/arbitrator, who would make a proposal to the court to resolve the dispute. Last, the family would be referred to ancillary services in the community, such as domestic violence programs, visitation supervision and monitoring, and community mental health and substance abuse programs.

NEW TREATMENT PROGRAMS FOR CHILDREN

The boom in the divorce rate in the 1970s and 1980s brought with it a new array of treatment methods for both parents and children. These programs are now so widespread that nearly every church has a divorce support group for parents, and most elementary schools have an ongoing group for children of divorce. For a comprehensive review, readers are referred to William Hodges's (1991) book *Interventions for Children of Divorce*.

Kid's Turn

One innovative program that has received much mention is Kid's Turn, widely popular in the San Francisco Bay area. Rosemarie Bolen (1993) wrote that the program was founded by Superior Court judge Ina Gyemont in 1988. Gyemont felt that it was time to "give the kids a turn" to speak out about their own experiences. The 6-week format of 90-minute meetings includes many of the psychoeducational features of other children's groups: videos, therapeutic children's books about divorce, drawings, a puppet show, and therapeutic board games.

Perhaps the most powerful activity of Kid's Turn is one in which the children write a newsletter to the parent group that runs concurrently with the children's group. John Stossel of ABC News did a segment on Kid's Turn in April 1995 ("Through the Eyes," 1995); he interviewed Judge Roderic Duncan, several parents and coleaders, and many of the children in the group. Duncan explained that he had joined the program in response to his frustration with parents who engage in high levels of conflict and domestic violence:

> You try to figure out some way to help them understand the corrosive effect this is having on the life of this little person that they've brought into this world. I've tried lecturing, and it doesn't seem to work. I've tried begging them, and I've tried putting them in jail.

Stossel asked Duncan why Kid's Turn would make a difference. Duncan replied, "When they sit down here with their kids in the other room and they see their kids talking to other kids who are going through divorcing, it seems to get through to their brain." Stossel noted to Gyemont that reading the children's letters seemed to make a greater impression on the parents than the judges' orders do. Gyemont responded that one parent had been planning on leaving the state and suing his wife for custody of the children. After going through Kids' Turn, he decided instead to get a job in the same town as his children and stay there.

Specialized Treatment Programs

Some clinicians have developed more specialized treatment programs for the children of highly conflicted divorces. Shelley Rooney and Todd Walker (1999) of Cincinnati, Ohio, described elements of individual psychotherapy in a case study format. Much of their approach centers around helping the child to differentiate himself or herself and his or her feelings and perceptions from those of the alienating parent. Also, the therapists help the child integrate and understand the good and bad parts of both parents in a way that makes sense and is more reality based. The goal of treatment is for the child to see parents through his or her own eyes rather than taking in the conflict.

Johnston and Roseby (1997) are perhaps the leaders in the field of new treatments for the children of highly conflicted divorces. They first published an article on their group treatment approach (Roseby & Johnston, 1995) and followed it up with a manual (Roseby & Johnston, 1997) and a book of therapeutic stories for children (Johnston, Breunig, Garrity, & Baris, 1997). This program runs for 10 weekly sessions, and younger children (7–9 years) are seen separately from older children (10–12 years). Early sessions focus on learning the language of feelings and how to express the intensity of feelings. Children go on to learn, through therapeutic play, how to distinguish inner feelings from the masks they wear. Learning to distinguish themselves from the alienating parent with whom they are often merged, the children are given a task—to go into a private room in their minds that only they can enter. Later, the children construct an identity shield that will project future aspects of themselves. In some of the final meetings, the children dramatize the impasse in the family and the role they play in it, through human sculptures and role play. These sessions help children to see the scripted rules and expectations that put them in a position of helplessness and anxiety.

One particularly dramatic intervention is the children's talk show. Children are videotaped while role-playing experts on a panel about children of highly conflicted divorces. They answer questions written by the leaders but read as though they came from other children who are seeking help and advice. The children give their answers with intensity and energy. They advise children to stay out of the middle, to talk to parents when they are upset, and to ask parents not to put such a heavy burden on them.

At several points during the 10-week program the parents stay after the close of the children's group and have a feedback session with the group leaders. The leaders report that when they describe to the parents some of the children's artwork and talk show advice, this alone has such an impact on the parents that they immediately begin to disengage from the alienating and begin to abide by the parenting plan. For others, still more group work and therapeutic mediation are needed.

In their closing note, Johnston and Roseby (1997) wrote that this program can be easily conducted in community centers around the country by trained mental health professionals.

CONCLUSION

At the beginning of this book, I addressed the outcome of the divorce revolution, particularly as it looks for children. After 30 years, we would have to conclude that the divorce revolution has not improved children's lives. Furstenberg and Cherlin (1991) concluded that although children of the 1990s may have higher levels of economic prosperity than previous generations, they have it worse overall than the children of the 1950s and 1960s. They suffer rates of parental loss comparable to those of the children of the 1920s and the 1930s, who commonly lost parents through the ravages of war, early death from disease and childbirth, and desertion.

Although divorces today are largely initiated by women, it is mothers who have borne the burden of the divorce most greatly. Mothers, as we have seen in this book, begin parenthood as the designated manager of the children's lives, and this role continues, even under joint custody. They continue to retain primary custody in greater numbers than fathers, yet they must also be the primary economic support of the family. Their economic standing declines while the father's rises (Maccoby & Mnookin,

1992). A major stressor on these mothers, and one that has not been measured, yet is seen often by clinicians, is that they must endure separations from their children, separations that can be acutely emotionally painful. Added to this is the fact that many of these women must surrender the care of the children to a father whom they divorced because they deemed him to be irresponsible, inadequate, abusive, or dangerous. Few mothers who initiate divorce are prepared for the particular emotional anguish they will experience during those intervals when the child is in the custody of the father. It is not surprising that Wallerstein and Blakeslee (1989) found that a dismal 10% of divorcing mothers and fathers reported that both were better off after the divorce.

We now know that the divorce launches the children on a trajectory through life that has many hazards ahead. The studies on the effects of divorce on children are legion, but we can sum them up by stating that divorce roughly doubles the risk for children of a host of emotional disorders (Zill, Morrison, & Coiro, 1991). Although the life courses of these children vary greatly from one family to another, we now know that the level of interparental conflict before and after the divorce will be a major influencing factor. Children who are exposed to high levels of conflict prior to the divorce, yet who witness an end to the conflict with the coming of the divorce, may benefit from the separation of their parents, at least in the short term. Children whose parents are in conflict for a long time prior to the divorce—conflict that continues into the postdivorce years—fare most poorly. Years of chronic conflict have a corrosive effect on the parent–child relationship, and these children feel progressively rejected, angry, and emotionally neglected.

The long-term effects of divorce on children are subtle, yet they have been documented in many studies. As parent–child bonds are weakened, children are opened up to socialization by their peers and by the mass culture in their teenage years. The family exerts less influence on these adolescents in terms of transmitting values. These young adults lose faith in the security and durability of all human relationships, which opens them up to a pattern of disordered behavior in their own relationships and contributes to higher divorce rates in the next generation.

Children caught in the crossfire attempt to cope with chronic conflict as they have attempted in the past to cope with other forms of loss and transition. Some do so valiantly, as we have seen, being, by nature, resilient individuals. However, many do not. Children who are caught up in the most insidious divorce wars often cope with confusion and loyalty conflicts by forming a strong alliance with one parent against the other that may last into adulthood or longer.

Over the past 30 years, many professionals have developed innovative programs to contend with this social problem. In the 1970s laws were introduced to end gender bias in the courts in favoring mothers for custody.

Although this was a victory for fathers, many see this as the trigger for a groundswell of custody battles, which continues unabated. Family mediation was developed to reduce conflict and, although it is effective in the short term, there appear to be neither long-term benefits from mediation nor improvements in children's adjustment. Parents who are locked in severe conflict do not benefit from mediation at all and view it as an obligation to endure on their way to divorce court.

Joint legal and physical custody were introduced as a way of enfranchising fathers to become full participants in their children's lives. This was founded on the belief that all children benefited from frequent contact with their fathers. Not only has joint custody not resulted in better emotional adjustment for children, or reductions in interparental conflict, but also a wave of studies has concluded, reluctantly, that children do not benefit from more contact with their fathers. Again, parental conflict appears to be the overriding mediating factor in predicting whether children benefit from joint custody or increased time with their fathers. Mandatory classes for divorcing parents have now been instituted in many jurisdictions —classes that focus on conflict resolution. Such classes have proved helpful in some cases, but they have little effect in the long run, especially on parents entrenched in postdivorce disputes.

The thread that runs through this discourse is that interparental conflict appears to be impervious to the efforts of well-trained professionals armed with new programs, treatments, and legal interventions. Why is this? We can speculate that it may be due to the enduring nature of the parent–child bond. All parents in all custody and access disputes view themselves as fighting desperately to protect their children from harm and to assert their influence over the raising of their children. It is a bond that goes deeper, and is more immutable, than any other human relationship. As we saw in chapter 5, the tension surrounding the threat of loss in custody cases often runs higher than that in murder trials. Second, as we saw in chapter 9, parents who are caught in the most entrenched conflict appear to have personality disorders or many traits of these disorders. Among emotional and behavioral disorders, the personality disorders are known to be extremely resistant to treatment interventions. Two decades of research suggest that they may be strongly genetically and physiologically based (see Cloninger, 1999; Cloninger, Svrakic, & Przybeck, 1993; Siever & Davis, 1991, for reviews). The intransigent nature of postdivorce conflict thus may be a result of the collision of these two factors—the parent-child bond and innate temperament, which may arise out of our own biology.

There is no going back on the divorce revolution. Furstenberg and Cherlin (1991) and Whitehead (1996) concluded that the right to divorce at will, to pursue one's happiness, is now a fundamental part of American society. There can be no ultimate solution in the courts, either. As Maccoby and Mnookin (1992) concluded, "the net is not fine enough" for the court to sort out the many small conflicts that arise between divorced families (p. 280). Johnston and Roseby (1997) concluded that the courts, by their adversarial nature, may exacerbate the sense of loss and narcissistic injury for parents, compounding their need for revenge.

As we enter the 21st century, we are seeing the aggregation of many services, all of which may be somewhat helpful, into multidisciplinary and multilayered programs. It has become clear to many professionals in the mental health, social service, and court systems that many legal problems cannot be viewed in isolation but must be seen and must be dealt with as the reflection of the unraveling of society. Recently, I attended a joint conference of the American Psychological Association (APA) and American Bar Association (ABA), "Psychological Expertise and Criminal Justice," in Washington, DC. At that conference I was struck by the proliferation of what are referred to as *wraparound* or *multisystemic* programs. For example, Assistant State's Attorney Pamela Paziotopoulos (1999), from Cook County, Illinois, described a program that has improved arrest and prosecution rates for domestic batterers. To do this, the program had to not only integrate investigators and prosecutors into a unified team but also provide advocacy for the victim and coordinate a whole range of services to support the victim with alternative housing, counseling, and financial support. Gene Griffin (1999), a psychologist and attorney with the Illinois Department of Human Services, described a program for intervention with juvenile offenders, the Federal Child and Adolescent Service System Program. This program not only focuses on the incarceration of juveniles, but it also integrates social services programs to assist the family: educational programs, health programs, and vocational programs.

Naturally, one would predict that model programs across the country that tackle the problem of chronic postdivorce conflict may inevitably become wraparound or multisystemic programs as well. Earlier in chapter 12 I described the Family Court program in Fulton County, Georgia. This program combines under one umbrella the many related disputes that these families bring to the courtroom. However, it provides much more: legal aid for the indigent parent; a law library for public use; and a court psychologist who can provide crisis counseling to the parents, court-ordered evaluations, and immediate consultation with the judges.

I would like to offer a modest proposal for the development of a model program along the lines of a Neighborhood Family Conflict Resolution Center. Such a center would provide the services of the Family Court but would be moved into the community and be less adversarial in nature. Professionals in the center might work on a fee-for-service basis, offering predivorce mediation, development of detailed parenting plans, and sexual abuse and custody evaluations. Group educational classes could be offered on a low-fee basis, covering topics such as conflict resolution, anger management, and effective parenting skills. Mediation could be offered, both through the divorce and after the divorce. Ongoing therapeutic mediation could be court ordered, as proposed by Johnston and Roseby (1997). Specific treatment groups could be offered both for children who experience chronic parental conflict and for their parents. Visitation services could also be offered for a fee. These could include the supervision and monitoring of highly conflicted visitations as well as enforcement of visitation orders. Special masters could be appointed at the entrance of each family into the center who would track cases and route them to the appropriate services. Legal aid could be provided to indigent families. Researchers on staff could obtain grant funding for ongoing studies, with some of the funding going to pay staff salaries. Families who wish to do so could hire attorneys to arbitrate cases to speed them through the court system. Otherwise, the cases would be heard on a regular basis by a Family Court judge, after all attempts at education, mediation, treatment, and dispute resolution have failed. The judge would have the authority to order the families into whatever services are deemed necessary.

Ideally, with good coordination of services, families would not have to feel that their cases will languish for months, awaiting a court date, but could begin to receive some assistance right away. The call goes out for an enterprising group of individuals to write a grant to obtain funding for such an innovative program.

DIRECTIONS FOR THE FUTURE

In his keynote address to the recent conference sponsored by the APA and ABA, Thomas Grisso (1999) outlined what he saw as the three phases of development in the role of psychologists in the criminal justice system. In Phase 1, the 1970s, psychologists entered the legal arena eager to demonstrate their skills in the courtroom. There were no standards for training at the time, as there were no graduate courses offered, and no postdoctoral opportunities existed. Thus, there were no standards for credentialing experts in the courtroom. There was no body of research in existence that had a direct bearing on psycholegal issues such as competency to stand trial, risk of dangerousness, and so on. Psychologists attempted to apply their clinical skills to forensic cases, although the psychometric instruments in existence at that time did not meet the criteria for the scientific validity that was needed in the legal arena. Neither did much of the clinical expertise that was offered have a direct bearing on psycholegal issues. Psychologists were not held to a high standard, and their opinions were not widely respected by the legal community.

In Phase 2, the 1980s through the 1990s, a large body of research has accumulated on psycholegal issues—research that has yielded an array of new methods for addressing psycholegal questions that are before the court.

We now have, for example, scientifically validated instruments for measuring psychopathology in adults and adolescents; the competency to stand trial; fitness to aid in one's defense; competency to waive one's Miranda rights; and dangerousness in adult criminal offenders, sex offenders, and domestic batterers. These measures are admissible under the Daubert standards of general acceptance, testability, and error rates. There now exist shelves of textbooks on forensic psychology, national workshops each year, and a dozen postdoctoral programs in forensic psychology around the country.

In Phase 3, Grisso (1999) proposed, lawyers and psychologists will collaborate on raising standards for the field. Psychologists should become involved in the training of lawyers, and attorneys should teach psychologists the law. In so doing, lawyers, and especially judges, will raise the expectations for psychological experts. As Grisso stated, "None of these advances will have a place in future courtrooms if attorneys and courts are willing to settle for mediocrity and the status quo in their use of forensic psychological experts."

Grisso's (1999) remarks focused on the use of psychologists in the criminal justice system. However, his thoughts bring into focus the current dilemmas in the field of child and family forensic psychology. This field is still in Phase 1. Perhaps that is because the expertise of the professionals who practice in this area comes out of the field of child and family psychotherapy, a more creative but less rigorous field than forensic practice. Perhaps, as we saw in chapter 11, it is because the standards of the juvenile courts and civil domestic cases are more relaxed than those of the criminal courts. Perhaps it is because the legal issue at hand—the loss of contact with one's child—is not regarded with the same level of seriousness as the loss of personal freedom.

Whatever the cause, in courtrooms around the country experts are still admitted in child and family cases who have no knowledge of case law, of psycholegal standards for the admissibility of evidence, or of the ethical standards of forensic psychologists. These experts conduct evaluations by using clinical instruments that have no scientific validity or functional relatedness to the legal questions at issue. There are no standards of training. Virtually any clinician can be admitted as an expert. Virtually any clinical opinion can be offered.

The field of child and family forensic psychology must move out of Phase 1 and enter Phase 2. We must embark on the same 10- to 20-year course of research and development that has gone on among our peers in the criminal justice system with regard to the training of experts, the development of scientifically validated measures, and new standards for the credentialing of experts. The following are some suggestions.

Research

Clinicians in the field of child and family forensic work are regularly called to court to testify as to the best arrangement for visitations for young children. There are virtually no guidelines in this area that are empirically based. In Atlanta, where I practice, clinicians simply propose whatever plan they favor. For example, one local expert is adamant that children not have overnight visitations with the noncustodial parent until the age of 4. On the other hand, judges routinely overrule the recommendations of courtroom experts and institute whatever visitation plan they see fit. Many judges rule that overnight visitations begin at the time of the divorce, regardless of the age of the child. One judge ruled that a 2-year-old child spend month-long visitations with her father in a distant city several times per year, regardless of the fact that the child spoke Japanese to her mother and was normally enrolled in a Japanese-speaking child care center. When with her English-speaking father, she was enrolled in an English-speaking child care center. In effect, a social experiment is taking place across the country with regard to how children might function in multiple living arrangements with multiple caretakers. Yet no one is measuring outcomes.

The field would be significantly improved by a longitudinal study in which the emotional and behavioral adjustment of these children could be tracked as they proceed through their various visitation arrangements. The independent variables could be the child's age, the child's temperament (easy or difficult), the number of caregivers, length of separation from the primary caregiver, and amount of hostility witnessed at transitions. We know from clinical experience that some of these may be important in predicting outcomes, but we do not know which variables are most crucial.

In addition, clinicians are also regularly called on to testify as to whether a child has parental alienation syndrome (PAS). Again, we are operating largely on clinical experience and personal bias. The field would be significantly enhanced by a study in which the criteria for PAS are agreed on by a panel of experts, then field tested.

Can the determination of PAS rise to the Daubert standard? To do so, we must determine if PAS is testable. Raters must review cases to determine if they meet the criteria and if there is a sufficient degree of interrater reliability. From there, we must determine the error rate. In other words, what is the rate of false positives? False negatives? With an effective measure, we can answer questions such as, At what age does PAS decline, such that adolescents are capable of differentiating from their alienating parent? Are separations from the alienating parent effective in resulting in improved emotional adjustment, or are they traumatic?

Furthermore, child and family forensic experts have been appearing in court to recommend parents for custody of their children over the course of the past 15 years. They have been doing so, again, largely on the basis of general measures of adult psychopathology, the parent's history, and clinical hunches. If the criteria laid out by the 1994 APA *Guidelines for Child Custody Evaluations in Divorce Proceedings* is the goodness-of-fit between one parent and the needs of a particular child, then research should be directed toward the development of a measure of the functional parental domain of goodness-of-fit. Grisso (1999) raised the issue of the need for measures of functional parenting abilities that were relevant to the legal issues at hand in court cases as far back as 1986. Yet we still do not have good measures in this area. Such an instrument would incorporate a measure of the needs of the child (i.e., with regard to educational needs, medical and rehabilitative needs, and temperament). It would also contain a measure of the functional parental capacities that might be needed and an index of the level of correspondence between the two.

This would be somewhat similar to the Parent Stress Index (Abidin, 1990), which yields a measure of correspondence between stress levels in the parent and stress-eliciting features of the child. Such a measure of goodness-of-fit would not be the only measure the evaluator might use in gathering information for the court, but it would have a functional relatedness to the psycholegal standard.

Moreover, most child and family forensic evaluators know little about the psychopathology of parents locked in chronic postdivorce disputes over access to the children. Most still use the MMPI–2—or, worse yet, projective measures—in an attempt to determine levels of psychopathology relevant to custody and parenting issues. Yet these measures have little to no functional predictiveness or discriminative value with regard to yielding valuable clinical insights that would be of use to the evaluator and to the court. Enough knowledge has been accumulated to suggest that such parents have numerous common traits of individuals with personality disorders, or at least subclinical levels of these disorders. The field could be improved by a personality measure, developed and validated on parents in chronic postdivorce disputes, that would yield information such as the parent's degree of flexibility with regard to adopting a parenting plan, the parent's ability to distinguish narcissistic needs from the needs of the child, the parent's ability to see the situation empathically from several viewpoints, and so on.

Last, the field would be improved by the development of a measure of the likelihood that child sexual abuse has been perpetrated by a parent, which could be used when the allegation arises in the midst of a custody dispute. Requests for evaluations such as these are common to clinicians in the field of child and family evaluation and treatment, yet guidelines in this area are minimal. Clinicians are still permitted to recommend to the court that a child's visitation with a parent be supervised, because of the presence of "sexual abuse indicators" in the child's artwork or sand-play.

Such evidence would never be allowed to be introduced in the criminal courts.

We have the beginnings of a method of validating the child's report of sexual abuse with the development of the Criterion Based Content Analysis/Statement Validity Assessment scoring system (Raskin & Esplin, 1991a, 1991b). We can go further than this by collecting actuarial data that have been compiled on true allegations and false allegations, much of which was described in chapter 10. These data can be incorporated into a scheme with subsections for information on such factors as the person making the allegation, the alleged perpetrator, the past relationship between the two, and the various categories of information gathered from and about the child. Items that are found to be particularly predictive of true allegations or of false allegations could be weighted more heavily. Such rating schemes have been developed for rating the risk of violence among offenders and have had good success (see Quinsey, Harris, Rice, & Cormier, 1998, for a review of several new measures).

These research projects would begin to bring the field of child and family forensic psychology well into Phase 2.

Training

The field of clinical psychology has been moving toward specialization over the past 20 years, with postdoctoral training fast becoming the standard for neuropsychology and forensic psychology (as it applies to the criminal justice system). Child and family evaluation and treatment are approaching the level of postdoctoral training as well. I hope that, in the next 10 years, there will be more opportunities for psychologists to attend postdoctoral training in forensic psychology, which includes practical experience in child and family evaluations and courtroom testimony in these cases.

Until that time, the APA should offer guidelines that raise the bar for experts in child and family forensic evaluations. These might include

- relevant graduate coursework in child development, developmental psychopathology, marital and family therapy, child psychopathology, and psychological evaluations of children and adults
- a PhD or PsyD from an accredited program
- a current license to practice in one's field
- five years of postdoctoral experience in child and family clinical work, as well as 5 years of experience in adult and marital psychotherapy
- a minimum of 50 hours of continuing education in forensic psychology through programs offered by the APA, the Amer-

ican Academy of Forensic Psychology, or the American College of Forensic Psychology

- a minimum of 12 hours of continuing education in family law in the state in which one practices.
- demonstrated proficiency in such standards in the field as the *Specialty Guidelines for Forensic Psychologists* (APA, Division 41, 1991), the *Guidelines for Conducting Child Custody Evaluations in Divorce Proceedings* (APA, 1994), the *Practice Guidelines—Use of Anatomical Dolls in Child Sexual Abuse Assessment* (American Professional Society on the Abuse of Children, 1995), and the *Guidelines for Psychological Evaluations in Child Protection Matters* (APA, 1998a), as well as a series of key articles in the field. (Such an exam could be administered by the APA through a home study course.)

If these standards were recommended by the APA through its national publications, they could be quickly disseminated and become the standard in the field. Such a standard could be used by attorneys to qualify or disqualify experts in the courtroom. As Grisso (1999) stated in his address, "Forensic psychologists will do no better than the courts demand."

REFERENCES

Abarbanel, A. (1979). Shared parenting after separation and divorce: A study of joint custody. *American Journal of Orthopsychiatry, 49*(2), 320–329.

Abidin, R. R. (1990). *Parenting Stress Index* (3rd ed.). Odessa, FL: Psychological Assessment Resources.

Achenbach, T. M. (1991). *Manual for the Child Behavior Checklist/4-18 and 1991 Profile*. Burlington: University of Vermont, Department of Psychiatry.

Ackerman, M. (1995). *Clinician's guide to child custody evaluations*. New York: Wiley.

Ackerman, M., & Ackerman, M. (1997). Custody evaluation practices: A survey of experienced professionals (revisited). *Professional Psychology: Research and Practice, 28*, 137–145.

Agopian, M. W. (1981). *Parental child stealing*. Lexington, MA: Lexington Books.

Ahrons, C. R., & Rodgers, R. H. (1987). *Divorced families: Meeting the challenge of divorce and remarriage*. New York: W.W. Norton.

Ahrons, C. R., & Wallisch, L. (1987). Parenting in the binuclear family: Relationships between biological and stepparents. In K. Pasley & M. Ihinger-Tallman (Eds.), *Remarriage and stepparenting: Current research and theory* (pp. 225–256). New York: Guilford Press.

Albiston, C., Maccoby, E., & Mnookin, R. (1990). Does joint legal custody matter? *Stanford Law and Policy Review, 2*, 167–179.

Allison, J. A. (1998). Review of the Parenting Stress Index. In J. C. Impara & B. S. Plake (Eds.), *The thirteenth mental measurements yearbook* (pp. 722–723). Lincoln: University of Nebraska Press.

Allison, P., & Furstenberg, F. (1989). How marital dissolution affects children: Variations by age and sex. *Developmental Psychology, 25*, 540–549.

Amato, P. (1996). Explaining the intergenerational transmission of divorce. *Journal of Marriage and the Family, 58*, 628–640.

Amato, P., & Booth, A. (1996). A prospective study of divorce and parent–child relationships. *Journal of Marriage and the Family, 58*, 356–365.

Amato, P., & Keith, B. (1991). Parental divorce and the well-being of children: A meta-analysis. *Psychological Bulletin, 110*, 26–46.

Amato, P., Loomis, L., & Booth, A. (1995). Parental divorce, marital conflict, and offspring well-being during early adulthood. *Social Forces, 73*, 895–915.

Ambert, A. (1982). Differences in children's behavior toward custodial mothers and custodial fathers. *Journal of Marriage and the Family, 44* (February), 73–86.

American Academy of Child and Adolescent Psychiatry. (1997). Practice parameters for child custody evaluation. *Journal of the American Academy of Child and Adolescent Psychiatry, 36*(10), 57S–68S.

American Professional Society on the Abuse of Children. (1995). *Practice guidelines —Use of anatomical dolls in child sexual abuse assessment.* Chicago, IL: Author.

American Psychiatric Association. (1981). *Child custody consultation: Report of the task force on clinical assessment in child custody.* Washington, DC: Author.

American Psychiatric Association. (1994). *Diagnostic and statistical manual of mental disorders* (4th ed.). Washington, DC: Author.

American Psychological Association. (1994). Guidelines for child custody evaluations in divorce proceedings. *American Psychologist, 49,* 677–680.

American Psychological Association. (1997). Report of the ethics committee. *American Psychologist, 52,* 897–905.

American Psychological Association. (1998a). *Guidelines for psychological evaluations in child protection matters.* Washington, DC: Author.

American Psychological Association. (1998b). Report of the ethics committee. *American Psychologist, 53,* 969–980.

American Psychological Association, Division 41. (1991). Specialty guidelines for forensic psychologists. *Law and Human Behavior, 15,* 655–665.

Arbuthnot, J., & Gordon, D. A. (1996). Does mandatory divorce education for parents work? A six-month outcome evaluation. *Family and Conciliation Courts Review, 34,* 60–81.

Arbuthnot, J., Kramer, K. M., & Gordon, D. A. (1997). Patterns of relitigation following divorce education. *Family & Conciliation Courts Review, 35*(July), 269–279.

Arditti, J. (1992). Factors relating to custody, visitation, and child support for divorced fathers: An exploratory analysis. *Journal of Divorce and Remarriage, 17,* 23–42.

Arditti, J. (1995). Review of the Ackerman–Schoendorf Scales for Parent Evaluation of Custody. In J. C. Conoley & J. C. Impara (Eds.), *The twelfth mental measurements yearbook* (pp. 20–22). Lincoln: University of Nebraska Press.

Ash, P., & Guyer, M. (1986, October). *A follow-up of children in contested custody evaluations.* Paper presented at the 17th annual meeting of the American Academy of Psychiatry and the Law, Philadelphia.

Ash, P., & Guyer, M. (1991). Biased reporting by parents undergoing child custody evaluations. *Journal of the American Academy of Child and Adolescent Psychiatry, 30,* 835–838.

Awad, G. A. (1987). The assessment of custody and access disputes in cases of sexual abuse allegations. *American Journal of Psychiatry, 32,* 539–544.

Awad, G. A., & McDonough, H. (1991). Therapeutic management of sexual abuse allegations in custody and visitation disputes. *American Journal of Psychotherapy, 45,* 113–123.

Bar, M. (1997). *The relationship of childhood trauma to adult adjustment to divorce.* Unpublished doctoral dissertation, Western Graduate School of Psychology, Palo Alto, CA.

Bargelow, P., Vaughn, B., & Molitor, N. (1987). Effects of maternal absence due to employment on the quality of infant–mother attachment in a low-risk sample. *Child Development, 58,* 945–954.

Baruch, G., & Barnett, G. (1983). *Correlates of fathers' participation in family work: A technical report* (Working Paper No. 106). Wellesley, MA: Wellesley College Center for Research on Women.

Bathurst, K., Gottfried, A. W., & Gottfried, A. E. (1997). Normative data for the MMPI-2 in child custody litigation. *Psychological Assessment, 9,* 205–211.

Baumrind, D. (Ed.). (1971). Current patterns of parental authority [Special issue]. *Developmental Psychology Monographs, 4.*

Baydar, N. (1988). Effects of parental separation and reentry into union on the emotional well-being of children. *Journal of Marriage and the Family, 50,* 967–981.

Baylor, B. (Executive Producer). (1993). Secrets of staying together. In: *ABC News 20/20.* New York: ABC.

Beck, A., & Freeman, A. (1990). *Cognitive therapy of personality disorders.* New York: Guilford Press.

Benedek, E., & Schetky, D. (1985). Allegations of sexual abuse in child custody and visitation disputes. In E. Benedek & D. Schetky (Eds.), *Emerging issues in child psychiatry and the law* (pp. 145–156). New York: Brunner/Mazel.

Bennett, B. E., Bryant, B. K., VandenBos, G. R., & Greenwood, A. (1990). *Professional liability and risk management.* Washington, DC: American Psychological Association.

Bernet, W. (1993). The noncustodial parent and medical treatment. *Bulletin of the American Academy of Psychiatry and Law, 21,* 357–364.

Biondi, E. D. (1996). Legal implementation of parent education programs for divorcing and separating parents. *Family and Conciliation Courts Review, 36,* 82–92.

Bischoff, L. G. (1995). Review of the Parent Awareness Skills Survey. In J. C. Conoley & J. C. Impara (Eds.), *The twelfth mental measurements yearbook* (pp. 735–736). Lincoln: University of Nebraska Press.

Blaisure, K., & Geasler, M. (1996). Results of a survey of court-connected parent education programs in U.S. counties. *Family and Conciliation Courts Review, 34,* 23–40.

Blau, T. (1997, May 18). *The psychologist as expert witness: Parts I and II.* Presentation at the annual conference of the Georgia Psychological Association, Atlanta.

Block, J., Block, J., & Gjerde, P. F. (1986). The personality of children prior to divorce: A prospective study. *Child Development, 57,* 827–840.

Block, J., Block, J., & Gjerde, P. (1988). Parental functioning and the home environment in families of divorce: Prospective and concurrent analyses. *Journal of the American Academy of Child and Adolescent Psychiatry, 27,* 207–213.

Blush, G. J., & Ross, K. L. (1987). Sexual abuse allegations in divorce: The SAID syndrome. *Conciliation Courts Review, 25*(1), 1–11.

Boat, B. W., & Everson, M. D. (1994). Exploration of anatomical dolls by non-referred preschool-aged children: Comparisons by age, gender, race and socioeconomic status. *Child Abuse and Neglect, 18,* 139–153.

Bolen, R. (1993). Kids' turn: Helping kids cope with divorce. *Family and Conciliation Courts Review, 31,* 249–254.

Bone, M. J., & Walsh, M. R. (1999). Parental alienation syndrome: How to detect it and what to do about it. *The Florida Bar Journal, 73* (March), 44–48.

Boothroyd, R. A. (1998). Review of the Parent–Child Relationship Inventory. In J. C. Impara & B. S. Plake (Eds.), *The thirteenth mental measurements yearbook* (pp. 717–720). Lincoln: University of Nebraska Press.

Braver, S. L., Salem, P., Pearson, J., & Deluse, S. R. (1996). The content of divorce education programs: Results of a survey. *Family and Conciliation Courts Review, 34,* 41–59.

Braver, S., Wolchik, S., Sandler, I., Fogas, B., & Zvetina, D. (1991). Frequency of visitation by divorced fathers: Differences in reports by fathers and mothers. *American Journal of Orthopsychiatry, 6,* 448–454.

Bray, J. (1991). Psychosocial factors affecting custodial and visitation arrangements. *Behavioral Sciences and the Law, 9,* 419–437.

Bray, J., & Berger, S. (1990). Noncustodial father and paternal grandparent relationships in stepfamilies. *Family Relations, 39,* 414–419.

Bresee, P., Stearns, G. B., Bess, B. H., & Packer, L. S. (1986). Allegations of sexual abuse in child custody disputes: A therapeutic assessment model. *American Journal of Orthopsychiatry, 56,* 560–569.

Bricklin, B. (1995). *The custody evaluation handbook: Research-based solutions and applications.* New York: Brunner-Mazel.

Briere, J. (1996). Trauma Symptom Checklist—Children. Odessa, FL: Psychological Assessment Resources.

Brodzinsky, D. (1993). On the use and misuse of psychological testing in child custody evaluations. *Professional Psychology Research and Practice, 24,* 213–214.

Brooks, C. M., & Milchman, M. S. (1991). Child sexual abuse allegations during custody litigation: Conflicts between mental health expert witnesses and the law. *Behavioral Sciences and the Law, 9,* 21–23.

Brooks, S. (1987). *Folie à deux* in the aged: Variations in psychopathology. *Canadian Journal of Psychiatry, 32,* 61–63.

Browne, A., & Finkelhor, D. (1986). Impact of child sexual abuse: A review of the research. *Psychological Bulletin, 99,* 66–77.

Bruch, C. (1992). And how are the children? The effects of ideology and mediation on child custody law and children's well being in the United States. *Family and Conciliation Courts Review, 30,* 112–134.

Bruch, C. (1993). When to use and when to avoid mediation. *Family and Conciliation Courts Review, 31,* 101–107.

Bruck, M. (1998). Reliability and credibility of young children's reports: From research to policy and practice. *American Psychologist, 53*, 136–151.

Bruck, M., & Ceci, S. J. (1995). Amicus brief for the case of. . . . *Psychology, Public Policy, and Law in the Public Domain, 1*, 272–322.

Bruck, M., Ceci, S. J., Francoeur, E., & Renick, A. (1995). Anatomical detailed dolls do not facilitate preschoolers' reports of a pediatric examination involving genital touching. *Journal of Experimental Psychology: Applied, 1*, 95–99.

Buchanan, C., Maccoby, E., & Dornbusch, S. (1991). Caught between parents: Adolescents' experience in divorced homes. *Child Development, 62*, 1008–1029.

Burks, H. F. (1977). *Burks' behavior rating scales preschool and kindergarten.* Los Angeles, CA: Western Psychological Services.

Burnham, C. P. (1997). Connecticut's child custody court. *Family Advocate, 22*, 43–45, 62.

Burrows, R. K., & Buzzinotti, E. (1997). Legal therapists and lawyers. *Family Advocate, 22*, 33–36.

Butcher, J. (1997). Frequency of MMPI-2 scores in forensic evaluations. *MMPI-2 News & Profiles, 8*(1), 2–4.

Caldwell, A. B. (1995, August). Interpreting MMPI data in custody evaluations: A clinical perspective. In S. Podrygula (Chair), *MMPI use in child custody evaluations: Integrating the data.* Symposium conducted at the 103rd Annual Convention of the American Psychological Association, New York.

Camara, K., & Resnick, G. (1988). Interparental conflict and cooperation: Factors moderating children's post-divorce conflict. In E. Hetherington & J. Arasteh (Eds.), *Impact of divorce, single parenting, and stepparenting on children* (pp. 169–195). Hillsdale, NJ: Erlbaum.

Camara, K., & Resnick, G. (1989). Styles of conflict resolution and cooperation between divorced parents: Effects on child behavior and adjustment. *American Journal of Orthopsychiatry, 59*, 560–575.

Carlson, J. F. (1995). Review of the Perception of Relationships Test. In J. C. Conoley & J. C. Impara (Eds.), *The twelfth mental measurements yearbook* (pp. 746–747). Lincoln: University of Nebraska Press.

Cartwright, G. (1993). Expanding the parameters of parental alienation syndrome. *American Journal of Family Therapy, 21*, 205–215.

Caruso, K. R. (1988). *Projective Storytelling Test.* Redding, CA: Northwest Psychological.

Ceci, S. J., & Hembrooke, H. (1998). *Expert witnesses in child abuse cases.* Washington, DC: American Psychological Association.

Chapsky v. Wood, 26 Kan 650 (Kan. 1881).

Cherlin, A. (1981). *Marriage, divorce, remarriage.* Cambridge, MA: Harvard University Press.

Cherlin, A., Furstenberg, F., Chase-Lansdale, P., Kiernan, K., Robins, P., Morrison,

D., & Teitler, J. (1991). Longitudinal studies of effects of divorce on children in Great Britain and the United States. *Science, 252,* June, 1386–1389.

Children's Rights Council. (1994). *Annual convention brochure.* Washington, DC: Author.

Church-based program helps mend marriages headed for divorce. (1995). Detroit News [On-line]. Available: http://www/retrouvaille-/org/publicity/helps/html

Clarke-Stewart, A. (1988). "The effects of infant day care reconsidered" reconsidered: Risks for parents, children, and researchers. *Early Childhood Research Quarterly, 3*(3), 293–318.

Cloninger, C. R. (1999). A new conceptual paradigm from genetics and psycho-biology for the science of mental health. *Australia–New Zealand Journal of Psychiatry, 33,* 174–186.

Cloninger, C. R., Svrakic, D. M., & Przybeck, T. R. (1993). A psychobiological model of temperament and character. *Archives of General Psychiatry, 50,* 975–990.

Cole, W. A., & Bradford, M. B. (1992). Abduction during custody and access disputes. *Canadian Journal of Psychiatry, 37,* 264–266.

Conger, J. (1995). Review of the Perception of Relationships Test. In J. C. Conoley & J. C. Impara (Eds.), *The twelfth mental measurements yearbook* (pp. 747–748). Lincoln: University of Nebraska Press.

Conners, C. K. (1990). *Conners' rating scales manual.* New York: Multi-Health Systems.

Cordes, R. (1993). Justice held hostage. Family feuds escalate into courthouse violence. *Trial,* June, 12–14.

A covenant for couples. (1997, August 13). *Wall Street Journal* [On-line]. Available: http://www.rmfc.org/up-cmpl1.html

Cummings, E. M., Zahn-Waxler, C., & Radke-Yarrow, M. (1984). Developmental changes in children's reactions to anger in the home. *Journal of Child Psychology and Psychiatry, 25,* 63–74.

Davies, P., & Cummings, E. M. (1994). Marital conflict and child adjustment: An emotional security hypothesis. *Psychological Bulletin, 116,* 387–411.

Dean, I. Deadly decisions. (1993, May 28). ABC News, 20/20. New York: ABC.

Denver Metro Community Marriage Policy. (1999). [On-line]. Available: http://www.rmfc.org/up-cmpl/html

Depner, C. E., Cannata, K. V., & Simon, M. B. (1992). Building a uniform statistical reporting system: A snapshot of California Family Court Services. *Family and Conciliation Courts Review, 30,* 185–206.

Derdeyn, A. (1976). Child custody contests in historical perspective. *American Journal of Psychiatry, 133,* 1369–1376.

Derogatis, L. R., & Spencer, P. M. (1982). The brief symptom inventory (BSI), administration, scoring and procedures manual—I. *Clinical Psychometric Research.* Baltimore, MD: Johns Hopkins University School of Medicine.

Deutsch, H. (1938). *Folie à deux. Psychoanalytic Quarterly, 7,* 307–318.

Dewhurst, K., & Todd, J. (1956). The psychosis of association—*Folie à deux*. *Journal of Nervous and Mental Disorder, 124*, 451–459.

Dick v. Dick (210 Mich. Ct. App. 576).

Dillon, P. A., & Emery, R. E. (1996). Divorce mediation and resolution of child custody disputes: Long-term effects. *American Journal of Orthopsychiatry, 66*, 131–140.

Dippel, B., Kemper, J., & Berger, M. (1991). *Folie à six*: A case report on induced psychotic disorder. *Acta Psychiatrica Scandinavia, 83*, 137–141.

Dixon, E. (1991, January). *A practical approach to child custody evaluations*. Presentation at the midwinter conference of the Georgia Psychological Association, Hilton Head, South Carolina.

Donahue, D. (1997, February 13). America's divorce culture sacrifices kids, author says. *USA Today*. p. 01D.

Downey, D., & Powell, B. (1993). Do children in single-parent households fare better living with same-sex parents? *Journal of Marriage and the Family, 55*, 55–71.

Dunlop, R., & Burns, A. (1995). The sleeper effect: Myth or reality? *Journal of Marriage and the Family, 57*, 375–386.

Dunne, J., & Hedrick, M. (1994). The parental alienation syndrome: An analysis of sixteen selected cases. *Journal of Divorce and Remarriage, 21*(3/4), 21–38.

Dwyer, M. (1986). *Guilty as charged: Or are they?* Unpublished paper, University of Minnesota.

Eckenrode, J., Powers, J., Doris, J., Munsch, J., & Bolger, N. (1988). Substantiation of child abuse and neglect reports. *Journal of Consulting and Clinical Psychology, 56*, 9–16.

Ehrenberg, M. F., Hunter, M. A., & Elterman, M. F. (1996). Shared parenting agreements after marital separation: The roles of empathy and narcissism. *Journal of Consulting and Clinical Psychology, 64*, 808–818.

Elliott, B., & Richards, M. (1991). Children and divorce: Educational performance and behavior before and after parental separation. *International Journal of Law and the Family, 5*, 258–276.

Ellis, E. (1995). *Raising a responsible child*. New York: Birchlane Press.

Elrod, L., & Spector, R. (1996). A review of the year in family law: Children's issues take spotlight. *Family Law Quarterly, 29*, 741–758.

Elterman, M. F., & Ehrenberg, M. F. (1991). Sexual abuse allegations in child custody disputes. *International Journal of Law and Psychiatry, 14*, 269–286.

Emery, R. (1982). Interparental conflict and the children of discord and divorce. *Psychological Bulletin, 92*, 310–330.

Emery, R. (1988). Mediation and the settlement of divorce disputes. In E. M. Hetherington & J. D. Arasteh (Eds.), *Impact of divorce, single parenting, and stepparenting on children* (pp. 53–71). Hillsdale, NJ: Erlbaum.

Emery, R., & Wyer, M. (1987). Child custody mediation and litigation: An experimental evaluation of the experience of parents. *Journal of Consulting and Clinical Psychology, 55,* 179–186.

Faller, K. C. (1991). Possible explanations for child sexual abuse allegations in divorce. *American Journal of Orthopsychiatry, 61,* 86–91.

Fantuzzo, J., DePaola, L., Lambert, L., Martino, T., Anderson, G., & Sutton, S. (1991). Effects of interparental violence on the psychological adjustment and competencies of young children. *Journal of Consulting and Clinical Psychology, 59,* 258–265.

Fauber, R., Forehand, R., Thomas, A., & Wierson, M. (1990). A mediational model of the impact of marital conflict on adolescent adjustment in intact and divorced families: The role of disrupted parenting. *Child Development, 61,* 1112–1123.

Feinberg, R., & Greene, J. (1997). The intractable client: Guidelines for working with personality disorders in family law. *Family and Conciliation Courts Review, 35,* 351–365.

Felner, R., Terre, L., Farber, S., Primavera, J., & Bishop, T. (1985). Child custody: Practices and perspectives of legal professionals. *Journal of Clinical Child Psychology, 14,* 27–34.

Finkelhor, D. (1984). *Child sexual abuse: New theory and research.* New York: Free Press.

Finkelhor, D., Hotaling, G., & Sedlak, A. (1991). Children abducted by family members: A national household survey of incidence and episode characteristics. *Journal of Marriage and the Family, 53,* 805–817.

Finlay v. Finlay, 148 NE 624 (NY 1925).

Fisher, R., & Uhry, W. (1981). *Getting to yes: Negotiating agreements without giving in.* Boston, MA: Houghton-Mifflin.

Forehand, R., Armistead, L., & David, C. (1997). Is adolescent adjustment following parental divorce a function of pre-divorce adjustment? *Journal of Abnormal Psychology, 25,* 157–164.

Forehand, R., Long, N., Zogg, C., & Parrish, E. (1989). Child abduction: Parent and child functioning following return. *Clinical Pediatrics, 28,* 311–316.

Foster, H., & Freed, D. (1973–1974). Divorce reform: Brakes on breakdown. *Journal of Family Law, 13,* 443–493.

Freed, D., & Foster, H. (1981). Divorce in the fifty states: An overview. *Family Law Quarterly, 14,* 229–283.

Freed, D., & Walker, T. B. (1988). Family law in the fifty states. *Family Law Quarterly, 21,* 421–571.

Friedrich, W. N., Grambsch, P., Damon, L., Hewitt, S. K., Koverola, C., Lang, R. A., Wolfe, V., & Broughton, D. (1992). Child Sexual Behavior Inventory: Normative and clinical contrasts. *Psychological Assessment, 4,* 303–311.

Fulton, J. (1979). Parental reports of children's post-divorce adjustment. *Journal of Social Issues, 35,* 126–139.

Furstenberg, F. (1987). The new extended family: The experience of parents and children after remarriage. In K. Pasley & M. Ihinger-Tallman (Eds.), *Remarriage and stepparenting: Current research and theory* (pp. 42–61). New York: Guilford Press.

Furstenberg, F. (1994). History and current status of divorce in the United States. *Children and Divorce, 4,* 29–43.

Furstenberg, F., & Cherlin, A. (1991). *Divided families: What happens to children when parents part?* Cambridge, MA: Harvard Universtiy Press.

Furstenberg, F., Morgan, S., & Allison, P. (1987). Paternal participation and children's well-being after marital dissolution. *American Sociological Review, 52,* 695–701.

Furstenberg, F., Peterson, J., Nord, C., & Zill, N. (1983). The life course of children of divorce: Marital disruption and parental contact. *American Sociological Review, 48,* 656–668.

Galinsky, E., & David, J. (1988). *The preschool years: Family strategies that work from experts and parents.* New York: Ballantine.

Gallagher, M. (1996). *The abolition of marriage.* Washington, DC: Regnery Publishing, Inc., Lanham, MD. Distributed to the trade by the National Book Network.

Gardner, R. (1982). *Family evaluation in child custody evaluation.* Cresskill, NJ: Creative Therapeutics.

Gardner, R. (1987). *Parental alienation syndrome and the differentiation between fabricated and genuine sexual abuse.* Cresskill, NJ: Creative Therapeutics.

Gardner, R. (1989). *Family evaluation in child custody: Mediation, arbitration, and litigation.* Cresskill, NJ: Creative Therapeutics.

Gardner, R. (1992a). *Parental alienation syndrome.* Cresskill, NJ: Creative Therapeutics.

Gardner, R. (1992b). *True and false allegations of child sexual abuse.* Cresskill, NJ: Creative Therapeutics.

Gardner, R. (1999). Differentiating between parental alienation syndrome and bona fide abuse–neglect. *American Journal of Family Therapy, 27,* 97–107.

Garmezy, N. (1987). Stress, competence, and development: Continuities in the study of schizophrenic adults, children vulnerable to psychopathology, and the search for stress-resistant children. *American Journal of Orthopsychiatry, 57,* 159–173.

Garrison, E. (1991). Children's competence to participate in divorce custody decisionmaking. *Journal of Clinical Child Psychology, 20,* 78–87.

Garrity, C., & Baris, M. (1994). *Caught in the middle.* New York: Lexington.

Gerard, A. B. (1994). *Parent–Child Relationship Inventory (PCRI) manual.* Los Angeles, CA: Western Psychological Services.

Glaser, D., & Collins, C. (1989). The response of young, non-sexually abused children to anatomically correct dolls. *Journal of Child Psychology and Psychiatry, 30,* 547–560.

Glassman, J. B. (1998). Preventing and managing board complaints: The downside risk of custody evaluation. *Professional Psychology: Research and Practice, 29,* 121–124.

Gleick, E. (1995, February 27). Should this marriage be saved? Many Americans are trying to make marriages more permanent—And divorce more difficult. *Time, 145*(9) 48–51.

Glenn, J. E. (1998). Divorce education for parents and children in Jackson County, Missouri. *Family and Conciliation Courts Review, 36,* 503–510.

Glenn, N., & Kramer, K. (1985). The psychological well-being of adult children of divorce. *Journal of Marriage and the Family, 47,* 905–912.

Glenn, N., & Kramer, K. (1987). The marriages and divorces of the children of divorce. *Journal of Marriage and the Family, 49,* 811–825.

Glenn, N., & Shelton, B. (1983). Pre-adult background variables and divorce. *Journal of Marriage and the Family, 45,* 405–410.

Glick, P. (1979). Children of divorced parents in demographic perspective. *Journal of Social Issues, 35,* 170–182.

Glick, P. C. (1984). Remarriage: Some recent changes and variations. *Journal of Family Issues, 1,* 455–478.

Glick, P. C. (1989a). The family life cycle and social change. *Family Relations, 38,* 123–129.

Glick, P. C. (1989b). Remarried families, stepfamilies, and stepchildren: A brief demographic profile. *Family Relations, 38,* 24–27.

Goldstein, J., & Solnit, G. (1984). *Divorce and your child.* New Haven, CT: Yale University Press.

Goleman, D. (1995). Intimate enemies. In *Emotional intelligence* (pp. 129–147). New York: Bantam.

Gonzalez, R., Krantz, S., & Johnston, J. (1984, April). *Predictors of post-divorce conflict.* Paper presented at the meeting of the Western Psychological Association, San Francisco.

Goodman, E. (1976, March 26). Child snatching. *The Washington Post,* p. 27.

Gottman, J. (1994). *Why marriages succeed or fail, and how you can make yours last.* New York: Fireside.

Gralnick, A. (1942). *Folie à deux:* The psychosis of association. *Psychiatric Quarterly, 16,* 230–263.

Gray, C., Verdieck, M. J., Smith, E. D., & Freed, K. (1997). Making it work: An evaluation of court-mandated parenting workshops for divorcing families. *Family & Conciliation Courts Review, 35*(July), 280–292.

Green, A. (1986). True and false allegations of sexual abuse in child custody disputes. *Journal of the American Academy of Child Psychiatry, 25,* 449–456.

Greif, G. L. (1990). Split custody: A beginning understanding. *Journal of Divorce, 13*(3), 15–26.

Greif, G. L., & Hegar, R. L. (1992). Impact on children of abduction by a parent: A review of the literature. *American Journal of Orthopsychiatry, 62,* 599–604.

Greif, G. L., & Hegar, R. L. (1993). *When parents kidnap: The families behind the headlines.* New York: Free Press.

Griffin, G. (1999, October). *Juvenile justice and mental health systems move toward integrating family and community in treating minors.* Presentation at the meeting of the American Psychological Association/American Bar Association, Washington, DC.

Grisso, T. (1986). Evaluating competencies: *Forensic assessments and instruments.* New York: Plenum.

Grisso, T. (1999, October). *Improving psychologists' assistance in criminal cases.* Keynote address, delivered at the meeting of the American Psychological Association/American Bar Association, Washington, DC.

Grych, J., & Fincham, F. (1993). Children's appraisals of marital conflict: Initial investigations of the cognitive–contextual framework. *Child Development, 64,* 215–230.

Grych, J., & Fincham, F. (1997). Children's adaptation to divorce. In S. Wolchik & I. Sandler (Eds.), *Handbook of children's coping: Linking theory and intervention* (pp. 159–193). New York: Plenum.

Gurwin, H. M. (1997). Divorce arbitration in the 90's. *Family Advocate, 21*(1), 29, 62.

Guyer, M., & Ash, P. (1986, October). *Child abuse allegations in the context of adversarial divorce.* Paper presented at the annual meeting of the American Academy of Psychiatry and the Law, Los Angeles.

Hagin, R. A. (1992). Review of the Bricklin Perceptual Scales. In J. J. Kramer & J. C. Conoley (Eds.), *The eleventh mental measurements yearbook* (pp. 117–118). Lincoln: University of Nebraska Press.

Halikias, W. (1994). Forensic family evaluations: A comprehensive model for professional practice. *Journal of Clinical Psychology, 50,* 951–964.

Halon, R. L. (1994). Child custody "move away" cases: McGinnis and psychology. *American Journal of Forensic Psychology, 12,* 43–54.

Hanson, G. (1988). The sex abuse controversy. *Journal of the American Academy of Child and Adolescent Psychiatry, 27,* 258.

Harris, E., Bennett, B., & Remar, R. (1997, May). *Advanced risk assessment, Parts I and II.* Presentation at the annual conference of the Georgia Psychological Association, Atlanta.

Hauser, B. (1985). Custody in dispute: Legal and psychological profiles of contesting families. *Journal of the American Academy of Child Psychiatry, 24,* 575–582.

Healey, J. M., Malley, J. E., & Stewart, A. J. (1990). Children and their fathers after parental separation. *American Journal of Orthopsychiatry, 60,* 531–543.

Hegar, R. L., & Greif, G. L. (1993). How parentally abducted children fare: An interim report on families who recover their children. *Journal of Psychiatry and Law* (Fall), 373–383.

Heinze, M. C., & Grisso, T. (1996). Review of instruments assessing parenting competencies used in child custody determinations. *Behavioral Sciences and the Law, 14,* 293–313.

Helping marriages last. (1997, August 14). *USA Today.*

Hess, R., & Camara, K. (1979). Post-divorce family relationships as mediating factors in the consequences of divorce for children. *Journal of Social Issues, 35,* 79–98.

Hetherington, E. M. (1972). The effects of father absence on personality development in adolescent daughters. *Developmental Psychology, 7,* 313–326.

Hetherington, E. M. (1973, February). Girls without fathers. *Psychology Today, 6,* 47–52.

Hetherington, E. M. (1989). Coping with family transitions: Winners, losers, and survivors. *Child Development, 60,* 1–14.

Hetherington, E. M. (1991). The role of individual differences and family relationships in children's coping with divorce and remarriage. In P. A. Cowan & M. Hetherington (Eds.), *Family transitions* (pp. 165–194). Hillsdale, NJ: Erlbaum.

Hetherington, E. M., Bridges, M., & Insabella, G. M. (1998). What matters? What does not? Five perspectives on the association between marital transitions and children's adjustment. *American Psychologist, 53,* 167–184.

Hetherington, E. M., Cox, M., & Cox, R. (1985). Long-term effects of divorce and remarriage on the adjustment of children. *Journal of the American Academy of Child Psychiatry, 24,* 518–530.

Hetherington, E. M., & Deur, J. (1971). The effects of father absence on child development. *Young Children, 26,* 233–248.

Hetherington, E. M., & Parke, R. D. (1979). Beyond father absence: Conceptualization of effects of divorce. In *Contemporary readings in child psychology* (pp. 456–463). New York: McGraw Hill.

Hetherington, E. M., Stanley-Hagan, M., & Anderson, E. (1989). Marital transitions: A child's perspective. *American Psychologist, 44,* 303–312.

Hightower, A. D., Work, W. C., Cowan, E. L., Lotyczewski, B. S., Spinell, A. P., & Guare, J. C. (1986). The teacher-child rating scale: A brief objective measure of elementary children's school behavior problems and competencies. *School Psychology Review, 15,* 393–409.

Hiltonsmith, R. W. (1995). Review of the Parent Perception of Child Profile. In J. C. Conoley & J. C. Impara (Eds.), *The twelfth mental measurements yearbook* (pp. 736–738). Lincoln: University of Nebraska Press.

The history of divorce in America, Parts 1–6. (1996, April 15–May 6). National Public Radio.

Hodges, W. (1991). *Interventions for children of divorce: Custody, access, and psychotherapy* (2nd ed.). New York: Wiley.

Hoorwitz, A. (1992). *The clinical detective: Techniques in the evaluation of sexual abuse.* New York: Norton.

Hoppe, C., & Kenney, L. (1994, August). *A Rorschach study of the psychological characteristics of parents engaged in child custody/visitation disputes.* Paper presented at the 102nd Annual Convention of the American Psychological Association, Los Angeles.

Horner, T. M., & Guyer, M. J. (1991). Prediction, prevention, and clinical expertise in child custody cases in which allegations of child sexual abuse have been made: Predictable rates of diagnostic error in relation to various clinical decisionmaking strategies. *Family Law Quarterly, 25*, 217–252.

Horner, T. M., Guyer, M. J., & Kalter, N. M. (1991). Prediction, prevention, and clinical expertise in child custody cases in which allegations of child sexual abuse have been made: III. Studies of expert opinion formulation. *Family Law Quarterly, 26*, 141–170.

Horner, T. M., Guyer, M. J., & Kalter, N. M. (1993). Clinical expertise and the assessment of child sexual abuse. *Journal of the American Academy of Child and Adolescent Psychiatry, 32*, 923–933.

Horowitz, S. W., Lamb, M. E., Esplin, P. W., Boychuk, T., Krispin, O., & Reiter-Lavery, I. (1997). Reliability of criteria-based content analysis of child witness statements. *Legal and Criminological Psychology, 2*, 11–21.

Ilfield, F., Ilfield, H., & Alexander, J. (1982). Does joint custody work? A first look at outcome data of relitigation. *American Journal of Psychiatry, 139*, 62–66.

Jacobsen, N., & Christensen, A. (1996). *Integrative couple therapy.* New York: W.W. Norton.

Jameson, B., Ehrenberg, M., & Hunter, M. (1997). Psychologists' ratings of the best interests of the child custody and access criterion: A family systems assessment model. *Professional Psychology: Research and Practice, 28*, 253–262.

Janvier, R., McCormick, K., & Donaldson, R. (1990). Parental kidnapping: A survey of left-behind parents. *Juvenile and Family Court Journal*, 1–8.

Jenkins v. Jenkins, 181 NW 826 (Wis. 1921).

Johnston, J. (1992). High conflict and violent parents in family court: Findings on children's adjustment and proposed guidelines for the resolution of custody and visitation disputes. Final report to the Judicial Council of the State of California, Statewide Office of Family Court Services, San Francisco, CA: Judicial Council. Referenced in: Johnston, J. (1994). High conflict divorce. *The Future of Children, 4*(1), 165–182.

Johnston, J. (1993). Children of divorce who refuse visitation. In C. E. Depner & J. H. Bray (Eds.), *Nonresidential parenting: New vistas in family living* (pp. 109–135). Newbury Park, CA: Sage.

Johnston, J. (1994a). High conflict divorce. *The Future of Children, 4*, 165–182.

Johnston, J. (1994b, November). Invited address, regional convention of the Association of Family and Conciliation Courts, Tucson, Arizona.

Johnston, J. (1995). Research update: Children's adjustment in sole custody compared to joint custody families and principles for custody decision making. *Family and Conciliation Courts Review, 33*, 415–422.

Johnston, J., Breunig, K., Garrity, C., & Baris, M. (1997). *Through the eyes of children: Healing stories for children of divorce.* New York: Free Press.

Johnston, J., & Campbell, L. (1988). *Impasses of divorce: The dynamics and resolution of family conflict.* New York: Free Press.

Johnston, J., Campbell, L., & Mayes, S. (1985). Latency children in post-separation and divorce disputes. *Journal of the American Academy of Child Psychiatry, 24,* 563–574.

Johnston, J., Campbell, L., & Tall, M. (1985). Impasses to the resolution of custody and visitation disputes. *American Journal of Orthopsychiatry, 55,* 112–129.

Johnston, J., & Girdner, L. K. (1998). Early identification of parents at risk for custody violations and prevention of child abductions. *Family and Conciliation Courts Review, 36,* 392–409.

Johnston, J., Gonzalez, R., & Campbell, L. (1987). Ongoing postdivorce onflict and child disturbance. *Journal of Abnormal Child Psychology, 15,* 493–509.

Johnston, J., Kline, M., & Tschann, J. (1989). Ongoing postdivorce conflict: Effects on children of joint custody and frequent access. *American Journal of Orthopsychiatry, 59,* 576–592.

Johnston, J., & Roseby, V. (1997). *In the name of the child: A developmental approach to understanding and helping children of conflicted and violent divorce.* New York: Free Press.

Jones, C. (1984). Judicial questioning of children in custody and visitation proceedings. *Family Law Quarterly, 18,* 43–91.

Jones, D. P. H., & McGraw, J. M. (1987). Reliable and fictitious accounts of sexual abuse to children. *Journal of Interpersonal Violence, 2,* 27–45.

Jouriles, E., Murphy, C., Farris, A., Smith, D., Richters, J., & Waters, E. (1991). Marital adjustment, parental disagreements about child rearing, and behavior problems in boys: Increasing the specificity of the marital assessment. *Child Development, 62,* 1424–1433.

Jouriles, E., Pfiffner, L., & O'Leary, S. (1988). Marital conflict, parenting, and toddler conduct problems. *Journal of Abnormal Child Psychology, 16,* 197–206.

Kagan, J. (1978, August). The parental love trap. *Psychology Today, 12,* 54, 57–58, 61, 91.

Kagan, J. (1984). *The nature of the child.* New York: Basic Books.

Kagan, J., Kearsley, R., & Zelazo, P. (1978). *Infancy: Its place in human development.* Cambridge, MA: Harvard University Press.

Kalter, N. (1977). Children of divorce in an outpatient psychiatric population. *American Journal of Orthopsychiatry, 47,* 40–51.

Kalter, N. (1984). Conjoint mother–daughter treatment: A beginning phase of psychotherapy with adolescent daughters of divorce. *American Journal of Orthopsychiatry, 54,* 490–497.

Kalter, N. (1987). Long-term effects of divorce on children: A developmental vulnerability model. *American Journal of Orthopsychiatry, 57,* 587–600.

Kalter, N., Kloner, A., Schreier, S., & Okla, K. (1989). Predictors of children's postdivorce adjustment. *American Journal of Orthopsychiatry, 58,* 605–618.

Kalter, N., Riemer, B., Brickman, A., & Chen, J. (1985). Implications of parental divorce for female development. *Journal of the American Academy of Child Psychiatry, 24,* 538–544.

Kasen, S., Cohen, P., Brook, J., & Hartmark, C. (1996). A multiple-risk interaction model: Effects of temperament and divorce on psychiatric disorders in children. *Journal of Abnormal Child Psychology, 24,* 121–150.

Keilin, W., & Bloom, L. (1986). Child custody evaluation practices: A survey of experienced professionals. *Professional Psychology: Research and Practice, 17,* 338–346.

Kelley, M. L. (1995). Review of the Parent Perception of the Child Profile. In J. C. Conoley & J. C. Impara (Eds.), *The twelfth mental measurements yearbook* (pp. 738–739). Lincoln: University of Nebraska Press.

Kelly, J. (1993). Current research on children's postdivorce adjustment: No simple answers. *Family and Conciliation Courts Review, 31,* 29–49.

Kelly, J. B. (1994). The determination of child custody. *The Future of Children, 4,* 121–142.

Kelly, J. (1996). A decade of divorce mediation research: Some answers and questions. *Family and Conciliation Courts Review, 34,* 373–385.

Kelly, J. (1998). Marital conflict, divorce, and children's adjustment. *Child and Adolescent Clinics of North America, 7,* 259–271.

Kendall-Tackett, K. A., Williams, L. M., & Finkelhor, D. (1993). Impact of sexual abuse on children: A review and synthesis of recent empirical studies. *Psychological Bulletin, 113,* 164–180.

Kessel, K. (1985). *The process of divorce.* New York: Basic Books.

Kim, L., Sandler, I., & Tein, J. (1997). Locus of control as a stress moderator and mediator in children of divorce. *Journal of Abnormal Child Psychology, 25,* 145–155.

King, V. (1994). Nonresident father involvement and child well-being: Can dads make a difference? *Journal of Family Issues, 15,* 78–96.

Klajner-Diamond, H., Wehrspann, W., & Steinhauer, P. (1987). Assessing the credibility of young children's allegations of sexual abuse: Clinical issues. *Canadian Journal of Psychiatry, 32,* 610–614.

Kline, M., Johnston, J., & Tschann, J. (1991). The long shadow of marital conflict: A model of children's post-divorce adjustment. *Journal of Marriage and the Family, 53,* 297–309.

Kline, M., Tschann, J., Johnston, J., & Wallerstein, J. (1989). Children's adjustment in joint and sole physical custody families. *Developmental Psychology, 25,* 430–438.

Koel, A., Clark, S., Phear, W., & Hauser, B. (1988). A comparison of joint and sole legal custody agreements. In E. M. Hetherington & J. D. Arasteh (Eds.), *Impact of divorce, single parenting, and stepparenting on children* (pp. 73–90). Hillsdale, NJ: Erlbaum.

Koopman, E., & Hunt, J. (1988). Child custody mediation: An inter-disciplinary synthesis. *American Journal of Orthopsychiatry, 58,* 379–386.

Kopetski, L. (1991). *Parental alienation syndrome: Recent research*. Paper presented at the 15th annual Child Custody Conference, Keystone, CO.

Kramer, K. M., Arbuthnot, J., Gordon, D. A., Rousis, N. J., & Hoza, J. (1998). Effects of skill-based versus information-based divorce education programs on domestic violence and parental communication. *Family and Conciliation Courts Review, 36*, 9–31.

Kuehnle, K. (1996). *Assessing allegations of child sexual abuse*. Sarasota, FL: Professional Resource Exchange.

Kulka, R., & Weingarten, H. (1979). The long-term effects of parental divorce in childhood on adult adjustment. *Journal of Social Issues, 35*(4), 50–78.

Kurdek, L., & Berg, B. (1983). Correlates of children's adjustment to their parents' divorces. In L. A. Kurdek (Ed.), *Children and divorce: New directions for child development* (pp. 47–60). San Francisco: Jossey-Bass.

Lachkar, J. (1986). Narcissistic borderline couples: Implications for mediation. *Family and Conciliation Courts Review, 24*, 31–38.

Lamb, M., Pleck, J., Charnov, E., & Levine, J. (1987) A biosocial perspective on paternal behavior and involvement. In J. B. Lancaster et al. (Eds.), *Parenting across the lifespan: A biosocial perspective* (pp. 111–142). New York: Aldine de Gruyter.

Lamb, M., Sternberg, K. J., Esplin, P. W., & Hovav, M. (1997). Criterion-based content analysis: A field validation study. *Child Abuse and Neglect, 21*, 255–264.

Lampel, A. (1996). Children's alignment with parents in highly conflicted custody cases. *Family and Conciliation Courts Review, 34*, 229–239.

Lazarus, A., & Folkman, S. (1984). *Stress, appraisal, and coping*. New York: Springer.

Lee, C., Beauregard, C., & Hunsley, J. (1998). Lawyers' opinions regarding child custody mediation and assessment services: Implications for psychological practice. *Professional Psychology: Research and Practice, 29*, 115–120.

Lee, C. D., Shaughnessy, J., & Bankes, J. (1995). Impact of expedited services, a court program that enforces access. *Family and Conciliation Courts Review, 33*, 495–505.

Lengua, L., & Sandler, I. (1996). Self-regulation as a moderator of the relation between coping and symptomatology in children of divorce. *Journal of Abnormal Child Psychology, 24*, 681–701.

Linehan, M. M. (1987). Dialectical behavior therapy for borderline personality disorder. *Bulletin of the Menninger Clinic, 51*, 261–276.

Long, N., Forehand, R., Fauber, R., & Brody, G. (1987). Self-perceived and independently observed competence of young adolescents as a function of parental marital conflict and recent divorce. *Journal of Abnormal Child Psychology, 15*, 15–27.

Long, N., Slater, E., Forehand, R., & Fauber, R. (1988). Continued high or reduced interparental conflict following divorce: Relation to young adolescent adjustment. *Journal of Consulting and Clinical Psychology, 56*, 467–469.

Lowery, C. (1981). Child custody decisions in divorce proceedings: A survey of judges. *Professional Psychology, 12,* 493–498.

Lubin, D. (1995, October). *Preparing for court/mediation.* Family Law Litigation in Georgia seminar, Atlanta.

Luepnitz, D. (1986). A comparison of maternal, paternal and joint custody: Understanding the varieties of post-divorce family life. *Journal of Divorce, 9*(3), 1–12.

Lund, M. (1995). A therapist's view of parental alienation syndrome. *Family and Conciliation Courts Review, 33,* 308–316.

Maccoby, E., Depner, C., & Mnookin, R. (1988). Custody of children following divorce. In E. M. Hetherington & J. Arasteh (Eds.), *The impact of divorce, single parenting and stepparenting on children* (pp. 91–114). Hillsdale, NJ: Erlbaum.

Maccoby, E., Depner, C., & Mnookin, R. (1990). Coparenting in the second year of divorce. *Journal of Marriage and the Family, 52,* 141–155.

Maccoby, E., & Mnookin, R. (1992). *Dividing the child: Social and legal dilemmas of custody.* Cambridge, MA: Harvard University Press.

Magazine is wedded to growth. (1996, December 8). *Atlanta Journal and Constitution,* p. B12.

Malmquist, C. (1994). Psychiatric confidentiality in child custody disputes. *Journal of the American Academy of Child and Adolescent Psychiatry, 33,* 158–168.

Mannarino, A. P., Cohen, J. A., & Berman, R. (1994). The Children's Attributions and Perceptions Scale: A new measure of sexual abuse related fears. *Journal of Clinical Child Psychology, 23,* 204–211.

Marchant, G. J., & Paulsen, S. E. (1998). Review of the Parent Child Relationship Inventory. In J. C. Impara & B. S. Plake (Eds.), *The thirteenth mental measurements yearbook* (pp. 720–721). Lincoln: University of Nebraska Press.

Marcus v. Marcus, 320 N.E.2d 581 (Ill. 1974).

Margolies, P., & Weintraub, S. (1977). The revised 56-item CRPB as a research instrument. *Journal of Clinical Psychology, 33,* 472–476.

Marriage and divorce. (1995, March 30). ABC News, *Day One.*

Masten, A. S., & Garmezy, N. (1985). Risk, vulnerability and protective factors in developmental psychopathology. In B. B. Lahey & A. E. Kazdin (Eds.), *Advances in clinical child psychology* (Vol. 8, pp. 1–52). New York: Plenum.

McArthur, D. S., & Roberts, G. E. (1990). *Roberts Apperception Test for Children.* Los Angeles, CA: Western Psychological Services.

McClenney, L., Johnston, J., & Wallerstein, J. (1994). *Prior loss and perceptions of the marriage as predictors of adult adjustment to divorce.* Unpublished manuscript.

McCombs, A., & Forehand, R. (1989). Adolescent school performance following parental divorce: Are there family factors that can enhance success? *Adolescence, 24*(96), 871–880.

McCord, W., & McCord, J. (1959). *Origins of crime: A new evaluation of the Cambridge–Somerville Youth Study.* New York: Columbia University Press.

McIntosh, J., & Prinz, R. (1993). The incidence of alleged sexual abuse in 603 family court cases. *Law and Human Behavior, 17,* 95–101.

McLanahan, S., & Sandefur, G. (1994). *Growing up with a single parent.* Boston, MA: Harvard University Press.

Melton, G. (1995). Review of the Ackerman–Schoendorf Scales for Parent Evaluation of Custody. In J. C. Conoley & J. C. Impara (Eds.), *The twelfth mental measurements yearbook* (pp. 22–23). Lincoln: University of Nebraska Press.

Melton, G., & Limber, S. (1989). Psychologists' involvement in cases of child maltreatment: Limits of role and expertise. *American Psychologist, 44,* 1225–1233.

Melton, G., Petrila, J., Poythress, W., & Slobogin, C. (1997). Child custody in divorce. In *Psychological evaluations for the courts* (pp. 483–505). New York: Guilford Press.

Mentjoux, R., van Houten, C., & Koolman, C. (1993). Induced psychotic disorder: Clinical aspects, theoretical considerations, and some guidelines for treatment. *Comprehensive Psychiatry, 34,* 120–126.

Mikkelsen, E. J., Gutheil, T. G., & Emens, M. (1992). False sexual-abuse allegations by children and adolescents: Contextual factors and clinical subtypes. *American Journal of Psychotherapy, 46,* 556–570.

Milk, L. (1995, November 8). Challenging Americans' attitude toward divorce: After two decades of no-fault laws, experts are rethinking the right way to end a marriage. *Atlanta Journal and Constitution,* p. G103.

Miller, L. C. (1984). *Louisville Behavior Checklist manual* (rev.). Los Angeles, CA: Western Psychological Services.

Mnookin, R., & Kornhauser, L. (1979). Bargaining in the shadow of the law: The case of divorce. *Yale Law Journal, 88,* 950–997.

Monahan, J. (1980). *Who is the client? The ethics of psychological interventions in the criminal justice system.* Washington, DC: American Psychological Association.

Morrison, D., & Cherlin, A. (1995). The divorce process and young children's well-being: A prospective analysis. *Journal of Marriage and the Family, 57,* 87–97.

Munro, A. (1986). *Folie à deux* revisited. *Canadian Journal of Psychiatry, 31,* 233–234.

Mussen, P., Conger, J., Kagan, J., & Huston, A. (1984). *Child development and personality* (6th ed., pp. 131–133). New York: Harper & Row.

My Two Homes' Calendar keeps lives straight for kids of divorce. (1997, January 2). *Atlanta Journal and Constitution,* p. B9.

Newman, L., Harrell, A., & Salem, P. (1995). Domestic violence and empowerment in custody and visitation cases. *Family and Conciliation Courts Review, 33,* 30–62.

Nicholas, L. (1997). *Does parental alienation syndrome exist? Preliminary empirical study of the phenomenon in custody and visitation disputes.* Paper presented at the 13th Annual Symposium of the American College of Forensic Psychology, Vancouver, British Columbia, Canada.

Nolen-Hoeksema, S., Seligman, M., & Girgus, J. (1992). Predictors and consequences of childhood depressive symptoms: A five-year longitudinal study. *Journal of Abnormal Psychology, 101,* 405–422.

Oberndorf, C. (1934). *Folie à deux. International Journal of Psychoanalysis, 15,* 14–24.

Palmer, N. (1988). Legal recognition of the parental alienation syndrome. *American Journal of Family Therapy, 16,* 361–363.

Paziotopoulos, P. (1999, October). *Domestic violence prosecution initiatives.* Presentation at the meeting of the American Psychological Association/American Bar Association, Washington, DC.

Pearson, J., & Thoennes, N. (1982). The mediation and adjudication of divorce disputes: Some costs and benefits. *Family Advocate, 4,* 26–32.

Pearson, J., & Thoennes, N. (1984). Mediating and litigating custody disputes: A longitudinal evaluation. *Family Law Quarterly, 17,* 497–524.

Pearson, J., & Thoennes, N. (1988). The denial of visitation rights: A preliminary look at its incidence, correlates, antecedents, and consequences. *Law and Policy, 10,* 363–380.

Pearson, J., & Thoennes, N. (1990). Custody after divorce: Demographic and attitudinal patterns. *American Journal of Orthopsychiatry, 60,* 233–249.

Pearson, J., Thoennes, N., & Hodges, W. F. (1984). *The effects of divorce mediation and adjudication procedures on children.* Unpublished report. Available from the Research Unit of the Association of Family and Conciliation Courts, 1720 Emerson Street, Denver, Colorado, 80218.

Pearson, J., Thoennes, N., & Vanderkooi, L. (1982). The decision to mediate: Profiles of individuals who accept and reject the opportunity to mediate contested custody and visitation issues. *Journal of Divorce, 6,* 17–25.

Penfold, S. (1995). Mendacious moms or devious dads? Some perplexing issues in child custody/sexual abuse allegations. *Canadian Journal of Psychiatry, 40,* 337–341.

People v. Humphries, 24 Barb 521 (N.Y. 1857).

Peters, J. (1976). Children who are victims of sexual assault and the psychology of offenders. *American Journal of Psychotherapy, 30,* 398–421.

Peterson, J., & Zill, N. (1986). Marital disruption, parent–child relationships, and behavior problems in children. *Journal of Marriage and the Family, 45,* 295–307.

Phear, W., Beck, J., Hauser, B., Clark, S., & Whitney, R. (1983). An empirical study of custody agreements: Joint versus sole legal custody. *Journal of Psychiatry and Law, 11,* 419–441.

Plass, P. S., Finkelhor, D., & Hotaling, G. T. (1997). Risk factors for family abductions: Demographic and family interaction characteristics. *Journal of Family Violence, 12,* 333–348.

Pope, H. S., Butcher, J. N., & Seelen, J. (2000). *The MMPI and MMPI-2, and MMPI-A in court: A practical guide for expert witnesses and attorneys* (2nd ed.). Washington, DC: American Psychological Association.

Posthuma, A., & Harper, J. (1998). Comparison of MMPI-2 responses of child custody and personal injury litigants. *Professional Psychology: Research and Practice, 29,* 547–553.

Quinn, R., & Staines, G. (1979). *The 1977 Quality of Employment Survey.* Ann Arbor, MI: Survey Research Center.

Quinsey, V., Harris, G., Rice, M., & Cormier, C. (1998). *Violent offenders: Appraising and managing risk.* Washington, DC: American Psychological Association.

Racusin, R., Copans, S., & Mills, P. (1994). Characteristics of families of children who refuse post divorce visits. *Journal of Clinical Psychology, 30,* 792–801.

Radovanovic, H. (1993). Parental conflict and children's coping styles in litigating separated families: Relationships with children's adjustment. *Journal of Abnormal Child Psychology, 21,* 697–713.

Rand, D. C. (1997). The spectrum of parental alienation syndrome (Part II). *American Journal of Forensic Psychology, 15*(4), 39–92.

Raskin, D. C., & Esplin, P. W. (1991a). Assessment of children's statements of sexual abuse. In J. Doris (Ed.), *The suggestibility of children's recollections* (pp. 153–167). Washington, DC: American Psychological Association.

Raskin, D. C., & Esplin, P. W. (1991b). Statement validity assessment: Interview procedures and content analysis of children's statements of sexual abuse. *Behavioral Assessment, 13,* 265–291.

Reidy, T., Silver, R., & Carlson, A. (1989). Child custody decisions: A survey of judges. *Family Law Quarterly, 23,* 75–87.

Remar, R. (1991). Consent to the provision of psychological services to minors and access to the records of psychological treatment of minors. *The Georgia Psychologist, 9*–11, 46.

Remar, R. (1998). *Risk management.* Presentation to the Georgia Psychological Association co-sponsored by the American Professional Agency, Atlanta, GA.

Rind, B., Tromovitch, P., & Bauserman, R. (1998). A meta-analytic examination of assumed properties of child sexual abuse using college samples. *Psychological Bulletin, 124*(1), 22–53.

Robins, L., & Rutter, M. (1990). *Straight and devious pathways from childhood to adulthood.* Cambridge, England: Cambridge University Press.

Rohman, L., Sales, B., & Lou, M. (1987). The best interests of the child in custody disputes. In L. A. Weithorn (Ed.), *Psychology and child custody determinations* (pp. 59–105). Lincoln: University of Nebraska Press.

Rooney, S. A., & Walker, T. F. (1999). Identification and treatment of alienated children in high-conflict divorce. In L. VandeCreek & T. L. Jackson (Eds.), *Innovations in clinical practice: A sourcebook* (Vol. 17, pp. 331–341). Sarasota, FL: Professional Resources Press.

Roseby, V., & Johnston, J. (1995). Clinical interventions with latency-age children of high conflict and violence. *American Journal of Orthopsychiatry, 65,* 48–59.

Roseby, V., & Johnston, J. (1997). *High-conflict, violent, and separating families: A group treatment manual for school-age children.* New York: Free Press.

Rosin, H. (1996, June 23). Nation's marriage woes go way beyond no-fault divorce. *Atlanta Journal and Constitution*, p. B4.

Ross v. Richardson, 143 S.E. 446 (GA 1928).

Rothberg, B. (1983). Joint custody: Parental problems and satisfactions. *Family Process, 22*, 43–52.

Rutter, M. (1971). Parent–child separation: Psychological effects on the children. *Journal of Child Psychology and Psychiatry, 12*, 233–260.

Rutter, M. (1987). Psychosocial resilience and protective mechanisms. *American Journal of Orthopsychiatry, 57*, 316–331.

Rutter, M., Tizard, J., Yule, W., Graham, P., & Whitmore, K. (1976). Isle of Wight studies, 1964–1974. *Psychological Medicine, 6*, 313–332.

Sacks, M. (1988). *Folie à deux. Comprehensive Psychiatry, 29*, 270–277.

Sagatun, I. J., & Barrett, L. (1990). Parental child abduction: The law, family dynamics, and legal system responses. *Journal of Criminal Justice, 18*, 433–442.

Saks, M. J. (1990). Expert witnesses, nonexpert witnesses, and nonwitness experts. *Law and Human Behavior, 14*, 291–313.

Salem, P., Schepard, A., & Schlissel, S. (1996). Parent education as a distinct field of practice: The agenda for the future. *Family and Conciliation Courts Review, 34*, 9–22.

Sandler, I., Tein, J., & West, S. (1994). Coping, stress, and the psychological symptoms of children of divorce: A longitudinal study. *Child Development, 65*, 1744–1763.

Sandler, I., Wolchik, S., Braver, S., & Fogas, B. (1991). Stability and quality of life events and psychological symptomatology in children of divorce. *American Journal of Community Psychology, 19*, 501–520.

Santrock, J. W., & Sitterle, K. A. (1987). Parent–child relationships in stepmother families. In K. Pasley & M. Ihinger-Tallman (Eds.), *Remarriage and stepparenting: Current theory and research* (pp. 273–299). New York: Guilford Press.

Santrock, J., & Warshak, R. (1979). Father custody and social development in boys and girls. *Journal of Social Issues, 35*(4), 112–125.

Saposnek, D. (1998). *Mediating child custody disputes.* San Francisco: Jossey-Bass.

Saposnek, D., Hamburg, J., Delano, C. D., & Michaelsen, H. (1984). How has mandatory mediation fared? Research findings of the first year's follow-up. *Conciliation Courts Review, 22*, 7–19.

Schaefer, E. (1965). Children's Reports of Parental Behavior: An inventory. *Child Development, 36*, 417–424.

Schenck, P. (1999). Reducing the risk of ethics complaints via careful documentation of informed consent in child custody evaluations. In L. Van deCreek & T. Jackson (Eds.), *Innovations in clinical practice: A source book* (Vol. 17, pp. 217–235). Sarasota, FL: Professional Resource Press.

Schetky, D., & Haller, L. (1983). Parental kidnapping. *Journal of the American Academy of Child Psychiatry, 22*, 279–285.

Schluderman, E., & Schluderman, S. (1970). Replicability of factors in Children's Report of Parent Behavior (CRPBI). *Journal of Psychology, 76,* 236–249.

Schnayer, R., & Orr, R. (1988–1989). A comparison of children living in single-mother and single-father families. *Journal of Divorce, 12,* 171–184.

Schutz, B., Dixon, E., Lindenberger, J., & Ruther, N. (1989). *Solomon's sword: A practical guide to conducting child custody evaluations.* San Francisco: Jossey-Bass.

Schwartz, P. (1983). Length of day-care attendance and attachment behavior in eighteen-month-old infants. *Child Development, 54,* 1073–1078.

Scott, E., & Emery, R. (1987). Child custody dispute resolution: The adversarial system and divorce mediation. In L. Weithorn (Ed.), *Psychology and child custody determinations: Knowledge, roles, and expertise* (pp. 23–56). Lincoln: University of Nebraska Press.

Seligman, M. (1990). *Learned optimism: How to change your mind and your life.* New York: Pocket Books.

Send them to jail. (1996, June 21). *ABC News 20/20.*

Sgroi, S., Porter, F., & Blick, L. (1982). Validation of child sex abuse allegations. In S. M. Sgroi (Ed.), *Handbook of clinical intervention in child sexual abuse* (pp. 201–235). Lexington, MA: Lexington Books.

Shaffer, D., Gould, M. S., Brasic, J., Ambrosini, P., Fisher, P., Bird, H., & Aluwahlia, S. (1985). A children's global assessment scale. *Psychopharmacology Bulletin, 21,* 747–748.

Shaffer, M. B. (1992). Review of the Bricklin Perceptual Scales. In J. J. Kramer & J. C. Conoley (Eds.), *The eleventh mental measurements yearbook* (pp. 118–119). Lincoln: University of Nebraska Press.

Shaw, D., & Emery, E. (1987). Parental conflict and other correlates of the adjustment of school-age children whose parents have separated. *Journal of Abnormal Child Psychology, 15,* 269–281.

Shaw, D., Emery, R., & Tuer, M. (1993). Parental functioning and children's adjustment in families of divorce: A prospective study. *Journal of Abnormal Child Psychology, 21,* 119–134.

Sheets, V., Sandler, I., & West, S. (1996). Appraisals of negative events by preadolescent children of divorce. *Child Development, 67,* 2166–2182.

Sheridan, R. (1990). The false child molestation outbreak of the 1980's: An explanation of the cases arising in the divorce context. *Issues in Child Abuse Accusations, 2,* 146–151.

Siegel, J. C. (1996). Traditional MMPI-2 validity indicators and initial presentation in custody evaluations. *American Journal of Forensic Psychology, 14(3),* 55–63.

Siegel, J. C., & Langford, J. S. (1998). MMPI-2 validity scales and suspected parental alienation syndrome. *American Journal of Forensic Psychology, 16(4),* 5–14.

Siever, L. J., & Davis, K. L. (1991). A psychobiological perspective on the personality disorders. *American Journal of Psychiatry, 148,* 1647–1657.

Simons, V. A., Grossman, L. S., & Weiner, B. J. (1990). A study of familiies in high-conflict custody disputes: Effects of psychiatric evaluation. *Bulletin of the American Academy of Psychiatry and Law, 18,* 85–97.

Skafte, D. (1985). *Child custody evaluations.* Beverly Hills, CA: Sage.

Solow, R., & Adams, P. (1977). Custody by agreement: Child psychiatrist as child advocate. *Journal of Psychiatry and Law, 5,* 77–100.

Soni, S., & Rockley, J. (1974). Socio-clinical substrates of *folie à deux. British Journal of Psychiatry, 125,* 230–235.

Sorensen, E., & Goldman, J. (1989). Judicial perception in determining primary physical residence. *Journal of Divorce, 12*(4), 69–87.

Sorensen, E., & Goldman, J. (1990). Custody determinations and child development: A review of the current literature. *Journal of Divorce, 13*(4), 53–67.

Sorensen, E., Goldman, J., Sheeber, L., Albanese, I., Ward, M., Williamson, L., & McDanal, C. (1997). Judges' reliance on psychological, sociological, and legal variables in contested custody decisions. *Journal of Divorce and Remarriage, 27,* 1–24.

Stahl, P. (1996). Second opinions: An ethical and professional process for reviewing child custody evaluations. *Family and Conciliation Courts Review, 34,* 386–395.

Stanton, G. T. (1996, June 23). Breaking up is hard to do. *Atlanta Journal and Constitution,* p. B1.

Steinman, S. (1981). The experience of children in a joint-custody arrangement: A report of a study. *American Journal of Orthopsychiatry, 5,* 403–414.

Steinman, S., Zemmelman, S., & Knoblauch, T. (1985). A study of parents who sought joint custody following divorce: Who reaches agreement and sustains joint custody and who returns to court. *Journal of the American Academy of Child Psychiatry, 24,* 554–562.

Stone, L. (1977). *The family, sex, and marriage in England, 1500–1800.* New York: Harper and Row.

Straus, M. (1979). Measuring intrafamily conflict and violence: The Conflict Tactics (CT) Scales. *Journal of Marriage and the Family, 5,* 75–88.

Sullivan, M. J. (1997). Have a problem? Hire a special master as decision-maker. *Family Advocate, 21,* 41–44.

Teleki, J., Powell, J., & Dodder, R. (1982). Factor analysis of reports of parental behavior by children living in divorced and married families. *Journal of Psychology, 112,* 295–302.

Teyber, E. (1992). *Helping children cope with divorce.* New York: Lexington.

Thoennes, N., & Pearson, N. (1992). Response to Bruch and McIsaac. *Family and Conciliation Courts Review, 30*(1), 142–143.

Thoennes, N., & Tjaden, P. (1990). The extent, nature, and validity of sexual abuse allegations in custody/isitation disputes. *Child Abuse and Neglect, 14,* 151–163.

Thomas, A., & Chess, S. (1977). *Temperament and development*. New York: Brunner/Mazel.

Thomas, A., Chess, S., & Birch, H. G. (1968). *Temperament and behavior disorders in children*. New York: New York University Press.

Thomas, A. M., & Forehand, R. (1993). The role of paternal variables in divorced and married families: Predictability of adolescent adjustment. *American Journal of Orthopsychiatry, 63,* 126–135.

Thomas, J. (1998, November–December). Governor's veto ends bizarre licensing case. *The National Psychologist, 7*(6), 9.

Thompson, L., & Walker, A. (1989). Gender in families: Women and men in marriage, work, and parenthood. *Journal of Marriage and the Family, 51,* 845–871.

Through the eyes of your child. (1995, April 4). *ABC NEWS, 20/20.*

Tompkins, R. (1995). Parenting plans: A concept whose time has come. *Family and Conciliation Courts Review, 33,* 286–297.

Tong, L., Oates, K., & McDowell, M. (1987). Personality development following sexual abuse. *Child Abuse and Neglect, 11,* 371–383.

Tschann, J., Johnston, J., Kline, M., & Wallerstein, J. (1989). Family process and children's functioning during divorce. *Journal of Marriage and the Family, 51,* 431–444.

Turner, J. (1984). Divorced fathers who win contested custody of their children: An exploratory study. *American Journal of Orthopsychiatry, 54,* 498–501.

Tuter v. Tuter, 120 S.W.2d 203 (MD 1938).

Tyson, A. S. (1996, September 10). States put minor speed bumps in divorce path: No-fault backlash [On-line]. *Christian Science Monitor.* Available: http://www/rmfc/org/newsitem.html

Tzeng, J. M., & Mare, R. D. (1995). Labor market and socioeconomic effects on marital stability. *Social Science Research, 24,* 329–351.

Uniform Marriage and Divorce Act, 402, 9, *Uniform Laws Annotated, 35* (1970, as amended 1971, 1973), American Bar Association.

Vaughn, B. E., Deane, K. E., & Waters, E. (1985). The impact of out-of-home care on child–mother attachment quality: Another look at some enduring questions. In I. Bretherton & E. Waters (Eds.), Growing points of attachment theory and research. *Monographs of the Society for Research in Child Development, 50*(1–2, Serial No. 209).

Vaughn, B. E., Gove, F., L., & Egelund, B. (1980). The relationship between out-of-home care and the quality of infant–mother attachment in an economically disadvantaged population. *Child Development, 51,* 1203–1214.

Verser v. Ford, 37 Ark 27 (Ark. 1881).

Wakefield, H., & Underwager, R. (1990). Personality characteristics of parents making false accusations of sexual abuse in custody disputes. *Issues in Child Abuse Accusations, 2,* 121–136.

Wakefield, H., & Underwager, R. (1991). Sexual abuse allegations in divorce and custody disputes. *Behavioral Sciences and the Law, 9,* 451–468.

Waller v. Waller, 136 S.E. 149 (GA 1926).

Wallerstein, J. (1985). Children of divorce: Preliminary report of a ten-year follow-up of older children and adolescents. *Journal of the American Academy of Child Psychiatry, 24,* 545–553.

Wallerstein, J. (1991). The long-term effects of divorce on children: A review. *Journal of the American Academy of Child Psychiatry, 30,* 349–360.

Wallerstein, J., & Blakeslee, S. (1989). *Second chances: Men, women, and children a decade after divorce.* New York: Ticknor & Fields.

Wallerstein, J., & Corbin, S. (1989). Daughters of divorce: Report from a ten-year follow-up. *American Journal of Orthopsychiatry, 59,* 593–604.

Wallerstein, J. S., Corbin, S. B., & Lewis, J. M. (1988). Children of divorce: A 10 year study. In E. M. Hetherington & J. D. Arasteh (Eds.), *Impact of divorce, single parenting and stepparenting on children* (pp. 187–214). Hillsdale, NJ: Erlbaum.

Wallerstein, J., & Kelly, J. (1980a). Effects of the divorce on the visiting father–child relationship. *American Journal of Psychiatry, 12,* 1534–1539.

Wallerstein, J., & Kelly, J. (1980b). *Surviving the breakup: How children and parents cope with divorce.* New York: Basic Books.

Warshak, R. (1992). *The custody revolution.* New York: Poseidon Press.

Warshak, R. (1996). Gender bias in child custody decisions. *Family and Conciliation Courts Review, 34,* 296–409.

Warshak, R., & Santrock, J. (1983). The impact of divorce in father-custody and mother-custody homes: The child's perspective. In L. A. Kurdek (Ed.), *Children and divorce* (pp. 29–46). San Francisco: Jossey Bass.

Weithorn, L. (1987). Psychological consultation in divorce custody litigation: Ethical considerations. In L. A. Weithorn (Ed.), *Psychology and child custody determinations* (pp. 182–209). Lincoln: University of Nebraska Press.

Weithorn, L., & Grisso, T. (1987). Psychological evaluations in divorce custody: Problems, principles, and procedures. In L. A. Weithorn (Ed.), *Psychology and child custody determinations* (pp. 157–181). Lincoln: University of Nebraska Press.

Wheaton, B. (1990). Life transitions, role histories, and mental health. *American Sociological Review, 55,* 209–223.

Whitehead, B. D. (1996). *The divorce culture: Rethinking our commitments to marriage and family.* New York: Vintage Books.

Williams, C. (1999, April 14). Yager foe recovers hidden daughters. *Atlanta Journal and Constitution,* p. C7.

Wolfe, V. V., Gentile, C., & Wolfe, D. A. (1989). The impact of sexual abuse on children: A PTSD formulation. *Behavior Therapy, 20,* 215–228.

Wolfe, V. V., Wolfe, D. A., Gentile, C., & LaRose, L. (1987). *Children's Impact of*

Traumatic Events-Revised. Unpublished manuscript. London, Ontario: University of Western Ontario.

Wolman, R., & Taylor, K. (1991). Psychological effects of custody disputes on children. *Behavioral Sciences and the Law, 9,* 399–417.

Woodbury, N. (1996). Pretrial interviewing: The search for the truth in alleged child sexual abuse cases. *Family and Conciliation Courts Review, 34,* 140–168.

Wyer, M., Gaylord, S., & Grove, E. (1987). The legal context of child custody evaluations. In L. A. Weithorn (Ed.), *Psychology and child custody determinations* (pp. 3–22). Lincoln: University of Nebraska Press.

Zaslow, M. (1988). Sex differences in children's response to parental divorce: 1. Research methodology and post-divorce family forms. *American Journal of Orthopsychiatry, 58,* 355–378.

Zaslow, M. (1989). Sex differences in children's response to parental divorce: 2. Samples, variables, ages, and sources. *American Journal of Orthopsychiatry, 59,* 118–141.

Zibbell, R. A. (1995). The mental health professional as arbitrator in post-divorce child-oriented conflict. *Family and Conciliation Courts Review, 33,* 462–471.

Zill, N. (1988). Behavior, achievement, and health problems among children in stepfamilies: Findings from a national survey of child health. In E. M. Hetherington & J. D. Arasteh (Eds.), *Impact of divorce, single parenting, and step-parenting on children* (pp. 325–368). Hillsdale, NJ: Erlbaum.

Zill, N., Morrison, D., & Coiro, M. (1993). Long-term effects of parental divorce on parent–child relationships, adjustment, and achievement in young adulthood. *Journal of Family Psychology, 7,* 91–103.

AUTHOR INDEX

Friedrich, W. N., 284
Fulton, J., 69, 140, 165
Furstenberg, F., 11–13, 21, 33–35, 47,
        68, 166–168, 248, 327, 328, 344,
        346

Galinsky, E., 155, 157
Gardner, R., 122, 137, 208–211, 220,
        221, 223, 292, 312–314, 318,
        341
Garmezy, N., 191
Garrison, E., 128, 129
Garrity, C., 157–160, 174, 220, 221, 224,
        225, 242, 333, 339, 343
Gaylord, S., 14
Geasler, M., 329, 330
Gentile, C., 284
Gerard, A. B., 124
Girdner, L. K., 258, 332, 340
Girgus, J., 196
Gjerde, P., 52
Glaser, D., 287
Glassman, J. B., 297, 300
Gleick, E., 324
Glenn, J. E., 330
Glenn, N., 30, 31
Glick, P., 11, 248
Goldman, J., 133
Goldstein, J., 159
Goleman, D., 65
Gonzalez, R., 179, 184, 185
Goodman, E., 253
Gordon, D. A., 330–331
Gottfried, A. E., 245
Gottfried, A. W., 245
Gottman, J., 63–65, 67, 79, 84
Gove, F. L., 156
Graham, P., 42
Gralnick, A., 218
Gray, 331
Green, A., 273, 277–279
Greene, J., 262, 263
Greenwood, A., 298
Greif, G. L., 97, 98, 256–258, 264
Griffin, G., 347
Grisso, T., 123–127, 137, 138, 312, 348,
        349, 351, 353
Grossman, L. S., 97
Grove, E., 14

Grych, J., 50, 195
Gurwin, H. M., 336
Gutheil, T. G., 277
Guyer, M., 121, 140, 167, 272, 292

Hagin, R. A., 126
Halikias, W., 312, 314
Haller, L., 253
Halon, R. L., 303
Hamburg, J., 74
Hanson, G., 273
Harper, J., 244
Harrell, A., 182
Harris, E., 297, 298, 301
Harris, G., 352
Hartmark, C., 194
Hauser, B., 68, 90, 98, 103
Healey, J. M., 167, 169
Hedrick, M., 212, 223
Hegar, R. L., 256–258, 264
Heinze, M. C., 124–126
Hembrooke, H., 280
Hess, R., 47, 167, 168
Hetherington, E. M., 20, 22–25, 28, 32,
        155, 167, 170, 192–195, 200
Hightower, A. D., 215
Hiltonsmith, R. W., 124
Hodges, W., 122, 157–164, 250, 342
Hodges, W. F., 76
Hoorwitz, A., 280
Hoppe, C., 246
Horner, T. M., 292
Horowitz, S. W., 286
Hotaling, G. T., 253, 254
Hovav, M., 286
Hunsley, J., 78, 140
Hunt, J., 72
Hunter, M., 135
Hunter, M. A., 247
Huston, A., 155

Illfield, F., 102, 103
Illfield, H., 102
Insabella, G. M., 32

Jacobsen, N., 66
Jameson, B., 135

SUBJECT INDEX

Behavior problems (*continued*)
children from divorced *vs.* intact families and, 32, 41–42
children from father- *vs.* mother-custody homes and, 94–95
intergenerational transmission of divorce and, 31–32
juvenile offenders, 347
parental conflict and, 42–44
visitation and, 169–170
See also Adjustment by children
Best-interests standard, 114, 328
Bethke-Elshtain, Jean, 322–323
Big Valley Grace Community Church, Modesto, CA, 324–325
Blankenhorn, David, 324
Boyan, Susan, 339–340
Boys
effects of divorce on, 21–23, 26–27
temperaments of, 52–53, 194
BPS. *See* Bricklin Perceptual Scales (BPS)
Brainwashing. *See* Parental alienation syndrome (PAS)
Branstad, Terry, 327
Bricklin Perceptual Scales (BPS), 126–127

California Children of Divorce Project, 237–238
Campbell, L., 238–242
Case management approach, and PAS, 225–226
Case studies
children's coping with conflict, 177–179, 186–187, 189–191, 204
confidentiality, 305–308
custody arrangements, 87–89, 110
custody evaluation, 111–114, 146–147
evaluation goals, 301–305
legacy of divorce revolution, 9–10, 36
noncustodial parents, 315–318
parental alienation syndrome, 205–208, 232–233
parental psychopathology, 235–237, 265–266
pathways to divorce, 61–63, 84–85
perils of average work, 308–315
privileged communication management, 299–301

problem resolution, 149–151, 175
professional involvement, 295–299
relationship between parental conflict and children's adjustment, 37–40, 59
role clarification, 305–308
sexual abuse allegations, 267–271, 293–294
stress responses in children, 177–179, 186–187, 189–191, 204
visitation plan, 149–151, 175
Catholic Church, 326
Caught in the Middle (Garrity and Baris), 242
CBCA/SVA. *See* Criterion-Based Content Analysis/Statement Validity Assessment (CBCA/SVA)
CBCL. *See* Achenbach Child Behavior Checklist
Center for the Family in Transition, 46, 169, 213, 238–242, 249
Child abduction by parents. *See* Parental abductions
Child adjustment and parental conflict, 37–59
case study on, 37–40, 59
clinical guidelines and, 55–58
deterioration of parent-child bonds and, 47–48
divorce as process *vs.* cause and, 54–55
divorce status and, 42–44
exposure to chronic conflict and, 48–52, 55, 345
importance of parent-child relationship and, 46–47
intact *vs.* divorced homes and, 40–42
postdivorce, 44–46
predivorce conflict and, 52–53
research summary on, 54–55
young adulthood and, 53–54
See also Adjustment by children; Behavior problems; Parental conflict
Child and family forensic psychology, as field, 348–353
Children of divorce
best and worst outcomes for, 57–58
court aid and, 328
impacts on, 19–34, 167–171
long-term effects and, 345
remarriage and, 26

treatment programs for, 342–344

vs. children from intact families, 19, 20, 31, 32, 40–42

See also Age of child; Boys; Child adjustment; Custody arrangements; Custody evaluation; Gender differences; Girls; Stress responses in children

Children's Attributions and Perceptions Scale, 284

Children's Impact of Traumatic Events Scale-Revised (CITES-R), 284

Children's Reports of Parental Behavior (CRPB), 127

Children's Rights Council, 164–165

Child Sexual Behavior Inventory (CSBI), 284

Child support, 328. *See also* Economic situation

CITES-R. *See* Children's Impact of Traumatic Events Scale-Revised (CITES-R)

Cognitive style
parents caught in divorce disputes and, 246–247
resilience in children and, 195–197

Cognitive theory, and divorce disputes, 242–243

Collaborative Law Program, 336–337

Communication patterns, and marital breakdown, 63–67. *See also* Conflict resolution

Community Marriage Policy, 324–325

Confidentiality, 299–301, 305–308

Conflict-avoiding couples, 63–64, 66–67

Conflicted parenting style, 103

Conflict resolution, 44, 63–64, 68. *See also* Parental conflict

Conflict Tactics Scale (CTS), 182, 184

Contempt, as element of marriage, 64–65, 67

Cooperative Parenting Program in Georgia, 339–340

Cooperative parenting style, 103, 105

Coparenting counselor. *See* Special master

Coping skills in children, 197–200. *See also* Resilience; Stress responses in children

Council on Families in America, 322

Courts. *See* Judicial system

Covenant marriage, 325–326

Criterion-Based Content Analysis/Statement Validity Assessment (CBCA/SVA), 285–286, 290, 352

Criticism, as element of marriage, 64

CRPB. *See* Children's Reports of Parental Behavior (CRPB)

CSBI. *See* Child Sexual Behavior Inventory (CSBI)

CTS. *See* Conflict Tactics Scale (CTS)

Custody and access disputes
co-occurrence of sexual abuse allegations with, 271–274
guidelines for clinicians and, 260–265, 290–293
mediation and, 72–73
parental abductions in, 252–259
personality traits of parents involved in, 243–248
remarriage and, 248–252
theories of parental psychopathology in, 237–243
See also Mediation; Psychopathology of parents in custody disputes; Sexual abuse allegations

Custody arrangements
court disposition of disputes, 116–119
gender considerations and, 95–97, 114, 133
historical trends, 89–91, 93–94
joint custody and, 99–104
outcomes for children and, 104–107
parental preferences and, 91–94
paternal custody and, 14–15, 94–97, 251–252
rights of mother and, 15–17
split custody and, 97–99, 107–108
treatment of PAS and, 224–225
See also Joint custody

Custody commissioner. *See* Special master

Custody evaluation, 111–147
APA *Guidelines* (1994), 120, 121, 123, 125, 135, 300–301, 307, 311–313, 351
case study on, 111–114, 146–147
child assessment, 128–129
data reliability, 312–313
defining a "good parent" and, 130–131

Emotional intelligence, 65
Empathy, lack of, 65, 66, 246
Equilibration coping strategy, 179, 188, 191
Ethical issues
    confidentiality and, 299–301, 305–308
    goals and, 301–305
    noncustodial parents and, 315–318
    perils of average work and, 308–315
    professional involvement, 295–299
    role boundaries, 290–291, 299–301, 305–308
Etzioni, Amitai, 325
Expedited Visitation Services (Arizona), 335

Family Advocate (journal), 335, 336
Family and Children's Evaluation Team in California, 225
Family and Conciliation Courts (journal), 329
Family conflict. *See* Parental conflict
Family Court program in Georgia, 334–335, 347
Family Solutions, Inc., 339–340
Fathers
    custody arrangement preferences and, 91–93
    effects of limited contact with, 24, 167–171
    visitation problems and, 164–167
    See also Joint custody; Parental alienation syndrome (PAS); Parent-child relationship; Paternal custody; Sexual abuse allegations
Federal Child and Adolescent Service System Program, 347
First International Congress on Parent Education Programs (1994), 330
Flexibility, 199
Folie à deux relationship, 208, 211, 218–220, 278
Formal mediation, 338
"Four Horsemen of the Apocalypse," 64–65

Galston, Bill, 323
Garrity, C., 242

Gender differences, child, 25, 31, 94–97, 105. *See also* Boys; Girls
Gender differences, parent
    acceptance of mediation and, 73
    in custody preferences, 91–94
    marital breakdown and, 67–70
    See also Fathers; Mothers
Getting to Yes (Fisher and Uhry), 72
Girls, effects of divorce on, 23–25, 27–29
Guidelines for Child Custody Evaluations in Divorce Proceedings (APA), 120, 121, 123, 125, 135, 290, 351
    ethical issues and, 300–301, 307, 311–313
Guidelines for clinicians, by topic
    children's stress responses, 200–201
    custody arrangements, 108–110
    custody evaluation, 134–144
    factors in divorce decision, 55–58
    legacy of divorce revolution, 35–36
    parental alienation syndrome, 228–232
    parental psychopathology in custody disputes, 260–265
    pathways to divorce, 80–84
    sexual abuse allegations, 280–288
    visitation, 151–164, 172–175
Guilt, 50
Gyemont, Ina, 342

Hartman, Merrill, 139
Helplessness, 50
Homosexuality, and custody decisions, 134
Human potential movement, 11

Identity shield, 344
Individual differences. *See* Stress responses in children
Infants, visitation guidelines for, 155–159
Informal mediation, 338
Insecurity, 49
Intact families *vs.* children of divorce, 19, 20, 31, 32, 40–42
Intergenerational transmission of divorce, 31–32
Interventions for Children of Divorce (Hodges), 342

See also Special master

Medical records, release of, 308–315

Mental health professionals
  future directions and, 348–353
  licensing board and, 297, 298–299
  new roles for, 337–342
  ranking of custody evaluation factors by, 132

Merging coping strategy, 188–189

Minnesota Multiphasic Personality Inventory-2 (MMPI-2), 122, 123, 221, 244–245

Missing children. See Parental abductions

MMPI-2. See Minnesota Multiphasic Personality Inventory-2 (MMPI-2)

Montagne, R., 324

Mothers
  burden of divorce and, 344–345
  custody arrangement preferences and, 91, 92
  effect of parental conflict on, 44
  right to custody, 15–17
  temperament of child and, 192–193
  See also Custody arrangements; Parent-child relationship

Multisystemic programs, 347

Munchausen syndrome-by-proxy, 278

Mutual acceptance, 66

"The Narcissistic Borderline Couple" (Lachkar), 247

Narcissistic vulnerability, 239–242. See also Personality traits of parents

Neighborhood Family Conflict Resolution Center, 347–348

No-fault divorce
  divorce revolution and, 11–13, 327–328
  repeal of, 326–327

Noncustodial parent
  decreases in visitations and, 166–167, 229
  denial of visitations and, 164–166, 229
  effects of limited contact with, 167–171
  rights of, 315–318
  stress factors at visitation times and, 203
  See also Parental alienation syndrome (PAS)

Optimism, and children's coping, 195–197

Paranoid schizophrenia, 278

Parental abductions, 252–260
  adjustment by children to, 256
  base rates of, 253–254
  common patterns in, 254–255
  intervention programs to prevent, 258–259
  risk factors for, 254, 264
  typology of, 256–258

Parental absence, impacts of, 40–41. See also Custody arrangements; Non-custodial parent; Parental alienation syndrome (PAS)

Parental alienation syndrome (PAS), 189, 205–233, 350
  associated features, 228–229
  case study on, 205–208, 232–233
  children who refuse visitation and, 212–218
  conceptualization of, 208–212, 227
  criteria for, 229–232
  degrees of severity of, 211–212
  formulation of, 220–223, 227–228
  guidelines for clinicians, 228–232
  research on, 212–218
  research summary, 227–228
  treatment of, 223–228

Parental attachment
  development of PAS and, 220–221
  measures in older children, 126–127
  measures in young children, 125–126

Parental conflict
  behavior problems and, 41–42
  children's adjustment and, 44–46, 54–55, 105–106, 170–171, 184–185
  children's coping strategies and, 179–180, 185–191
  custody arrangements and, 103, 328, 346
  divorced vs. intact families and, 42–44
  effects of chronic exposure to, 48–52, 55, 345
  effects of temperament of children on, 195
  as impervious to intervention, 346
  parental abductions and, 252–259

children who refuse, 212–218
decision tree on, 152, 153
development of guidelines for, 151–155
disputes involving, and the courts, 335
divorce process and, 82–83
effects of limited paternal contact and, 167–171
factors in stress of, 202–204
guidelines for, by age group, 155–164
problems with, 164–167, 201–204
See also Parental alienation syndrome (PAS)
Volatile couples, 63–64

Wallerstein, J., 237–238
Washington, 334
Whitehead, Barbara Dafoe, 323
Wilson, J., 323
Wiseperson. *See* Special master
Withdrawal
  as element of marriage, 65, 67
  visitation problems and, 181
Wraparound programs, 347

Young adult children of divorce, 26–29, 53–54
Young children, 125–126
  visitation and, 155–162, 180–181

ABOUT THE AUTHOR

After obtaining her PhD from Emory University in 1977, Elizabeth M. Ellis worked for several years as a research director with the University of Georgia. Since 1980, she has been in private practice in a suburb of Atlanta, working with children, adults, and families. She has published over 20 scholarly papers in the fields of psychological trauma, psychotherapy, and forensic assessment.

Her parenting book, *Raising a Responsible Child* was published in 1995. Dr. Ellis has done assessments in hundreds of child and family forensic cases and testified as an expert witness in 11 counties in Georgia. She lives in Atlanta with her husband; her son, age 13; and her daughter, age 9.